THE STREETS ARE BLUE

THE

STREETS

ARE BLUE

*True Tales of Service
from the Front Lines of the
Los Angeles Police Department*

Gary Farmer

iUniverse LLC
Bloomington

THE STREETS ARE BLUE

iUniverse books may be ordered through booksellers or by contacting:

iUniverse LLC
1663 Liberty Drive
Bloomington, IN 47403
www.iuniverse.com
1-800-Authors (1-800-288-4677)

ISBN: 978-1-4917-2249-7 (sc)
ISBN: 978-1-4917-2251-0 (hc)
ISBN: 978-1-4917-2250-3 (e)

Library of Congress Control Number: 2014902048

Printed in the United States of America.

iUniverse rev. date: 05/28/2014

This book is dedicated to the
men and women within these pages
and
to those past, present, and future
members of the
Los Angeles Police Department.

Then I heard the voice of the Lord say,
"Whom shall I send? Who will go for us?"
I said, "Here am I. Send me."
—Isaiah 6:8

Contents

Note: Dates in brackets indicate years on the
       Los Angeles Police Department

Front Cover: Partial image from the February 1, 1956 cadet class of the Los Angeles Police Department. The image was taken on May 4, 1956 prior to graduation. Full image on page 70.

Acknowledgments

This book contains the words of others, and it required a great deal of sensitivity to allow the words to stand as spoken. Abella Carroll edited my preliminary drafts with just such sensitivity. We worked together to ensure that each person's story respectively reflected what was essentially a major part of his or her life. It was important to me to offer the stories just as they were told, and I believe we achieved that.

Each person provided me photos that came in varying degrees of condition: spots, wrinkles, fading—you name it. Bryan Weaver, my cousin, worked tirelessly to restore the photos to as close to their original condition as possible. It is an absolute shame for the reader to not see the before and after of a restored photo, because it is truly an art to image edit a damaged photo for a credible presentation. Kevin Turcotte, a friend of the family, provided his touch on the cover of the book. My daughter gave me an idea for the book cover and I passed it along to Kevin. He created a cover worthy of the individuals portrayed in the book. Both Bryan's and Kevin's expertise and professional level of assistance were truly inspirational and motivating.

The interviews of each person ranged from two to seven hours. My wife and I tried to transcribe the interviews, but it became overwhelming. Two friends, Jean Mourn and Ginny Holloway, both transcriptionists, took on the task. Both told me that they had thoroughly enjoyed transcribing the interviews, as it was unlike anything they had ever done before.

Two others of note—Glynn Martin, the executive director of the Los Angeles Police Historical Society, and Dennis Doyle, an English professor at Glendale Community College—are both family friends whose insights, suggestions, and support helped this project move forward.

They say to always save the best for last. My family is the best, and forever we will last. During my career, the faith of my wife, son, and daughter was ever present and unwavering. In all of our family endeavors, with the support of one another, there was a level of confidence that whatever task was at hand, it would be accomplished or completed. That certainly happened here.

To those I have mentioned, to others who have had some part in this project, and especially to and on behalf of the officers in this book, I offer my sincere and heartfelt appreciation and gratitude.

From the Author

As a young boy, I was given two books: *Baseball When the Grass Was Real* by Donald Honig and *The Glory of Their Times* by Lawrence S. Ritter. Each book is a collection of oral histories by former professional baseball players from the turn of the century through the 1940s. The players provided accounts of how they became baseball players and offered various stories of their baseball careers. I have always treasured each book because I felt as if each ballplayer, while telling his story, was speaking directly to me. The players' stories gave me a glimpse of the past—a past whose events few people living today were there to witness. The events became stories, and the stories, because of the interest of Honig and Ritter, are still with us.

During my career with the Los Angeles Police Department, I often thought about using the same format as the baseball books to present the stories of former Los Angeles Police Department officers. Once I retired, a former partner I had always considered as a subject for my book passed away. His death motivated me to start this endeavor before more history and experiences were lost in time.

The former officers in this book include people I worked with or around; people whose reputations I was aware of; people whom others suggested; people whom the officers in the book talked about; or people I contacted purely at random. It didn't matter what their experiences were—the police department has had thousands of officers, and each one's career is unique unto itself. When I walked into their homes, I had no idea what stories or experiences were forthcoming. I was captivated by their stories and their recollections of events that, for most, occurred half a lifetime ago. If it was a significant event, I researched as much as I could to ensure the accuracy of the story. More often than not, the story had happened just as it was told to me. One fascinating aspect was the mention of certain individuals by multiple persons in the book. One can almost follow the career of the individuals solely by these random mentions.

I gave each former officer as much time as he or she was willing to take to share his or her stories. Hence, I acquired pages and pages of material. I omitted a good amount to improve the readability of the book, while still offering a flavor of the individuals' overall careers. Editing was minimal to keep their spoken words intact so that readers can share what I experienced while listening to each individual. As you read the book, hopefully, you will appreciate, as I did, the sacrifices these extraordinary individuals made and, through their stories, the sacrifices others have made during their careers with the Los Angeles Police Department.

What Is a Cop?

All at once, you've lost your name. You're a "cop," a "flatfoot," "John Law." You're "the fuzz," "the heat" . . . you're bad news. They call you everything but never a policeman.

Then there is your first night on the beat . . . you'll rub elbows with all the elite: pimps, addicts, thieves, bums, winos, cheats, con men, the class of Skid Row. You'll walk the beat and pick up the pieces.

You'll do time in the patrol car and get an "unknown trouble" call . . . never knowing who you'll meet . . . a kid with a knife . . . a pillhead with a gun . . . two ex-cons with nothing to lose.

As a detective . . . you'll have few facts and a lot of hunches . . . you'll work stakeouts that could last a week . . . you'll run down leads that dead-end . . . do legwork until you're sure you've talked to everybody in California . . . people who saw it happen but really didn't . . . people who don't remember . . . those who try to forget . . . those who tell the truth . . . those who lie.

There are over five thousand men in this city who know that being a policeman is an endless, glamourless, thankless job that must be done. I know it too. And I'm damned glad to be one of them.

—Sergeant Joe Friday, excerpt from the
February 9, 1967, episode of *Dragnet*

Roy Bean

Roy Bean

Birthplace: Spanish Fork, Utah
Career: 1941–1965
Rank at Retirement: Sergeant
Divisions: Harbor, Hollywood, Training, Administrative Vice, Robbery

I'm going back fifty or sixty years, but we used to tell this story in the academy. There was a streetcar situation in Los Angeles back in December 1942. This streetcar was full of women and children. Also on board was a drunk, Stanley Beebe, who was mistreating the women. The motorman saw a policeman on the corner, stopped the streetcar, and hailed the officer. The policeman could see that Beebe was drunk and obnoxious. He got Beebe off the streetcar, and in doing so, Beebe fell and hit the back of his head on the street. The policeman reached down to pick him up, and Beebe spit in the officer's face. The policeman stepped back and kicked Beebe hard in the stomach. The kick was enough that the man later died as a result of a ruptured bladder. The policeman was charged with murder, but the trial resulted in a hung jury, and the charges were dismissed. We told that story in the academy to impress upon the cadets, "Don't do this."

My dad and my grandfather were attorneys, and later, my grandfather became a judge. My dad died when I was twelve, and my mother passed away when I was thirteen. I went to live with my dad's brother, but he wasn't like my dad. I guess from birth, there were probably never two people closer than me and my dad. Just before my parents passed, we lived on Brighton Avenue in Los Angeles. One day, I was on my way home, and a neighbor was standing on his front-yard knoll, watering across the sidewalk onto the parkway. When I walked by, he didn't turn his hose away, and I got the full brunt of that water. Of course, I was a typical snot-nosed,

1

spoiled little brat. I went home and got a big bucket of hot water. I took the bucket of hot water over to this neighbor, rang his doorbell, and he got the water. One of the last defense cases of my dad's life—me.

When I was twenty-one, I read in the newspaper that there was an examination for the police department. I had always been attracted to the police—to get a pension more than anything, but I also liked the legal aspect because of my dad and my grandfather. I passed the examination enough to get an appointment in the fall of '41.

I don't think I was a standout except physically. I was physically capable of doing more than most in my class. I was fast; there wasn't anybody who could outrun me in the seventy-five-yard dash. There was an obstacle course at the academy, and I held the record for five years or so, until some young kid who was a hurdler came along. This kid beat my time, so his picture replaced mine in the main hall of the academy.

While I was at the academy, there was a big strike on Terminal Island in San Pedro. On Terminal Island there was a big shipyard with four hundred men working inside and four hundred outside on strike. The unions had something to do with the strike, of course. At noon, the whistle was set to blow, and the monstrous gates would open. A clash between those inside and those outside was expected. Initially, there were only fifty policemen there, so men were brought in from other divisions. The department also knew where they could get a hundred men in a hurry—right from the academy. We had 105 in my class. All we were told to do was to keep these guys from killing each other. It was stupid to allow this thing to take place, but it did.

When the gates opened, fistfights and mayhem began. A policeman named Reeves and I saved one man from drowning. There was water in a big, deep ditch, and one guy was drowning another guy. We had to fight one to keep him from wanting to get more of the other. I don't know if that's a save or not, but the man didn't drown. Guys were fighting for different reasons, and some didn't know what they were fighting about. We always thought some jackass union leader had decided to do this, and some other union leader had said, "No, you have to do that." That was a problem: the unions fighting each other. The situation was over that afternoon. On the way to the shipyard, I had wondered what in the heck was going to happen. I was sure glad to be going home.

After the academy, I went to Harbor Division and was there until late '42. I don't remember having any training officers. We learned as we went along. My classmate and I worked a radio car for four or five months until I got a detective job inside. We thought young policemen working together was normal. We were expected to be policemen.

I was working uniform patrol when the attack on Pearl Harbor occurred. We tried to secure Terminal Island because the shipyards were vital to the defense of our nation. Hundreds of Japanese lived and worked there. There was concern that the Japanese would conduct sabotage of the shipyards and refineries. We evacuated the Japanese off Terminal Island, and it was my understanding they went to camps. I spent most of my time either evacuating the Japanese or examining and registering people as members of the neighborhood watch. That was the process for many months.

When I finished probation, I was invited to work as a plainclothes detective in the Detective Bureau. One case in particular stood out—the rape of a seven-year-old boy.

Longshoremen used a hand tool called a longshoreman's hook, which had a sharp, curved piece of steel attached to the handle. It was common for a longshoreman to carry one on the street. We'd arrest him for it, or if he relinquished it to us, we took it to the station and put his name on it. He could pick it up later on his way to work. It was a perfect tool for handling hay or picking up bundles, but it was a terribly dangerous thing when used against a human being. I'd already had some experience with those hooks on that union strike when I was in the academy.

In the case of this seven-year-old boy, our process was to find whoever had committed the crime before the family found him. If the family found him first, you can guess what might happen to this guy. We worked day and night for two days to try to find the perpetrator of this crime. On the second day, we found the person lying on the steps of a hotel in downtown San Pedro. He was ripped from the rectum up to the top of his head with a longshoreman's hook, and he had bled to death. The family had found the perpetrator before we had.

In late '42, my number came up, and off I went into the navy. I went to San Diego for processing, training, and so forth. After two or three months of training, if you boxed two or three rounds with any opponent from any of the other classes, you got the weekend off. So I was the Friday-night entertainment for the fellas and got some weekends off. I trained to operate LCM boats, and by '43, I was in Hawaii. In '45, the atomic bomb went off, and the whistle was finally blown. When I returned, I went back to work at Hollywood detectives in Robbery.

I never got into a gunfight with anybody, but I was in several physical confrontations, mostly with people who didn't want to go to jail. In the middle of town was the Hollywood Ranch Market, which was open 24-7 and never closed. One time, we were looking for a guy who frequented this market. Bookmakers, prostitutes, and other types also frequented the market. It was late at night, and we were driving by the market when my partner, Meredith Bimson, said, "Roy, pull over—I think we got this guy."

I pulled over, and the guy started to run. I was still in reasonably good shape and chased him into a dark parking lot, and he stopped between two cars. I showed him my badge, and he said, "Yeah? Where do you want me to put that badge?" That sort of conversation went back and forth. I put the badge away, and the next thing I did—I later taught this at the academy because I thought it was effective—was get his hand up behind his back with my arm around his neck, choking him. He was as big as I was. I was about to break his arm when he gave up. Meredith pulled the car around, and off to jail we went. We didn't have all the rules that officers have nowadays. If we saw somebody who needed to be interrogated, we went and did it. There wasn't all the worry. I don't think I could be a policeman today. Anyway, it was a constancy of "It's time for you to go to jail."

"Oh no. Not me—I'm not going to go."

"Well, you're going."

I don't remember losing a fight.

One night, my partner and I got a call to come to the station. My regular partner, Meredith, was off that night. The watch commander of the uniform part of Hollywood Division happened to be a rather close friend. He had seen my ability to control belligerent people in various sets of circumstances, and he liked the way I worked. We arrived at the station, and there was a taxicab with a nude woman in it parked in front. The cabbie had picked up the woman in Huntington Park, and she wanted to go to Hollywood Boulevard. She was drunk—far drunker than most women get. She'd thrown her shoes out the window. Next had been her dress, then her bra and her panties, and so forth. She was totally nude, and the cabbie hadn't known what to do, so he'd driven her to the police station. At least two radio cars were there; they couldn't get this woman out of the cab. She had locked the doors and was kicking at the windows.

The watch commander called old Roy Bean. "Roy, I got a problem here. Can you solve it?"

I said, "Well, give me a couple of minutes." Right next door to Hollywood station was an emergency hospital. I asked my partner to get a blanket and a roll of gauze from the hospital. He came back, and we got the cabbie to open one door. I told my partner, "Go open one of the other doors, and when you get that door open, I'll jump in with this blanket, put it over her, and then get her cuffed." He did, and we threw the blanket over her, and immediately she was covered head to foot. I told her, "Turn over, and give me your hands behind your back." She wasn't cooperative at first until I had her hand and her hair. We got her handcuffed, and we wrapped her feet together with the roll of gauze. At the city jail, we walked in with this gal bare—she didn't want any blanket around her. Up to the jail she went, eyes and wonderments galore.

In '48, I asked to go to the academy. I wanted to get into the physical-training aspect of police work. I was at the academy for a good fifteen years, and I really enjoyed working with those young men. We put through classes of policewomen too, but not as often as the men's classes. I was a physical-training instructor. I also taught the penal code, the vehicle code, and chemical agents, and I was a shooting instructor. I had a sincere desire to make sure what I taught them was effective.

Roy Bean

My philosophy as an instructor was protection of the officer first: "What can you do in this case?" I told them that when physical force was necessary, it must be quick and easy. That was why the LAPD always had two officers. It was a lot harder for one man to take another man down and handcuff him than it was for two men. Two men were going to take him down easier and get the job accomplished without anybody really getting hurt. One on one, chances were that one of them was going to get hurt. You just didn't want it to be a policeman.

When I was in charge of the unit, all the instructors knew my position: "If you can't do the exercise, don't call for the cadets to do it." I believed if an instructor was going to call for fifty push-ups, he needed to make sure he could do them right along with the cadets. My instructors could always do one hundred if we had to keep going. I would not allow anyone who worked for me at the academy to stand back and count. The instructors did the exercises along with the cadets—or more than the average cadet did. A cadet could never say, "Well, he stood there and blew the whistle."

I thought the attitudes of the cadets were always good; I was never disappointed. If I saw a change in someone, I'd call him aside. I would say, "Find yourself, and realize what we're trying to do here is to make you a better, more capable, physical specimen. We can't adjust our program for a guy like you. You better adjust to it, or you're going to find yourself out on the street. If you don't like it or if I think you can do better selling shoes or picking tomatoes, I'm going to tell the captain that's what I think you ought to do." I did that with a couple of them.

Roy Bean and Don Nowka, LAPD
Exhibition Shooting Team members

We also did some retraining of policemen with ten or more years on the department. Well, nine out of ten of them thought the academy was of no particular value one way or another. I'd say, "I recommend this type of hold."

"Well," they would respond, "that won't work."

"If you don't like this," I would say, "you had better make sure you got something that you know will work. Because I know this works."

Regarding staying in shape, I tried to make it clear to these policemen: "You could be sitting in that radio car for five, six, seven hours, and all of a sudden, you have to chase somebody. Not very many of you will be able to get out of that car and chase one of these fleet-footed escape artists. So what do you do? Now here's something you can do," and I'd go from there.

I was on the department's exhibition shooting team for about three years. We put on lots of exhibitions. Those were the days when we shot chalk out of each other's fingers, ears, and mouth. We considered ourselves exceptional marksmen, and we had the utmost confidence in each other. You had to in order to stand there and let a guy shoot at you.

From the academy, I went to Administrative Vice as a sergeant. I investigated bookmaking. About every fourth weekend, you and your partner had to cover the office for the weekend. One weekend, my partner and I were in the office, and it was raining cats and dogs. The phone rang, and my partner said, "Roy, you better answer this."

"Hello?" I said.

"This is Lieutenant So-and-So in Inglewood. We got a young man here that has some information regarding bookmaking that you might be interested in."

"About bookmaking?"

"Yeah. I wouldn't bother you, but it sounds to me like he knows what he's talking about, and I think you ought to come and talk to him."

"All right, we'll be there as soon as we can get there."

We got the guy out of jail and started chatting with him.

The kid said, "You know so-and-so?"

"Do I ever—he's one of the biggest fish in the pond."

"Well, I slept with his daughter for six months."

"You what?"

"I slept with his daughter."

"Well, did you know they were bookmakers?"

"Of course."

"What was your part in it?"

"All I was there for was to be a partner to his daughter."

"Was she bookmaking?"

"Of course."

"Well, you must have some names and information."

"Better than that—I was with her when we dumped a whole sack full of names and addresses and so forth in an underground waterway down in Huntington Park."

"Can you take me there?"

"Yeah."

He told us they had lifted a big sewer lid and dropped the information down into the sewer. Well, we got there in time before the floodwaters got to all of the material. We came back to our office, and we had a twenty-foot-long table with nothing but bookmaker information on it. Within a day or so, we knocked down a door and found the daughter sitting there, bookmaking. We arrested and booked her.

The next night, we were at Taix's Restaurant. I saw her dad, the bookmaker, and he came over to the table. He said, "I just wanted to thank you, Sergeant. My daughter told me how decent you were with her. I appreciate that. Let me pick up the tab here."

"No, no, that's all right."

A week later, we kicked in another door. Dang, if it wasn't his mother. She made a big fuss—oh, was she mad. Off to jail she went. We had the benefit of a relationship between this kid in jail and a bookmaker's daughter for the information that was thrown down a sewer. We kicked a few doors on that case for quite some time.

Eventually, I ran out of information in general, and we weren't knocking down many doors. I called Chief Robert Houghton and asked if he had an opening somewhere. He said, "How would you like to go to Robbery?" I went to Robbery for the rest of my days—about three years. The first thing they did was take me to the hat store.

They said, "You get two of these and one of those, and if you buy two of these and one of those, you get this one free." I had never worn a hat in my life, except as a policeman, before working Robbery. We wore our hats everywhere. All of Robbery was the "Hat Squad" at that point, the whole bunch of us.

l to r: Clarence Stromwall, Edward Benson, Harold Crowder, and Max Herman: Los Angeles Police Department Robbery Division "Hat Squad," 1960

Jerry Moon and I worked the academy for several years, and we went to Robbery together. They called us the "Choke-Hold Elite." We had some good stakeouts together. One time, we were looking for some robbers of liquor stores; this was about the fifth holdup in about two days. The robbers were working a certain area, so we started staking out different liquor stores. Big ones, little ones—it didn't matter. They hit big ones, and they hit ma-and-pa ones. Jerry and I were staked out in this one liquor store. It was medium sized and had maybe two employees. Inside the store, gallon jugs of wine were stacked in a pyramid approximately eight feet wide and maybe seven feet high. In came two men. Both of us were aware of them. *This is the twosome,* I thought. As soon as they entered, one of them pointed a gun and started yelling, "Get your hands up!" So we knew we had a robbery. Jerry had the shotgun and had loaded it with what was called a slug round. That was the first one that came out of the gun. Then the next one was a scatter round, maybe fifteen or twenty pellets, each about the size of a pea. At fifteen yards, the pellets spread quite a bit—that was what the scatter round was designed to do. But the first one Jerry had in the shotgun that night was a solid slug. As soon as this suspect got on the other side of this pyramid of wine, off went this shotgun shell—right through the wine and then through him. It made about a three-inch hole out of the wine bottles and took about a half a pound of glass into this guy. The pyramid stayed intact, but not him. We got the other guy in a hurry; immediately he was ours. That put an end to the robberies.

Jerry Moon: "They called us the 'Choke-Hold Elite.'"

Soon after I retired, the Los Angeles County Superior Court put out an invitation for anyone interested in becoming a juvenile court referee to submit a résumé and so forth. Thirty-two hundred people—men and women from all over the United States—applied for the positions. The applicants knew going in that there were only going to be ten appointments to the juvenile court. I came out second on the list. Another LAPD officer was first. We got the black robes, and I was there for fifteen years.

George Adams

Birthplace: Genesee Corners, Wisconsin
Career: 1945–1966
Rank at Retirement: Policeman
Divisions: War Emergency Relief Program, Accident Investigation, West Los
    Angeles Accident Investigation, West Valley Accident Investigation

During World War II, I was in the army military police stationed in Los Angeles. I worked with LAPD special investigators for accident investigations involving military personnel. The LAPD made their report, and I, in turn, would make a report for the army. I got acquainted with many policemen, including Ray Lauritzen, Louie Wyckoff, and Jeep Jensen.

After the war, my wife and I went to dinner with Louie Wyckoff. He asked me, "What are you going to do?" I told him there was a job at one of the movie studios in security. He said, "Why don't you come on the police department?" It was the War Emergency Relief Program at the time. They paid fifty dollars a month for fifty weeks in addition to the regular policeman salary. I decided to take advantage of that.

I went to Traffic Division, and Lieutenant P. K. Miller was working. Looking in the time book, he said, "Do you want to work morning watch?"

I said, "Sure," and he hired me. There was no exam. I got the job based on nothing other than the reputation I had from the special investigators I'd worked with when I was in the army. So I joined the police department but was not certified. You were a policeman, but you were not certified until you received formal training. I worked the War Emergency Relief Program as a policeman for fourteen months.

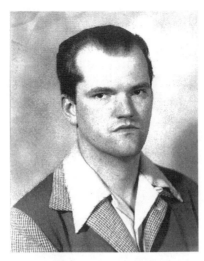

George Adams

My first night was December 5, 1945. You couldn't buy uniforms or equipment. I wore my army field jacket and my military overseas cap. You also couldn't buy guns during the war or just after, so I carried a chrome-plated revolver that belonged to my wife's father in a shoulder holster. That night, we handled a call and went into the University Division station to make a report. As the clerk was typing away, she did a double take when she saw me. She said, "What the hell police department do you work for?" For the first three days on the job, that was what I wore. Finally, I bought a uniform and hat from a guy who had made detective. Of course, the police department, in their generosity, had given me a hat piece. I worked out of Accident Investigation Division, and we filled in at any division that needed an officer. I did that for six months until two guys got hurt in West Los Angeles Division in a traffic accident. I was sent to West LA Accident Investigation as a replacement. I stayed in West LA until I went into the academy in the early part of '47.

The academy was four to six weeks. I was the oldest man there, and while running those hills, a few times, I didn't know whether I was going to make it or not. At our graduation, the cadets had to stand inspection. I still had the gun I carried—the chrome-plated revolver. I knew it had a pit in one of the grooves inside the barrel. My wife's brother had shot it when he was a kid and hadn't told his dad about it; a pit had formed in the barrel, and I couldn't get it out. I had even taken it to a gunsmith to see if he could scour it out.

We were lined up with our guns out for inspection. Chief Clemence Horrall spotted that chrome-plated gun about four men before me, and he skipped those lucky guys. He grabbed the gun out of my hand, looked through it, and jammed it back into my hand. He talked directly to me and said, "That barrel is pitted." The thought hit my mind to say, "Well, I could have told you that before you looked." But fortunately, my better judgment took over my instant response, because I don't think he would have liked that. Later, my wife's brother, Lawson Snyder, came on the job, and he carried that revolver until he could buy one. When he went to Metropolitan Division, he had the barrel cut to two inches, and that took care of the pit.

I had been getting the War Emergency Relief pay of an additional fifty dollars from Uncle Sam. Once I graduated from the academy, I got a letter that the government wanted my last fifty dollars back. I threw the letter away. I got a second letter and then a third letter and threw them both away. No more letters arrived, and I thought, *Ha-ha—outlasted the government.* I came to find out that Mrs. Adams had decided she didn't want any more of those letters, and she had sent the government its fifty bucks.

We were never issued guns, but I was able to buy a skinny lightweight-frame .38 revolver. Then on his last night at end of watch, before he retired, Lieutenant P. K. Miller said, "Anybody that's got fifty dollars in their pocket can buy this gun." The gun was beautiful. I bought it, but how in the world I had fifty dollars, I don't know. It must have been payday, and I must have cashed my check first. The gun was a heavy-duty six-inch Smith and Wesson with a big, fat grip. The first time I qualified with that gun, I hit the two-dollar bonus money. A few months later, I was sent back to West LA Division. AI worked out of the West LA station but covered both West LA and Venice Divisions.

At that time, AI officers wore the regular dark hats. It wasn't until the mid-1950s that we went to the white hats. About the same time we went to the white hats, the department eliminated the shoulder belts for our Sam Brownes. The bad guys were yanking on those belts, although sometimes the good guys were the ones doing the yanking. One night, Jeep Jensen and I heard a radio call of a silent burglary alarm at a closed market. We looked inside and saw no signs of a disturbance. We went around the back, and there was a storage door. I tried it, and it was unlocked. I started to open the door, and all of a

George Adams, left, administering intoximeter test

sudden, I went flying back, my shoulder belt crushing against my chest. Jeep had taken hold of my strap from behind and yanked me back, and he profanely said, "Don't *ever* open a door and stand in front of it." If somebody was in there, then I would have been a goner. I was learning.

One night, three young air force pilots were bringing a C-47 into the LA airport, which was called Mines Field then. There were some lights on the field on the other side of Aviation Boulevard before the runway to let pilots know the runway was coming. But this young pilot didn't realize that those were just warning lights, so he started to land in a plowed field, short of the runway. As soon as he realized the field wasn't a landing strip, he tried to pull up. But the undercarriage caught the cyclone-wire fence and dragged it out across Aviation Boulevard. The fence scooped up about four parked automobiles before it broke loose as it hit a train on tracks parallel to Aviation. We handled the investigation. One of the pilots had reached back into the airplane for his duffel bag and had burned his arm on the wreckage, but that was the only injury from the incident. These guys all walked away from it.

"These guys all walked away from it."

One time, a guy drove right over a cliff off Manchester Boulevard. He was driving down Manchester and didn't realize that it ended at a T intersection. He went straight through the intersection and over the cliff. A department photographer asked me to shine my light on the hood so that he could get a good picture of the car. When the picture came out, it looked as if I were holding the car up with my flashlight. The guys said, "Boy, you're really strong—holding up that car." My partner on that one was Francis Torres.

We investigated another traffic accident on Manchester involving the death of a California highway patrolman's daughter. She had been celebrating her graduation, and her father had given her a beautiful diamond wristwatch as a graduation present. She and her girlfriend had been out in her girlfriend's car. They had been speeding and had crashed, and both had been killed. That was a tough one. I remember going to the morgue, taking her picture for identification, and then making the notification to her father. It was difficult news to give to a fellow officer.

George Adams, left, Francis Torres, right: "Boy, you're really strong—holding up that car."

Near the end of '47, my partner, Tom Houchen, and I were patrolling near Robertson Boulevard. It was nighttime, and I was the passenger. We saw a guy run a boulevard stop sign. We got behind him, and he wouldn't stop for the horn or the red lights. After a couple growls of the siren, he still didn't stop. So Tom pulled up alongside him, and I said, "Hey, pull the car over. You just ran a stop sign." The man slowed down and then stopped. Tom stopped behind him, and just as I was getting out of the police car, I could see he was holding a gun that was reflecting off the headlights of oncoming cars. I yelled, "Look out, Tom! He's got a gun!" I thought he was going to turn and try to get Tom, but instead, he shot himself in the head. This guy was taken to the hospital, where he died. We found a note in his car. The note said,

> To John Law: Greetings, John. Our relations, to the best of my memory, in the past were never overaffectionate. It's all been strictly business, so let's keep it that way. My name is Donald

I. Smith. My address is Nebula M-17. Any astronomer can tell
you it's too far to bother going there. Nebula M-17 is quite a
journey, and it may tire your flat feet. Happy New Year, and
may all your kids be born with flat feet. I was educated at three
prisons. I've been in jails too numerous to mention. I've got a
long prison record.

Here, I had just told him to pull over, and he'd had that gun lying
on the seat. He had previously served time in Folsom Prison and he
was wanted for the kidnapping of his stepdaughter.

When some of the younger officers would get an investigation with
a fatality, they would ask me to make the notification. I was considered
the old man of West LA. Well, in fact, I was all of twenty-seven years
old. One time, I was asked to make the notification to a Mexican lady
whose husband had been killed in a traffic accident. The lady insisted
I come in the house. In the house, she had a regular altar, like in a
church. There was a picture of her husband under a canopy on the
altar. She was crying and saying, "He can't be dead. I love him." She
loved him so much that she had made a shrine to her husband while he
was alive.

One night, we had an accident call on Sepulveda Boulevard coming
over from the San Fernando Valley; this was before there was a freeway.
The accident involved a young football player, and he must have been
good, because he had just signed with the Los Angeles Rams. He had
gotten a bonus and bought himself a convertible. He had been coming
down Sepulveda from Mulholland Drive, and he oversteered and tried
to correct it. He tipped over, and because the top had been down, he'd
almost been beheaded by the side of the car when it landed. It had
choked him to death and broken his neck. I learned later about his
signing with the Rams.

We booked Edward G. Robinson Jr., son of the actor, for drunk
driving. He hit four parked cars in fraternity row at UCLA. Lieutenant
Sid Barth's kid, Martin Barth, was also in the car, and he lost sight in
his right eye, which made the crime a drunk-driving felony. Edward
had been driving with a probationary license. We spent seven days
on the first trial and had a hung jury. The next trial lasted four days,
and the jury found him guilty. Because his father was so popular, the
incident was pretty well hushed up.

Bob Sauter and I investigated an accident on Pico at Camden, where there was a storm-sewer excavation site with barricades all over the place. A drunk driver in his Cadillac didn't see it or didn't care. He drove through the barricades and into the hole. One of his passengers was killed and the other was seriously injured. The irony of this was that the guy killed was Bob's buddy from high school. When we got back in our car after we had finished our investigation and turned in the report, Bob said, "That was a high school buddy of mine." I hadn't known prior to that moment. He had calmly handled the investigation. We had been busy completing the reports and waiting for the doctor to verify the death. It was quite a few hours before he told me. Bob had never shown any signs of having known the person who was killed.

George Adams, top, Bob Sauter, below: "Bob had never shown any signs of having known the person who was killed."

When I moved to Thousand Oaks, I transferred to West Valley Division. Sometimes I worked what we called the Freeway Flyer. The flyer was a small Oldsmobile with a big engine. It was the patrol car for the freeway because it could go like a bat out of hell to catch speeders. One day, a unit had a traffic-accident investigation on the freeway, and we drove over to help. The driver had been hurt pretty badly in the car, and the officers were waiting for an ambulance and a tow truck. As we were waiting, I heard *tickety-tickety* behind me, and I looked around and saw a car driving up against the fence—the *tickety-tickety* had been the fence posts going down. The man driving almost hit the back of the police car. One of the posts had come up underneath the car, missed all of the underpinnings, and lodged in this guy's throat. He was sitting in the driver's seat with his neck broken and the post in his throat. Later, after that accident, I told my wife that was the last notification I ever wanted to make. We went to make the notification, his wife came out, and I saw four little brown eyes peeking through the window right next to the driveway—the sons. We didn't have to tell her; she knew. But the strange thing was what she didn't know, what we didn't tell her. Her husband's pants had what we thought was a brown insert at the hip on each side, but later, after we talked to the hospital staff, we found out the inserts were the pockets of his pants. His pants were inside out, as if maybe he'd had to put them on in a hurry.

I got a radio call of a traffic accident late one day. All of the traffic cars were going end of watch, and I was still on the air. I saw the car up over a curb, with the front end against a tree; there was no driver, and a lady was seated on the passenger side. The lady was older, and she was knitting. She was knitting away and didn't know what was going on; she had Alzheimer's. Her husband, the driver, was outside the car with what I thought was blood on his face and his sleeve. The glove compartment was open, and there looked to be blood on the glove compartment door. At the time, I couldn't figure out how the blood had gotten there. At the hospital, we discovered that he was a diabetic. We told the doctor, and he gave the guy a shot. In minutes, the man was shaking his head and asking, "Where's my wife? Where's my wife?" He had been in a diabetic coma. His wife was sitting in the waiting room, still knitting. He got up eventually, went into the waiting room, and talked to her. She was glad to see him, but she had no idea what he had gone through. The "blood" turned out to be chocolate from a candy bar. Apparently, he'd had a diabetic attack and reached into the glove compartment for the sweet candy bar. He had grabbed the candy bar and gotten some in his mouth, but not enough to help him.

Twice I had partners who had wives who were about to have babies while we were working. One time, my partner Elmo Metz's wife, Bonnie, went into labor and called the station. They lived close by, and when we got to his house, we put her in the police car. I wouldn't let him drive. On one turn on our way to the hospital, there was a dip. As we approached the dip, I told her, "Cross your fingers."

She said, "Hell, I'll cross my legs!"

We just barely got her to the hospital, where she delivered in the emergency room. That was their only child.

The other time, my partner Paul Brodowy and I were handling a traffic accident near the LA airport. While at this accident, a department photographer drove up to us and yelled to Paul, "Come on—your wife's having a baby!" Paul went with the photographer to Paul's house, which was near the airport.

After I finished the investigation, I met up with Paul at the hospital. His wife hadn't delivered yet. There was a little restaurant near the hospital, and I suggested we go get a cup of coffee. He said, "Okay." I swear the coffee was scalding, and he just chug-a-lugged the coffee and said, "Let's go." We got back to the hospital, and the kid arrived.

After I left West LA and went to West Valley Division, I didn't see Paul again. When I retired, my wife and I moved from the Los Angeles area. Many years later, while at a grocery store, someone in the next aisle started laughing and said, "I think that's George Adams," and sure enough, Paul walked around the aisle. He had heard me talking and also had smelled my pipe tobacco. Small world.

I met a lot of nice guys on the police department. At West LA, our wives all knew each other so well that when one was going to have a baby, the others would give her a baby shower. All the guys would play poker together. In March 1966, I was sitting in roll call one day when it suddenly occurred to me that I had been at this work a long time, and I'd had enough. I took the rest of the day off and went downtown and retired. I did not use any sick time or get credit for overtime—I just retired. I went to the college library where my wife worked, took her out for coffee, and announced to her that I had retired. We had not talked the decision over beforehand. I didn't have any special reason for retiring, but my wife said the last notification I had made was the main reason I quit. I don't know.

George Adams LAPD retirement identification card

Lomie May Hall

Birthplace: Tuskegee, Alabama
Career: 1951–1978
Rank at Retirement: Sergeant
Divisions: Juvenile, Jail, Hollenbeck, Seventy-Seventh Street, Parker Center
    Business Office, Wilshire, Highland Park

I grew up in Tuskegee, Alabama. My granddad, William Cornelius Daniel, was elected sheriff three times of Macon County, Alabama. The town jail was the back part of his house, and I used to play cards through the window with the trustee. My granddad also used to supervise the prisoners on the work farm in the cotton fields. He let us pick cotton too as long as he was there. In 1945, my first husband, who had been in the navy, and I came to California. He became a Pasadena Police Department motor officer. My friend was a Pasadena policewoman—there were only five at the time—and one was going on maternity leave. I thought that would be a good job for me for a few months until she returned. Pasadena would not hire me, because they would not hire two who were in the same family. I had never planned to be a policewoman, but I thought, *They can't tell me I can't be a policewoman.* I took the policewoman exam for LAPD. I passed the exam, the physical agility test, and the interview.

When I took the medical exam, I was sure I would pass. I was twenty-seven years old. The doctor poked around my stomach and then called another doctor in. I thought, *Am I gonna die before I get outta here?* I said, "What's the trouble?"

The doctor said, "I can feel your backbone."

I said, "You can feel everybody's backbone."

Lomie May Hall

He said, "Not from the front."

So I went to the gym.

When I went back to the doctor's office, Dr. Vance, a mean old codger, said, "What did you do to get some muscle?"

I said, "I went to a gym."

He said, "You'll be a better policewoman for it. See you later." That was it.

In the academy, about twenty women were in my class. Eight graduated from the academy, four made it past probation, and one quit the day after graduation. She said she had known as soon as she'd gotten started that she didn't want to do it but that she had wanted to prove to herself that she could. At the time, policewomen were required to be at least twenty-five years old. By that age, as a general rule, you had a smarter group of people, because people either had a job or had continued to go to school. I did a little bit of both. We had to sign an agreement that we wouldn't seek advancement beyond sergeant. When I came on the job, there were about one hundred policewomen, including the sergeants. A new men's class started a few weeks after us, but we did not intermingle with them.

Sgt. Leola Vess

Our academy class was one month long. We learned three things in the academy: first, always have a nickel in your pocket in case you have to use the phone in an emergency; second, never give orders to a male officer; and third, don't expect your partners to open doors for you.

Sergeant Leola Vess, the first female sergeant on the department, was in charge of our class. She was good and fair. We couldn't have our fingernail polish darker than hers, though. If someone did, you had to change it. Sergeant Vess had been a circus performer—a trapeze artist, I believe. She was the only person I had ever seen climb the rope hanging in the gym hand over hand all the way to the top. I thought that was a pretty grand feat.

The academy did not have any guns at the time, so I bought a secondhand gun for sixty-five dollars. It was a Colt, but as soon as I could, I swapped it for a Smith. I already knew how to shoot a gun. My granddad let us shoot guns, even a shotgun. The Smith was a two-inch .38, and I carried it in my purse. The policewoman's purse had a built-in holster. I carried my gun out in the field, but I never shot anybody.

When we graduated from the academy, Chief William H. Parker presented our diplomas to us. We didn't have formal uniforms at graduation. I graduated in a dress. Policewomen didn't have to buy formal uniforms until they got off probation. When I worked the jail, I wore a white nurse's uniform. June Lang was in my class, and after several years, only the two of us stayed on the job. Every time we saw each other, it was a class reunion.

Georgia Street police station and hospital, circa 1930s

After I graduated from the academy, I went to Juvenile Division at the Georgia Street station. When a policewoman worked with a policeman, even though he might have graduated from the academy the day before, he was in charge. The first night, I worked with a guy who was a real hotshot policeman. He didn't really like to be in Juvenile, and now he had a policewoman who was one day out of the academy in the car with him. A robbery-in-progress call came out at a Safeway Market. He pulled up in front with no help—with a hindrance, really. There was another car assigned, and they got there quickly. We went into the market. There had been a robbery, but the suspects were gone. My partner told me to let Communications Division know the suspects were gone, and I did. That was my first hot call, and for me, although I was scared, it was pretty exciting.

After a while, I went to morning watch. There was only one Juvenile car for the whole city on morning watch. One of my partners was Rudy De Leon. He was fun to work with. The best thing about Rudy was that if you weren't too busy, he'd start telling you the story about his family living on this big property with cows and gauchos and all that. After about an hour, I'd say, "I saw that movie, Rudy. What others have you seen?" He was really a prince of a fellow to work with. I'm glad they named the new Hollenbeck station after him.

While at Juvenile Division, I saw my first dead person. There was a homicide at one of the little houses in Chavez Ravine. This was before Dodger Stadium was built. We went by, and a few detective cars were there. Well, when curiosity gets the better of you, you really want to know what's going on, so we went in. The detectives were waiting for the coroner. The dead guy was leaning on a table with a big butcher knife stuck in his back—very dead, not bothering anybody. That was quite an experience. I would be scared now. I didn't have enough sense to be afraid then.

At Juvenile, our duties included working the desk that handled missing juveniles. The policemen at Communications Division would receive calls, and if the conversation began with "My kid . . ." they transferred the call to Juvenile. One mother called all the time. Her little girl was about fourteen years old, and her name was Lovey. The mother would start the conversation by saying, "That Lovey's done gone again." Lovey would just take off, and later, she would go home, and her mother would call to cancel the missing report. When Lovey reached eighteen, she got pregnant. She lived with somebody else, but nothing bad ever happened to her. Why kids ran away all the time, I could never understand. I used to think everyone's life was normal— people had a mother and dad, the dad loved the mother, the mother loved the dad, he went to work and gave the money to the mother to run the house, and everything was fine. I found out not everybody had that.

I was still on probation when they transferred me to Lincoln Heights jail. I wasn't there long, but long enough to know they had good food, and I gained four pounds. Well, the bad thing—the really bad thing—was that I learned to smoke while working the jail. I had never smoked when I was in college, because I hadn't been able to afford it. It seemed to me that every time somebody came into the jail who was filthy, loud, drunk, or fighting, everybody would take a break. It was always my turn to search and print. Well, I learned to smoke too, and take a break. Years later, I said to myself, *Stupid! You were the one on probation. You were supposed to get the dirty, loudmouthed fighters anyway.* It was an expensive habit, but that was why I started smoking.

Frank Guayante and Hollenbeck DAP unit

Once off probation, I went to Hollenbeck Division and worked the DAP program, the Deputy Auxiliary Police Program. The program was for girls and boys, and they wore uniforms. I had a drill team and a rifle club. The policeman in charge of the unit was Frank Guayante. He would not allow the kids to speak Spanish in the station, because he thought they might talk and laugh about us and we wouldn't know it. That was a good idea and a bad idea but was the best thing at the time. We took the kids many places, including the beach, the skating rink, and dances. The Catholic church let us use their big room all the time to have our dances. I worked Hollenbeck for almost five years, and I haven't been back. They've worn out two stations since I left, and I've not seen either one of them.

Captain John "Two Gun" Powers was the captain of Juvenile Division, and the DAP program was under Juvenile Division. One day, we were at a mountain camp, and Captain Powers came for a visit. At some point, while he was sitting out in the sunshine, I went to sit with him, and we had a chat. I told him that I would like to get back to Juvenile Division, that I hadn't done police work in a long time. He asked me how I liked DAP, and I told him I really liked it—I didn't have to go in early, the kids were nice to me, and I got to spend a lot of time with my son. I told him all the good things about the job. I was on the next transfer to Juvenile; I guess maybe I liked the job too much.

The policewomen at Juvenile would walk footbeats in high heels, hats, and gloves. When we went to court, we dressed the same way. Policewomen were the last to wear hats to court. One of the footbeats was at the bus station. The main thing was to meet the buses and capture the kids—the runaways—before the bad guys got them. We would take them to Juvenile Hall. If the parents sent money, we'd put them on the bus or train for home.

We also checked downtown movie houses for kids with families or runaway kids sleeping in the theaters. Main Street movie houses were open all night, and one night, we arrested a whole family at one of them—a mother, a father, and three little kids. The mother and father were sitting in the middle so that they could lean on each other. The kids were on either side of them, which was against the law. If the kids were in between the parents, then it was okay. These people wouldn't have known if somebody had picked up their three-year-old and gone off with the kid or if someone had petted the kid right there during the movie. One night, we took our Code 7—our meal break—and saw a half hour of a movie starring a Swedish actress. The next night, we came back to see the second half of the movie. We were in the back, sitting in seats made of plywood and nailed to the floor—like those in old school auditoriums. A guy was sitting on one end of the row of seats, and the whole row of seats was shaking. He was scratching like a dog. We got outta there before we could get his lice and fleas. We never did see the rest of that movie. We didn't particularly like checking the movies—there were always drunks and derelicts—but we did. It was surprising to see the kids in there. We also checked the Main Street hotels for runaway kids.

There were people, sometimes families, who slept in their cars, and we would try to find them shelter. There were many shelters for men, and those would fill up, but it was hard to find a place that would take the entire family. Some shelters, such as the Sunshine Mission, would take mothers and babies or small children but no men. One couple said they'd never been apart a night since they'd gotten married, and they had a string of kids. If they couldn't go together, then none of them would go, they insisted. We finally persuaded them to soften their stance, and we got the mother and children into a mission and put the father in another mission. The Indian Mission would always take people, and you didn't have to have a passport that said you were Indian. If someone called them, they would say they were full, but if we took somebody there, they would keep the person. We used to drive around the corner and wait to see if the people we dropped off were sent back out, but the mission always kept them.

My partner, Andy Evans, and I used to drive around MacArthur Park after ten o'clock at night to see if kids were there. If they were, we'd stop them. They'd say they were on their way home. "Why aren't you on the bus? Don't you have any money?"

"No."

If it was at all feasible for them to catch a bus or streetcar, we'd tell them to wait right there for the next bus, and we'd give them a dime or whatever it cost to get them on the bus to go home. What were we to gain by taking an ordinary kid who was going home from the park and had stayed out a little too long to the station and by having his father come to the station if the kid was not really doing anything that we knew of? We did that many times. There was no point in giving a kid a record unnecessarily. We worked the same area and saw the same kids. We knew who was and was not doing anything. A different brand of kids were around then. If a policeman would see kids at ten thirty or eleven o'clock at night and say, "Hey, come over here," they'd come. They wouldn't call the officer a name and just walk off. Even the bad kids respected policemen.

Occasionally, I was loaned to Ad Vice Division to work undercover. One time, Leroy Goforth, who worked bookies, had me walk on the corner of Third and Figueroa posing as a streetwalker. I had to walk the street to see if I could find out who was taking bets at that corner. There was a small café there, and a bar. The bar was just one long bar; it had no tables or anything. I was there every day for a week. I must have been doing my job of looking like a streetwalker well, because the beat officers kept writing FIs—field-interview cards—on me. The only identification I had was my Social Security card, which had my full name on it. Leroy would go to roll call each day to find out what the beat officers had seen. The beat officers gave him the info from the FI cards, and one told him, "All she had was a social security card, but this is a phony name if I ever saw one."

Lomie May Hall

On the last morning, I went into the café; stayed a few minutes, having coffee; came back out; and sat on the bus bench. An old man sat on the bus bench by me and said, "Don't go back in the restaurant or the bar, because the people in there know you are a policewoman."

I said, "Thank you very much."

The next time my partners came by, I got in the car with them and left. I found out there were more good people there than bad people.

Ad Vice was investigating a group of gypsies, and they sent me to the gypsies' house to get my fortune told. The gypsies would listen to clients the first time because they wanted them to come back with money. But this particular time, they couldn't do the reading there. The gypsies wanted me to go with them because the main gypsy was at another place. They were going to take me somewhere else, but I wouldn't get in the car with them. My backup partners had terrible cars left over from before the war. In some, we had to put the key in a certain way to make the car start. That day, we had one of those cars that wouldn't start good. So I just said, "Not today."

In '66, I made sergeant. I went to Wilshire detectives and worked a year at the detective desk. I was fond of Captain Ed Jokisch. Jokisch was polite, and he would not criticize women. One time, something went wrong, and he gave the policeman involved holy hell. I said, "Captain, I'm the sergeant. I'm the one that told him to do it, in my ignorance."

"Okay." He never said a cross word to me.

One day, everybody walked past my desk with a shotgun. They didn't say "We're going bird hunting or rabbit hunting" or "We're going to catch a robber" or anything. They came back later and put the guns back. I said, "Captain, what happened?" He told me what had happened, and I said, "You know, you hired me here to do a job. I'm supposed to tell the chief where you're going and what you're going to do."

"Okay."

So the next morning, Captain Jokisch walked by my desk, put his newspaper under his arm, and said, "I'm going to the library." We laughed. I enjoyed working for him.

When Captain Jokisch left Wilshire, Bob Perry became the captain of detectives, so I worked for Perry. When he went to Highland Park Division, there was no policewoman sergeant there, so I went with him. That was a good job and a really good place to work. For years, I hadn't been willing to work there, because I didn't want to work in my own neighborhood. I had gotten a divorce, and when I was looking for a place to live, I wanted my boy to go to school in South Pasadena.

I couldn't rent an apartment in South Pasadena, because I had a big dog—a Great Dane—so we lived in Highland Park. I had a small boy and a large dog instead of a small dog and a large boy.

After I retired, my former DAP kids had a barbecue for me. These kids were grown and had families. One boy became the head of the board of education for a school district. Some of their parents also came. More than one mother came up to me and thanked me for helping their girls grow up having some manners and not getting in trouble, as other girls did. Before we went anywhere, I used to tell my girls that we knew that because Hollenbeck had the prettiest girls, we had to act the nicest. I always considered it a feather in my cap that not one girl got pregnant during a DAP activity. We went to a lot of places, including camp, the beach, and dances, and had a lot of Friday-night events. None of the kids told their parents that they were going to a DAP activity and then went somewhere else. We didn't have any of that. I was given a special award, and I was the proudest person that evening. Can you imagine? I worked DAP between '51 and '56, and they honored me when I retired in '78.

Calvin "Cal" Drake

Birthplace: Glendale, California
Career: 1952–1976
Rank at Retirement: Detective III
Divisions: Parking and Intersection Control, Newton, Administrative Vice,
    Metropolitan, Bunco-Forgery

Do I remember how much money I made when I first came on? I certainly do. I made $319 a month, gross. When I graduated from the academy, we were given a raise from $319 to $340. It was a cost-of-living index raise—the first time they had ever had one. When we got up to around $500 a month, Chief Parker said, "One of these days, a cop will make a thousand dollars a month."

I said, "Chief Parker's gone crazy. No cop is ever going to make a thousand a month."

My mom introduced me to law enforcement. My dad was killed in World War II, and before my mom remarried, she got a job working for the Los Angeles Police Department as a civilian in the accounting office. Her office was on the twenty-first floor of city hall. Occasionally, I met her there, and she would introduce me to policemen. I never told them I wanted to be a police officer, but I thought that might not be a bad job. When I was sixteen years old, not too long after my mom remarried, I told her I wanted to go into the Marine Corps. She fixed my birth certificate to make me look seventeen rather than sixteen, and I went into the Marine Corps with her permission. I promised her that when I was done serving, I would finish high school and get a diploma. At the end of my two years in the Marine Corps, I went back to high school and graduated.

Cal Drake

My oldest son was one month old the day I started the academy in '52. The academy was a lot like the Marine Corps boot camp, except cadets got to go home at night. It really wasn't a shock to my system, as it was to some. There was one who had never been in the military, and he was also the youngest, at twenty-one. I was twenty-two. The oldest, Ken Green, would later retire as the captain of Burglary Auto Theft Division. Kenny was a former marine, and during World War II, he had ended up on Guadalcanal as an armorer for Pappy Boyington's outfit. When someone was going to be let go, the class door would open, an officer would call someone out, saying, "Bring your stuff and come with me," and we'd never see the person again. It scared the heck out of us. We all wanted the job; it wasn't a matter of this was just another job.

In class one day, the instructor was writing on the blackboard, giving us information as we took notes. The door opened, and two shots were fired—blanks. Someone entered, shoved the instructor up against the blackboard, and took the instructor's wallet. The guy ran out the door, and after the door closed, the instructor said, "I want you to write down everything you saw."

LAPD.CADET CLASS - DEC. 9, 1952

Cal Drake, seated, far right: "We all wanted the job; it wasn't a matter of this was just another job."

I thought, *What does the floor look like?* because I had been digging a hole in the floor when the shots were fired. I could only say I had heard two shots. The lesson was an eye-opener for us. We learned that when someone asked for a description, people's memories of an event that just happened were not going to be good most of the time. If an officer got a good description, he or she should question how accurate it was. I don't remember if anybody came up with a good description in the class. I know I didn't.

One guy in my class was Sam Sirianni. We didn't know that Sam had already worked an undercover assignment. Ever hear about the Mabel Monohan murder? Mabel Monohan was an elderly lady who lived alone in Burbank. The rumor was that she had a lot of money in her house. Barbara Graham, Jack Santo, and Emmett Perkins broke into her house and searched it, but they could not find any money. They pistol-whipped her to find out where she kept her money and finally killed her. They never did get any money, but they were arrested. Because Sam was Italian and looked like a gangster, he was introduced to Barbara Graham through her cellmate, an informant. He met with Graham in the county jail a few times. Finally, she said to him, "I want you to come to court and testify that on this particular night, you and I were in this motel shacked up."

He said, "What do I get for that?"

She said, "You get twenty-five thousand dollars and all the sex you can handle."

That was what he testified to in court. She didn't know until he walked down the aisle in court that he was an undercover cop. She was convicted and later executed. Sam was now my classmate. He didn't say anything, and the instructors didn't say anything about his undercover work. We learned about it later. He had to come back through the academy before they could send him out in the field.

When I graduated, I went right to PIC—Parking and Intersection Control—directing traffic. I got to stand downtown and suck up all the smog from the buses and cars. I stood at Fourth and Hill the whole time. PIC was actually boring except for one day when my relief came down. We were standing there talking when a guy walked up to us and asked where the press club was. My relief guy said, "You're Jim Thorpe, aren't you?"

He said, "Yes, I am."

We chitchatted for a minute. That was about six months before Thorpe passed away. I had never met a person of that stature from the sports world before that.

While I was at PIC, I worked the Rose Parade in Pasadena and got paid twenty-five bucks for the day. I had never seen the Rose Parade until I was paid for it. That was January 1, 1953. The department let us work the parade part-time and in uniform. I had a spot right on Colorado Boulevard. One little kid sitting on the curb, named Johnny, saw Hopalong Cassidy coming down the street as part of the parade, and he said, "Wow, Mommy—there's Hoppy."

Barbara Graham, left, Sam Sirianni, far right: "She didn't know until he walked down the aisle in court that he was an undercover cop."

I said, "You want to meet Hoppy?" I picked him up and carried him out into the street. I said, "Hoppy, this is Johnny. Johnny, this is Hoppy," and they shook hands. That kid was walking high off the ground after that.

After five months at PIC, I went to Newton Street Division. On the first night, I remember getting in the car, and my partner said, "You want something to eat or you want to go to the bathroom, let me know. Otherwise, stay there, listen, and keep your mouth shut. I'll tell you what I need from you." He also said, "What you learned in the academy—forget it. Most of it's not going to work out here." In a sense, he was right. The academy gave you a good basis to work from to be a policeman, but you had to be on the street to actually figure out what you're doing.

You remember the name Marion Hoover? Hoover and I were partners on night watch, and he later was involved in a number of shootings. Before he came to Newton, he had been assigned to Motor Transport Division and had been the driver for Mayor Norris Paulson. Our lieutenant had also come to Newton from Motor Transport, and Marion used to report to him. Marion told me the lieutenant would ask him, "What does the mayor talk about when you're out driving around? Who's he talking about? When there are other people in the car, what are they saying?"

Marion told me he would tell this lieutenant, "I can't tell you that."

The lieutenant would say, "If you're loyal to the department, you can tell me that."

Marion said he told the lieutenant, "The mayor's going to fire me if I do that." Marion and the lieutenant did not get along.

One night, near the end of roll call, we lined up in the hallway for an inspection. Marion had a Distinguished Expert shooting medal, and he'd just had a diamond placed on it. The lieutenant walked up to him, took hold of Marion's shooting medal, and said, "Oh, Distinguished Expert," and he kept holding it.

Marion said, "Am I under arrest?"

The lieutenant said, "Well, no."

Marion said, "Then get your damn hands off me."

The whole roll call started laughing. The lieutenant's bald head went red. He said, "That's it," and he left.

I looked at Marion and kidded, "Hoover, you're really a piece of work. I hope it doesn't rub off on me."

I had one partner, Jack Howlett, who later retired out of the academy. He was six foot four and weighed 240 pounds. One night, we were chasing a car with a young guy driving it. We were just about ready to go in pursuit when the guy got to an intersection and rear-ended a car in front of him. We had real bumpers on cars then, so there wasn't any damage. I walked up to the driver's-side window and said, "Let me see your driver's license."

He started chipping at me. "Look at what you made me do. You made me run into this car."

I said, "I didn't make you do anything. Get out, and let me have your driver's license."

After I asked him a third time, Jack's arm went over my shoulder, and he pulled the guy right through the open window and out of the car. Jack held the guy up and said, "You should do what the policeman says. When he says he wants your driver's license, you should give it to him."

The guy was screaming, "Put me down!"

I looked at Jack and said, "Jack, you take all the fun out of this job!"

Jack was a big, easygoing policeman. He was always there to do what you needed him to do. You never felt like you needed more backup than that.

The sergeants today, I guess, are out in the field all the time, following up on calls. Our sergeants hardly ever did that. They left us alone to do our jobs, and as long as we were doing them right and not getting in trouble, they were good to us. One night, I was working with a guy who was senior to me. We had an incident, and he said, "I'm going to call a sergeant. I think we need advice." We were working morning watch.

He called for a sergeant, and this sergeant pulled up, rolled the window down, and said, "What do you have?"

My partner explained to him what we had.

The sergeant said, "What's your badge say?"

He said, "Huh?"

"What does your badge say?"

He said, "Policeman."

"Then dammit—be a policeman." He rolled the window up and drove off.

Jack Howlett

In 1956, there was a train wreck involving a two-car passenger train in Newton. It was a commuter train that ran from Los Angeles to San Diego and back. The two cars were bigger than the average car and carried a lot of passengers. There was a curve in the track near Washington Boulevard and east of Santa Fe Street. The speed limit for the curve was twenty-five miles per hour. The engineer, I believe, had a heart attack, fell on the throttle, and hit the curve at over sixty miles per hour. The train turned over and slid on its side. You could imagine what it looked like. There were bodies everywhere and a whole bunch of people with broken arms and legs. Thirty people died and over a hundred were injured. I was working a one-man car and was the first unit on the scene, but other units arrived shortly after. I took three carloads of walking wounded with broken bones to Central Receiving Hospital, Code 3. It was a mess. A wrecker was brought in, and the cars were up-righted. A motor cop was standing down from me, and a deputy coroner came up to him and said, "Here—grab this cardboard box. We're going down the tracks; start picking up pieces."

The motor cop said, "I can't pick up dead body parts; I'm not authorized to do that. That's got to be a coroner to do that."

The deputy coroner said, "You're deputized—let's go."

Sante Fe train wreck, 1956

I heard this exchange, and I turned around and quickly walked away. I was not going to go pick up body parts if I could help it. I went home at about four thirty the next morning.

About a year later, I went from Newton to Metropolitan Division. Part of Metro's job was to saturate an area with policemen to suppress crime and to work stakeouts for detectives. On one case, a nurse who worked at a local hospital and lived in an apartment building on Los Feliz Boulevard was murdered inside of her apartment. Someone broke into her apartment and killed her. We set up a rolling stakeout of two or three cars. I worked it, and it went on for several months. I remember sitting in the car during wintertime, and it was cold. There was no heater in the car. We would put a blanket around us to keep warm. It was so cold that our breath would fog the windows. And I had a partner who smoked cigars. The suspect was finally caught.

We worked a fishermen's labor strike for a month and a half in San Pedro. On the first day, we blocked off a pier at Twenty-Second Street where all the fishing boats came in. Only the people working the boats could go in and out. The strike was against the packinghouses because they weren't paying enough for the fish. Well, the longshoremen decided they were going to get involved, brothering up with the fishermen. Captain Joe Stephens of Metro was also the Labor Relations officer. Joe was a big, tall, husky cop and had been in Metro and Labor Relations for most of his career. He probably had twenty-five years on the job then. He had been through some really nasty strikes. During a strike in '37, some longshoreman had taken a swipe at him with a shipping hook. The hook had ripped his uniform and cut him across the chest. He picked the guy up over his head and threw him off the dock and into the ocean. Every time the man had come up, Joe kicked him in the face and knocked him back in. Joe told us, "I just kept kicking him back."

A longshoreman union leader told Joe as we were standing there, "Tomorrow morning, we'll have a thousand longshoremen down here." He said, "The first thing we're going to do is throw you cops off the dock; then we're going to go in and settle our problems."

Stephens looked at him and started poking him in the chest. He said, "Let me tell you something. If one of my cops gets hurt, I'm holding you responsible."

The guy said, "No, I can't be responsible; I can't stop those guys."

Stephens said, "You are responsible, and I'm going to beat the living shit out of you if one of my people gets hurt." Nobody got hurt.

Policemen at Metro were occasionally loaned to various units, and I went on several loans to detectives. One loan was to Forgery Division. Eventually, an opening in Forgery came up, and I went there in '60. I spent the next sixteen years there. I had worked Metro for about a year and a half. One of the reasons I left Metro was because I got tired of the constant changing. In a week's time, officers could work morning watch, day watch, and night watch and go from soft clothes to uniform, from rags to a suit, depending on what they were doing.

While I was at Forgery, the Watts riots started. The day after the riots started, we were told to report downstairs to Central Division to work patrol. We didn't have uniforms at the station. We worked in a radio car that day, and we handled calls in suits—no helmets, nothing. Being out there with suits on was going to get us hurt. That night, I went home and told my wife, "Get that uniform out, and let's make it fit."

METROPOLITAN DIVISION L.A.P.D. 1959

Capt. Joe Stephens, front row, fourth from left: "During a strike in '37, some longshoreman had taken a swipe at him with a shipping hook. The hook had ripped his uniform and cut him across the chest. He picked the guy up over his head and threw him off the dock and into the ocean."

The next day, I was in uniform, and we got helmets. We were working four men to a car. It was the middle of August, it was hot, and the police cars did not have air-conditioning. We had to keep the windows up because there was word that rioters were throwing bottles of acid at policemen. We had four shotguns in the car, which had come from other departments. We were out there answering calls, although Communications Division wasn't assigning them. The process was "Any unit in the vicinity, handle this call."

After the riots were over, detectives from all over the city were tasked with recovering stolen property. When I drove down around 103rd Street in Watts to recover property, the scene reminded me of pictures from World War II of German cities that had been bombed. Some of the buildings had been burned to the ground.

"Black Owned" was written on the fronts of some of the buildings that were all busted up.

In '66 or '67, Willie Gough from Forgery said to me, "We're putting together this group—a sniper-type thing," and asked me if I was interested. He was on the police pistol team and was a great shooter with almost any kind of weapon.

I said, "Sure."

So I ended up going to the forerunner of SWAT. It wasn't called SWAT at first; actually, it wasn't called anything. We got together on weekends or after work and practiced. We used our own equipment on our own time. After about a year of practicing and training, the department decided to make the group an official department unit. There were sixty of us from across the department. We talked about what to call the unit. The consensus was to call it Special Weapons and Attack Team. That name was presented to Daryl Gates, who, I believe, was a deputy chief at the time. He said, "You guys are crazy; you can't call it an attack team." Ideas were kicked around some more, and the name Special Weapons and Tactics Team was selected. We formed four-man teams, like a military fire team. I was a rear guard position.

The first major thing we got involved in was with the Black Panthers. In December '69, we got a call to bring our gear and meet at the armory in Elysian Park at four thirty in the morning. We were told that search warrants were going to be served at several Black Panther locations. Lou Riker and I got the job of ramming the front door at the Black Panther headquarters on Central at Forty-First Street.

At the location, we had rifle teams on the roof of the building across the street and officers in the back of the building. It was a quiet morning, and there was nobody around. There was a screen door in front of a wood-framed door with a glass center. We hit the door with the ram, the glass shattered, and the screen hung up a little on the ram. We missed the actual jam on the first hit, and we hit it a second time. The door opened, and we backed off and hit the deck. Our job wasn't to go in; there was a team behind us tasked with making the entry. When we hit the deck, all of a sudden, the world exploded. There was shooting everywhere. I was lying down next to a foundation wall just in front of the door. There was shooting coming from inside the place through the door and portholes in the windows. The rounds were going over my head. One round hit me in my ankle.

l to r: Bob Arnold, Dan Mahoney, Larry Buonocristiani, Cal Drake, and Lou Riker, kneeling: SWAT team members, 1970

Ed Williams's team was going in a door just north of the door we had hit, which led to a stairway to the second floor, where the Panthers slept. The team took that door down, and he entered and started up the stairs. Somebody upstairs fired a shotgun, and Ed caught a load of buckshot. He didn't have a flak vest. Fortunately, most of the buckshot hit the shotgun. He was brought out, and he was bleeding rather profusely. Some guys came down to me, and I said, "Grab my shotgun, and give me a pull." As they were pulling me, I didn't realize it at the time, but I was being pulled right through Ed's blood. They loaded me into an ambulance, and away we went.

At the hospital, I had blood all over me, and the nurses were having a fit, asking me, "Where else were you hit?"

I said, "I was only hit in the ankle. That's somebody else's blood."

Black Panther headquarters: "When we hit the deck, all of a sudden, the world exploded."

I ended up being in the hospital for about three days with my foot and ankle in a cast. The doctor told me he found pieces of my boot and cloth from my sock inside the wound. The bullet had entered the right side of my ankle and traveled over the bone, underneath the tendon, and out the other side. For thirteen years, the injury caused me problems when I walked. Apparently, the bullet had cut the tendon, and the two bones were rubbing together. I had my ankle operated on, and the doctors made a new tendon using muscle from another part of my leg. Dick Wuerfel and Jim Segars were also wounded.

The shooting went on for almost four hours, and the Panthers finally surrendered. The search warrants were served, and a lot of weapons were recovered. Six Panthers were arrested. Once inside, we discovered that the Panthers had been digging a tunnel to a city sewer system behind their building. It was going to be an escape route. They had poured the dirt from the hole into the walls to make them tough to shoot through. It was a business building with storefront windows for displays. They had sandbagged the windows and hidden the sandbags behind posters in the windows. They had put gun ports in the side windows next to the front door.

Jack Webb, left, Cal Drake, and family: Medal of Valor ceremony, 1972

Eleven of us got the Medal of Valor for the Panther shoot-out. We did not get the awards until '72 because the district attorney's office asked the department not to issue the medals until after the trials were over. They thought awarding the medals before then would cause some problems. Chief Ed Davis said later he would never again delay giving officers recognition for valor.

When officers first go to Forgery, they work the front desk, take reports, and handle the phones. One day, a gal came in, sat down, and wanted to make a report. She had a thirty-five-dollar check that had bounced. I said, "Okay, now what did you give for the check?"

She said, "Service."

I said, "Service? Well, what kind of services did you give?" She mumbled back and forth, and I said, "Honey, are you a prostitute?"

"Yes."

"Was this check from one of your tricks?"

"Yes."

I said, "I can't make a report on that."

She said, "Well, why not?"

I said, "Because prostitution is illegal, and that would stop the whole transaction. You can't give a bad check for something illegal and expect to prosecute the person that gave it to you. It's just not done." She walked out.

We went out to serve a warrant in University Division in the Liemert Park area. This guy had tried to pass a bad check at Bank of America. When the bank had found out it was a bad check, they had tried to have him arrested. He'd taken the guard's gun away from him—pulled it right out of his holster—and of course, he'd gotten away. We went out to his apartment and verified with the manager that it was still the guy's apartment. We got the manager's key, and when we went in, there was evidence that the suspect had been there recently. His wallet was lying on a table, and his pants were lying on the bed. We searched the apartment, but he was not there. My partner, Jim Carter, looked in the closet and said, "Cal, come here—look at this."

There was a cut out in the floor. We pulled the cover up, and we were looking at the foundation area underneath the apartment. We figured he was armed with the security guard's weapon. Willie Gough had also come out, and he and I went under the building. I went one way, and he went the other. He looked around with the flashlight and saw the guy. The guy said, "Don't shoot! Don't shoot."

Willie said, "All right, you get your butt over here and get out of that crawl hole." He did, and we took him to jail. We never did find the gun.

Bob Arnold and I worked patrol together in Newton, and we worked together in detectives for a long time. He was a damn good cop and detective. Bob and I worked on one case where we had an old-time crook who was check kiting. For check kiting, criminals would open two or three accounts, and then they'd take checks from one account, deposit them in another account, and keep depositing. None of the accounts actually had any money in them. The scheme worked because of the check-clearing time. We got a call from Bank of America one day, and we went to the branch office and were told about this case. They gave us a stack of cashier's checks. The suspect was getting cashier's checks on deposits that were nonexistent. The cashier's checks amounted to a little over a million dollars. I asked the bank official for a description of the suspect and asked if he would recognize the suspect if he saw him. He gave us a description and said he could recognize him. I came back in the morning with a photo spread, and he pointed to one of the photos and said, "That's the guy."

"That was who I figured it was."

He said, "You know him?"

I said, "I put him in jail before on a kiting case."

At that time, while he was sitting in jail, he got a deputy sheriff to go out and make deposits for him. The deputy sheriff was arrested, and he went to jail. The suspect had also involved a policeman from a small police department. That policeman was caught and fired. The suspect was a rotten person. We arrested him on the Bank of America case, and he went back to prison. The guy was so smart that he probably could have made a lot of money honestly, but he didn't want to do that. That was work. To him, it was fun taking money away from other people.

Over the years working detectives, I did fifty to sixty extraditions. One time in Florida, I picked up an old guy on our fugitive warrant—an old con man who had been in prison forever. As we were walking through the airport terminal to our gate, he bumped into me. I figured, *Okay.* Then he bumped into me again. I said, "If you're looking for the gun, it's on the other side. You bump into me again, I'm going to knock you flat on your ass." He thought all policemen carried a cross-draw holster.

My career as I look back? I loved it. Not everybody can be a policeman; some are just not cut out for police work. Officers have to learn how to handle the stress of the job without driving themselves nuts, and not all people can do that. I'm as proud of being a policeman as I am of being a marine. There's no such thing as an ex-marine or an ex-policeman. The job was good for me.

The day I retired, it was a little scary turning in my badge. I had known for two months prior that I was leaving, because I had accepted an offer for another job. But as I was standing there, I thought to myself, *You have had a good job for twenty-four years. Do you really want to do this?*

Augusta "Gustie" Bell

Birthplace: Los Angeles, California
Career: 1954–1979
Rank at Retirement: Detective III
Divisions: Jail, Juvenile, Intelligence, North Hollywood, Devonshire

They called us the "Gangster Squad," but it was Intelligence Division. The name was a carryover from the '30s. We gathered information; that was our primary function. One time, we rented an apartment right next door to where a gangster lived. We would watch his apartment from our apartment. One day, our neighbors were doing something to their door, so one of the fellas said, "Gustie, go see what they're doing."

I opened our door and said, "Can I help you?"

"No, thank you. We're just having a little problem here." It was the gangster, Mickey Cohen.

I wanted to get a degree in sociology, but my father didn't think women should go to college. He was an old German. "What do you want to go to college for? You go get married and have kids. That's what women should do," he told me. So that was what I did; I stayed home, and I had two children. I was a housewife. My husband, John Reagan, was a police officer on LAPD. We later divorced, and I had to work. I couldn't get into sociology, because I didn't have a degree, so I applied to LAPD to be a policewoman. I was accepted, and I went into the academy in '54.

Sergeant Daisy Storms was in charge of us. She was good. She wanted us to be ladies, not to take on the men's way. She always said, "Retain your femininity."

Our physical-training instructor was Warren Aronson. His nickname was Beezy. He had us do a lot of running and other exercises. Some of the girls got shin splints; they weren't used to such physical training. It was easy for me, though; I had always been active.

Sgt. Daisy Storms conducting academy class, with Gustie Bell, third from right

At the time, there were sixty women on the department. In our class, there were about twenty of us. Some dropped out, and some were let go. The academy was two months long, and we graduated six policewomen. There was a separate male class, but at graduation, both the men and the women were together. After we graduated, we had a party in the academy gym.

When I graduated, I went to the Lincoln Heights jail. I had never been to a jail, and I was somewhat shocked by what I saw: women who were locked up. There was a lot of foul language, and some of the women were pretty rough. The ones we had problems with, we put in separate cells. We couldn't turn our backs on them, because we'd risk one striking us or using some type of violence. Fortunately, no one struck me. When it was mealtime, we had to escort the women to the dining room. Once in a while, a few would be irritated at each other and start throwing food. To pass the time while they were in jail and to give them a skill, we conducted sewing classes. Most of the women wanted to sew or learn sewing. A few were not interested; they'd refused to sew and would throw the bobbins we used for sewing. I worked the jail for a while and then transferred to Juvenile Division.

Jim Hillman and Gustie (Regan) Bell receive valedictorian awards from Chief William H. Parker at academy graduation, 1954

Juvenile Division was at the Georgia Street station. Al Ackerman used to work the first-floor missing kids desk. He was an old-timer and knew everything about juvenile investigations. He took the time to explain things to me. He was a big help and a great guy, but he was a jokester. We had to watch ourselves, because he'd play jokes on us. He'd tell us something that wasn't true, and once he saw us get all excited, he knew he had us, and he'd laugh. I spent part of my time at the missing persons desk and the rest of my time upstairs doing investigations. We also had a jail at Georgia Street for the male juveniles, if needed. I usually had a female as a partner, and we worked in plainclothes. Most of the cases were runaways or kids picked up for shoplifting. Once they were arrested, they were cited to us for counseling. We'd sit with them and their parents and discuss what they had done. We would decide whether or not we were going to file their case with the Probation Department. In most cases, we did.

Later, I was reassigned to the section that handled the filings with the Probation Department. One time, as I was driving to the Probation Department, I heard cats screaming from somewhere in the car. When I got to the department, I opened the hood to the engine compartment,

Gustie Bell, far left, and fellow policewomen with raccoon-skin caps from actor Fess Parker, a.k.a. Daniel Boone, at Lincoln Heights jail

and cats jumped out. I couldn't believe it. At Georgia Street, we parked our cars in the parking lot next to the building, and sometimes cats got into the engine compartments of our cars, where it was warm.

At one point, I went on loan to Intelligence Division. They needed women because they wanted to pair up their male officers with females so that they looked like couples. It was a good job, and I later transferred in. I had a couple female partners: Nan Allomong and Jean Wilford. Nan has since passed away, and Jean and I are still good friends today.

At Intelligence, one of our responsibilities was to follow the gangsters around to see who they met. Cohen, Battaglia, Dragna, Sica—we followed them all. If they went into a bar or elsewhere, my partners would say, "Gustie, go in and see who they're meeting." Because I looked Italian, I had to go in. One time, we followed a suspect into a restaurant that also had a bar. This suspect managed to get behind the cash register at the bar and somehow opened it. He grabbed the money and ran out of the restaurant, and I ran after him. I had my gun out and said, "Stop."

He said, "Don't shoot, lady. Don't shoot." By that time, my backup guys were there, and they helped me take him into custody. That was the only time when I had to pull my gun on someone.

I was working with Dick Unland and Robbie Robertson one day, and we were following Joe Dippolito. He had a vineyard that was open to the public out in the San Bernardino area. He went down a road off the main highway that led to his vineyard, parked his car between two buildings, and then entered one of the buildings. We saw some Cadillacs there, and we decided to get the license numbers. We got the license numbers and left. Dippolito apparently saw us, and he followed us out onto the main road. He pulled up alongside us and said, "What are you doing here?" He made some verbal threats and brandished a gun. He warned us not to come back onto his place. We figured he knew who we were, although he didn't say. We called the San Bernardino sheriffs, and they arrested him. We went to court, but the charge was dismissed. He said he'd thought that the two guys I was with were going to kill me and dump my body on his property and that he would be blamed. How he came up with that, I don't know, but it was enough that the charge was dropped.

Whenever they had visiting dignitaries in Los Angeles, Intelligence Division would provide personal security for them unless they brought their own. In '63, I was part of the personal security when the Shah of Iran and Empress Farah were visiting Los Angeles. We went to Disneyland with them for the opening of Walt Disney's Enchanted Tiki Room. They were nice. In '64, I was the personal security for Mrs. Lyndon Johnson, wife of President Lyndon Johnson, when they were here. The president of Mexico, Mr. Adolfo Lopez Mateos, and his wife, Mrs. Eva Lopez Mateos, with Nan as her personal security, were here at the same time.

In '68, I was promoted to sergeant. I had to leave Intelligence Division because they did not have authorization for a female sergeant. I went to North Hollywood Division, and when there was an opening for a female sergeant at Devonshire Division, I transferred there. Devonshire Division at that time was housed in an abandoned Thrifty drugstore until the actual station was built.

I was working Devonshire when the Black Student Union took over the school president's office at San Fernando Valley State College. The students held about thirty administrators hostage and gave a list of

Gustie Bell, back left, Nan Allomong, back right, providing security for Mrs. Eva Lopez Mateos, front row, center left, and Mrs. Lyndon Johnson, front row, center right

demands. Their demands included an increase in black student enrollment and a larger presence of black teachers. It was our investigation, we came to a resolution, and they released the hostages.

Before anyone knew about Charlie Manson and his followers running around killing people, I went out to the Spahn Ranch on a missing juvenile investigation. The Spahn Ranch was where Manson stayed. This mother of a runaway kid said her son often went to the ranch. I talked to one of the guys who was in charge there, and he told me he hadn't seen the kid. As I was ready to leave, the kid popped up behind a haystack. The kid was returned to his home, and shortly thereafter, the Manson case hit. The guy I had talked to could have been the foreman, Shorty Shea—I'm not certain. I went out there by myself, which was kind of stupid. Afterward, it was scary thinking Manson may have been there.

When I retired in '79, I worked for the district attorney's office as an investigator. One case I worked on was the Virginia McMartin case. It was a sexual abuse case against the owner, McMartin, her son, and some teachers at a private preschool. I interviewed some of the kids and accompanied them to court. It was a bad case, and the whole thing was eventually dismissed. I also worked the 1984 Olympics, where I was in charge of the security at Exposition Park. A commander from the department asked me if I wanted to be in charge of security at the park. I said, "Sure." I wasn't doing anything at the time. He recommended me, and I got the job. That was an interesting experience. That was what really marked my career with the police department—just a lot of interesting experiences. For someone without a sociology degree, I thought I did pretty well.

Thomas "Tom" Rogers

Birthplace: Hollywood, California
Career: 1954–1979
Rank at Retirement: Lieutenant II
Divisions: Jail, Central, Traffic Enforcement, Seventy-Seventh Street, Hollenbeck, Central Traffic

You're in the academy, you're full of piss and vinegar, you want to knock down doors and make arrests, and all of a sudden, you're working the jail. I'm fingerprinting drunks that are pissing in their pants and throwing up on my shoulder. Some of these guys' hands were like horses' hooves; I could hardly fingerprint them. Then I worked in the felony section, and one of the first situations I had made me think, *Wow, I have to be careful. I'm wearing a badge.* They had a guy in isolation who was with the Mafia. He kept pushing me to do things for him, trying to get next to me, and I wouldn't do it. When he got a phone visit, I took him down to the main floor, and he talked on the phone. The conversation was being tape-recorded, and I was listening to him with the tape operator. He was pissed off at me for not doing what he wanted. He was saying, "I want you to get this kid. I don't care how you do it, but get him." So for the next month, I went home a different way each night; I was afraid to go home. What a way to start the police department.

My first year in college, I got married. My wife's father owned a big heavy-equipment outfit in Yorba Linda, and during the summers, I worked for him. He told me that when I graduated, I could take over the business. After I graduated, I was on the back of a bulldozer twelve hours a day, and on Sundays, I was out estimating new jobs. This went on for about six months. I was thinking on Wednesday at high noon, *Oh boy, the week's half-over.* That was bad. So one rainy day, I was really down; I didn't like what I was doing. I got in my car and drove around. I ended up at Los Angeles City Hall. I looked at bulletins, and there was one on LAPD. I thought, *Man, that sounds good.*

Were there any instructors in the academy who were hard on us? Yeah, Ray Ruddell. He was not only a physical-training instructor but also our law instructor, and he was tough. He became one of my best friends. A lot of guys didn't like him. It was either white or black with that guy, but I liked him a lot. Then there was Roy Bean, who was a legend. He was rough on us. With him, you just never got a chance to stop.

After graduation, I was sent to Lincoln Heights jail for about a year. Then I made a trade with a policeman from Central and started working Central patrol. That first night in patrol, I was excited that I was finally doing what I was paid to do. After learning search and seizure, laws of arrest, shooting policy, and what and what not to do, all of a sudden, I was there.

Central Division police station

Charlie Reese was my regular partner, and he later became a deputy chief. One night, we had a man-with-a-knife call in a slum apartment building. We walked down a long hall and followed blood all the way to an apartment. The guy wouldn't open the door, so we knocked it down. This guy was standing there cut from ear to ear, and the blood was running down the side of his T-shirt. I thought he was hiding something under his shirt, and as I lifted it, a big glob of blood hit the floor and splashed all over my pants. At first, we didn't know if he was a suspect or what; turned out he was the suspect. There were two bedrooms. We went into one bedroom, and the pictures on the walls had blood on them. There were four little kids—the oldest one about five years old—with blood all over them, as if they had been christened. We thought at first they were all dead, but they were asleep. I almost dropped to my knees when I saw them. We took the guy and booked him.

At Central, there were lots of old-timers. They were at the end of the road, they got lousy ratings, and they were just putting in their time. One night, I was with this one guy who was really cocky and wore his hat down the back of his head. We pulled over a drunk driver. My partner gave him a field sobriety test, and I figured we were going to take him in. All of a sudden, I heard, "Okay, see you later." The drunk got in his car and drove away.

I said, "What happened?"

He said, "Tell you later."

We drove to a liquor store, and he went in. I later figured out he had changed a twenty for two tens. He got back in the car, turned to me, and said, "Here, this is yours."

"What's that?"

"That's your part of the deal."

"What deal?"

"Well, I let the guy go, and he gave me a twenty. Here's ten for you."

"No, I won't take it," I said. "Drive me to Property Division; I'm going to book it as found property."

"What!"

"I'm going to take my ten dollars, and I'm going to book it as found property." Well, when we got there, we booked the whole twenty as found property. I never worked with that guy again.

Tom Rogers

After I had worked patrol almost ten months, I put in for motors and was accepted. At motors, I worked freeways for about eight years. LAPD had the freeway system until about 1969, and then the California Highway Patrol took over.

We had a party with the CHP at the academy to celebrate the change. It was a big party. LAPD motor cops and the CHP—like handing over the baton.

I'd been on the job five or six years and was divorced from my first wife. I didn't have anything. I lived at my mom's house in San Gabriel in a room over the garage. Right next door was a gas station, and I got acquainted with a mechanic there—a really nice guy. I told him I had always wanted to buy a gas station because I had worked in them a lot when I was a kid. I asked him if he would go in with me if I got a gas station. He said, "Yeah." Union Oil had one station available in South Pasadena for $2,500 bucks. This was 1961. I took a couple weeks off, went to the Union Oil dealer school, and then opened up my gas station. I had it for about twenty years. In fact, when I retired, I had three Union Oil stations and a transmission shop. The gas station was in South Pasadena, at the end of the Pasadena Freeway. Since I was working the Pasadena Freeway, I had the best of all worlds. I was single, I had moved to an apartment off the Pasadena Freeway, I had my gas station, and I had my beat.

And so what happened? I usually had a regular partner at night. I'd say, "Okay, meet me out at the gas station, and we'll walk across the street to the bowling alley and have a cup of coffee." It was a routine I did every night.

One night, I had an extra guy working with me, not my regular partner. I told him the same thing. He said, "Okay, I'll be there." We met and had coffee and then worked the night. That was the only time I worked with him. About three months later, he made sergeant. About a year later, he was back as a motor sergeant. I was still doing my thing and was happy. The first night back, he staked out my gas station. Here came Tom Rogers in the driveway, as always. He put me on the south end of the Harbor Freeway. He couldn't have gotten me any farther away. I was really pissed. The next day, I bought about $300 worth of books: legal, search and seizure, evidence—all this stuff. I started studying. I studied hard and came out eighteen on the sergeants' list. I thought, *This was easy. I think I'll make lieutenant.* I studied, and I made lieutenant. A year after making lieutenant, I was back as the officer in charge of motors, and he was one of my sergeants. He went on vacation, and when he got back, he was transferred to patrol. Everyone knew what I was going to do. They were just waiting for the ball to drop. Anyway, that was what happened.

One day I heard a call come out about two suspects who had just robbed a bank and were driving a panel truck. I was on the Pasadena Freeway, and the transition ramp going over to the Golden State Freeway was jammed up. That was unusual for ten o'clock in the morning. I worked my way up and saw a panel truck turned over on its side. People were telling me the guys were both armed, and they had jumped off the side of the bridge. I put out my location to Communications Division and requested some help. I ran over to the side and saw the two guys running. I jumped off the bridge and worked my way down toward the riverbed. The suspects ran and hid behind an abutment. They were in a little alcove. I worked my way down, but before I got to where they were, one of them came around and started to aim at me with his gun. As soon as he aimed, I shot, and he ducked back in. I went a little farther toward them, he came out again and aimed, and I shot once more. I did this about three more times, and I finally got right up next to the abutment.

When he came out again, I grabbed him, disarmed him, and handcuffed him. The other guy took off and jumped down into the riverbed. Here I had this guy, so I just kicked him in the nuts as hard as I could, and he went down. I jumped down into the riverbed and captured the other guy and brought him back. For that, I was awarded the Medal of Valor.

A few weeks later, on the Pasadena Freeway, I pulled over a '55 T-Bird on a shoulder area that was all gravel. As I was walking up behind the driver, all of a sudden, he drove off, blowing gravel all over me. He hit the Pasadena Freeway; it was about ten o'clock in the morning, and there was little traffic. I was on a spare motorcycle, not my regular bike, doing about eighty miles per hour, chasing him, and he was staying ahead of me. I radioed that I was in pursuit, and then I dropped the mic. It bounced on the pavement like a yo-yo. Then the right footboard fell off, and I had one foot hanging. He was getting away, so I pulled my gun out and shot at him twice. I could see the bullets hit the bumper and come right back at me. I thought, *I better quit shooting or I'm going to kill myself.* He took the off-ramp at Orange Grove, went airborne, and then went back onto the freeway. He was off again at Fair Oaks and went straight through the intersection and out into South Pasadena. I backed off at the Fair Oaks intersection; I had lost him. I drove back down the freeway and sat at the Avenue 64 overcrossing, reloading. I looked over my shoulder, and my sergeant was right there.

Tom Rogers, front row, second from left: Medal of Valor ceremony, 1964

"What are you doing?" he said.

"Oh, nothing."

They gave me two days off for unauthorized shooting. In fact, the day I was told I was going to get days off for that shooting, as I was walking out the door, the captain said, "Oh, by the way, you've been awarded the Medal of Valor."

"Oh, thanks." It all balanced out.

A call came out of a robbery one day, and the suspects were driving a '57 Chevy. I saw the car in Highland Park by this big old apartment building. An AI officer was there about the same time. The guys saw us, went inside an apartment, and slammed the door. We put out a call for assistance. I said to the AI guy, "I'll go around the back, and you go in the front."

He said, "Okay."

We were gung ho in those days. We didn't have SWAT and all that stuff; you either handled a situation yourself or forget it. He was out in the front, and I was waiting to hear him yell or something. I looked through a window—there were about eight of them in there. One guy looked at me, and all of a sudden, he dived under the bed. I thought he was going after a gun. I climbed through the open window and dragged him out from under the bed, and he had a shotgun under there. Several other guys were in the bathroom, flushing narcotics. We had more stuff going on. By the time other policemen got there, we had all eight guys up against the wall. The suspects had a little of everything, including money that they had taken in the robbery. Later, whenever the AI guy and I saw each other, we'd laugh and say, "Boy, what a bunch of dummies we were— almost in over our head."

One time, a car was pulled over on the Golden State Freeway, and a guy was standing outside the car, waving his arms at me. I recognized him. He worked at the armory. He was yelling, "My wife's in the car having a baby!"

I pulled over and went back to the car, and there was his little wife, lying across the front seat of this Corvair. He didn't know what to do, so I said, "We'll get on my mic and call for an ambulance, and I'll see if I can help your wife." I was in there trying to get her taken care of, and my ear was about that long waiting to hear that ambulance coming. When I first reached underneath her, I pulled my hand out and had a whole handful of feces. I had my head over the backseat, and I was trying to keep from throwing up. I never did throw up, but I damn near did. Anyway, I finally delivered the baby. The ambulance got there and took her and the baby away. Another time, I delivered a baby at Adams and Western in the back of a Chevron gas station. The mother was some old gal who weighed about three hundred pounds; it was her ninth kid. About all I did was catch it.

In '65, during the Watts riots, we escorted the fire department because the rioters were shooting at the fire trucks to keep them from putting out the fires. They were burning down their own houses, schools, and grocery stores. In a group, people lose their identities. One guy by himself wouldn't do anything, but get fifty guys together and they'll do just about anything.

Several years later, I was working in Watts, sitting on a corner. I saw a white guy who was about forty-five years old walking down the street with a bag in his hand, and he kept looking back. When he walked down an alley, I worked my way down to watch him. As he started to go through a gate in this alley, I said, "Hey, buddy—hold on a second. What are you doing down here?"

He said, "I came to see my aunt," or something like that.

I asked for some identification. He gave me something; I was not sure what it was. I grabbed the mic and asked for the air, the frequency, so that I could run this guy. Well, something was going on; I waited and waited, and I couldn't get the air. *I can't leave this guy sitting here forever,* I thought, so I said, "Well, you're in luck. I'm not going to run you." I think I wrote him a ticket and then left.

A couple hours later, I was at the main jail, booking somebody, and there on the wall was a Wanted poster with a picture of this guy, listing him as armed and dangerous. He was wanted for masquerading as a cop. I got hold of Central detectives, and we all went down there. They went into this guy's place, and I stayed at the back just in case he came out. He was taken into custody without any problem. Later that night, one of the detectives called me at home and told me, "The guy had a loaded .45 in his hand inside that bag, and if you were going to get the air, he was going to blow you up." How about that? That was how close you get sometimes.

Norm Sulflow: "He was a great partner."

Norm Sulflow and I were partners for years. He was a great partner. We were working Wilshire one night, and a television crew was out looking for news. We picked up a guy for drunk driving, and this television crew came swooping in with lights and cameras. The reporter was talking to Norm, and he was describing how it had all happened, what was going to happen, and all kinds of stuff. I was over there impounding the car, itemizing the stuff in the car, and taking care of everything. I looked over at Norm and didn't see our arrestee. I said, "Hey, Norm, where's our 502 guy?"

The news reporter said, "You mean the guy that just got in a cab and drove away?"

He had taken off. We had his car, but he was gone.

I was on motors until I made sergeant. After I made sergeant, I went to the jail, back to motors, and then to Seventy-Seventh Division as an assistant watch commander and a tour in vice. When I made lieutenant, I went to Hollenbeck and then back to motors as the OIC of motors. I put in the rest of my time in motors, so out of twenty-five years, I probably had twenty-two-plus on motors. I enjoyed it.

When I first started on motors, I had a Harley-Davidson, later a Moto Guzzi, and my last bike, a Kawasaki 1000. When I made lieutenant, every year, I got the first new bike. I had the Kawasaki, and I was coming in from a meeting with a sergeant in Rampart. It was about eleven o'clock at night, and I was on Beverly Boulevard. A guy whipped a left in front of me. I didn't mean to, but I wasn't used to the brake system, and I hit the front brake ahead of the back brake and—just like that—went eighty feet sliding down that street. I dislocated both my shoulders and tore up my knees. There was a bar right there, and the patrons from the bar carried me out of the street and laid me down on the sidewalk. I looked straight up, and all of a sudden, I saw a little light—a tiny light that got bigger and bigger and bigger. Then a voice said, "Leave that officer alone." I thought it was God coming after me. It was the police helicopter. I didn't know what was going on. This happened the day after Christmas. They took me over to Orthopedic Hospital. When my wife walked in and saw my uniform all torn up and bloody, she thought I was dead.

The department had a motor drill team, and as the only motor lieutenant, I was head of the drill team. We used to do a drill at the academy for graduations, and I would lead the graduates in. I was not going to do much—just ride in, cross, turn around, and stop. The team was going to do the drill. I rode a Moto Guzzi, and while going around, all of sudden, it kicked itself out of gear, and I went right over on my side—in front of the chief, the mayor, *everybody*. I pulled the bike back up quickly and went on about my business, as if it were just normal procedure. The next two months, every time I walked through Parker Center, someone would tell me about it. I was so embarrassed. These guys did this drill and never had a problem, and all I had to do was drive in, and I fell over.

Howard Bogusch, a great guy, was the drill master, and I decided I wanted to learn how to do the drill like he did. I worked at it pretty hard and got to where I could do it in practice. We went to Palm Springs to perform in a parade, and the guys thought they'd play a trick on me. On the day of the parade, Bogusch was missing. We were getting ready to go, and I asked, "Where's Bog?" Pretty soon, he came walking out, his uniform disheveled, as if he were drunk. I thought, *Now I've got to lead this drill,* and I about died. Then he started laughing. They really set me up. We went all over the state of California doing drill exhibitions.

I had more trouble off the job than on the job. My wife and I used to go to Chinatown almost every Thursday for years to a place called Quan Mon for dinner. When we walked in, we were like king and queen. While we were eating dinner one night, some guy walked into the bar, kicked about seven glasses onto the floor, turned around, and walked out. The guy behind the bar, of course, knew me and said, "Hey, Tom."

"Okay."

Next door was a little novelty store. Three guys were in there, including the guy who had kicked the glasses at the bar, and they were pulling toy guns out of cellophane bags. The little gal behind the counter—I knew her. She said, "Tom, Tom."

"I'll take care of it."

I walked up to two of the guys and got my arms under their elbows and said, "Come on, guys—let's walk on outside and talk this thing over." We got just about to the door, and the third guy copped a Sunday punch on me. It didn't knock me out, but it knocked me back, and then I started wrestling with these guys. I was fighting all three of them when some gal jumped on my back. My wife got hold of a doggone bottle or something and hit her with the bottle. Now my wife was in the fight. They finally ran across the street, picked up some little metal sheets used for signs, and started throwing them at me. I had to wait to avoid the sheets, and two of them took off. The main guy ran up one street, and I started chasing him. I knew I wasn't going to catch him; I couldn't catch him. I yelled, "Oh, my leg," and I got down and crawled around. He looked backed and saw me lying there on the ground. When he came back, that was the last thing he remembered. I caught him right in the throat with my elbow. About that time, of course, the cops had been called, and about nine million cops showed up, and most of the guys knew me. They took him to jail. The other two guys were arrested, and all three went to court. They were all deserters out of the army—mean guys. Orientals don't like to get involved in things like that. Officers can never get them to be witnesses for them or anything. When we showed up in court, that place was packed. There must have been two hundred Chinese in there to back me up. That was the last fight I had that my wife knew about.

I used to play on the department's intramural baseball and football teams every year. One time, I broke my leg playing baseball. The choice was to either fuse it or have no weight bearing on it for a year.

Norm Piepenbrink

I decided on the year. When I came back, I worked light duty for a while, checking traffic citations for errors. We had one helicopter on the department, and it was down for repairs, so the pilots were working with me to give them something to do. I became good friends with one of the pilots, Norm Piepenbrink. He was married, but I didn't know his wife then. In '64, he was killed in a helicopter accident. Some years after that, I met his former wife, and we ended up getting married. We were married for forty-four years, and she passed away a few years ago. She and I were reading a department magazine one day, and it had pictures of officers who had been killed in the line of duty. For Norm, they had listed his name correctly but had printed the wrong picture. My wife saw that and almost collapsed.

I thank God that I did what I did, because I could have been in fifteen or twenty different jobs and still had nothing. I'm just so thankful that I made it, went through it, and didn't get fired or worse. I always felt you make what you can for yourself. It's up to you. I was on the captain's list when I retired. I could have gone pretty far if I had applied myself and gone to the right places. You can't go very far when you've got years on motors behind you. My problem was that I was having so much doggone fun. I never even thought about taking a promotion test until that guy pissed me off.

Edward "Ed" Meckle

Birthplace: Bayonne, New Jersey
Career: 1956–1976
Rank at Retirement: Lieutenant II
Divisions: Jail, University, Metropolitan, Seventy-Seventh Street, Wilshire,
    Hollywood, Organized Crime Intelligence

MacKinlay Kantor won a Pulitzer Prize for writing a book called *Andersonville*, which is about a Confederate prisoner-of-war camp. He also wrote the book *Signal Thirty-Two*, which is about two guys who come back from World War II and get on the police department in New York. One gets in trouble, and he goes bad. The other one works with an old-timer. The old-timer tells the kid, "Police work is like having a front-row seat to the greatest show in the world." I've used that line a hundred times, and it always seems appropriate. In police work, wherever the action is, you're right up front. You're not in the back, trying to see what's going on. You're in charge. You're holding the crowd back. You're the guy who's going to solve the mess—good, bad, or indifferent. You're the one everybody looks to. You are the man. I thought, *How damn true. How absolutely true that is.*

I've always been called Ed. The only person who ever called me Edward was my mother. I was born in Bayonne, New Jersey, but I was raised in upstate New York in the Catskills, back in the middle of nowhere. I graduated from high school during the Korean War. Guys were being drafted and I thought, *I'm not going to take a chance; I'm going to join the Marines.* I was on an aircraft carrier for two years, and my last duty station was Quantico, Virginia. I was in Guard Company, which was the military police. I really enjoyed it. One day, I was reading a magazine called the *Leatherneck*, which had an article about the LAPD. There were photos of a couple marines going through

69

Ed Meckle, front row, third from left

the police academy. I thought that really looked good. To make a long story short, I got out of the Marines, went home to my small town, and earned enough money to move to California in November 1955.

My class started on February 1, 1956. Of the thirty-four in my class, thirty-one were from out of state. When we graduated, everybody in those days went to either the Lincoln Heights jail or PIC—white hats, white gloves, downtown, directing traffic. I can't say I looked forward to either one, because I wanted to go out and crush crime. I went to the jail, and I was running an elevator, working the main desk, or fingerprinting drunks. One night, I was working the main desk, and a gentleman came in. I thought, *Geez, that guy looks familiar.* It was Broderick Crawford. At the time, he was starring in a TV series about the Highway Patrol. The scene was right out of a bad movie; he had the camel-hair coat on with the collar turned up and was wearing a snap-brim hat and dark glasses, and it was the middle of the night. He had a little agent with him, who said, "We're looking for Willie Jackson."

I said, "Yeah, we got him."

"Where's the car?"

"Swanney and McDonald's Tow." And I gave him the address. I found out later that Broderick Crawford had had so many drunk-driving arrests that he'd lost his license. The studio had hired a driver for him, with a studio car, and the driver had gotten busted for drunk driving, so now the car was in impound. They couldn't have cared less about the driver; they just wanted the car.

There were two courtrooms in the old main jail for the arraignment of drunks. Somebody got the idea to hold a mock courtroom in the middle of the night. The courtroom was dark from four o'clock in the afternoon until eight o'clock the next morning. An officer went in, turned the lights on, put the judge's robes on, and sat up there at the judge's bench. The other officers ran the drunks through, and he was sentencing them. Everybody had a big laugh until the next day when the real judge, Judge Robert Clifton, gave this drunk thirty days. The drunk said, "Well, that ain't right. The other judge gave me fifteen." That exposed that—a couple of policemen got their tail feathers burned.

One night at the jail, my classmate Ray Espinosa said, "You know, I want to get married, but my girlfriend is really concerned about me getting hurt. I'm a police officer, and you can get shot."

I said, "Ray, what are the chances, for gosh sakes? How often do coppers get shot?" Well, that was in '56. Ray did get married. In '58, he and his partner, Tom Scebbi, a friend of mine, were working a radio car, and they stopped a guy at Third and Kingsley in Wilshire Division. The guy shot both of them. He killed Scebbi and shot Ray in the gut. The guy was caught, and he eventually went to the gas chamber. Ray had to retire on disability and later became an investigator for the state bar. And I had told him, "Go ahead. What are your chances of getting shot?"

A decade after World War II, most street cops were war vets who had seen and done it all. What were the streets of Los Angeles like compared to what they had been through? There were no training officers in those days; the department just put you with a couple of older guys. I was now at University Division, and I wound up as third man on a radio car with Hal Brasher, who had flown B-25s during World War II, and Ward Fitzgerald, who had been in the navy. They were good guys, and I learned a lot from them. I listened to everything they had to say.

Although I was not there when this happened, I saw evidence of it the next day. Across the street from the station was a row of businesses, including a great chili spot and a barbershop. The morning watch was waiting for the night watch to come in when there was a pursuit. Some guy had stolen the buy money from a narco team. They were chasing him, and right behind them were several black-and-whites. The whole thing was coming right by the station, and there had been shots fired during the pursuit. Well, in those days, the shooting policy wasn't nearly what it is today. So, some morning watch guys lined up, and as the pursuit went by, shots were fired, none of which hit the suspect's car. Two shots hit the car with the narcotic guys in it, one shot hit a black-and-white behind that, and the rest blew out all the business windows across the street. When I came in the next day, the windows were boarded up, so I knew something had happened. I went to roll call, and even though I hadn't been there and it hadn't been our watch, we got the lecture. The incident never made the press. They were able to keep some things in-house in those days.

In roll call one night, I was assigned to a radio car. Leo Wise was part of a two-man footbeat. His partner didn't show up, and Leo said, "I'll walk it alone." He was shot to death that night. He broke up a barroom brawl, took the two drunks outside, and told them to leave. Later, Leo encountered one of the drunks, Marion Linden, again outside of the bar. As Leo went to a Gamewell to call for transportation, Linden pulled a gun and shot him twice at point-blank range. Leo got off two rounds before he died. Linden left in his car, but witnesses to the shooting followed him and told two motor officers, who captured him. Linden was convicted and later executed at San Quentin.

One day Frank Isbell and I were in heavy traffic on Adams Boulevard, and the guy in the car next to us kept eyeing us. At one point, the guy jumped out and started running toward the bridge over the freeway. I jumped out and chased him.

We got up onto the overpass. I grabbed him, he pulled me, and I fell down. He kicked me in the head and took off running. I fired, and by the time I fired, he was almost all the way across the overpass—and I hit him in the shoulder. The distance was well over a hundred feet. Lucky shot. He ran for a little while, and then he got tired and sat down. It turned out he had just been released from prison and had just scored heroin.

Frank Isbell

Frank and I got an unknown-trouble radio call one night. We got to the house, and the front door was open. I went in, and it was dark. I shined my flashlight across the living room, and on the other side was a woman in a chair. Her head was back, and there was a spray of blood from her face all the way to the ceiling and onto the far wall, as if her face had exploded. I figured she was dead. Frank came in, and all of a sudden, she moaned. We learned her boyfriend had just left. We found her boyfriend's car a block away at a T intersection. It was the middle of the night, nobody was around, and we had our headlights on it. We got out, and Frank walked around the front of the car. I went around the back, and the suspect was behind the car, crouched over, trying to close the bolt on a rifle. I yelled for him to drop it. He turned toward me, and I could've shot him, but for some reason, I didn't. I said, "Drop it," and he did. He was trying to put the wrong size of ammo in the gun.

He admitted shooting his girlfriend. He'd shot her because she had broken one of his music records. He said, "I had my choice between a twelve-gauge and a twenty-gauge. I used the twenty because I love her," the twenty gauge being the smaller of the two guns.

When we went to court, she was on the stand, an awful mess, all bandaged up. The DA said, "You saw him walk in with a gun—then what happened?"

She said, "I heard bells."

"You heard bells?"

"You know, like *ting-a-ling, ting-a-ling*." That was when he'd shot her. That was all she remembered—hearing bells.

My partner and I got a radio call at a furniture store. In those days, the buildings were one or two stories max, with flat roofs. As we pulled up out front, my partner and I both smelled it—a dead body. We walked in, and our eyes watered. The clerk in the furniture store said, "Something is dripping through the ceiling, and we had to move the furniture."

The store was one of those buildings that had an apartment on the roof. We climbed an outdoor stairway to the roof and walked across the roof to a small structure. We knocked, an elderly European woman opened the door, and the smell was overpowering. Her husband had died and was lying flat on his back on the kitchen floor. We later determined he had probably been dead about three days in the heat. She said, "He is not eating his soup." She'd been spooning soup into his mouth the whole time. That was my first experience with a real stinker; you never forget the smell.

I did my time in the radio car, and then I went to Vice. I worked with Frank Isbell and Dick Sullivan. We worked gambling mostly. One time, we tried to take down a game in the middle of the night. They hoisted me up through an open window, and I lost my balance and fell in. This was around midnight, and it was dark, dark, dark. I landed on some guy who was asleep. Now, I don't know what you would do if somebody landed on you in the middle of the night. I know what I would do. This guy woke up, looked me in the face, and said, "Jesus, Officer—you scared the hell out of me." I was in plainclothes!

One time, we were outside the window of a gambling location—a dice game—and we heard an alarm clock go off. The guy inside said, "Okay, quitting time. Vice squad is coming to work." He knew what time we came to work, and they had set the alarm. Unfortunately for them, we were early, so we got them. Between Seventy-Seventh, Newton, and us, over three months, we probably put a thousand people in jail for gambling, just the three divisions—mostly dice, sometimes cards. It was as if we were trying to empty the ocean with a teaspoon.

Ed Meckle, University Division Vice

Ida May Adams was an old judge and very moralistic. One day, one of our arrestees for prostitution, a trick, decided to go to trial. This guy testified, and Judge Adams found him guilty. She asked him, "Are you married, sir?"

"Yes."

"What is your wife's name?" And he told her. She said, "What is your phone number?" From the bench, she called his wife and said, "This is Judge Ida May Adams. I don't know if you're aware of it or not, but your husband is in my courtroom, and he has just been found guilty of consorting for the purposes of sexual intercourse with a prostitute. He'll be home in three days." She slapped him in jail for three days. Nobody ever went to jail, but she gave him three days.

Dick Sullivan—or Sully, as we called him—was a funny guy. One night, he stopped a drunk driver, and instead of booking the guy, he decided to throw the car keys up in the ivy and let him go. At the end of the night, he went to get in his own car and discovered that he had the suspect's keys. His own keys were in the ivy. We had to drive back out to find his keys at three o'clock in the morning. We found the keys. Sully was a hell of a guy. We worked a lot of places together, including Metro and Robbery. One time, I came back from court, and I walked into the room and saw a guy I didn't recognize typing. I said, "What?"

Sully said, "That's the suspect. He's typing his own arrest report." He said, "Look how fast he can type." Is that great or what?

In '59, I went to Metropolitan Division. We did crime suppression in high-crime areas and stakeouts. The F-cars, the felony cars, wore suits. We wore sport shirts and coats, so we were called the "No Tie Heat!"

There was a guy sticking up See's Candies stores downtown. It was the holiday season, with a lot of people and traffic, so no shotguns—handguns only. I was working with Sid Nuckles. We were assigned one of the See's stores, and we sat in the back of the store behind latticework with phony ivy on it. We were not there ten minutes before we heard *bang, bang, bang* from outside. There was an independent candy store across the street. Out the front door of this candy store came a stickup man with a policeman right on his tail and no second officer. I took off after them, and Sid went to the store to locate the second policeman. As I got to the corner, the suspect made a turn and started running northbound. The policeman stopped, shot, and put him down. I rode in the ambulance with the guy and got his statement, but he died before we got to the hospital. They pulled the stakeout. The next night, another See's Candies got hit. It turned out the first guy had just been a stray. So they put us back on. Two stores got hit in the same night. At one store, they caught the guy, and at the other one, they wounded a guy. One dead, one wounded, and one not—that put an end to it. The whole thing lasted three or four days. We had every store in the downtown area covered, and the only reason they put policemen across the street at the independent store was because we had extra teams.

Narcotics Division would send young-looking officers into the schools to work undercover, making buys of narcotics from dealers. Narcotics would obtain indictments and then have a "roundup" to arrest the drug dealers. They would call Metro, and we would meet in the Parker Center Auditorium. It was almost like a secret mission—"Don't open the orders until you leave port." I was working with Billy Tibbs. Billy and I knew the south end really well, so naturally, they sent us to Hollenbeck on the east side. They gave us an envelope containing an instruction sheet and two photographs; these guys were known to hang out in Hazard Park. We finally found it, and while we were sitting there, a car went by, and I said, "You notice anything unusual about the car, Billy?"

He said, "Yeah, it's on fire." This guy was so drunk that he'd hit a telephone pole and sheared it off, and part of it had gone through the side of his car. He was driving twenty miles an hour and had no idea in the world that his car was on fire. We hooked him up. The only time he ever realized what was happening was when the fire department arrived. "Do you know why they are here? Because your car's on fire!"

Metro often loaned us to detectives, and I was loaned to Newton detectives. I worked with William Pinkston. Everybody called him Pinky; he was a good old detective. He knew everybody, and he knew everything about everybody. Anybody we talked to, he would tell me to write a shake—a field-interview card. At day's end, he would say, "Run 'em."

While doing this one day, I said to Pinky, "Remember when we stopped at the rooming house over there on Central Avenue and talked to that really old guy, the witness?"

He said, "Yeah."

I said, "He's wanted for escaping from a prison train in Texas in 1927." I said, "You wanna go get him?"

He said, "We'll get him in the morning."

Long gone. The proprietor of the rooming house said, "That guy lived here thirty years! You guys weren't in the car yet, and he was packing up and out the door."

We got a gun that was booked into evidence, and Pinkston gave me the report and said, "You want to be a detective?"

"Yeah."

He said, "Detect. Find the owner."

I searched and discovered that the gun was taken in a burglary in 1943. This was now 1959. We were a little closer than 1927. I finally found the owner living in some retirement community out in the middle of nowhere. He answered the phone, and I said, "Are you so-and-so?"

He said, "Yes."

"Yeah, this is Detective Ed Meckle, LAPD. We found your gun."

He said, "What gun?"

I said, "The one you reported taken in a burglary in 1943."

There was dead silence. He said, "You just found it?"

I said, "Yeah, we've been working the case full-time, and we just got it!"

I made sergeant and went to Seventy-Seventh. I was working morning watch with a brand-new lieutenant, Stan Modic, who was a funny man. One night, the two of us were in the watch commander's office, and the jailer said, "A prisoner wants to see a supervisor." Well, it was a choice between me and the lieutenant, so who was going to go?

I went, and the prisoner said, "I gotta talk to you."

I took him out of his cell and into one of the little interrogation rooms and said, "What's your problem?"

He said, "The guy in the cell with me is wearing my suit."

I said, "That's an interesting start, but where are we going with this story?"

He said, "I was burglarized about two weeks ago, and this son of a bitch is wearing one of my suits."

I said, "How do you know?"

He said, "He was sleeping. I lifted the coat up, and my name is on the inside pocket." I took him back to his cell, and I found the burglary report. The next available radio car was going to get a really easy burglary pinch.

Rudy De Leon retired as the captain over at Hollenbeck. Everybody loved Rudy. When I was a sergeant at Seventy-Seventh, Rudy was a sergeant working AI, and we were both on morning watch. One night, we were sitting side by side in our police cars in a parking lot, talking, when a car went by doing about eighty miles an hour. Rudy was facing the right way, and he pulled out and gave chase. I pulled out but was a little behind. Just about the time Rudy got behind him, the guy pulled over. Rudy got out and approached the passenger side. I pulled up right behind Rudy's car. I found out later that when Rudy got out of his car, he could hear a woman screaming in the vehicle. I didn't know about it, because Rudy was already on the passenger side. I was walking up on the driver's side when the driver popped out, ran toward me, and then turned to go behind the car—right to Rudy. There was a guy in Newton who used to make saps that looked like paddles for a canoe. I still have mine. It was a monster. Well, I couldn't let this guy jump on Rudy, so I dropped him with the sap. I mean, he went down hard. Then we discovered the guy's wife was having a baby. So we called for a G-unit—the ambulances were called G-units then. The G-unit showed up. They not only delivered the baby but also patched the bump on the head of this guy, who was apologizing to me for having made me hit him. And being a magnanimous guy, I accepted the apology, and that was the end of that.

In March '63, I was on morning watch, doing whatever sergeants did. There was an officer-involved-shooting call, and I went to the scene. The officers were driving down a street and passed an all-night café. Just past the café, they saw a car parked with a towel over the rear license plate. They stopped, walked back to the café, and peeked through the window. A guy inside was pulling a stick-up. He ran out. *Bang, bang, bang.* Down and dead. Good shooting. I got on the radio and requested detectives, photo lab—everything. Nobody was available. Everybody was in Bakersfield. That was the night Ian Campbell and Karl Hettinger were kidnapped and taken to Bakersfield. That was where I was that night, and it wasn't until the next day that I found out what had happened. I'll always remember that night forty-nine years ago.

I then transferred back to Metro. I was working nights, and Charlie Appleton was the other sergeant. We each had five teams. It was the night that Charles Monaghan and Robert Endler were killed at Sears. This was February 1964. Monaghan and Endler were two detectives, both working nights at Wilshire. Endel Jurman, a uniformed officer in plainclothes, was end of watch, and the three of them were shooting the breeze. Sears was right next door to the old Wilshire station. An employee from Sears called and said, "We got a forger over here in the security office."

Monaghan and Endler walked over to Sears, and Jurman went with them. The three of them walked into the security office. The suspect, Leaman Russell Smith, was seated and had not been searched. He pulled a gun, and he shot Monaghan, he shot Endler, and he shot Jurman. When I got there, I saw two bodies—Monaghan and Endler—both of whom I knew, both dead. Jurman had already gone to the hospital. The boss at Wilshire station was Lieutenant Ed Jokisch, who a couple years later would be my boss. I told him I was from Metro and had five teams. "They're yours," I said. "Charlie Appleton has five teams. They're yours."

So he put us to work. Smith had escaped. We thought he might have gone to a location in Long Beach. I took three Metro teams with me. We went to Long Beach and met a sergeant and two uniform officers from the Long Beach Police Department. The house was little and there was a big yard all the way around it. It was two or three o'clock in the morning, and we were looking for a guy who had just shot three policemen. It was one of the few times in my life on the police

2 L.A. Policemen Slain by Gunman

Killer Escapes After Wounding Two Others in Pico Blvd. Store

department when I was concerned. Normally, we did what we had to do, but this time, I was thinking, *Wow!* I sent the Long Beach policemen to cover the back of the house, and my teams and I were going to take the front. I booted the door, and the door went down on my first kick, along with part of the doorframe. The room was pitch black. We all came in with lights, and in one corner was a guy sleeping. Our suspect wasn't there, so we apologized to the guy, put the door back, and left. Smith was caught a couple days later in Chicago. He was sentenced to life in prison.

In '65, I was working Robbery at Wilshire detectives for Jokisch. When the Watts riots started, I was in Houston on an extradition. I had a suspect who had been arrested by the Houston Police Department. We were coming back on Friday, August 13, and as we were flying in over Watts, the pilot said, "If you look out either side, you will see over a thousand fires." He said, "That is Los Angeles burning." We landed, and the next day, I was back in uniform.

When I was at Wilshire detectives, there was a suspect known as the Remorseful Rapist. The reason he was known as the Remorseful Rapist was because he immediately felt terribly guilty for what he had done and would apologize to the woman. He was eventually caught. It turned out that one of the guys in Homicide had been married only a year before, and the Remorseful Rapist had been one of his ushers. He was in the wedding pictures. This guy was convicted and went to prison. Afterward, we used to kid this detective every time there was a crime: "Hey, bring in your wedding album. We'll use it for a photo lineup." He did not appreciate that.

l to r: Ed Meckle, Jim Nichols, Dale Brown, Ed Jokisch, Dick Sullivan, Tom Ferry, and Dwight Stevens: Wilshire Division Robbery, 1966

I made lieutenant and worked Hollywood and then Wilshire, and in 1969, I went to Organized Crime Intelligence Division, where I finished my career. I was at OCID for eight years. I ran the surveillance squad and the airport squad. We didn't have the capabilities to do wiretapping, so we used to pretend we did. These guys were so paranoid that they would go out and use phone booths. Our guys, with earphones on, would sit in a car where they could be seen by the suspect and point a hair dryer at the phone that he was using. We made it look as if we were listening to the telephone call. We didn't know what the hell the suspects were saying, but we knew we were driving them crazy. We were just messing with them.

I wasn't going to tell this story, because it sounds as if I'm tooting my own horn, but I might as well end with it. It's probably my best piece of police work, and I'm proud of it. On Memorial Day weekend in '67, I was working Wilshire Division, and a call came in—a homicide. It was on Gramercy Place, in a four-story brownstone just north of Wilshire Boulevard. Harry Horkin and I went out there and found an elderly woman lying on her back. She had a semicircular cut right between her eyes, and she was nude from the waist down. She had been raped and strangled. We knew she had scratched her attacker, because her nails were bloody. Uniforms were there, and we had them canvass for witnesses. A guy had been seen hanging around the building. On the corner, about three hundred yards away, was a bar called the Jade Room, and I knew the owner. I told Harry, "I'm going to walk down and talk to her." I said, "Off chance." So I went down, and I described the guy.

"Yeah, he was in here." The place was deserted; it was Sunday and a holiday weekend.

"What's your impression?"

She said, "He's a sailor, and he's from Oklahoma." Sharp gal.

I went back to the apartment building and told Harry what I had; it was now getting on late afternoon. Harry and I were both former marines. *Where do servicemen go on Sunday afternoons?* we asked ourselves. *They try to get back to the base.*

Harry said, "I'm gonna play a long shot. I'll try the bus depot."

He got one of the other detectives, and they went to the bus depot. I stayed at the location. The place had been ransacked, and one of the things we found was an empty watch box for a lady's Hamilton wristwatch. Someone in the building said, "Yeah, she had a watch she was really proud of—a retirement gift from when she retired from Water and Power in 1949." The watch was not there.

Harry and the other detective saw a guy in line for the bus. He had scratches on his face and was wearing a ring with a crescent, and when they stopped him, they found a Hamilton watch in his pocket. They brought him to the station. When I talked to him, he admitted to being in the building, but he would not admit to having done anything else. That was as far as he would go. Okay, we had him in the building.

The bartender said, "Yeah, that's him."

The wristwatch he had was the same make as the box, but was it her wristwatch? We knew it was, but we had to prove it. She had blood and facial hair under her fingernails. We shaved him so that we could get some of his stubble. His underwear had blood spots and semen on it. She had semen on her, but we couldn't match it—this was before DNA testing.

The watch was our best bet. I called the watch company factory in Connecticut. They found their report. The watch we had had been sent to a jewelry store in Los Angeles in 1948. When a watch was worked on by a jeweler, he put his initials on the back. This watch had no initials, and the jewelry store no longer existed. The owner had moved to Sun City, Arizona. I called over there and discovered the owner had died. I talked with the son, and he said, "I just burned all those records not two months ago."

We went to Water and Power. "Is there a receipt for the watch in the folder?"

"No."

"Was there a photographer?"

"Yes."

"Let's look at the pictures." In the photos, the victim was holding her plaque, and she was showing off her watch. We had the pictured enlarged at the photo lab, but we got to the point where the watch was so huge, it lost context because it was so big in the photo. We went to the Sears next door to Wilshire station and borrowed some watches. We had a watch show-up with the people in her building. "Do you think you see her watch?"

"Yeah, I think that's it."

The man's ring was a match to the cut on the victim's forehead.

We did everything we could do to that point. We went to the DA's office, and they filed the case. We put on the entire case at the preliminary hearing. He was held to answer, but we had to put on our entire case. The DA's office called me later and said, "The public defender wants to plead him to murder one, life without parole, no gas chamber. How do you feel about it?"

"Go for it." That was the end of that.

A couple of years later, the DA's office gave Harry and me an award. I felt almost embarrassed because many guys investigated hundreds and hundreds of homicides, and I probably only did half a dozen in my entire career.

Ed Meckle: "I was just a kid right off the farm and from a small town."

As I tell my story, I reflect on what incredible luck and timing brought me to this place and time. The mid-1950s to the mid-1970s had to be part of the glory years for the LAPD. William H. Parker was the greatest who ever served as chief. I worked for probably one of the best homicide detectives ever to draw breath, Pierce Brooks. I even met my future wife on the job. When I was working Wilshire detectives in 1965, I asked Chief of Detectives Thad Brown for the hand in marriage of his secretary, Mina Canales. He granted it, and we were married.

Police work is almost a calling, like the priesthood. It becomes an all-consuming way of life that you live and breathe and take home with you every night. Even after all this time, as I drive, I still read license plates and look down dark alleys. You just can't separate yourself from the job; it's part of you. I still meet with retired policemen from the department, and we share love and respect for each other. I was just a kid right off the farm and from a small town. I did my three years in the Marines, and all of a sudden, I was exposed to all this—and I just enjoyed the hell out of it. As I said at the start, I had a front-row seat to the greatest show in the world. Is that great or what?

Jimmy Sakoda

Birthplace: Seattle, Washington
Career: 1958–1984
Rank at Retirement: Lieutenant II
Divisions: Narcotics, Central, Wilshire, Juvenile, Asian Task Force

In 1941, my family lived in a small farming community near Santa Maria. Many Japanese Americans were living there, doing farm work. When I was six years old, the attack on Pearl Harbor happened. I didn't know about Pearl Harbor, but I remember that one day, two big men came to the door, talked to my parents for a brief period, and left. Shortly thereafter, my parents seemed worried, and we were all of a sudden packing things in suitcases and putting our furniture outside. People later drove by and took the furniture away. We got into my dad's old, beat-up Model T Ford and drove to Tulare, California. It was one of several reception areas for Japanese Americans living on the West Coast. From there, the Japanese Americans were ordered to different centers for ultimate transportation to ten different camps that the US government had constructed. We were sent to Gila Bend, Arizona, in the middle of the desert. In 1943, we were put on a train and taken to a high-security camp at Tulelake, California. There were eighteen thousand or more people in the camp. My brother and I went to Japanese school, where we learned not only the Japanese language, including how to read and write it, but also the culture and the history of Japan. I took all of the martial arts. After the war in 1945, I came back on the train with my mom and my brother to Los Angeles, but my dad had to stay at the camp for a while. We got off the train at Union Station, and I remember—as clear as day—walking through the station carrying suitcases that my dad had created out of canvas. The

Jimmy Sakoda

station was huge, and the other passengers and people in the station were looking at us as if they didn't like us.

We lived in a flophouse on Bunker Hill. My dad worked the midnight shift at a business in Little Tokyo where Parker Center now stands. I used to walk with my mother and my brother to take him dinner. We walked past the old Central police station at First and Hill. I was curious one day, and as we were walking by, I looked in the door of the station. A policeman said, "Come on in." There were other kids there who were part of the DAP youth program—the Deputy Auxiliary Police. I was somewhat hesitant, but I did spend some time in there a couple of times when we walked by. That was my first contact with the LAPD.

I went to UCLA, but I didn't really enjoy it there. I joined the army, and after I left the service, a buddy of mine suggested I go to Los Angeles City College. He said I should take a particular administration of justice course. I took the course, and Sam Posner, a lieutenant at Central Division, was teaching the class. Posner encouraged me to take the test to join LAPD. I did, and I entered the academy in February 1958.

The academy was three months long, with about seventy in my class. The instructors were Roy Bean, Jerry Moon, Dick Scheeders, Bill Jordan, and Warren "Beezy" Aronson. Bean was the lead physical-training instructor. He looked like a Hollywood gangster. I mean, he just had that look that said, *Don't mess with me or I'm going to squash you.* My classmates elected me as president of the class. I think my athleticism had a lot to do with it. Bean picked me a couple of times to go one-on-one with different classmates. I didn't know if he was trying to see if I could take care of myself, because I was one of the smallest guys in the class. I remember he put me against my classmate Bob Smitson a couple of times. He was the biggest guy in the class. After going against Smitson, I thought, *Okay, it's all right; I'm still walking. Gingerly, but walking.*

It was graduation, and we were in our blues and were looking sharp. My classmates were asking each other where they were assigned. When I was asked, "Where are you going?" I had to respond, "I don't know. They haven't told me yet." My assignment was working undercover in Narcotics Division, and I couldn't say anything. My classmates didn't know where I went until months later.

Roy Bean: "He just had that look that said, 'Don't mess with me or I'm going to squash you.'"

At the academy, they taught cadets how and when to shoot. They didn't teach how to work undercover. I was twenty-two years old, and I had never used drugs. Now I was being asked to pose as a druggie. *How do I do that?* I wondered.

I was told, "Just go out there and buy drugs."

"Okay, what do they look like, and how much are they?"

"Oh, you'll find out."

It all amounted to on-the-job training. If you were lucky, your partners would put you together with an informant and he would teach you. I had none of that. The first thing they did was put me in jail. I was "busted" in Little Tokyo, as planned. Two other new undercover officers and I were taken with a group of actual arrestees to jail at Parker Center. I was processed and placed in a detention cell. All these dopers were in there, and I didn't look or feel like a doper. I was sitting there thinking, *What if they ask me something and I don't know how to answer?* There were a lot of things going through my mind. One thing I was thinking: *My classmates are out there in nice uniforms, looking good with their badges shining, and I'm sitting here with a bunch of dirtbags.*

That first night, the guys in my cell were huddled around another guy who was trying to pass his dime bag of heroin that he had swallowed just before the police had arrested him. I spent the weekend

Jimmy Sakoda with parents: academy graduation, 1958

in jail. My backup detectives would take me out under the guise of an interview and have a Tommy's burger waiting for me. That was good.

We would make buys of all kinds of drugs—anything from pills to marijuana to hard stuff, such as heroin. I spent a couple of months doing that. Some guys were into it, but it was not for me. Then a sergeant from the Central Division Vice Unit said to me, "We want to use you for a couple of undercover operations," so I was loaned to Central Vice. I stayed for almost two years.

At the time, there was a city ordinance that if a woman was having sex for money and officers caught her in the act, they could arrest the girl and the trick, her customer, for a misdemeanor. However, the officers had to observe the activity; they couldn't just make assumptions. We followed prostitutes and their tricks into the old hotels. If we saw a prostitute go into a hotel room with

a trick, we would take a gimlet—a little corkscrew with a handle—
and drill through the door and peek through the hole. If we made
an observation of them having sex, we had the violation. There were
some doors on East Fifth Street with so many holes that it looked as
if somebody had shot the door with buckshot. Most of the time, we
would try to plug up the hole.

At some hotels, there would be gambling, and they would lock the
front door. If the hotel clerk saw us, he would warn the gamblers the
police were there. Some of the hotels had alleys in the back and fire
escapes on the backs of the buildings. To get access to a hotel, I would
stand on the roof of the car, jump onto the fire escape, go into the hotel,
and open the back door so that the clerk would not see us. Then we
would find the gambling game and make the arrests.

There was one big gambling game where we had a complaint. My
partners took me to the Twentieth Century studio makeup department.
Ben Nye, a famous Hollywood makeup artist, made me look older
by coloring my hair gray and creating wrinkles on my face. That
afternoon, my future wife said, "What happened to you?"

"Do I look like I'm fifty or sixty years old?"

"No, you don't." She stuffed some pillows under my shirt so that I
had a potbelly. That evening, I walked past two lookouts, one of whom
I had gone to high school with, but he did not recognize me. I went
in, and there must have been thirty people gambling. I was supposed
to remember who was doing what, but there was a lot going on. After
fifteen minutes, my backup officers came in, and we made the arrests.
Thankfully, they all pleaded guilty.

There was one thing that happened when I worked Central Vice
that was bad initially but turned out good. It was nighttime, and my
partner, Gil "Sandy" Sandoval, and I saw a prostitute standing at the
entrance to a hotel at Sixth and Ceres. Usually I did the operating.
Sandy said, "Okay, drop me off, and I'll walk down to the hotel. You
watch me from the car."

He had a two-inch Smith, but he asked for my Derringer. I had
a two-shot .22-caliber Derringer as my backup gun. Sandy put the
Derringer in his jacket pocket and kept his hand on it. It was dark, but
there was a light at the entrance to the hotel, illuminating the prostitute.
I was watching with my binoculars, maybe fifty yards away, and I could
see Sandy walking to the hotel. Then I saw three white guys walking

Gil "Sandy" Sandoval

toward the hotel from the opposite direction. I thought they might be tricks. When these guys got close to the hotel entrance, the prostitute walked into an alley next to the hotel. Sandy was now in front of the hotel, and he and the three guys faced each other. All of a sudden, all four of them walked into the alley. I wondered if they were all going to try to hit on this girl. I didn't have a good feeling about it. About a minute passed, and I thought, *I don't like this, and I can't see them.*

I started the car and drove across the face of the alley. I looked down the alley and saw one guy with his hands against the wall, and I saw silhouettes. I didn't know if it was Sandy against the wall. I whipped in there with my high beams on, and I could now see it was Sandy at the wall. The three guys took off. Sandy ran over to me, saying, "Give me my gun. They just robbed me, and they got the Derringer."

I drove after them, and Sandy was trying to pull his gun out of my pocket. One guy ducked into a dark alcove, and the other two ran into another alley just south of Sixth Street. I screeched on my brakes, and Sandy now had his gun. *Bam! Bam!* He was shooting. I jumped out of the car, and I didn't know whether this guy in the alcove had a gun. I ran over to the alcove, and the suspect started to raise his hand. I hit him with my gun barrel. He was screaming and fighting. I heard more shots as Sandy shot down the alley. I got the guy under control and handcuffed. Sandy came back and told me the other two had taken off. He got on the Gamewell and told Communications Division that he had been robbed and described the suspects. Now there were Central and Newton police cars all over the place. We were close to the border of Newton. One of the suspects hid in a vacant lot where there were a bunch of abandoned cars, and the patrol guys got him. Sandy and I were looking on Seventh Street, and I saw the third suspect. He fought, but we took him into custody. I found my Derringer on the ground near where I had caught the first suspect. He'd had the Derringer in his hand when he'd raised his hand. There are marks still on my Derringer from when he dropped it. That was my first and only real involvement in a shooting. Sandy was a great partner, and fortunately, he was not hurt.

I left Vice in 1960 and went to Central patrol. Finally, I was in uniform. My first assignment was working the B-wagon, and then I walked a footbeat. On the footbeat, I learned how to twirl my baton with the leather cord. The baton was just a straight eighteen-inch stick. In fact, we used our batons as measurement tools to see if cars were parked eighteen inches or more from the curb. If so, it was a violation. I remember walking into some of the burlesque theaters on Main Street. The girls would be in the back, practicing their bumps and grinds, and they teased me because they knew I was young. It used to embarrass the heck out of me. Then I left the footbeat and worked patrol. My partner, Horst Wendt, spoke with a strong German accent. They used to call us the "Axis car." I took it as a friendly acceptance.

I wheeled to Wilshire Division and later went to Juvenile Division, and in '65, I made sergeant. I returned to Wilshire Division, and in August '65, the Watts riots occurred. During the riots, the hardest part for me was trying to keep the policemen from going to the riots. Everybody wanted to go help his brother officers. All of the divisions had a loss of manpower, but eventually, more of us were sent to Seventy-Seventh. Looters were all over the place, and the National Guard was there. I'd come home, sleep, get up, and go back again. This was the first major riot, so the department didn't seem to know what to do. What made it worse was that we were having problems with communications. The frequencies were different for each division. Later, because of the Watts riots, there was an effort toward getting a tactical frequency so that everybody could talk to each other regardless of his or her division.

One of the original Robbery Division "Hat Squad" guys, Clarence "Red" Stromwall, was working Wilshire. He was a huge man, imposing but soft-spoken—a gentleman in uniform. He didn't try to impress us with the Hat Squad thing; he was always willing to help. He helped me a lot as a probationary sergeant. We became fishing partners with a group called the Lundy Lake Loonies up in the Sierras. After he retired, he became a municipal court judge. He asked me several times to come to his courtroom and talk to him about narcotics so that he could be prepared for those types of cases. He also had me testify as an expert in narcotics. When he worked the Hat Squad, I didn't personally know him then. I remembered him, though, because he, along with other guys on the Hat Squad, always dressed impeccably. Everything was tailored; their clothes fit them like a glove, and they wore nothing outlandish.

I made detective and worked residential burglaries in Wilshire detectives, and in '67, I went to Narcotics Division. Tragically, a couple of detectives in Narcotics were shot, one of whom died. Kelly Key was serving a search warrant at a drug location. Kelly was standing by the door when the suspect shot from inside, hit Kelly in the spine, and paralyzed him. He became a quadriplegic. How many times have we stood near a door, be it serving a search warrant or answering a radio call?

Blackie Sawyer was the detective who died. I worked many cases with Blackie and used him as undercover officer making buys of narcotics. On the day he was killed, I spoke with him as he was having a wire placed on him before the operation. Normally, I would have been there with him, but I was now working another team. I said, "Hey, Blackie, you're going out?"

"Yeah, we've got this deal, you know. A couple of kilos that's going to be a buy/bust."

The operation was at a hotel. Blackie was in one room of this little hotel, and his cover was in the next room, listening to the wire. The suspect came in, he and Blackie had a conversation, and as the suspect was leaving, he turned and shot Blackie. The cover officers broke into the room and arrested the suspect, but Blackie was dead. Blackie had an engaging personality. I had some good laughs with him, and we enjoyed working together. You never know when something like that is going to happen. You just never know.

We were working the street-level dealers. Even though we kept arresting dealers and they went to jail, somebody else would take their place, and the flow of narcotics stayed constant. When Ed Davis became chief of police, he said, "We're going after the suppliers."

Davis created Administrative Narcotics Division and, within it, a unit called Major Violators. We kept the divisional narcotics units to get the street peddlers, but Major Violators went after the big boys. I decided to work Major Violators, and they made me a squad leader. We made one of the first major boat seizures in San Pedro Harbor. We seized multiple tons of marijuana off a boat called the *Roughneck*. It was a huge seizure. Of course, as the case was being developed, the Federal Bureau of Narcotics was saying, "This is a case that should be ours—what is LAPD doing?" Because we were now going after the suppliers, initially, there was some bickering over which was going to be the lead agency.

I had an informant who was a Caucasian guy who could speak some Spanish. He didn't look like a doper; he looked like an engineer— pretty clean-cut. But he had contacts. I got to know him because his girlfriend used narcotics, and I helped him get her into rehabilitation. He gave me this one case. He had a contact in Mexico who was a supplier of brown heroin. One day, he called me and said, "They're going to be making a pretty good-size delivery."

I said, "Well, do you think we can buy it?"

He said, "No. They already have a buyer, but I can tell you when and how it's going to be done."

I said, "I'll take that."

Later, my informant called me and said the heroin would be in the gas tank of a tan Dodge. The car came across the border, and we were following it on the freeway. All of a sudden, the engine sputtered, and the car came to a stop. We had wanted to follow it to identify and arrest the buyer, but now we had to initiate contact. We had the car towed to a place where we could get underneath and take the gas tank off. What had happened was that the brown heroin was inside condoms; the gasoline had eaten through the rubber lining, and the heroin had gotten into the gas line. The car had essentially overdosed on heroin.

As my career progressed, people in the Asian community would call me with questions about crimes, everything from extortion to "I had my car broken into."

I'd say, "Why didn't you call the police department?"

They would reply, "They don't understand me," or "It's embarrassing," or "It wouldn't do any good to report it." Whatever the reason, they would not report the crime.

One day, a friend of mine invited me to attend a City Employees Association meeting. Those in attendance were primarily Asian city employees. Chief Davis was going to talk to the group. I attended and, at one point, spoke with Chief Davis. During our conversation, he stated, "Groups like this are helping us have good citizens in the community—a community that never has any crime."

I said, "You're wrong. The crime is here."

He invited me to his office, and the next day, I told him about the problem. He asked me what we could do. I said, "Well, I think if you set up some kind of a unit that can find out what's really going on, then we'll have a better picture of the crime that's occurring."

He said, "I like that. We're going to have a staff conference, and I want you to write a paper about your idea."

Shiro Tomita, who also worked Narcotics, and I wrote a paper on our idea. I made the presentation at the conference, but some were reluctant because they thought it would create more specialized units. After some discussion, Chief Davis said, "We don't want to start any new units because of the budget. What I'm going to propose is that we have the unit on a temporary basis. Let's see what Jimmy finds out." That was the beginning of the Asian Task Force. Eventually, there were eight officers in the unit: two Chinese, two Filipino, two Korean, and two Japanese, including myself. We started in October 1975.

One day, a buddy of mine from the US Secret Service called me and told me that the emperor of Japan was coming to the United States and wanted to visit Los Angeles. He put me in touch with the Secret Service agent handling the emperor's visit. He was receptive to our offer for help, because we could do both intelligence work and help provide security. That was our first assignment—intelligence and security for the visit of the emperor of Japan.

Then in '78, I was promoted to lieutenant and went back to Wilshire and, after six months, back to Narcotics to the boat squad. In '80, I was asked to return to the Asian Task Force. I was told there were some internal problems between the unit and the chain of command. Some of the command staff thought the Asian Task Force was only good for translating. That mentality was something we'd had to deal with initially when the unit had started. Over time, we had become a valuable resource. We worked various undercover assignments, from divisional vice units to specialized investigations with Major Crimes. We assisted with many investigations, obtaining information or making arrests of suspects that other detectives were unable to get. A prime example: in 1984, Officer Duane Johnson was killed, and his partner, Officer Archie Nagao, was shot in the eye at a jewelry store robbery in Chinatown. Central detectives handling the investigation called on the Asian Task Force for assistance. Two Chinese officers from the unit knew the Chinese community, but even more so, they knew many of the gang members in the Chinese gangs. Through their investigation, they came up with the names of suspects. Several suspects were ultimately arrested as a result of the intelligence gathered by the Asian Task Force officers.

In 1981, a shooting occurred in Central Division, adjacent to the Harbor Freeway on Fremont Avenue, between Temple and First. A Japanese couple was shot while taking pictures in a small dirt parking lot at about eleven o'clock in the morning. The wife was shot in the head, and the husband, Kazuyoshi Miura, was shot in the thigh. Central patrol officers responded, and Miura related what had

Jimmy Sakoda, center right: Asian Task Force, 1983

happened: two guys in a green car had shot both of them and tried to take his wife's purse and his wallet. That was his story. Because Miura's English was limited, the investigators contacted us. Mitch Kato, from my unit, and Dave Gray, a detective in Robbery at Central detectives, after interviewing Miura, thought Miura was a good witness because he could describe in detail the car and the suspects. At the hospital, a department artist drew a composite based on Miura's description of the suspects.

As the investigation progressed, Gray and Kato began to have doubts about Miura. At the time this happened, I was in Japan, speaking at the US Japan Organized Crime Conference. Kato called me and asked me if I could confirm if Miura had a criminal record. I contacted a friend who was a Japanese policeman, and he confirmed Miura had a record of arson, theft, a weapons violation, assault, attacking a guard in prison, and insurance fraud.

Miura's wife was comatose, and he wanted to take her back to Japan. The doctor advised him not to transport her to Japan, that her condition was critical. He took her anyway, and she died a year to the date after she was shot. The Japanese media ultimately picked up this case and did their own research. It was discovered that three months before the shooting, Miura's wife had been a victim of a hammer attack by an Asian woman in Los Angeles. The woman, a mistress of Miura, confessed to the Japanese media that Miura had approached her with a plan to kill his wife, telling her they would split the insurance money. Miura and his wife had been staying at a hotel in Los Angeles. He'd told his wife that he had ordered a dress for her and that a seamstress would be coming to their room to measure her. When the mistress had arrived posing as the seamstress, he left, and the mistress had tried to hit Miura's wife over the head with a hammer. But the wife had fought her off, and the mistress fled. Miura returned to the room after the attack and told his wife that they should not report it to the police.

By 1984, this case had been going on for three years, and I was getting frustrated with the investigation and the reluctance by the command staff to allow us to take over the investigation. After the 1984 Olympics, I retired. I had written a novel, and it became a best seller in Japan. In Japan, the Miura case was now the equivalent of the O. J. Simpson case. While I was there on a book tour, the parents of the wife came to me and expressed their frustration with the progress of the case. They wanted me to investigate it, but I told them I was now a private citizen. I set up a meeting for them with Ira Reiner, the new district attorney in Los Angeles.

Later, in 1985, I went to work for the DA's office. Jack White, a former academy classmate, was the chief of the bureau of investigation for the DA's office, and my new boss. He said, "You want to work the Miura case?" I said yes. Jack knew the frustration I had, and he believed it was a good case.

Miura and his mistress were convicted in Japan of the attempted murder of Miura's wife at the Los Angeles hotel. He received six years in prison, and the mistress received two years. In Japan, a Japanese citizen could be tried for a crime committed outside of Japan. In 1988, we got a felony arrest warrant for Miura for murder and conspiracy to commit murder. We believed that Miura had his wife shot to collect insurance money. But we were unable to extradite him, and eventually, we took our evidence to Japan. Miura was convicted for the murder of his wife, but his conviction was overturned by the Japanese high court in 1998. He was released, and he boasted to the media that he had been wrongly accused. Japan had no conspiracy law, and he was not prosecuted for that.

Our evidence was returned to us, but the arrest warrant remained active. I kept track of Miura's movements, and in 2008, I found out he was going to Saipan. When he was leaving Saipan, he was arrested on our warrant. He fought extradition for several months, but we finally got him here. Detective Rick Jackson, now assigned to the case, brought him back from Saipan and booked him into the jail at Parker Center. I thought I'd be able to talk to him after he was booked in, but he committed suicide that night.

Miura had taken out four insurance policies—close to $800,000—on his wife. He'd had an import-export business that was failing, and he'd tried to collect fire insurance by burning the building down. He'd also had another mistress, who turned up as a Jane Doe in Los Angeles in '79. We believe she was suffocated. He had been using her ATM card and had taken out all of her money after her death. He was one bad guy who preyed upon women. There were many intricacies to this case, and someday, I may write about it.

Robert "Bob" Smitson

Birthplace: Los Angeles, California
Career: 1958–1986
Rank at Retirement: Captain III
Divisions: Central, Training, University, Metropolitan, Wilshire, Hollenbeck,
  Southeast, Northeast, Hollywood, Anti-Terrorist Division

All the men in my family were Los Angeles City firemen. In fact, my uncle, Ray Hill, rose to the rank of fire chief of the Los Angeles Fire Department. But I wanted to be a Los Angeles policeman because of LAPD sergeant Gil Burgoyne. He worked Highland Park Division, and on his off-duty time, he was a youth sports coach. He was an all-around great role model for all of us who played sports for him. As a result of his influence, about twelve of us became policemen.

After I graduated from high school, I took a police science class at LA City College, and Lieutenant Sam Posner was the instructor. He became another mentor to me, like Burgoyne. He was the watch commander at Central Division and allowed me to walk with the footbeat officers on their beats. Posner was also a wrestler. He invited me to wrestle at the academy, and I wrestled both him and Sergeant Warren Aronson, whom everyone called Beezy. The two of them developed some outstanding self-defense techniques for policemen. In fact, Posner was the one who developed what they call the "police sleeper," which we know today as the carotid hold. It was applied differently then. You would bring your hip into the person's body and bend the person over your hip, and that elongated the neck. Using your arm around the neck, you choked the person out. That was why it was called the police sleeper. Because of the reductions in height requirements, it was a difficult maneuver for a shorter officer against a taller suspect. The department then went to the bar arm control. Today, we have gone back to a progressive carotid hold.

Sgt. Gil Burgoyne

Lt. Sam Posner

But Posner was the first one to develop that maneuver, and it became a critical part of an officer's self-defense techniques. I also had the pleasure to meet other academy instructors, including Roy Bean and Jerry Moon. Both of those guys were just physically overpowering.

I applied and was accepted on the LAPD. On the first day of the academy, we were all lined up in our dress suits, standing at attention. I was one of the first ones in line, because of my height. As I was standing there, Roy Bean walked over to me, put his hand out, and said, "Bob, I'm really happy to see you made it here." My new classmates' eyeballs went over to me, and they were wondering, *Why is this monster of a man shaking this recruit's hand?* I was honored that he did that, but by the same token, everybody's focus was on me. That was my first moment in the academy.

After we graduated, I was sent to Central Division and briefly worked a radio car before Lieutenant Posner put me on a footbeat. In those days, we didn't have handheld radios. On the footbeat, we would call in on the Gamewell every hour. If we missed our call in, they would wait ten minutes and then send a car looking for us. When you're walking a beat you had to learn good tactics because during that

Don Stanley and Bob Smitson

seventy-minute time, you were on your own. No one knew where you were; no one was going to call for help. You had to react quickly to the actions of suspects. The longer you were engaged with a suspect, the greater chance you had for other people to be on your back.

One night, Bob Jarvis and I stopped some suspects, and one of them came right at Bob. He stepped in and threw this guy. I've never seen a body travel so far up into the air, and this guy hit the ground hard. This was Bob's first day out of the academy. He had been on the Milwaukee Police Department, and he was into judo. His takedown of this guy made a big impression on the other suspects, and we had immediate control.

A brand-new footbeat was established on Alvarado, near MacArthur Park, for a row of bars that had become a problem. I was placed on the footbeat, and over time, we got into many fights with ex-cons who lived in that area. Because of the pressure we put on the bars to clean them up, they were losing money. Unbeknownst to us, the bar

Bob Jarvis

owners hired some union strike busters. On one night, four of them ambushed us in an alleyway. My partner and I walked down this alleyway, and there was a guy lying facedown. He looked like a downed drunk. I went up to him, and all of a sudden, he came up off the ground and three more guys came in from the shadowy areas of the businesses. Now the fight was on. Ultimately, two suspects died, and the other two went to jail. One died of a broken neck, and the coroner could not make a determination on what caused the death of the second suspect, except that his heart had stopped. After that, we worked harder and applied more pressure, and there were no more problems. Our good tactics and training saved us that night.

I worked the F-cars at Central for a while, and then in March '63, I went to the academy as an instructor. At about that time, the Onion Field incident happened with Ian Campbell and Karl Hettinger. Pierce Brooks, the lead investigator, in his report, actually referred to it as the Onion Patch, not the Onion Field. Up until that time, a shooting or the death of a police officer was not really critiqued on a department-wide basis. A few weeks after, Inspector John Powers wrote a paper on officer survival because people just assumed officers wouldn't give up their guns. Campbell was the senior officer in the car, and he told Karl, "Give

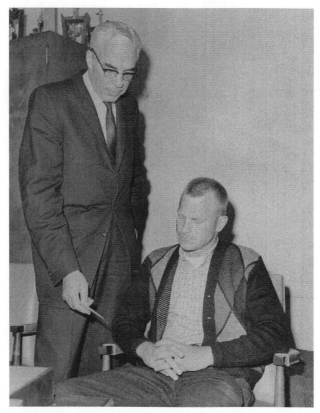

Inspector John Powers and Karl Hettinger on night of kidnap/murder investigation, 1963

up your gun." It was said once. It was said again. It was said again. It was said again. Finally, Karl turned the gun over to the one suspect. Campbell was later killed, and Karl blamed himself for Campbell's death. He was devastated.

Chief Parker made Karl his driver, which changed the minds of a lot of officers about Karl. Chief Parker then said that the shooting would be critiqued and would be taught to officers and recruits so that they could learn from the incident. It was my responsibility to do the teaching, and that was when we started a course called Officer Survival. I talked with Karl, and he said every night he went to bed, he would relive the incident and wonder what he would do if faced with that situation again. Would he give up his gun? He contemplated suicide and needed help to shed the guilt. I firmly believe—because he felt so responsible—that was why he died in his sixties and did not live a longer life. There was a reunion of Metro policemen at the academy, and Karl was there. The policemen told him how much he meant to them with what he'd done and gone through. It was great to see Karl receive the recognition. Karl's ability to escape and avoid being shot after Campbell was shot was truly commendable, as most people put in that situation would be in a state of shock and unable to react.

In '64, Inspector John Powers and John Nelson, who worked the academy as an instructor, formed two-man sniper teams that would ultimately be the beginning of SWAT. Nelson had been a sniper in the Marine Corps. The two-man setup progressed into four-man teams: one at the academy, which I was on, and one team at University Division within the detective bureau.

While at the academy, I made sergeant and went to University Division. Captain Charlie Reese started a special operations squad of eighteen policemen in plainclothes and me as the supervisor. At that time, the Black Panthers were really active. The Panthers were trying to take over the community with gifts and with fear—primarily fear. The reason they took policemen on was to show the community that individuals could take on the so-called "man" and kill him. Their way of looking at it was that then they were just that much more powerful in the community. We also expanded the SWAT program by forming additional teams. I had a team at University Division with Pat McKinley, Rich Szabo, and Everett Gossett, whom Terry Speer later replaced. Eventually, SWAT was divided into three sections. Willie Gough, Dave McGill, and I were the section leaders.

In the early part of '69, I returned to the academy and became the supervisor of the new Physical Training and Self-Defense Unit. I brought in Terry Speer, Dick King, Rik Violano, Bill Henry, and Bill Gilstrap. Harvey Eubanks and Bob Koga were already at the academy. I also taught officer survival, but eventually I had Terry take over the officer survival class. I felt he would be the best one to teach it, and true enough, he was.

On December 8, 1969, SWAT was going to serve search warrants on three Black Panther locations. Dave McGill's team was assigned the Panther headquarters, a business building on Central at Forty-First Street. A team led by Dave Wissman, was given the second location, the residence of Elmer Pratt, a Black Panther leader. My team was assigned a Black Panther stronghold, a two-story house divided into a two-family residence on Exposition Boulevard. Charlie Reese, the field commander, got no-knock warrants for each location. In those days, a no-knock warrant was something that people thought you could never get, but due to the extreme danger presented by the Panthers, they issued him no-knock warrants. It wasn't going to be a walk in the park.

At the Exposition location, the Black Panthers occupied the front side of the residence, both the first floor and all of the second floor. A family unrelated to the Panthers lived in the back of the residence, but they didn't have access to the second floor—only the Panthers did. The windows were boarded up with plywood and wire meshing. The door leading to the Panthers' side of the residence was a double door; one opened out, and the other opened in. The entire wall on the front side on both levels was sandbagged. They had cut the four-by-fours underneath the side wooden porch so that if anybody stepped on it, it would collapse.

At four thirty in the morning, we started the operation on Exposition. Ron Barnes's job was to cut the phone lines. He later told me he saw two black lines and didn't know which was phone and which was electricity. He said, "I just prayed that I got the right one, because if I snipped the electrical ones, I was going to be in a deep world of hurt." But he snipped the phone line.

We had a fire ax from the fire department, and Ron put it right through the wire meshing and the plywood of a window on the west side of the building. I fired tear-gas shells right over his head and through the hole he had created. I just fired, fired, fired. I could never fire that many rounds that quickly with a gas gun if I were asked to do it again. Then I heard Rik Violano yell, "Gun!" I came running around the corner along with Jerry Brackley, who was armed with an AR-15 to protect my backside. A Panther had extended his shotgun out of the firing port between some sandbags and was trying to turn the barrel toward the policemen knocking down the door. The barrel hit Violano's leg, and he felt it, looked down, and yelled, "Gun!" I fired two tear-gas shells right through that firing port. We made entry and took eight suspects into custody. We hit the place so hard and so fast that the Panthers didn't have time to gather themselves and react. They were disoriented from the tear gas and were quickly neutralized. We put so much tear gas in that place that they later had to tear down the entire building. We served the search warrant and recovered guns, pipe bombs, and other weapons. When the operation first started, we had a

"We put so much tear gas in that place that they later had to tear down the entire building."

team take the family out of their side of the residence. Nobody got shot. No officers were injured. Everyone did one fantastic job.

Ultimately, a decision was made to make SWAT a part of Metro Division. I went to Metro for a short period of time, made lieutenant, and went to Wilshire Division. From Wilshire, I went back to Metro as the first full-time lieutenant in charge of SWAT. On one of our first callouts, an armed individual had broken into an apartment on the second floor of an apartment building in Foothill Division. The person was mad at his common-law wife and her sister, who lived in this apartment, and he wanted to kill them. There were also a third woman and six children in there. The third woman jumped out of the second-story window, and that was what brought the police to the location. We had a negotiator trying to talk to him, but he was not giving up. We had an entry team ready and a sniper in place. We were trying to talk to the guy on the phone, and all of a sudden, *bam!* He started shooting inside this apartment. Our guys went up a ladder, onto the porch, and through the front door. Even through all the confusion and the screaming of two women and six children, the officers—like surgeons taking out cancer in a human body—weeded through the chaos and put him down. Neither the women nor the children were injured.

Lloyd Woller, center right: Watts riots, 1965

Lloyd Woller was working Metro as a sergeant, and he was a classmate of mine. On his way home one night, he stopped to help someone who had pulled over to the shoulder on the freeway. Lloyd saw a car coming right at them, and as he threw the motorist out of the way, he got hit. By all rights, he should have died. He had numerous surgeries and eventually came back to Metro. One time, there was an emergency at the Coliseum, and we had to park a ways from the entrance. We were running, and Lloyd, who could barely move on one leg, was moving and trying to keep up. He was a gutsy human being. Later, when he made lieutenant, he came to work for me at Southeast Division. He couldn't sleep because of the pain in his leg, so he would come in at three in the morning, work about three hours, go home, sleep a little bit, come back, and work a few more hours. The people who worked with him loved him. When he retired, his leg was amputated. He and his wife moved to Grass Valley, and when I heard he had gotten cancer, I flew up to see him. I can still see him and his wife waving good-bye to me out of his second-story bedroom window. The week after I visited him, he passed away. I had the pleasure of giving his eulogy. Some policemen from Metro who had worked for him were the honor guard at the service.

With a lot of prayers and lit candles, I made captain. I was now at Southeast as a captain, and the Eulia Love shooting occurred. Lloyd O'Callahan and Edward "Mike" Hopson responded to a dispute at Love's residence, and she confronted them with a knife. The officers were trying to get her to drop the knife when she threw the knife at the officers, and they shot. It was a difficult tactical situation for the officers. As a result of the shooting, there were demonstrations in front of the station in protest of Love's death. Both Lloyd and Mike took it really hard, but we kept working with them. Late one night a few days later, Mike was working the front desk. I happened to be there when he got a telephone call from his daughter. She was about nine years old. She told him, "Daddy, I love you. You're not a bad man. You're a good man." And he just broke down at that point, which was good. I mean, sooner or later, you've got to let it out. I sent him home. The shooting became political, and two outstanding policemen's lives were turned into a living hell. I presented the circumstances of the shooting to the Shooting Review Board. From a board of three, two voted that the shooting was in policy, and the third voted that it was out of policy. Chief Daryl Gates showed his grit and insight by taking the majority opinion.

After that, whenever an officer was involved in a shooting, I sent the officer home for three to four days. I would tell them, "Spend time with your family, and then come back to work."

One time, I called the home of an officer whom I had sent home for three days. His wife answered the phone, and she became worried because her husband wasn't there. She thought her husband not being there meant he was in trouble. I said, "No, no. He's not in trouble. I'm just calling to see how he's doing." I then said to her, "How are you doing?" There was a moment of silence, and she all of a sudden started crying uncontrollably. Finally, it was out, and I said, "You okay?"

And she said, "Yes, thank you for that." She said, "I know he may not come home. I know he can get shot. I know he can get killed, but I don't want to dwell on that, because that's not going to make it good for our marriage." In this particular situation, her husband had been shot at, and he'd shot the suspect. She said, "What happened just brought it all home. I didn't want to break down in front of him, because he's going through so much himself."

A side story: My twin sons attended a Catholic high school, and one day, the teacher, who was not yet a priest, brought up the Eulia Love shooting. He said it was a bad shooting, described the policemen as white, said Love was black, and so on. My sons came home and told me about what the teacher had said. They asked me questions, so I went over the situation with them. They went back the next day and said, "Excuse me, sir, but my dad was involved in that Eulia Love shooting. Did you know that one of the officers was black and the other was half Mexican and half white?" I mean, that didn't change the shooting, but they also offered some facts about the distance the knife had been thrown, what the knife could have done if it had hit either officer, and the amount of time they had spent talking to her.

The teacher had made it sound as if they had just driven up, she'd had a knife in her hand, and *boom, boom, boom*—they'd shot her. He apologized to the whole class. He said, "I told you some things yesterday about this shooting of Eulia Love. I was mistaken on just about all of it, and I apologize for bringing it up." I thought that was classy on his part. But it showed the whole spectrum of how the incident was viewed. It was an emotional time for everybody.

In '81, there was a scandal at Hollywood Division involving two officers committing burglaries. Chief Gates called me at home and told me they had arrested the two officers. He said, "I want you to go to Hollywood Division and take over command." Overnight, I was sent to Hollywood.

People around Chief Gates had essentially convinced him to transfer the entire division—I mean just clean the whole place out. I asked Chief Gates not to send everyone out of Hollywood Division and said, "The majority of the men and women who work Hollywood are good, and I honestly believe they didn't know what was going on. If you transfer all of them, then for the rest of their careers, they will have to explain why they left Hollywood." The chief agreed and helped me get some lieutenants, sergeants, and officers transferred in. Over time, the division bounced back.

During the 1984 Olympics, I was in the command post, and President Reagan had just arrived for the opening ceremonies at the Coliseum. I got a telephone call from the person in charge of the Coliseum. I couldn't understand what the man was saying. All I heard was "Bob, bomb. Bob, bomb." He was frantic. I finally got him to calm down, and he told me that at the east end of the Coliseum, they had seen what they believed was a bomb inside the tower of the Olympic torch. There was a ladder going up to the area, and they had seen a black box that had never been there before. They also believed the equipment for the lighting device for the flame to travel through and light the Olympic torch had been sabotaged. The president had just arrived, and the Coliseum was filled. We had an evacuation plan, but how would we clear thousands of people out of there in time? Arleigh McCree and Ron Ball—who, in 1986, would both be killed diffusing two pipe bombs in a garage—rode with me Code 3 to the Coliseum. Arleigh and Ron climbed the ladder up into the area in question and determined that the black box was not a bomb. It was part of the equipment for the lighting device for the Olympic rings and the torch. There had also been no sabotage. The president of the United States was there, my own family was seated at the east end, and it was thought there was a bomb in the Coliseum. This was just before Rafer Johnson was set to run up with the torch to light the Olympic rings. Stress comes with the job, and I can personally testify to it.

l to r: Chuck Higbie, Eddie Garcia, George Haynes, Pat McKinley, Bob Smitson (all retired LAPD): Fullerton College Police Academy staff

Once, back when I was walking a footbeat, an old-timer said to me, "There will come a time when you'll know when it's your time to retire." I didn't really understand what he was talking about at the time. But he was right. In '86, I decided it was time to retire and become a full-time teacher. Teaching had always been a passion of mine. In '61, I started teaching at LA City College. In '66, I started teaching at Fullerton College, and I've been there ever since. I also taught at the Rio Hondo College Police Academy for twenty years, Glendale College, Golden West College Police Academy, California State University at Fullerton, and the United States State Department. I'm now a full-time professor and coordinator of the Fullerton College Police Academy. Teaching has allowed me to remain current with a profession I love and be around people I have shared experiences with during my police career. And like Gil Burgoyne and Sam Posner, teaching has given me an opportunity to introduce the police profession to others.

James "Eddie" Watkins

Birthplace: Sanford, Florida
Career: 1958–1983
Rank at Retirement: Lieutenant II
Divisions: Parking and Intersection Control, Venice, University, Highland
 Park, Burglary Auto-Theft, Special Investigation Section, Training,
 Metropolitan, Newton, Devonshire, Narcotics

After high school, I served two years in the army, and after the military, I worked for the steel industry, welding on high steel buildings. But I had always wanted to be a policeman. I applied to LAPD and flunked my first attempt. I recognized that there were certain things that I had to know, so I put a lot of effort into educating myself. I reapplied and was accepted, and I went into the academy in '58. When I got there, I was in a lot of trouble because I had to *really* study. I never really worked hard on my physical capabilities, because I had always been physically fit. One of my classmates, Jimmy Sakoda, was the only one to beat me on the physical-fitness tests. But I had to develop study habits to get me through the academics of the academy. I did, and when I graduated, I was in the top third of my class. I was proud of that.

When we graduated, I was really looking forward to going to patrol. I was sent to PIC, and I thought, *My goodness, here I have lived all my life wanting to be a policeman, and where did they send me? Directing traffic in downtown Los Angeles.*

One day, after I had been there about three months, the sergeant said, "Hey, Watkins, we've got to have a talk." He said, "The businesses at your intersection say you blow your whistle too much. It's aggravating to them because you are always blowing your whistle."

Eddie Watkins

I said, "Well, you know, Sergeant, I can cut that out a little bit." As soon as he left, I started blowing that whistle like crazy. I blew that whistle as much as I could, and three weeks later, I was transferred to Venice Division patrol. I succeeded in escaping PIC.

I was in Venice Division for over a year. It was an odd place, and you have to remember that this was 1959 and 1960. On morning watch, there were generally three cars and a sergeant. By two o'clock in the morning, we stopped working and went to the sleeping hole. The sleeping hole was in a field with a few ponds and oil wells. There was a night watchman to watch the oil wells, and the policemen would bring him a newspaper. I was on probation, and I couldn't go to sleep. When my classmate Arvid Keidser and I got off probation, we worked together. On any given night, we would be 14A1, 14A7, 14A99. We would answer every call for those units. They thought, *This is great. Those two rookies are out there answering the calls, and we can sleep.* I always wondered about the dispatchers when they heard Arvid or me answering the calls as 14A1 or 14A7 or 14A99 all in the same night.

Venice Division police station

The last part of my time at Venice, I was working Vice, when the beatniks were around. The first time anybody ever made an arrest out of a beatnik store, I made it. It was for possession of marijuana and narcotics paraphernalia. That created a bit of a disturbance in the area because nobody had ever messed with the beatniks. It was a political thing going on at the time, and there was a big write-up in the local paper: "Vice Officer Arrests People from Beatnik Shop." I also made the first arrest of a prostitute in Venice Division. With that, it was time to go, and I went to University Division.

At University Division, those guys knew police work. I was doing police work now and was a happy soldier. It didn't take me long before I was assigned to the felony car, the F-car. On the night Ian Campbell and Karl Hettinger were missing, I was working an F-car. We were a neighboring division, and we searched for them that night. The car was found but not the policemen. At the end of the night, we didn't conclude anything. The next day, when I came back to work, we were told a little bit, but nobody really had a lot of information. When the story came out, it kind of disturbed me because I had gone through the academy before those two policemen had. I had been taught you didn't give up your gun. Holding on to your gun was the only reason the other policeman was going to stay alive. If you gave up your gun, you

Ian Campbell and Karl Hettinger police vehicle at location of kidnap, 1963

both could die. I could not imagine them going through the academy and not hearing the same thing I had heard. It was a tragedy. I felt really bad for both of those policemen. One was dead, and one was mentally dead because of the way it affected him.

One night while working the F-car, my partner, C. B. Westergard, and I got a call on Pico Boulevard of a robbery in progress at a bar. As we got there, a guy came across the street toward us from the bar; he was a dishwasher at the place. He said, "There's a robbery in there. One guy has a gun, and one has a knife."

C. B. went to the back door, and I went to the front door. In California, there was no visibility into a bar from the outside. It was against the law. I decided since I was in plainclothes, I could go in the place and maybe see what was happening in there. I wasn't using my head, as I should have. I opened the door. It was one of the old oak doors about three inches thick, solid oak wood. As I opened the door, a person was coming out. Well, there was only one person who would be coming out that slowly. If it was somebody escaping, he would have been barreling out of there. He backed up and reached into his waistband, and I knew this guy was going for a gun. He

C. B. Westergard

backed right up against a table with four people seated, drawing his gun out. I thought, *I can't shoot here—they're four people there—but I can get out.* As I grabbed the doorknob, he shot, and the first bullet hit between my feet. When he brought the gun out, he was squeezing the trigger already, and the bullet missed me. The next bullet went into the door that I had shut between us. About that time, other police cars arrived. I said, "My partner is in the back, and I've got the front here." One policeman went around the back, and C. B. was down behind some garbage cans. The shooter was now coming out the back. The officer, not recognizing C. B., yelled for C. B. to drop his gun. The shooter, thinking the policeman was yelling at him, dropped his gun. C. B. and the officer took him into custody. At the same time, the guy with the knife came out the front door, holding two females around the neck, with a knife to one's throat. He wanted us to get him a car and bring it to the front, or he was going to cut their throats.

As another policeman and I were talking with him, a sergeant came up behind him. The sergeant stuck his gun to the head of the suspect and told him, "The only way you're going to live is if you give that knife up."

I yelled at him, "Give me that knife." He turned the knife over and handed it to me, and we took him into custody. Well, that was a situation when I really learned about using the wrong tactics. You can't do everything perfectly all the time. It didn't take anybody else to tell me that. There were only two of us—me and C. B.—and I shouldn't have gone inside. We had them in there. We could have talked them out, gotten them out however we had to, without risking a life. It's better to let whatever happens happen, unless there is some circumstance where you have to go in. But you do it with more than just one person. It was a real time of learning for me.

I was working auto-theft detectives at University Division when I made sergeant. I went to Highland Park Division patrol. By this time, I had about six years on the job. Marion Hoover worked for me at Highland Park. He had been involved in about six shootings. One night, Marion and his partner came upon a rape in progress. There were two suspects raping this young girl in a car parked up on the mountain in a lover's lane. Marion interrupted them in their rape and started dragging them out of the car. One jumped over the cliff—not a long drop or anything—and got away. Marion hit the other, split his head open, and took him into custody. Well, this lieutenant thought that was conduct unbecoming of an officer—to split this guy's head open—especially when a complaint came in about it. Marion was part of my mid-watch but was working morning watch when this happened. The lieutenant called me in and said, "I have a complaint here on Marion Hoover for this dastardly deed that he did. You have to investigate it."

"Very good. I'll do that," I said.

Marion, in his statement to me, said, "They're raping a young fourteen-year-old girl. I could have shot them both, but I chose to take them into custody, which caused one to get away—but at least I got one of them. Hopefully, he won't get a chance to rape another girl."

I said, "That's pretty good, Marion." I wrote a long investigative report, and I made out a commendation report. I explained how great a job Marion Hoover had done and said that I found him not in violation of anything. I turned the reports in to the lieutenant, and he went haywire. I said, "Well, you know, Lieutenant, you asked me to investigate this, and I did, and these are my findings. I thought he did such a good job that I wrote him a commendation. You can do anything you want with that report, and you can do anything you want with that commendation, but I did what you told me to do." Well, the good captain accepted my recommendation, and he accepted my commendation for Marion.

After Highland Park, I went to Burglary Auto-Theft Division. I hadn't been there long when I got my job in SIS, Special Investigation Section, in '66. It was a tremendous blessing to work surveillance in its opening stages. SIS had only been going a couple of months when I joined the unit. There was not a more prestigious or rewarding place to work. We received information on suspects from all kinds of sources. A few times, defense attorneys called in and said, "I just defended these guys, but they're still robbing places." Those were the kinds of guys we worked.

There were a couple of guys who robbed banks, and one of the suspects would fire an automatic weapon. We had good information from a snitch that they were going to pull a bank robbery in Foothill Division, and we would know when they left their house to do the robbery. We staked the bank instead of following them. We got the call that they were on their way. It was happening. Meanwhile, Foothill Division was having training that day, preparing their division for handling a major incident. As these outlaws came into town to rob this bank, they saw police cars running everywhere and called it off. Shortly thereafter, they set up to do a bank robbery over in Wilshire Division. We knew which bank they were going to hit, and our units set up on the bank. The suspects showed up. One suspect wore a Nairobi-style robe and a big head rag, and he had a Thompson submachine gun. His partner had a handgun. The guy with the handgun walked into the alley, and the one with the submachine gun went to the front. Previously, they had both gone in together and hadn't separated, but this time, they did. The officers inside were told, "One's coming through the front door with a submachine gun, and the other one's in the back." We had the back door locked. The guy in the alley tried the back door, but he couldn't get in. The first guy went through the front door, took the submachine gun out from under his Nairobi robe, and announced a robbery, and he was put down. The officers in the back got into a shoot-out with the alley suspect and wounded him. The news guys at two television stations were bad-mouthing us because they thought we had shot this bank robber in the alley twenty-three times. They found out after they had been blabbing all this that we had used shotguns, and there were eleven pellets in each shell, so that was why there had been twenty-three hits on this guy. We hadn't shot him twenty-three times, but we had put him down. You put people down to stop them from what they are doing. If you do that, you have succeeded. If the suspect dies, that's unfortunate, but that's what your mind-set is—to get him to stop doing what he's doing.

We were given three years to operate that unit. In three years, the unit arrested in excess of three hundred suspects committing felonies, and about 90 percent of them were armed at the time they were committing crimes. In the three years, only seven suspects were shot and killed. That's pretty good; that's a good standard to have only shot that many. It's still a great unit today, even though the politicians of Los Angeles have, on several occasions, tried to get the unit disbanded. A sergeant ran the unit in the beginning, and when they finally gave us a lieutenant, it was Danny Bowser. Danny did an excellent job of running that outfit. It was a great crew to work with.

I missed one year with SIS to help set up BAD Cats at Burglary Auto Theft Division. BAD Cats was set up to investigate commercial auto thefts. I was one of the first six people assigned to the unit. We had some great cases. On one case, we took down a big operation run by a schoolteacher. They would buy a piece of junk that couldn't be rebuilt, go steal a car like it, switch VIN numbers, and sell the stolen car with a counterfeit pink slip in Texas. We filed a good number of cases on the schoolteacher.

After my one year at BAD Cats, I went back to SIS. One day, Ted Breckenridge and I heard a Robbery-Homicide team chasing a robbery suspect in the Hollywood area. The guy they were pursuing had robbed a jewelry salesman and had taken his car. He was going back and forth on the Hollywood Freeway. He'd go south, get off, get back on the other side, and go north. One of those times, he was headed toward downtown, got off the freeway, and got right back on, and that was right in front of where we were, so that was good. I saw one of the Robbery-Homicide guys' cars in the center divider, where he had crashed, and there was a bullet hole in his window. As we drove by him, I asked him on the radio if he was okay, and he said he was. We came up behind another Robbery-Homicide guy, and I said, "Do you want us to take it?"

He said, "Yeah, take it."

We passed him, and there were a couple of bullet holes in his window. I was driving and Ted was in the passenger seat. I was thinking this was a guy who had robbed a jewelry salesman, had stolen the car, and was shooting at police officers. This guy was no good. This guy was a bad guy. We were coming up behind this guy, and Ted had a shotgun. On the Hollywood Freeway, there were a couple of places with overpasses with big cement walls along the sides. You were fairly well protected in those places from losing a shot that could hurt somebody. As we came up behind him, I had a pretty good angle on him, and Ted leaned out the window with the shotgun. He blew the back window out of the car. This caused the guy to panic a little bit. He got the word that we really wanted him. When the shot blew the back window out, his car started wiggling, and he spun out. When he spun out, I was going a little bit faster and passed him up. I threw on my brakes and cranked the wheel around so that my back end came around. Now we were facing this guy sliding down the freeway backward, and he was still coming in my direction. We both stopped. He sat up a little bit and then leaned back down, and I thought, *This guy is looking for his gun.* I popped a round through the windshield at him. The bullet missed him because of the slant of the windshield and lodged in the body of his car. We took this guy into custody. I talked to a couple of the Robbery guys later and found out that all of the bullet holes in their cars were from them shooting at this guy without rolling their windows down. And I had been thinking this guy was a bad guy and was shooting at police. Well, no, he hadn't been shooting at police. The police had been shooting at him. He had been trying to save his life, get away from them, and keep from getting shot.

That was a significant day for me. That was a great lesson: don't prejudge anything. You can't go out on the streets and be a policeman without knowledge. I had lots of probable cause to shoot that guy. To me, he was going for a gun. I had already seen bullet holes in the police car windows, and if I had shot him, I don't think I would have had any problem, knowing what I knew and thinking what I thought, considering the things that had gone on. People understood why I shot. Thank goodness I didn't kill him. It was a day of really growing up for me. Things like that incident and like going into that bar and having a guy shoot the bullet between my feet became a driving force for me to teach. I made a mistake, and I didn't want anybody else to make one.

Throughout my career, I wanted to teach, and I got the opportunity at the academy. As a detective at Burglary Auto-Theft Division, based on reports that I had read, I knew detectives were getting incomplete

Los Angeles Police Department Academy, circa 1950s

reports. It was my opinion that they were not teaching recruits at the academy how to investigate, what a report required, and how to write it. I set up field scenarios for recruits to do. I would lecture on a scenario and then have them investigate it and write a report. Over time, we got feedback from the field that the recruits were better trained. They knew more about investigations and report writing than any recruits before. To me, that was a great thing. I did two years of report writing and three years in the physical fitness and self-defense unit and eventually set up the Field Problems Unit and put three years in there.

Whenever there was an officer-involved shooting, I would review the shooting for training purposes. There was one such shooting when the Training Division captain asked me to answer a question about the operation of a revolver. A young kid and his class were scheduled to graduate from the academy. He would've been one of three brothers on the job at one time. The police commissioners and the councilman from his area were going to be at the graduation, where this kid was going to give his valedictorian speech. On the day of the graduation, Captain Rudy De Leon was going to bring him and the officer's family to the academy. The officer, his kids, and his wife were in the breakfast room of the kitchen. The wife was sitting at the end of the table, and the officer was at the other end, making sure his uniform and gear were good—everything shiny and bright. He took his gun out of the holster and opened the cylinder. He wiped the gun clean, loaded it back up, and closed the cylinder. His finger was on the trigger. The gun went off, and the bullet struck his wife in the mouth and killed her. My captain wanted to know if a revolver would go off if someone was holding the trigger back and dropped the hammer. The answer to that is yes—it will do that. If a person has the trigger back, causing the hammer to cock back, loads it, shuts it, and lets the hammer loose, the firing pin is out and it's going to strike. That was what happened. A few days after the funeral, the officer said, "I can't go back. I can't be a policeman." He couldn't pick up a gun after that. He couldn't hold it, wouldn't hold it. We brought him back to the academy and spent some time with him, trying to get him to use a gun and be confident with it again. After a while, he thought he could do it. He tried to report to the job, but he could not. He never came back. He had really wanted to be a policeman, his brothers really wanted him to, and the department wanted him to. It was a tragic story but, at the same time, a gun-safety story.

I had taken a couple of tests to make lieutenant and decided that I needed more experience to get promoted. Eight years was enough at the academy, although it was the best eight years of my life. I think I did as good a job there against crime as I would have if I had been working the field. I knew there were people going out of the academy who had a deeper understanding of their duties as police officers and the critical thinking that was required for police work.

From the academy, I transferred to Metro Division as a sergeant, later made lieutenant, and went to Newton Division. There was an officer who was on loan to detectives but had gone beyond the time period for the loan. When officers were on loan to detectives, they were expected to take and pass the detective test. If they did not, then they returned to patrol. He was coming back to patrol. He was five foot ten and weighed close to three hundred pounds. He was obese. He came into the office and said, "Hey, Lieutenant, do I get my regular car back?"

I looked at him and said, "No. No, you don't get it. We're going to put you on the desk."

"You can't put me on the desk!"

"Yes, I can put you on the desk," I said. "Until you lose some weight, you're a danger to me out on the street. You have a partner, and if there's a chase or you have to go over a fence, you're useless to him. Best you can do is get back to the car and ask for help. So you're not going to go out there until you're safe."

He said, "Well, you can't do that. I'll have to see the captain."

I said, "That's okay. Go ahead."

Now, I had not discussed this situation with the good captain. The officer went in to talk to the captain about it. While he was in there, the captain called me in and said, "I understand you've placed him on the desk?"

I said, "Yes, sir."

"What's your reason for that?"

I told him my reason, and he turned back to the police officer and said, "You're our desk officer. You're not going back in the field until you lose some weight and make yourself safe as a patrol officer. You're excused." And he left.

I said, "Thank you very much, Captain."

He said, "That's okay; it's about time things around here were run in a police orderly way."

I was happy he had backed me on that decision. That story went through the troops really quickly because there were a lot of guys who didn't want to work with that guy. I looked back at his record, and there was a time when he had shot at a suspect versus chasing him, and it hadn't been a good shooting. In another incident, he'd lost a suspect because he couldn't chase him, and that had been when he was getting heavy before he'd gone to detectives. That put me in a relatively good frame.

Eventually, I went to Narcotics Division for the last three years before I retired. One time, one of my detectives, Richard Vincent, had an informant who told him about a guy he knew who had a couple of kilos of cocaine. Vince said, "Set it up with your friend so that we can make a buy."

The following Sunday, the informant called Vince and said, "Hey, a buddy of mine went over to this guy's house, took the cocaine out of the house, and brought it home to me. We need to get this to you." Well, Vince was highly irritated over that. I mean, here this informant had had his buddy burglarize this place, get the stuff, and bring it out to him. The house was built on a steep bank. To get into the house, the guy climbed up onto a telephone pole receptacle, stood on it next to an open window, and climbed through the window to get inside.

Vince said to me, "What do we do? We got the cocaine."

"Well, here's what we do. Go up to their house where they live, pin a note to the door, knock on the door, and run like heck."

The note read, "I got your stuff. If you want it, give me a call back," and we wrote a phone number. They called Vince the next day. They wanted their stuff, and Vince told them he wanted money for it. Of course, these were outlaws. These were ugly folks we were dealing with. Vince was asking them for money to get their own cocaine back. They wanted to meet with him to bring him the money. He told them he was not going to have the stuff with him, that he wanted to see the money before he would make a call and have someone bring the stuff. He told them he didn't want to meet in a private place. They agreed to meet at Taix's Restaurant.

The first thing I did was set up countersurveillance. Sure enough, my guys arrived far ahead of time, and one reported, "Ed, I got a car parked down here off the main street. There's two of them in the car, and they both have long guns. I think they're shotguns."

Another car said, "We got another guy over here. He's been driving around looking for a place to park, and he's trying to park so he can see the parking lot of Taix's."

Based on our countersurveillance, there was no question about it; this was going to be a shoot-out. I told Vince, "You go in and meet with these guys. You don't want to do the deal. You're afraid that he's got people around there, and they're going to hurt somebody."

After they met, the suspects went back over to their pad where the narcotics came from, and we arrested them. No problems— everything went down fine. We took it to court, and Vince ended up having to take the jury out to the scene because these guys said, "Well, nobody broke my door down, and they can't get in." The informant testified as to how all of this had gone down, and the defendants were convicted. That was a fun case—trying to see who was going to do what.

I retired from there. It was a good time for retirement and a time to really think back over almost twenty-six years and see what I had accomplished. When I retired, we moved to Missouri. I became the chief of police for Rockaway Beach, Missouri, and the training officer for the county. In 1985, I became a California Fish and Game warden until 1998. I was sworn in as a game warden in the backseat of an undercover car in a peach orchard in Bakersfield, California. I worked undercover investigating the commercialization of wildlife and ran the undercover unit for the last ten years that I was there. And as I said, I enjoy teaching, and I'm still teaching police work today.

Jim Martin

James "Jim" Martin

Birthplace: Hollywood, California
Career: 1960–1986
Rank at Retirement: Detective III
Divisions: Narcotics, Central, West Valley, Metropolitan, Devonshire,
    Foothill, Internal Affairs, Organized Crime Intelligence

In '46, my best friend and neighbor, Bill Richmond, and I joined DAP, the Deputy Auxiliary Police, at Hollywood Division. We were in the program for a year, and we did camping, swimming, and field trips to the academy. Bill went on to become a police officer with the Burbank Police Department, while I went into the air force, assigned to the military police. I served two years in Japan, where I experienced my first riot long before the Watts riots. Because of my experience with the DAP program and the military police, I decided I liked police work. I applied to LAPD and was hired in August 1960. I was ready for the academy because I had been in the military police for four years and was attending college, studying police administration.

Once out of the academy, I worked undercover in Narcotics Division for four months. The hypes on the street thought I was Mexican and called me Green Eyes, because Mexicans usually had brown eyes. My dad was Mexican, but my mom was white. I didn't speak Spanish, but I got by saying my dad had died early, so I hadn't learned the language. I also used the story that I was on parole out of the Vacaville prison. When I was in the air force, I had actually been through the prison at Vacaville, because I was going with a girl whose dad worked there. I was familiar with the facility. I used that a couple of times when I got in spots where I had to make an excuse to leave, such as before the hypes started shooting heroin or using other drugs. One time, I was in a guy's house, and there were probably ten hypes, all shooting up. They were cutting a big bundle of heroin, so I was trying to get some of it for evidence. They thought it was strange that I wanted to leave, but somehow I managed to get out of there. When it came down to it, I was out there with just a handful of money and my wits.

One time, I was in a car with five hypes, and we had just made a buy. I had a balloon of heroin in my mouth, and we were pulled over by the police on Main Street. Everyone ran from the car and into a furniture store, but they were all arrested. I pulled one of the policemen aside, and I said, "I'm an undercover cop, and I need to talk to you. Get me away from the rest of these people." He took me aside, and I told him, "I have a balloon of heroin in my mouth, so don't choke me out or anything." I told him to call Lieutenant Roger Guindon. The policeman did as I asked, and it all worked out. Roger Guindon was the best supervisor I ever worked for, and he later became a captain. Neat guy.

It was a tough assignment, and I learned who the crooks were on the street, including the shoplifters, the burglars, and the robbers. I was walking the streets with hypes, and they were open about what they did. One guy wanted me to pull a robbery with him. I said, "Sure, you going to get some guns?"

"Yeah, I'm going to get some guns."

I found out where he lived and turned the information over to the detectives, and they took it from there. I never found out what happened.

There was a Mexican dealer who wore a suit and a hat and carried a briefcase, looking like a businessman. What set him apart, though, was that he had his baby with him when he was selling. He had the heroin tucked in the baby's diapers. Because he used the baby, even the hypes didn't like him. His wife told us about him. I made a couple of buys from him, and we arrested him and got him off the street.

Before I left Narcotics, I was shown a picture of a drug dealer wanted for murder and robbery. That same day, I was on Broadway and saw the guy. He had distinct tattoos on his arm. I called it in to the office and kept following him. When he got down to Seventh and Broadway and nobody was there yet, I approached a white hat—a traffic officer directing traffic—and I pulled him aside. I told him that I was an undercover officer and pointed out the guy who was wanted for murder. He believed me and arrested the guy. It was a little excitement and change of pace from directing traffic for him.

Jim Martin, Narcotics Division: "When it came down to it, I was out there with just a handful of money and my wits."

When I left Narcotics, I was sent to Central Division patrol but spent most of my time in court for the narcotics arrests. I made seventy buys of heroin on the street and arrested fifty dope peddlers. Evelle Younger was a superior court judge then, and I had most of my cases before him. One time, I had a case before Judge Younger, and the dealer pretended not to speak English. Well, I had testified that the deal had been done in English. Judge Younger stopped the proceeding, leaned over, and asked the dealer what his name was and where he lived. The guy answered in English. Then Judge Younger looked at the guy's attorney and said, "Do you have anything else before I find him guilty?"

I was working Central patrol one day as a one-man car. I stopped four guys in a car in Elysian Park, just south of the academy. I could smell marijuana when I got up to the car, so I grabbed the driver and the car keys and took him to the back of the car. I handcuffed him, and the other three jumped me. That was a mistake on my part—not calling for backup when I was first making the stop. When I did get to my radio, I called for assistance when I should have called for help. When officers got there, we ended up arresting three out of the four guys. One of the three had his shirt torn off, so he was easy to spot. I got help from one of the park visitors too. He was trying to hold one of the guys down, but the suspect got away temporarily. I was just coming off probation, had four years in the military police, and had worked undercover for four months. I had figured I could handle myself in a one-man car. Well, I sure could have used a partner.

One day, I saw six drunks sitting on the curb at Fifth and Main, all holding short-form drunk slips in their hands. They said they were waiting for the B-wagon, as Officer Ralph Gillet had instructed. I asked them, "Since neither Officer Gillet nor the B-wagon is here, why not leave?"

They stated, "No, no, Mr. Gillet would not like that!"

In 1963, I transferred to West Valley Division, about the time Ian Campbell and Karl Hettinger were kidnapped. I knew Campbell because I was going with a girl he knew from before he was married. Ian was really good friends with her brother, so I had been introduced to Ian. It was a real tragedy, and of course, things changed after that.

In 1964, I applied and was accepted to Metro Division. There were good police officers and supervisors there. My partner was Bob Gilmore. One of the things Metro did was bank stakeouts. If there was an increase in bank robberies, we would pick out the bank that was most likely to get hit. One time, Bob and I did a stakeout at a Bank of America on Main Street. Three guys pulled up in a car, and two entered the bank while the third one stayed in the car. The two approached a bank teller who had just handed a lot of money to a customer. The two suspects hit the customer, took his money, and ran out of the bank. Bob and I caught one outside of the bank, and he resisted us. As we were grappling with him, he grabbed my gun. Bob and I both fired and wounded the suspect; the other one surrendered on the spot. The third suspect took off in the car, but the two we captured copped out on him, and he was later arrested. The customer who'd had his money taken said to us, "Good, you saved my money."

On the day the Watts riots started, we were sent to Seventy-Seventh Division. One of the days during the riot, I was working with Carl Kundert and Marty Yturralde. We had arrested a burglar and were driving down the street with him in the backseat. We heard some shots and thought someone was shooting at us. Two guys then came running around a corner. We got out of the car, and the two guys flopped down on the sidewalk next to us. One was bleeding profusely from his leg. Carl tied off the guy's leg to stop the bleeding, which probably saved his life. We put out an assistance call and requested an ambulance. It turned out a policeman had shot at these guys, but the two guys claimed we did it. Fortunately, we had our burglar witness in the backseat.

After the National Guard was deployed, we teamed up with a National Guard lieutenant and two soldiers. One night, we were on Western Avenue when some shots were fired at us. We thought the shots were coming from the Veterans of Foreign Wars Club. There was no evidence someone had gone through the doors or windows, so the National Guard lieutenant and I went up on the roof and saw that a vent had been kicked in. We figured somebody was inside the club. The lieutenant said, "I've got a gas pack."

I said, "We don't want to burn the building down."

He said, "It won't catch on fire." He tossed the gas pack through the vent. By this time, more cops, highway patrol, sheriffs, and soldiers had

l to r: Jim Martin, Carl Kundert, and Marty Yturralde, Watts riots, 1965: "Carl tied off the guy's leg to stop the bleeding, which probably saved his life."

shown up. Ralph Gillet, who was now working Metro, shot out a streetlight to make it dark. Unfortunately, everyone else thought the shot came from the building. They all opened up, and the lieutenant and I were still up on the roof. I went to the end corner of the roof and shrunk my six-foot, 190-pound body into a little ball until they finally stopped shooting. It felt like wartime. We eventually determined nobody was inside. We walked through the club, where there were pictures of World War II heroes, generals, and admirals on the walls. The pictures were now riddled with bullet holes. I thought the city was going to pay big-time for the damage. As it turned out, Carl's dad, who had served in World War II, was a member of the VFW Club. I later asked Carl about it, and he said his dad had told him the vets loved it. They fixed everything but left the wall with all the bullet holes through the pictures. Those World War II guys were just happy as hell about that.

In 1968, I made sergeant and went to Devonshire Division. The station was temporary, and the division was part of the old West Valley area where I had worked before. One day, two FBI guys came to the station. This was about the time of the antiwar discontent on the campuses. One of the FBI guys said, "We got some dynamite we picked up at the San Fernando Valley State college campus." They opened the trunk of their car, and they had two cases of dynamite that were leaking.

I said, "That leakage is a real bad sign for sticks of dynamite, and you're bouncing around with this stuff in your car." We called the bomb squad and evacuated the area. Those two got their backsides in a sling for that one.

One night, I rolled on a call of a naked man in a yard. This guy was stark naked, fifty to sixty years old, eating bark off a tree. Turned out he was a professor at the college. This was before we knew anything about PCP. But that sure seemed like what he was on based on what I saw with other PCP suspects later in my career.

I then went to Foothill Division as an assistant watch commander. That was a routine job, but there was one particular incident. A motor officer had been hassling some teenagers hanging out on Foothill Boulevard. We'd had complaints on this motor officer before. The lieutenant called him in, and we had a talk with him. "You know, you got to stop this; there are too many complaints."

Well, he gave us a "That's how I do my job—I'm the best policeman there is" kind of response.

I said, "The lieutenant and I would probably disagree with you on that. What exactly have you done?" After he told us, we told him that maybe we had a little more knowledge about police work than he did. He was put on parking-lot duty. "March around that lot for eight hours until you can finally decide that you're not the best damn policeman around and you know how to treat people correctly."

After a week or so, he finally came in and said, "I can't stand this anymore. I give up." That helped him. Actually, that helped him a lot.

A former partner of mine, Neil Spotts, was at OCID, Organized Crime and Intelligence Division. He knew I was looking for a job, and he called me up and said his partner was retiring. I had to take a demotion, but I went there. We did special investigations for Chief Ed Davis and then for Chief Gates. I worked there from 1974 to 1986, when I retired.

There was a guy who wrote a book about Marilyn Monroe and claimed Monroe had been murdered by the Kennedys. We were assigned to reinvestigate her death. Luckily, a lot of the records were still available. We were able to disprove this guy's theory on the death of Marilyn Monroe and prove that she had died as the official record showed.

Our secondary job was VIP dignitary protection. When Japanese Emperor Hirohito came to the United States, we were assigned as part of his dignitary protection. While he was here, he wanted to see John Wayne, Charlton Heston, and Iron Eyes Cody, the Indian actor. These guys all stood over six feet tall. It was interesting watching the emperor interact with them.

Neil and I were not assigned to the surveillance unit, but we filled in if needed. One time, there was a major Mafia guy, John Roselli, who was going to meet with another Mafia guy, Jimmy Fratianno, at a restaurant in Beverly Hills. This was 1976. There was going to be a surveillance of the meeting, and Neil and I were asked to fill in. The restaurant was next to some tennis courts, so we dressed as tennis players and sat next to Roselli and Fratianno in the bar. They had a fairly open conversation, and we got some good information. Shortly thereafter, Roselli went back to Florida, disappeared, and was later found inside a steel drum floating in Dumfoundling Bay, near Miami. We later saw crime-scene photos of his death—pretty gruesome. He had been strangled, and part of his legs had been chopped off. Not too long after that, Fratianno turned himself in to the FBI and wanted protection.

We also provided security for President Ronald Reagan. I knew Ronald Reagan quite well. We were both members of the Beverly Christian Church, and I provided security for him when he ran for governor of California. When he became president, I told his Secret Service guys that Reagan was the only US president I would sacrifice myself for and protect from a bullet.

It was a long span of time from the DAP program to my retirement. A good part of my life was associated with the Los Angeles Police Department. My buddy Bill chose to go with the Burbank Police Department, but for me, LAPD was the only choice.

Bill Richmond and Jim Martin

William "Bill" Schmidt

Birthplace: Dell Rapids, South Dakota
Career: 1960–1973
Rank at Retirement: Sergeant I
Divisions: Central, Hollenbeck, Seventy-Seventh Street, West Los Angeles, Rampart

My father came on the LAPD in '40 or '41 and left in '42. He was only making seventy-five dollars a month and had two boys—me and my brother, Jack. He couldn't make it financially, so he left the department to work in the oil fields, rig building. The job paid more, and due to the war, rig builders and carpenters were needed. He was also a carpenter. Shortly after he left the department, the pay was raised to $125 dollars per month. He said if he had known that they were going to raise the pay, he would have stayed and made a career with the department. He had a family to take care of, and at the time, you could not do it on seventy-five dollars a month.

In 1955, at age fifteen, I started working at Knott's Berry Farm as a busboy. I was promoted to broiler cook and then to manager of the Cable Car Kitchen. At the time, Knott's had cable cars around the parking lots. One day, one of the security guards, a retired navy chief, said to me, "You know, you're not going anywhere. You are just going to be working here as a manager and a cook. What are you going to have in life? Why don't you try the police department?" He said, "I bet you can't make it."

I said to him, "What do you want to bet?"

He said, "A steak dinner."

"Okay."

I applied to LAPD, and three months later, I was in the academy. It was just boom, boom. I started October 24, 1960.

Bill Schmidt

Roy Bean was the head instructor at the academy and was in great shape. But the one who really stood out was Joe Ferrell. He was built like a brick house and had shoulders like a fullback. He could run backward up the hills faster than we could run forward. That was what kind of shape he was in. I wasn't much of a runner, so I was on the goon squad. That meant I had to come in an hour early every morning and run for an hour to get myself in better shape. The funny part about it was that I started the academy at 185 pounds, and when I left the academy, I weighed 195. On the shooting range, they didn't have earplugs. We used toilet paper. After a while, I got smart and used some spent cartridges to try to deaden the sound. A lot of guys from my generation have impaired hearing because earplugs were not provided in the academy. They didn't have eye protection either.

"A lot of guys from my generation have impaired hearing because earplugs were not provided in the academy. They didn't have eye protection either."

We graduated February 7, 1961. I went to Central Division, and the captain called me in to congratulate me on graduating from the academy and said he was proud to have me in Central Division. He said, "In Central, it is a little bit different than what they told you at the academy." He told me I would be going into different restaurants and that some were going to give me free food. To not embarrass the department, he didn't want me to say anything; he told me to just put a quarter on the table to pay for the meal.

I said, "Yes, sir." Here I had spent sixteen weeks in the academy, and they had said, "No gratuities," and the captain was telling me this was how we were going to do it.

My first assignment was the B-wagon, and Kenny Baker was my partner. He had three more months on the job than I did. The first night, he said, "You like to fight?"

"Well, I guess."

"Well, all you do is you fight drunks. You fight to get them in the B-wagon, and you fight to get them out of the B-wagon."

I did that for about six months. One time on the B-wagon, while I was working with another partner, a robbery call came out, and the suspect's car came right by us. My partner said, "Let's go." We went in pursuit down Hill Street with drunks in the back of the B-wagon. We had no siren; all we had were red lights. My partner told me, "Just tell them where we're going and what we're doing."

Once I put us in pursuit, a sergeant came on the air and said for us to cancel the pursuit. My partner said, "No. No. We're almost on them." Then we were hung up in traffic. He stopped the B-wagon, jumped out, and ran down the street after the guys, who were at least a block away. I laugh about it today, but we should have never been doing that. The suspects got away.

Then I walked a footbeat on Main Street with Tom Weller, an old-timer. He could make his nightstick dance down the street. All the old-timers could do certain tricks with those sticks. Each baton had a strap that an officer wrapped around his little finger. They taught me how to twirl it, and we'd just go down the street twirling our batons. Working a footbeat, I got to know everybody—every drunk, every hooker, and all the business owners. In fact, I had some really great dinners at Mike Lyman's, next to the Biltmore Hotel. The meals were good—and only a quarter.

I worked a patrol car for a while. I was working the night Ian Campbell and Karl Hettinger were kidnapped. The call came out when they started looking for the car: "Officer needs help. We are missing a unit from Hollywood." They gave us a description of their car and the license plate number. It was spooky. We found out at roll call the next day what had happened. Then we were given roll-call training on what to do and what not to do if somebody got a drop on your partner.

I wheeled out of Central Division to Hollenbeck Division and worked a footbeat there for a while. But I wanted more action, so in '63, I transferred to Seventy-Seventh Street Division. I had a ball at Seventy-Seventh because on any given night, we had thirty, forty, sometimes fifty radio calls.

I worked with Bill Davis. They called him "Mr. Cigar." He was really knowledgeable, and all the blacks respected him. It was tremendous, the amount of respect given him. He was totally fair with people, and we put a lot of people in jail. He always had that cigar in his

Bill Davis awarded Medal of Valor by Chief Tom Reddin, 1968: "They called him 'Mr. Cigar.'"

mouth, and it was always lit. I swear I never saw him put a new one in his mouth; it just seemed as if he continuously smoked the same one. And he always wore his hat inside the car. In the old days, the officers were trained to always wear their hats because the hat was a sign of authority. We were in pursuit one time down Alameda Boulevard. We were doing about one hundred miles an hour, and our car started backfiring. Bill was driving, and I was broadcasting. I yelled to him, "Shots fired."

He said, "No, we're just backfiring."

It happened again, and I yelled, "Shots fired."

And he said again, "No, our car is backfiring."

Finally, the suspect spun out and hit a tree.

I asked Bill, "Did he shoot at us?"

He said, "Well, he might have, but he didn't hit us, did he?" That was Bill. We didn't find a gun in the car.

I got a federal subpoena to go to Omaha, Nebraska, once. I had arrested a girl at Sears for forgery and fraud who was later arrested in Omaha. When I returned, I found out I had been transferred back to Hollenbeck Division. I was told they wanted me to walk a footbeat on Brooklyn Avenue during the Christmas season. They wanted somebody who knew the businesses. I was supposed to be "Smiling Bill." It was in the newspaper, and there was a big to-do over it with the civic leaders in Hollenbeck. So that was what I did for a month—walked up and down Brooklyn Avenue, just being a cop on the beat. After that, they put me back in patrol, but again, I wanted more action. The only opening was Central Division, so I went back and worked there from late '64 to September '65.

At Central, I was put right back on a footbeat. Again, I got to know all the drunks, thieves, and prostitutes. One night, I arrested one hundred guys for being drunk. Another time, I arrested a guy at Sixth and Hill for begging. We got him to the station, and he had a money belt with over a thousand dollars in cash on him. According to his bankbook, he had $250,000 in the bank. Here he was begging, and he had a quarter of a million dollars in the bank. He said, "People give me money, and I just put it in the bank." Well, he probably had been doing that for twenty or thirty years.

During the Watts riots in '65, I was sent to Seventy-Seventh for seventeen days. We were brushfire units—three-man cars responding to all the shots-fired calls. The first night, though, twenty of us wearing our white helmets were at 103rd Street and Wilmington Avenue and saw people running in and out of furniture stores and liquor stores, stealing everything. Buildings were burning. The lieutenant said, "No, we can't move." There were felonies being committed in our presence, but he said, "No, you can't move."

We had to guard that intersection, and I was thinking, *What are we guarding the corner for? Is somebody going to steal it?* I said to the sergeant, "Come on, Sarge—we can capture some of these guys." I mean, people were running down the street; one guy even had a small couch on his head. We surely could have caught him. It was never explained to us.

Rioters were shooting at us, but we were told not to shoot back. We could hear the bullets going over our heads. About the third day, they said we could start shooting back. That was also when the National Guard came in. For three days, we had let the rioters burn and steal everything. Then all of a sudden, if they threw a rock at us, we could shoot. I don't know what the powers that be were trying to do. I felt that if we had been able to do our job at the beginning, the city would not have been burned to the ground, and there wouldn't have been all the deaths.

After the riots, I transferred back to Seventy-Seventh Street. I worked a plain car in uniform with Jerry Doyle. He was known as "Mad Dog Doyle." One night, he and I were at Eighty-Fifth and Figueroa, and three guys started fighting us. We were there because they had been causing a disturbance. Jerry was swinging his baton. Well, he swung his baton, the one guy ducked, and Jerry hit me right on my kneecap. It put me down, but I grabbed one of the guys as I was going down. All of a sudden, from nowhere, a big security guard who was about six foot seven and three hundred pounds, named Robinson, yelled out, "Officer Smitty, I'll help you." He stood me up and said, "Now you can hit him." We took all three into custody. It was funny—I was two hundred pounds, yet Robinson just picked me right up. I was called Smitty because most could not pronounce Schmidt.

When President Lyndon Johnson came to Century Plaza for a fundraiser, the department was expecting a big demonstration and brought sixty of us up from Seventy-Seventh. We were in the front line when the demonstrators all of a sudden started pushing. Well, we broke their line. We pushed the demonstrators back and moved them right out. We didn't mess around; we just moved them right down the street. There was a black guy with an Afro trying to direct people, and we thought he was one of the ringleaders. We tried to get to him to move him back, but he stayed away from us. We later found out he was an undercover policeman. He was trying to help us by directing part of the crowd away.

On Christmas Eve in '68, I was working with Mark Turnipseed. We were just getting ready to eat when some officers put out a help call around Sixty-Eighth and Main. As we got there, I heard two shots, then screaming, and then three more shots, and I saw a police car in the middle of the street. I ran up and looked over the police car, and there was a policeman lying in the driveway of a house. I shined my flashlight on a window of the house and saw a head go back. All of a sudden, the door opened, and a guy came out with a rifle or a shotgun—I didn't know which at the time. He turned toward the policeman who was down, and I screamed, "LAPD—over here, asshole!" He turned toward me, and I fired two rounds and put him down. I went over and kicked the weapon away from him. The policeman in the driveway was okay. I went into the house, and there were two little girls. One was about six years old, and she had been shot three times with a shotgun up close. The other one was four years old, and she was also dead.

The man I'd shot was the father. The mother was in General Hospital, having a baby. The father was supposed to be babysitting the girls and had gone crazy. Apparently, the wife had called the station to do a welfare check on the children because the father had been unstable. A patrol unit and a sergeant had gone there and started talking with the father. The guy had told the sergeant, "No, I don't have to put up with you," and closed the door. He had fired one round through the door at the policemen. One of the policemen had fallen off the porch, and the round had passed over him, and he'd stayed down. The sergeant and the other policeman had called for help. The girls were still alive when the policemen and the sergeant had first gotten there. The father had slammed the door and put the round through the door, and then he killed the little girls. The next morning, I was with my kids, and it was Christmas. It was a heartbreaker to think about those little girls.

At Seventy-Sixth and San Pedro, by Fremont High School, there was a shooting, and a guy was killed. The coroner showed up, and as usual, a crowd gathered around us. He told the crowd to back up because he had to get the temperature reading of the liver. Everybody was leaning in as he pulled the dead guy's shirt up and pushed a meat thermometer right into the liver. A woman fainted, and people started puking. I was thinking, *Policemen see this all the time.* Policemen see dead bodies of adults and kids, people who have been raped, and people who were brutalized. Some people just don't understand what a policeman sees during his career.

Most of the sergeants at Seventy-Seventh were good guys. The one who stands out, though, was Sergeant Stan Uno. He was Japanese and the neatest sergeant I had ever seen in my life. After work, he would have us come over to his house, and we would have watermelon. He was just a really neat and unique individual. He was in superb shape, highly intelligent, and a person anybody would love to have as a sergeant. He was just a stand-up guy. I was impressed with him.

Sgt. Stanley Uno: ". . . a person anyone would love to have as a sergeant."

One night at home, my wife woke me and said the girl across the street had told her there were people in her garage. I jumped out of bed, grabbed my sidearm, and went across the street. I went up to the garage door, and there was stuff inside that had obviously been stolen from offices and businesses. The items had been haphazardly thrown in the garage, and with a policeman's sixth sense, I thought, *These are burglarized items.* I told the two guys to come on out and to get down on their knees. I told my wife to call the local police department. About that time, the girl had called her husband, and she relayed to us that her husband had said it was okay, that these two guys were friends of his. The police came, and sure enough, her husband and the other two guys had been burglarizing businesses.

In '69, when I made sergeant, they sent me to Rampart Division. It was funny in a sense because Rampart used to be part of the old Central Division, so I knew the area. One night, a Rampart unit received a child-welfare call and met Children Services at the location. I went there as well. There was dog crap with fuzz on it all over the house, so we knew it had been there for a while. There was nothing in the refrigerator; the conditions were horrible, so we took the children into custody. When the parents showed up at the station, I was standing behind a desk in the back of the lobby. This big, fat white woman demanded, "Who took my children? You can't do that." She had her little, skinny husband with her.

I said, "I took them, and you're under arrest."

She went berserk. I jumped the counter and choked her out. We arrested her for child endangerment, and she was convicted too. Those were the kinds of arrests I felt good about.

One day, I saw a guy acting suspicious with a bag in his hand. I stopped him, and he tried to hide the bag. Well, it was full of jewelry. Come to find out, he was a butler for a guy, and he was stealing the guy's jewelry and selling it. I gave the jewelry to a young policeman named Michael Parker, and he booked it as evidence. Three weeks later, Mike was involved in an on-duty traffic accident and killed. I had to testify that I had seen Mike put his initials on the property, and the guy was convicted. Mike was a good young policeman with just four or five years on the job.

About a week or so later, I was in a black-and-white, responding to a disturbance call. I was stopped by some people on a corner who told me, "There are some guys fighting at Eighth and Vermont. One of them has a gun."

I told myself, "I won't go straight there; I'll go the back way around," and I went over to Westmoreland. By the time I got over there, the guy with the gun was walking on the sidewalk and had reached Eighth and Westmoreland. I could see a gun in his hand. He went around the corner. I crossed the intersection and hit my red lights. The guy started running, and I caught up to him. I got out of the car, and he fired at me. It was a shoot-out; he hit me once, and I hit him three times. He got me in the shoulder, and the bullet entered my chest cavity. In fact, it went through my shoulder and through my armpit and busted two ribs. The bullet took out my lung, and it stopped in my heart sac. When he shot me, I thought he'd shot the gun out of my hand, because all of a sudden, I was lying down on the trunk of a car, and my gun was out in the middle of the street. I picked it up and tried to fire it, but it was already empty. I had fired all six rounds in about five seconds. I went back to the police car and called for help. One of my shots had broken his pelvic bone, and he could not walk. I hit him three times—in the arm, the pelvic bone, and the head. He crawled under a car and was trying to hide, but he was still armed and had fight left in him. The troops showed up, and they subdued him and dragged him out from under the car. I went into shock and didn't know where I was. He turned out to be a deserter from the Russian army, and he was wanted for murder in Toronto, Canada.

SGT. DOUGLAS NELSON EXAMINES SCENE WHERE FELLOW OFFICER FELL
. . . Sgt. William Schmidt was rushed to surgery after being felled by gunman in shootout

L.A. OFFICER WOUNDED IN SHOOTOUT

Kenny Baker, my old partner from Central, was a sergeant at Rampart. He showed up and called for ambulances. Both the suspect and I went to Central Receiving Hospital. He was in one ambulance, while I was in another. I survived because when they brought me in, a little nurse named Hope saw that my artery had been severed. She stuck her finger in the hole and pressed down to stop the bleeding. The doctor could not get any blood pressure and said, "I can't find any pulse."

Lieutenant Charles Applegate of the hospital detail said, "Well, try his legs." Here was this lieutenant telling the doctor where to check for blood pressure. Meanwhile, a priest had already given me my last rites. The doctor checked my legs and found a pulse. I was given sixteen pints of blood. They opened up my chest and busted two more ribs in doing so. The doctor reached up under my heart, and the bullet dropped into his hand. I have the bullet to this day, encased in glass.

My brother, Jack, who was working Metro at the time, showed up and kept saying that if I died, he was going to shoot the son of a bitch. His partner said that maybe he should take Jack's gun for safety's sake, because the suspect was in the next room, being patched up.

Jack worked Metro for about eighteen years, which included SWAT. I encouraged him to come on the job. He worked twenty-five years and retired in '87. We got to work together a little bit in Central Division and a day during the Watts riots. When we were at Central, if people came in and made complaints about tickets or something on either of us and one of us was standing right there, they would say, "No, that's not him; it's the other guy."

I credit the nurse for saving my life. I only knew her by her first name: Hope. After about six months, when I was better, I went back to Central Receiving and thanked her. She was a little Irish nurse, a godsend. She kept telling me that I was her crowning joy. I thanked the priest as well, telling him, "You might have helped a little bit too." He said I was sure looking better than the last time he had had seen me. I was sent to Canada to testify against the guy who had shot me. I was a guest of the Canadian government for two months. I didn't stay on the job after that, because I didn't want to work a desk job. I was given an option to work inside or retire. Since I still had medical problems, I retired. I was awarded the Medal of Valor.

Bill Schmidt awarded Medal of Valor by Chief Ed Davis, 1971

During my career, I had the opportunity to work detectives a couple of times, but I always preferred the blue suit. The men in blue were on the front line. People came to you for help. They didn't go looking for a detective; they wanted the man in blue. For me, that was the most rewarding position in the police department. You're out there helping people and keeping people safe, and you feel good when you go home at night. And yes, I got that steak dinner at Knott's.

Dudley Varney

Birthplace: Long Beach, California
Career: 1961–1984
Rank at Retirement: Detective III
Divisions: Narcotics, Central, Harbor, Seventy-Seventh Street, University, Detective Headquarters, Special Unit Senator (Robert Kennedy Task Force), Robbery-Homicide, Homicide Special (Hillside Strangler Task Force), Major Crimes

One night, we got a man-down radio call in the projects. We went to the address, and they let us in the front door. Lying on the floor was a dead middle-aged man. Around the room were at least a dozen children, from about one year old to twenty years old. The mother was there too. I got down on the floor with this guy, and there was no question about it—he was dead. I looked around the room at all the faces. I rolled him over and started doing resuscitation on him, the old-fashioned type—just pushing. An ambulance came rolling up, and Andy, the ambulance driver, whom we were quite well acquainted with, came up, leaned over, and said, "Dudley, he's dead."

I said, "Yeah, I know. Do you want to tell them?"

"No!" It was a natural death, and Andy took him to the hospital.

I left home at fifteen years of age and went to work as a ranch hand on a cattle ranch. I earned just enough money for college. My grades did not qualify me for the school of veterinary medicine, so I tried engineering courses. That didn't do much for me either. I dropped out and joined the army. When I got out of the army, I went to Washington State University and enrolled in police science. I worked the campus police, which gave me a taste of police work, and I decided to try for the LAPD. My wife and I packed our bags and went to Los Angeles. During the background investigation, my neighbors were interviewed.

One neighbor told me, "I was interviewed by your background investigators the other day. I'm an ex-con, and I don't want to screw up your chances of being on the police department." I told him he hadn't known me when he was a crook, and I thanked him. I made it to the academy.

From the academy, I went into the Narcotics Buy Program. I was from out of state, no one had seen my face in Los Angeles, and I hadn't been on patrol. I was also twenty-six years old, the second-oldest guy in my class, and I had some street smarts. There were three black policemen and me. The four of us worked together, and we did well. We got indictments on 104 dope dealers, with 102 convictions. During my undercover work, I let my hair grow, shaved with barber shears, and wore clothes from the Salvation Army. I was scroungy looking. On one narcotics roundup in Harbor Division, I recognized a young policeman from my high school in Washington. I asked him how he was doing. He later told me that I had scared him to death when we first met. It had been his first night out, and he'd been afraid the department would become aware he knew someone who appeared to be a drug addict.

Some of my neighbors were worried about me. They called one day, sat my wife down at a coffee klatch, and said, "Okay, what happened to your husband?" She couldn't tell them I was working undercover, so she said she didn't know. Another day, my neighbor, the ex-con, sat me down and tried to straighten me out. We eventually moved before I left Narcotics, so those people probably thought they knew a cop who had gone bad.

Hubie Much

After Narcotics, I worked Central Division patrol morning watch with Hubie Much and Bud Kourowsky, two good, straight officers who worked by the book. They taught me how to relax. We worked East Fifth Street, and you learned really quickly what life on East Fifth Street was like—it was raw. There was a derelict who died in a hotel on East Fifth. It looked like a natural death. When Bob Danbacher, from the coroner's office, and I came downstairs carrying the gurney, there were a bunch of derelicts standing out front. We heard one ask another, "Billy, did you see who it was?"

The other replied, "Yes."

We walked about forty feet to the coroner's wagon between these derelicts lined up on both sides of the sidewalk. They all had taken their hats off. It was the only funeral this guy would have. I had greater respect for the derelicts after that.

There was a bar on Main Street, and one night, a hell of a fight went on inside. We got the call, and Hubie and I rolled up to the place. We got everybody out, and they all lined up against the wall in a parking lot next to the bar. Hubie talked to them, and I was the guarding officer. The press rolled up and took our picture. The next night, we were in the station, and Stan Modic, the lieutenant, said, "The press sent us a picture of you guys from last night at that bar." He said, "Look at that," and he had a picture of us standing near a black-and-white police car and a line of people standing against a wall. Modic said, "It's a good thing you had your hats on!"

One day, we had a jumper at the Hotel Cecil on Main Street. The hotel was about fourteen stories tall. The jumper was up on the roof, standing on a parapet, and I wasn't about to get out on that parapet. I talked him down, and once we had him in custody, I told him if he ever did that again, I'd let him jump. I've never liked heights since that day.

Hotel Cecil: "The jumper was up on the roof, standing on a parapet, and I wasn't about to get out on that parapet."

One day, I was working day watch as a one-man car, and there was a call: "Prisoner escape—federal courthouse." I positioned myself behind my black-and-white, with the entryway to the courthouse in front of me. I was looking for a guy to come running out of the building when a car screeched to a stop behind me. The doors popped open, and four of the biggest detectives I'd ever seen in my life got out of that car, hats and all. These guys made a shotgun look like a toy. They came marching up beside me, a flank of four across, and one said, "Anyone come out this side?"

"No, sir," I said.

He said, "You stay here, and we'll take care of it," and they marched into the building. I was impressed—yes, impressed. It was the Hat Squad.

At that time, every officer had to work three divisions. For me, the first division was Central, then came Harbor Division, and last was Seventy-Seventh Street Division. It was called the wheel.

Seventy-Seventh was a hoot because we'd handle, on some nights, up to thirty radio calls. We worked hard. One of the legends of Seventy-Seventh was Bill Davis, "Mr. Cigar." He would irritate the station staff by having a cigar sticking out of his mouth. I never worked with him, but later, when I was assigned to the officer-involved-shooting team, I handled the investigation when he was shot.

One night, I delivered a baby. Roger Gibbard and I were patrolling late at night when a man hailed us down at Manchester and Main. "My wife's having a baby!"

I looked over in the backseat of the car, and the baby was about to crown. Well, having been a cowboy, I knew how with calves, right? So I said, "Don't worry, ma'am. I'll take care of it." I got in the backseat and helped with the birth. It was an easy birth. Well, for me anyway. The baby was messy, and it was cold. I said, "Roger, give me a T-shirt." He pulled his T-shirt off, and we wrapped the baby in it.

The sergeant rolled up and said, "What's going on?"

"Well, we just had a baby here."

He got on the radio and said, "We need an ambulance at Manchester and Main—an OB."

The RTO said, "We don't send ambulances on OBs."

He said, "On this one, you will. We have a bouncing baby girl here." The ambulance came and took the baby and the mother to the hospital, and we went back to patrol. A couple days later, I got a Father's Day card from all the girls at Communications Division.

Lee Castruita and I were working on this crummy, rainy night, and there was a three-car traffic accident. We put the drivers in the backseat behind us in the police car. Lee was filling out a report, and I ran the cars over the air. When we heard "felony want" on one of the cars, we both dove out of our car. One of the drivers in our backseat was wanted for kidnapping. He had taken a guy out to the desert, kicked him in the head, left him for dead, and taken his car. The victim had lived. We arrested and booked the guy and later got a subpoena to the court in Blythe, California. After our shift ended, we drove to the Blythe police station. They had a brand-new jail, never been slept in. We went in one section of the jail and went to sleep. When we woke up, there was the judge, the sheriff, the public defender, and the prosecutor, all sitting at a big, round table in a back room. The whole case was settled right there at that table over breakfast. I'd never seen justice done that way before, but it worked out fine.

Avalon and Fifty-Ninth Street was a dope dealer's paradise. I had worked undercover at that location in Narcotics, and the dealers didn't think it was fair that I came back. I knew all their operations. One night, Art Hansbrough and I, working a Z-car—a crime-suppression car—saw a female dealer by a pool hall. We parked the car down the street and walked up the alley about a block. Sure enough, there was a dope deal going down; this gal was dealing out of her bra. We sneaked up on her and said, "Howdy."

She started screaming, and she pulled her blouse up so that everybody could see her chest and all. A hostile crowd gathered; we were surrounded, and we had no radio. Two big guys stepped out of the crowd and said to the crowd, "You have to take us first." I had arrested both of them when I worked Narcotics.

One of them pointed to me and said, "He treated me right. He didn't put anything on me." The crowd dispersed, and we walked out with our skin. Those two guys saved our bacon.

Seventy-Seventh was quite different before the '65 riots. We maintained rule down there, but I can't say much more than that after the riots. The first day of the riots, we were on Manchester, and all of a sudden, someone was taking some shots at us. I dove into a doorway, and a really young officer followed. He was just out of the academy. The shooter kept firing, and we had to keep our heads down. The young policeman said to me, "I might not make probation." Someone took out the sniper and yelled that it was all clear.

I said, "Now you will."

The next day, Art and I were working with a third guy. We drove out, and not too far from the station, someone shot out our back window. We returned to the station and replaced the window, and back out we went. We didn't get halfway across the division, and somebody shot the back window out again. We went back to the station and cleaned it up, but there were no more windows. We put the backseat directly against the back of the front seat and gave the third officer a long-barreled shotgun that Sears had loaned us. We drove around with that shotgun sticking out the back window, and no one shot at us again.

Art and I went to a market where looters were inside, and we chased the looters out. As soon as we stepped out through a side door with the last of the looters, the whole front of the store blew up. Someone had put a bomb in there. It was a big blast, and the whole front—all the glass and doors—blew out. We had only been out of there for twenty or thirty seconds.

One other time, Art got acid bombed. A big group surrounded us in front of a laundromat. Someone from the crowd threw a bottle of acid, and it hit the pavement, splashed on Art's foot, and started eating his pants up. He ran into the laundromat for water to dilute the acid and stuck his foot into a tub of water. I stayed in the doorway to hold off the crowd. Of course, they stayed back. When he was ready, we just walked out of there. They didn't bother us after that. We never found out who threw the acid.

In '66, I made sergeant and went to University Division. When President Lyndon Johnson came to the Century Plaza Hotel, my crew was assigned to be around the president. We had orders that nobody got to the president. We worked with Secret Service agents and moved the president to his suite. The Secret Service took it from there. When we left the hotel, there were a bunch of police recruits from the academy at the entrance. Sergeant Bob Smitson was behind them. There were about ten thousand screaming hippies across the street, and these recruits appeared more afraid of Smitson than they were of the crowd. At one point, part of the crowd started moving, with one guy in front of them. He wore sandals and a robe of some sort, and he had a big Afro hairdo. Most of them followed him. That guy was an undercover cop, and he moved most of the crowd out of the way. I can't remember his name, but he did a hell of a job.

Lieutenant Roy Keene was at Seventy-Seventh Division when I was there. He was now a lieutenant at Detective Headquarters Division and offered me a job. I accepted, transferred, and worked the K-car. The K-car handled all the dead-body and detective calls for the divisions during the off-hours—midnight to eight o'clock in the morning. There were several big cases while I was at Detective Headquarters, but the most important one to me was the Robert Kennedy assassination. I was sent to the Ambassador Hotel and reported to a lieutenant from Rampart Division. He said, "Just stay with Kennedy." I went to Central Receiving Hospital, caught up with Kennedy, and stayed with him. They stabilized him, and he was transferred to Good Samaritan Hospital. I stayed in the waiting room while he was in the operating room. There was a squad of uniform officers there as security. I was with him until the next day, and then I went home. I came back the next night and again stayed with Kennedy. The family, including his wife, Ethel Kennedy, and his brother, Senator Ted Kennedy, were there. After he died, he was taken on his bed to the elevator, and we were on our way to the morgue. Kennedy supporters and workers from his campaign filled the elevator. They told me I had to take the next one, but I pulled an individual off the elevator and stepped in. We took him to the morgue for his autopsy. After Dr. Thomas Noguchi, the LA coroner, got there, that was the end of my detail.

The next day, I was called in and told I was now assigned to the Special Unit Senator Task Force. I was on one of two teams. We were to determine if Sirhan Sirhan had acted alone or if he was part of a conspiracy associated with Kennedy's assassination. Sirhan had acted alone and with intent, and there were no conspiracies. Dave Brath and I both participated in writing the final report. There were two copies— one for the chief of police and one for the attorney general of the United States. At the time, we were not told the report was to remain confidential or that it would not be released to the public for twenty-five years. I had no idea how they arrived at twenty-five years, but after that time had passed, the report was made public.

After the task force, I went to Homicide. My first case was the same hotel on East Fifth Street where the derelicts had lined up for the one derelict who had died. I was sent to investigate a homicide and was working with an officer on loan from Metro. We got to the location, and it was pretty ugly. It was a homosexual thing. We made some quick inquiries, found out who the lover was, and snatched him up. When we came back to the station, we had the body at the coroner's office and the suspect in custody. I solved the first case I went out on.

Ed Henderson was assigned as my regular partner, and right off the bat, we picked up a Mafia killing by the airport. Julius Petro was found in his car with a bullet in his head in '69. Petro was muscle for the Mafia. John "Sparky" Monica had hired the hit, but he died in an automobile accident in Arizona. I had his fingerprints and picture taken at the funeral home to make sure it was him who had died. So one mafioso showed up at the pearly gates with ink on his hands. We put him back in the casket and sent him on his way. Jimmy Fratianno confessed to me years later that he had been involved in the killing.

In '75, Jack Molinas, the attorney and former basketball player who'd been involved in a shaving-points scandal in college and then bet on the pro team he played on, was killed. My boss said, "Dudley, it's yours." His partner in a trading business, Bernie Gusoff, had been killed a year earlier, and I had that case too. So I had two more Mafia cases I was working on. Sid Nuckles and I went to New York to talk with some Mafia figures about the Molinas case. I was given an address and told, "You come here—you come alone, second floor."

I went alone—no guns, no recorders—and an old guy met me. "Have a seat," he said. There were a light and two chairs. The rest of the floor was bare, and the windows had curtains, but the windows were painted over on the outside. I sat down on one chair, and this guy sat down on the other.

I said, "I want to talk to you about Jack Molinas. My word is that you were his protector."

He said, "I'm not going to tell if I am or I'm not. I'll tell you this: if anyone in the family is going to do a hit, I have to give permission. I did not give permission." When I retired, neither the Molinas case nor the Gusoff case was solved.

One of my first contacts with an organized-crime person was during one of my first court appearances on the job. I was brand new to the court system. I had a case, and I got there early. I'd been up all night. There was a nice, well-groomed gentleman standing by the table, and I said, "Are you the district attorney?"

He laughed and said, "No, I'm not." He said, "There's the district attorney. I'm Mickey Cohen."

One time, a suspect telephoned Walter Matthau, the actor, and told him he had kidnapped Matthau's son. Matthau tried to call his son, who was in England, but was unsuccessful. He then called some guys he knew who worked in Homicide. They found out Matthau's son was on a

Dudley Varney

plane home, so they contacted the airline to make sure he was safe. In the meantime, this suspect wanted money. I was working with a female FBI agent. A suitcase was put together for the suspect, and the drop was made. The suspect picked up the suitcase and ran into a field by Occidental College; he just couldn't wait. When he opened the suitcase, *boom*! He had socks on his hands to avoid leaving fingerprints, and the socks were burned off. He was sitting there burned and caught.

I was called out on the Charles Manson case to Sharon Tate's house on Cielo Drive to assist with the investigation. I worked it for a brief period of time. I didn't do anything spectacular, but I did discover a fingerprint in the bedroom that had been overlooked. In the bedroom, underneath the venetian blinds, I found a bloody fingerprint on the wood. It was a discovery that placed one of the Manson girls at the scene. She later came out naming Manson. So I'd like to think I had something to do in helping to solve that.

We had a gangbanger who was an informant for my partner, Larry Byrd. He testified for us on a case and did a good job. After the trial, we took him back to the state prison in Iowa to finish out his life sentence. He had gangrene, his feet were falling off, and he was barely alive. We got on the plane and landed in Phoenix. As we were transporting him to the deputy sheriff's office, he said, "Can I get a request?"

"Sure."

"I'm not going to get any kosher food where I'm going, and I'd like to get a kosher meal."

The deputy sheriff directed us to a kosher restaurant, where we had a nice dinner.

"One more request. I need some stuff for my false teeth. They don't get me any in prison."

We stopped at a drugstore. Robbing drugstores for forty years was how this guy had made his living. So we were sitting in front of the drugstore, and he leaned over and asked the deputy, "Can we keep the motor running?"

"Why?"

"Oh, for old times' sake." He died shortly after we returned him to prison.

When I worked Homicide, television reporter Warren Wilson came to see my partner and me and said, "Someone is killing prostitutes." We started to look at the tip, and sure enough, within a few days, a young woman was found dead in a field near downtown. She had a record of prostitution in Hollywood. At the autopsy, the doctor said, "She's had a baby."

"How long ago?" I asked.

"Recently."

We pulled field-interview cards at Hollywood Division, and there were some recent ones on her and whom she had been with. My partner and I knocked on a few doors and questioned a few people about the baby. We found the baby in a motel room with some dopers. The baby was clean, fed, and warm, lying in a dresser drawer with a pillow in the bottom and some clothes they used for covers. We took the baby into custody, and the grandmother eventually got custody of the child. Shortly before I retired, I got a phone call from the grandfather. He said, "There's someone I'd like you to meet." My wife and I met him at a restaurant, and he had his granddaughter with him. She was a little eight-year-old girl, cuter than a bug's ear, nicely dressed in a pinafore dress—just a darling little girl. It was fulfilling to meet someone you saved from who knows what some years before.

That prostitute's death led to the formation of the Hillside Strangler Task Force. This was around October '77. I became the coordinator of the investigations. We looked at thirteen cases, but two of those were later determined not to be involved with the Strangler, including one of my cases. We pared it down to eleven cases, including two from the Los Angeles sheriffs and one from Glendale. More than eighty guys worked the task force, and they were a hardworking, dedicated team. We worked through the winter into the spring. I was called out every time a girl was killed in LA County. I spent a lot of time just looking at bodies to see if there were any connections. There were a couple of attempts to make the murders look like the work of the Strangler.

Kenneth Bianchi and his cousin, Angelo Buono, were the suspects. When Bianchi moved to Bellingham, Washington, the killings in Los Angeles stopped. Then two female university students were killed in Bellingham. Bellingham's chief of police, Terry Mangan, thought the cases looked familiar to our cases. He contacted our task force. I called my boss and said, "We're going to Bellingham."

Dudley Varney, right, briefs Chief Daryl Gates, left, at Hillside Strangler murder scene. Detective Sherman Oakes in background.

Lt. Ed Henderson at Hillside Strangler press conference

They held the crime scene for us and kept the bodies at the coroner's office so that we could view the autopsies. We collected Bianchi's prints—he had been arrested by Bellingham police—and went back to Los Angeles, where I gave the prints to George Herrera. I had just left his office and pushed the button to the elevator when one of the print guys came roaring out and said, "We got him!" He'd just linked Bianchi's prints to one of our crime scenes. Bianchi confessed to the murders; he was proud of his work. We indicted him and Buono. Bianchi testified against Buono, and Buono was found guilty of nine of the murders. When Buono died in prison of a heart attack in 2002, I got a call from the press: "Do you want to make any comments?" I told them we had done what we'd said we'd do: kept him in prison for the rest of his life.

In '77, I was diagnosed with multiple sclerosis. I was told to retire and take it easy, but I told them what they could do with it, and I stayed seven more years. I went to work, I did my job, and I went home.

Dudley Varney with arrestee Kenneth Bianchi

Gary Thomas

Birthplace: Wyandotte, Michigan
Career: 1963–1987
Rank at Retirement: Sergeant I
Divisions: Seventy-Seventh Street, Parking and Intersection Control, Metropolitan, Central, Wilshire, Southeast

Back in Michigan, before I was born, my dad ran booze in the days of Prohibition. When Prohibition ended, he became a cop. By the time I was born, he and my mother were divorced. He always told me about his being a motor cop, and ever since, I was determined to be a policeman too. After high school, I went into the army, the military police. When I left the service in '63, I came out to California and joined the LAPD.

In the academy, we went on ride alongs with traffic and patrol. In traffic, my training officer and I received an accident call on a freeway on-ramp. A drunk woman had hit a bridge pillar, and she had a baby in the car. We went to the hospital, and the first thing she asked about was her car. Her baby was dead. She never asked about the baby, only her car. That shocked me at the time. Here she was, drunk with a baby in the car, and the first thing she worried about was the car.

When we graduated, I was sent to Seventy-Seventh Street Division. I worked with Charlie King and Bill Mockette. These guys were from the '40s, they still did patrol work, and they were good cops. Charlie was a full-blooded Indian with a photographic memory. One time, we were driving down the street, and Charlie saw a car in a motel parking lot with a license plate he recognized. He asked the manager, "Whose car is that?"

"Room so-and-so."

The two guys in the room were wanted for burglary. Charlie had remembered the car and the license plate number. It was just a gift he had.

Gary Thomas

Charlie also had great eyesight. One night, we were on a roving stakeout. He said, "That woman walking down the street—it's late, and this is a dangerous place."

I said, "What woman?"

"Just down the street there."

"No woman down there."

"Oh, for Christ's sake—can't you see a woman down there in the long brown coat?"

We drove about two blocks, and sure enough, there was a woman in a long brown coat. I worshipped that guy. He was fantastic. Of course, both of those guys were friendly to everybody, but they didn't take crap from anybody. "You're under arrest. You don't debate this now. Put your hands behind your back"—that was the way they taught me to do police work, and then the '70s came along, and the rules changed. All of a sudden, the old way was not the right way. They taught me a lot of good stuff, but they taught me the old way of police work.

Charlie King: "I worshipped that guy."

Charlie chased a burglar one night and got hurt. The burglar jumped over a fence, and Charlie jumped after him. There was a twenty-foot drop on the other side to the pavement, and when Charlie landed, he injured his arm. The suspect died from the fall. Charlie was told he needed surgery and that the surgery would entail cutting a sensory nerve. The surgeon cut a motor nerve by mistake. Charlie's hand was all curled up and useless. He pensioned off and became a private investigator.

From Seventy-Seventh Division, I was wheeled to PIC. I hated that place! I wanted to do police work, and I was stuck at Third and Grand, directing traffic. I was in PIC during the Watts riots. We rode around in a bus, went to the command post, and didn't do a whole lot of anything. Attitudes changed after the riots. When I was first at Seventy-Seventh Division, we'd get a call in the projects, and we'd just park the police car, windows down and doors unlocked. We would go handle our call, and when we came back, nothing had been touched. The Watts riots changed all that. After the riots, we had to keep an eye on the car. We really became the enemy, I guess.

After three months at PIC, I was wheeled to Wilshire Division. I worked with this old-time cop. He had been on the department during

World War II, and he carried a .357 revolver. We couldn't carry .357s, but nobody bothered him. I asked him why he carried that gun, and he said, "During the war, a guy went AWOL from the army, and he robbed a place. The guy was behind a car on one side of the street, and I was behind the police car on the other side of the street. We were exchanging gunfire. I'd shoot and reload, and I kept shooting, thinking I was missing the guy. He finally fell down. He had six or seven bullet holes in him." He had been using a .38-caliber revolver with bullets that were going right through the suspect. He'd carried the .357 since that shooting. I wish I could remember his name. He was a good ole guy.

Policemen used to serve traffic warrants in those days. We would receive a traffic warrant, go to the person's address, and arrest him. We kept trying to get this one woman, but there was always no answer at the door. One night, just before end of watch, we saw lights on inside the residence and a car parked in the driveway. We knocked on the door, and a man answered. We explained that we were there to see this lady. "She's in bed—just a minute," he said, and he left. He came back and said, "Well, she's not here now."

We knew she was there, and we walked in. He reached into a closet and came out with a shotgun. I grabbed the shotgun and wrestled around with him over it and took the shotgun away from him. The shotgun was not loaded. We arrested him and booked her for the warrant. We went to court, and his lawyer told him that he was the luckiest man who had ever lived, pulling a shotgun on a policeman and not getting shot. He had been about to get himself killed over a traffic warrant—a traffic warrant for her. I understand wanting to protect your wife, but you can't do that by pointing a gun at a policeman.

From Wilshire, I returned to Seventy-Seventh—back home again. I worked with Bill Davis, "Mr. Cigar." He was a great guy. We'd stop, and people would say, "Hi, Mr. Cigar." Everybody knew him. He'd been down there in Watts for years. Bill was a hell of a cop and a tough guy. He was old when I worked with him, but I don't think I could have whipped him. He was a big man, and everybody respected him.

Bill and I had an altercation one time with a guy. Well, I should say *I* had an altercation with this guy. Bill stood there and observed. He would have jumped in if it had appeared I was not able to handle myself. He tested guys that way. He wanted his partner to be tough—that was Bill Davis. He was also an excellent softball pitcher. He was an old man, but he still played softball; he was a great athlete. He died of cancer. I sure admired him. The department couldn't replace him; he was a legend. People in the community would have done anything for him.

One night in '67, my partner, Fred Romero, and I were in the Nickerson Gardens projects. There was a burglary call at a closed day-care center, which was an apartment. As we arrived, I turned out the car lights and we coasted to a stop. My partner went around the back, and I went to the front. All of a sudden, the suspect ran out of the apartment. He came right at me with a crowbar in his hand. He swung the crowbar and hit me on my shoulder. It just missed my head, only because I had ducked to avoid the blow to my skull. I shot, and he went down. It was a good burglary, and he had used the crowbar to break into the day-care center apartment.

Richard Iddings and I received a man-assaulting-a-woman radio call out on the west side of Seventy-Seventh one night. We went to the door and questioned the husband, who was hostile. He told us he and his wife had had an argument and his wife had left. We returned to the police car and were getting ready to go when the wife drove up. We could tell she had been smacked around and beaten. "Do you want to arrest him?" I asked.

"No." In those days, we didn't have to arrest anybody.

"What do you want to do?"

"I want to go in and get my stuff."

We stood by as she got her things, and then she left. I was getting ready to drive away when Rich saw the husband with a shotgun at the kitchen side door. Rich said, "The guy's got a shotgun in his arms. He's standing in the doorway, and he's staring at us."

I said, "Well, we can't drive away now." We got out of the car and walked up the driveway. He took his shotgun and aimed it at us. Rich jumped to one side, and I went down onto the driveway; I had no other place to go. I shot and put him down. I firmly believe that it was a case of suicide by cop. He had shells in the shotgun but none chambered.

In '68, I was selected for Metro—good guys and good sergeants. Ralph Gillet and I worked Metro together. He was a character and the only guy I knew who had a nine-inch barrel on his revolver. I don't know how he got to keep it. He was one of the old-time street cops.

One time, we did a stakeout of a hamburger stand across from USC that had been robbed several times. There was no place to sit, so we parked behind some bushes off Santa Barbara Boulevard. That was the best that we could do to hide ourselves, but some people came by and said, "Hi, officers." We had the binoculars and we're watching, but nothing happened all night long. Then we saw the clerk get ready to close. A woman came up to the door, but he waved her off, indicating they were closed. He did let in a guy that appeared to be a friend. The clerk had a bag in his hand at the cash register. I saw something going in the bag. The clerk was talking and laughing with the friend at the counter, and the clerk handed him the bag. Pretty soon, a call came out that a robbery had just occurred, but we were right there. We went in, and the clerk said he had just been robbed. We knew that wasn't the case—the clerk had put the money in the bag and given it to his friend. We'd been there all night, but the clerk hadn't seen us across the street, and no one had told him we were watching the place.

Before I went to Metro, I had been making more money at Seventy-Seventh, attending court and working overtime. My wife was going to court reporter school, and we were short of money, so I decided to go back to Seventy-Seventh. One night, my partner and I responded to a robbery in progress at a mom-and-pop liquor store. When we got there, two suspects had been shot and were down inside the store. They had entered the store with guns. A single clerk and the female owner usually operated the store. This particular time, the owner's son was visiting and helping in the store. One of the suspects had grabbed the clerk around the neck, pointed a gun at his head, and demanded money. The son, who had been behind the cash register, had reached under the counter, grabbed a .44 Magnum revolver, shot one suspect, killed him, and then shot the second suspect, who had been holding the clerk. I rode in the ambulance with the second suspect, and he was later booked for robbery. The suspect had all of his clothing except for his shoes. We later returned to the liquor store, and we found the shoes exactly where he'd stood before he was shot. We had found his body three feet from the shoes. The suspect had absorbed the full force of the Magnum round, knocking him clean out of his shoes. He later died, proving that armed robbery was a dangerous business. The son was formerly in the Marine Corps, and we tried to recruit him for the department, but he declined.

A nurse came home late from her job at a hospital one night. A suspect had broken into her apartment and was waiting behind the front door. He grabbed her around her neck and started dragging her to the bedroom, but he had to pass through the kitchen to get there. She grabbed a butcher knife from the countertop and started slashing him. He ran outside the apartment and died on the front lawn with over a dozen stab wounds. Her quick thinking and survival instinct saved her.

Another call we had, an old woman was working in her front yard when a guy hopped the fence and tried to drag her into her house. She pulled a .32-caliber revolver from the pocket of her apron and killed him. Who would have expected a little old lady to be carrying a gun in her apron while working in the front yard?

Finances were a little easier at home now, so I went back to Metro Division. One day, Larry Graham and I were working in uniform in an unmarked car. We drove by an old hotel that was now a halfway house, a place for ex-cons with drug or alcohol problems, at Sixth and Alvarado. There was a drug deal going down in front of us. A male suspect was holding open a paper bag, and another male was looking in the bag. When the guy holding the bag saw us, he dropped it and took off running. Larry jumped out and chased him while I recovered the bag and discovered heroin inside. I handcuffed the prospective buyer, put him in the car, and searched for Larry. About two blocks away, I found him. He was struggling with the suspect. Larry had him on the ground, but the guy was trying to grab Larry's gun. Metro had just issued us experimental batons that were much longer than the normal batons. I hit the guy to

Gary Thomas with arrestee at termination point of vehicle pursuit

Gary Thomas: Anti-war protest, 1970

stop him from getting Larry's gun. The baton was effective, and we took the guy into custody.

In July '74, I made sergeant and went to Wilshire Division. Later, I transferred to Southeast Division when it opened, and it was my last division. The first day, I was on my way back from Seventy-Seventh station when I heard a call come out of a guy walking on the street with a rifle in Southeast Division. I responded, and other police units were there. The guy pointed the rifle at the officers, and *bang, bang, bang*—the officers shot, and I did too. I had been in the division for twenty minutes, and I had gotten involved in a shooting.

I was forty-one years old now, and I was a field sergeant. I responded to back a unit that had received a radio call of "family dispute, shots fired, baby in the house." That was a good call to go to. I responded, figuring I'd go in with the unit. I was about two blocks from the location when two women—the victim and her friend—waved me down. The victim told me her husband was in the house. They had had an argument, and he had grabbed a gun and fired shots into a wall. The baby was still in the house, and she wanted to get her baby out. As I was talking to her, she said, "There he is now," and pointed to a white car backing out of a driveway. I was two blocks away, but I tried to catch up to him. He made a right turn onto San Pedro, and when I got there, I saw a white car at the curb and a guy walking across to the liquor store. A little farther down was another white car parked at the curb. I was thinking the guy in the car going to the liquor store was him. I walked in while the guy was at the counter. I stood behind him and asked him if he had heard a gunshot in the area. He said he had not. I then said, "You don't mind if I search you to make sure you don't have a gun?"

All of a sudden, the female clerk was looking at the guy's waistband, and her eyes got big. I saw his hand coming up, and I grabbed his hand. The fight was on. I figured I was a big guy, but he turned on me and started turning a gun in my direction. I grabbed him, ran him down the counter against some racks, and knocked a bunch of stuff over. I got my gun and put him down. I suppose the guy had been so upset that he hadn't cared whether he lived or died. He would have probably spent a night in jail, but instead, he decided to try to shoot a policeman.

Two guys who worked for me at Southeast were Mike Sillers and Randy Cochran. Mike was one of the best street cops you'll ever find. Hell of a street cop—he should have been in some specialized unit. Randy Cochran was a young cop, but he was probably the best cop I had ever seen. Anytime I had a chance, I would ride with him because it was just fascinating to watch him work. He never got mad at anybody; he was always calm.

Mike Sillers   *Randy Cochran*

Gary Thomas, right, spotting for weightlifter during weightlifting competition

I spent the last couple of years sitting in as the assistant watch commander at Southeast Division, and then I retired. It was a great career. I was in several shootings, but if officers spent enough time on the street, the odds were that they would likely be involved in situations requiring them to draw or shoot their weapons. I have great admiration for all cops who face the potential of a deadly force situation. They do a remarkable job, considering the scrutiny they endure and the pressures they face.

The department had a weightlifting team, and I was on the team for years. I have always been an advocate of weightlifting. I started when I was thirteen years old. My brother and I went with my father to his friend's house. He had a set of weights, and I was fascinated by those weights. I got myself a set of dumbbells and, later, an old barbell set. My brother went to work at a steel factory, and he made some one-hundred-pound plates for me.

Even a year after I retired, I competed in the Police Olympics. I had never really been able to deadlift, so I had to get a great big lead on those guys in the bench press or I'd lose. A 550-pound dead lift was the best I ever did, and there were guys deadlifting seven hundred pounds in my weight class. However, I could beat them all in the bench press. Since I retired, I continued lifting. In 2003, I broke the world record in the sixty-plus age group for my weight class. I bench-pressed 447 pounds. Then I hurt my shoulder for the umpteenth time, and I haven't been bench-pressing for five or six years now.

Ferdinand "Ferd" Wunderlich

Birthplace: Soerabaja, Java, Dutch East Indies
Career: 1963–1989
Rank at Retirement: Detective III
Divisions: Parking and Intersection Control, Central Traffic Accident
    Investigation, Seventy-Seventh Street

After the Watts riots, I handled a major traffic accident on the Harbor Freeway—about eight cars were involved—with two fatalities. The most difficult time that I had in accident investigations was death notifications. I hated it. Other guys hated it too, but it was part of our job. I had to do that for this accident, and it didn't go down well. Both fatalities were from the same family. You're dealing with a lot of emotions and drama in those situations. We were not suited for that, but it was something we had to do.

I was born in the Dutch East Indies in 1936. In 1942, during World War II, the Japanese built a bamboo fence around the perimeter of our residence; we couldn't freely go in or out. There were Japanese guards at a checkpoint, and when we passed the guard, we were supposed to bow. My mom refused to bow. One day, when she didn't bow, a Japanese guard hit her with the butt of a gun, causing my mom to lose her hearing in one ear.

I had an infection in my ankle; it was some kind of bacteria that would eat through bone. We had no medication for it, and I was in total pain and agony. I didn't get medication for it until the Americans defeated the Japanese and freed our people. After the war, we went to Singapore for a short time, and from Singapore, we went back to Holland, where my family was from originally.

In 1957, the United States had a special quota for victims of the war to immigrate to the United States, and I took advantage of it. We were

Ferd Wunderlich

required to have a medical exam, a sponsor, and a job. All three had to be in place before an individual could actually leave for the United States.

I ended up in Wisconsin on a farm. I didn't like the conditions in Wisconsin, so I left and eventually moved and settled in California. I married, and my wife's father was a retired captain from the Los Angeles Fire Department. We would talk about my future, and he said, "If you want job security, get into either the fire department or police department." I applied to the Los Angeles Police Department and entered the academy on April 29, 1963. Another guy and I were the oldest in the class. I couldn't get on the police department any sooner because I had to wait for citizenship. That was one of the requirements.

We had a big class, almost one hundred. In the academy, they left me alone. I was in good shape, and I didn't draw any attention to myself. I remember sitting in the classroom, and one of our instructors called out a name and said, "Sergeant wants to see you." My classmate got up and was almost to the door when the instructor said, "Might as well pick up your books. You're not coming back." That made an impression on me. The month before we entered the academy, Ian Campbell and his partner, Karl Hettinger, were kidnapped and taken to an onion field. The instructors talked about it in the academy—about not giving up our guns if we got in a situation like that.

One of the shooting instructors, Jim Dougherty, had been married to Marilyn Monroe. Of course, their marriage hadn't lasted long, and he didn't talk about her. He wore a big diamond ring, and he would focus on the shooting target through his diamond ring and hit a bull's-eye every time. How he did it, I don't know, but that was his little trick on the firing range. He was a good guy.

After I graduated, I spent my probationary time at Seventy-Seventh Street Division. A few days after going to Seventy-Seventh, I worked with an old-timer, and we chased two grand-theft-auto suspects. Being the gung-ho guy that I was from the academy, I thought I was going to show this old-timer how to do it. I started chasing the passenger as the old-timer started to chase the driver. He immediately called me back: "Boot, get over here. Let the guy go. Let's go chase the driver instead," and we caught the driver. He sat me down after we made the arrest and said, "Look, we have no portable radios. Of utmost importance is officer safety. If you chase that guy, I don't know where you're going, and you don't know where I'm going, and if you need help and I need help, we're outta luck because we can't communicate. Nobody knows where we're at. Communications knows our initial location, but that's all they know." So that was my first lesson in officer safety, and I remembered that well, because working Seventy-Seventh, that was of the utmost importance—officer safety. When we went out in the field, the only radio we had was in the car. When we left the car, we were on our own.

One day, I observed a juvenile in the back of a store with a handgun. I pointed my gun at him and told him to drop his gun. Just because he was a juvenile didn't mean he was less dangerous than an adult with a gun. He looked in my direction and started to raise his gun. I pulled back the trigger of my gun and hesitated. Why, I don't know. About that time, he dropped the gun. I arrested the kid and examined the gun. It turned out to be a BB gun, but from a distance, it had looked like a genuine .45. I don't believe he realized how close he had come to being killed, and I would've felt terrible, even though shooting him would have been justified.

Another time, we responded to a radio call of "burglary suspects there now." My partner went to the back. I went to the front, and the suspect came out the front door. I pointed my gun at the guy and told him to stop. For some reason, he started reaching into his pocket, and I was concerned he might be pulling a gun on me, so I fired. I missed the guy. I'm glad I missed, because he didn't have a gun. The guy said, "Man, that was close. I could hear the bullet whizzing by me."

I said, "Well, you know what? You are no gladder than I am!"

We were pursuing a stolen car on Figueroa from Seventy-Seventh Street one night, and then the stolen car we were pursuing collided with another car. It turned out the other car was also a stolen car. We got two for the price of one!

Most of the officers I worked with were positive. We had some old-timers, and I don't care what was said about the old-timers, I liked every one of them. I mean, they were down-to-earth. Bill Davis—I worked with him. We called him "Mr. Cigar." He was like the old-timer in the movie *The Onion Field*—in the back of the roll call room, smoking a cigar. In the movie, when the lieutenant says that it was a mistake for them to give up their guns, the old-timer gets in his face and says, "Well, you know what? Don't criticize these kids. You're not in their place. When somebody sticks a gun in your ribs, you don't know what to do." That was the kind of guy Bill Davis was—always smoking a cigar and outspoken. I also worked with Phil Sheidecker, another old-timer. Both were good guys.

In '65, during the Watts riots, I was working Accident Investigation out of Central Division, and we were sent to Seventy-Seventh Division. My partner and I stopped a guy in a Volkswagen who had just broken into a butcher shop. His car was loaded with meat. I talked it over with my partner and said, "We can't take this meat. We have no place to book it."

He said, "To hell with it. Just leave it in the car."

We took one piece of meat for evidence and took the guy to the station. I can't imagine what the car smelled like by the time he got out of jail.

Later, when I worked detectives, I went to the impound yard, and I was looking at a van. The guy said, "The van is junk."

I said, "What happened?"

He said, "There was a dead body in there."

I said, "Just steam clean the inside and repaint it."

He said, "Can't be done. The smell gets in all the metal and all the crevices. You just can't get it out." I can imagine the guy in the Volkswagen probably had the same experience.

During the Watts riots, so much was happening, and we were undermanned. There was a lot of chaos. We would just go from one scene to the next, make arrests, put people in jail, and go out again. We would work twelve hours, go home, and come back again. That was what it was like working the riots. In fact, strangely enough, when I was working Seventy-Seventh detectives years later, I came across a yard full of bricks. I asked the guy who owned the yard, "Are those bricks for sale?"

He said, "Yeah," and he told me the bricks were from buildings destroyed in the riots. I bought the bricks and faced my fence and my house with them. The bricks had been sitting in his yard for years. He called them "riot bricks."

Watts riots, 1965: "He called them riot bricks."

I left AI and transferred back to Seventy-Seventh Division. I worked 12A99, which covered the south end of Seventy-Seventh Division, including Watts and the projects. We spent most of our time in the projects, though. The projects were just a big maze. You really had to know the projects, because you could get lost in there. When we did go in foot pursuit of someone, we also had to be careful of the clotheslines. The clotheslines were made of steel, and you could cut your head off or take your teeth out if you ran into one of the lines.

There were many purse snatches on Imperial Highway next to the projects. These kids living in the projects would wait until a car stopped at a traffic light next to the projects. If the window was open, they'd reach in and snatch the purse out of the car.

A guy once refurbished a bunch of apartments in the projects and put in all-new appliances. He was doing something nice for the community. I told him, "They're going to steal you blind."

He said, "I have faith that they won't."

They did. They stole all the appliances, and they took all the copper lines out. It was a total disaster. It was a shame because he was really trying to improve the neighborhood.

We got a call one time about a kid who was trying to break into a liquor store. He tried to crawl through the window above the entry door. The window had bars on it, and somehow he managed to spread apart the metal bars and squeeze through. But he got to a point where he couldn't go forward and couldn't go back. In time, his body started to swell, and of course, he expired. We called the fire department to cut the bars. He was some young kid—maybe fourteen or fifteen years old—just trying to steal something, and it didn't pay off.

One day, I got a call to see a woman about an odor coming from underneath her house. I told her an animal had probably crawled underneath the house and died. I removed the cover on the crawl space and shined my light in the area. Lo and behold, I saw a hand sticking up from the soil. It was a dead body. What she had smelled was the odor of death. I called the detectives, and they came out. Somebody had buried the body underneath the house, and for some reason, the hand had come up. I don't know what the outcome was or how long the body had been under there. She certainly did not feel good about having a dead body underneath the house.

Ferd Wunderlich questioning two youths, Watts, 1966.

On Sundays, we could hear the gospel music as we drove by the churches. After church, the congregations usually had barbecues. Occasionally, they would invite us to share in their barbecues. We'd sit on some milk crates and have barbecued meat or catfish. It was nice. The community, for the most part, appreciated the police being there.

One night, we were on Main Street when a car parked at the curb all of a sudden took off. We went in pursuit for about six blocks, and the car hit a light standard. The driver was a juvenile, and he was out late. I thought he was up to no good. We took him to the station and called his mom. I counseled the kid about the consequences of what he had done. Of course, as with many families in South LA, there was no father in the picture. For years, even when I was in detectives, the mom would call me and ask how I was doing and how the family was doing. She once told me, "The reason I'm calling you is because I was so grateful for what you did for my son." That made me feel good. I think the son ended up okay, and we didn't see that often in South LA. I was impressed with that. She was a nice lady.

Vice was one detail that I never liked to work. I knew more guys who got in trouble working Vice. I was working what was called an SOS detail, a specialized unit within the division. Occasionally, we were loaned to other units. I was loaned to Vice one night, and the detail that night was to pick up a prostitute and see if you could get a solicitation. I told my partner, "I didn't volunteer for this detail."

He said, "Well, it is what it is."

I said, "Okay."

So we went to a known hangout for prostitutes, and we approached one. I rolled the window down, and she said, "You must be the police."

I said, "You know, we are!"

My partner said, "That's it. You're done!" So mission accomplished. Needless to say, I was not in favor of working Vice.

After several years in patrol, I went to Seventy-Seventh detectives while I was still a policeman. To get in, an officer's name was circulated among the detectives, and they had to be in agreement that they wanted the person in there. If somebody said, "I don't want him," he didn't get in.

My detective training officer was Vic Eliott. The first day, he said, "There's your arrestee; you're on your own." That was how I was broken in: "There's your body. Go take care of it." I worked my way through, and I was able to finish what I needed to do.

One day, someone from the Homicide Unit said to me, "Let's go." He had gotten a call about a stowaway who had fallen out of an airplane and landed in a school playground not too far from the freeway. A plane that had been making the approach to land at the Los Angeles airport had lowered the landing gear. This guy had concealed himself in one of the wheel wells, and when they'd lowered the wheels, he had fallen out and landed on the playground. Luckily, no kids had been on the playground. Body parts were scattered all over the place. We went through all of his personal belongings, and this guy had been an admirer of kamikaze pilots, with pictures and stories about them. I didn't think he'd chosen purposely to fall out of the airplane, but he liked kamikaze pilots. It was ironic that he met his demise that way. The experts told us the guy was probably dead by the time he left Mexico City, because once you reach a certain altitude, there is a lack of oxygen. He probably never knew what hit him. I was glad no kids were on the playground and no kids saw the incident.

Ferd Wunderlich receiving sergeant's badge from Deputy Chief Robert Houghton at promotion ceremony.

Andrew   *Tim*

Kyle

I have two sons and a grandson on the job. My son Tim came on the department, and after that, my other son, Andrew, came on the department. At one point, all three of us worked Seventy-Seventh Division together. My sons would impound a car, and the report would show impounded by Wunderlich. I was now in charge of the auto detectives, and the owner of the car would have to get the vehicle release form from me, another Wunderlich. They'd say, "What's going on here?" I used to tell them, "Didn't you know? We own the station." Then Tim's son, Kyle, my grandson, joined the department. He's been on almost a year, and he also worked Seventy-Seventh. He's wearing my policeman badge number. When Kyle went in the field, people wanted to know how he'd gotten such a low badge number. He'd say, "It's my grandfather's."

Pete Haynes

James "Pete" Haynes

Birthplace: San Fernando, California
Career: 1964–1989
Rank at Retirement: Policeman II + II
Divisions: Wilshire, Traffic Enforcement, Central Traffic, West Los Angeles
    Traffic, Traffic Coordination Section

Chasing people in West Los Angeles was like chasing the stars. One day, I was working a speed beat, and Mort Saul, a famous comedian and actor, came by. I caught him doing about sixty miles an hour, so I pulled him over and gave him a ticket. About three days later, I was sitting in the same place, and there he went again. I pulled him over and said, "Mr. Saul, what are you doing?"

He said, "I'm sorry. I'm sorry. I'll never let it happen again."

I said, "Fine."

I let it go; I didn't write him a ticket. A couple of days after that, there he went again. I stopped him, and he said, "What's your name?"

I said, "Pete Haynes, sir."

He said, "Why don't you and I do a comedy act together?"

I said, "Get going, but next time, I'm gonna give you another ticket."

My dad came on the California Highway Patrol in 1946 and retired in '74. In '49, he became the resident CHP officer in Malibu. He rode motors as an officer and as a sergeant from '54 to '67. I grew up in Malibu. At ten years old, I was sweeping the Malibu pier for five dollars a day. Later, I was a deckhand on one of the fishing boats, and when I turned twenty-one, I got my license to run sport boats. In '62, I began running the *Lenbrooke* out of Malibu. I was running a sixty-five-foot boat, half days, that could carry seventy-three people. I was getting paid twenty dollars a day with no benefits. We had a baby on the way, and I thought, *I'm going to have to see about doing something else.* I

The Lenbrooke

applied to the LAPD, and of course, it broke the old man's heart that I was not applying to the CHP. In February '64, I was in the academy. When I graduated, I went to Wilshire Division.

There were some notable officers at Wilshire, and I've got to believe Joseph Wambaugh might have chosen one as his model for Bumper Morgan. That guy, I'm positive, was Joe Rieth. Joe always sat at the back of the roll-call room with his hat on cockeyed, smoking a big old cigar. His partner was Connie Babilonia, whose daughter, Tai Babilonia, was an Olympic skater. They worked a Z-car, a crime-suppression car. One night, Joe was sitting in the back, and he said to the watch commander, "Connie is off tonight. I'm going to work with the kid," and he pointed at me. I was all spit and polish, brand-spanking new.

There was a club called the If Club at Ninth and Vermont. Growing up in Malibu, I had no clue what the rest of the world was about. We walked into the If Club, and it looked like a *Star Wars* bar scene. Transvestites, homosexuals—it had them all. While we were in there doing a bar check, a man—I think it was a man, but I could be wrong; maybe it was a female— walked up to us and said, looking at me, "Joe, what have we here?"

Joe Rieth

Joe said, "George, get the hell away from him. Leave him alone."

After a few minutes, we walked out of the club and started walking back to the patrol car. We heard a ruckus over to the right of us, about fifty feet away, in the club parking lot. I saw two women arguing back and forth, and all of a sudden, one pulled out a .22 pistol—a little automatic—and shot the other one right in the stomach. As soon as she saw us, she dropped the gun and threw her hands in the air, and we arrested her. We called for an ambulance and had everybody coming. I was thinking, *Where in the hell have I ended up?*

One night, I was working with this other guy, not my regular training officer. I had been working at Wilshire for about four months. It was about two o'clock in the morning, and we were driving along Eighth Street. We saw an inebriated woman walking along near an apartment building. My partner pulled the car into the apartment parking lot and told me, "You stay here and finish up the paperwork, and I'm going to walk her up to her apartment to make sure she gets in okay."

I said okay. About fifteen minutes later, he came back to the car. I said, "Everything okay?"

"Yeah, she's fine." That was it. We drove back to the station and went end of watch.

The next day, I got into the station and was told, "Haynes, don't bother going to roll call; you're going to Internal Affairs."

I wondered what this was all about. Then I talked with a classmate of mine. He said, "There was a show-up on morning watch. This woman was in there looking at everybody." It was the inebriated woman.

My partner was off, and I called him at home. I said, "What's going on? They had this woman in here looking at everybody. Do you have anything to tell me?"

He said, "No, nothing happened. That's all you need to know."

At Internal Affairs, the captain from Wilshire was there. He and the Internal Affairs investigators were interviewing me. "What were you doing?"

I said, "I did what I was told—stayed in the car and started doing the reports."

The captain said, "That's bullshit. I know you know what went on up there, and probably you're in collusion with your partner. We know exactly what happened, so don't give me any of this crap."

I thought, *You're taking the word of this person over a policeman?* Of course, I was giving my partner the benefit of the doubt, being naive.

I was down there for what seemed like hours. Finally, the captain said, "You sign these resignation papers. If you sign them right now, you'll probably be able to get another job somewhere. If you don't sign them, we're going to fire you." Just like that. I was on probation, and this was a captain telling me this. What was I going to do? Like an idiot, I signed the papers. I was gone.

Lieutenant Wally Nesbitt at Wilshire really liked me a lot. He heard about this business and that I had been forced to resign. I didn't know this until he told me later, but Lieutenant Nesbitt's classmate had been Chief William H. Parker. So he called him up, and Chief Parker intervened. I was at Supply Division, turning all my stuff in, when the captain called me there. He told me not to turn my property in and to come back to the station. "We are going to have a chat." Just like that.

At the station, the captain was all of a sudden nice. I thought to myself, *What in the hell?* but I didn't push it.

He said, "Take a couple days off, and then come back." William H. Parker saved my bacon. I was a witness, and I testified at the grand jury hearing. The charge against my partner was forced oral copulation. He didn't go to jail, but he was fired.

One evening in August '65, I was working Traffic Enforcement Division in West Los Angeles, and everyone was called in to the station. The Watts riots had started. I had never experienced anything but a fistfight in high school up to that point. Four of us got in a car, and we headed toward Seventy-Seventh Division. I had never been there, and no one else in the car had either. We made a couple of errant turns in Seventy-Seventh, trying to find the station. Around the corner on one turn, there were probably two hundred people in the street. They saw us, and by the time we backed up, the whole windshield was completely shattered from rocks and bottles. From the backseat, I said, "Let's get outta here." We finally got to the station.

On one of the days, I was assigned to the command post at the Ninety-Second Street Elementary School. Chief Tom Reddin was there, although he might have been an inspector at the time. The word went out to every state in the union that we needed shotguns. As the shotguns came in, it was my job to open the crates, catalog the shotguns, and then issue the shotguns and shells to the policemen. As I was cracking open the crates, I came across one from Mississippi. I looked inside, and Reddin was looking over my shoulder. Inside was a Confederate battle flag over the guns. Reddin reached in and grabbed the flag. I thought to myself that had he not been there, I'd have grabbed that battle flag and would never have said a word. Tom Reddin has it, and you can quote me—he has that battle flag.

At one point, I was part of a four-man car assigned to follow the fire trucks around. They were getting sniped at. A number of times, the firemen would pull up to the site of a fire, and if they were shot at, the order was "Wrap it up, boys; we're out of here—let it go." That was why everything burned down. Those idiots were keeping the firemen from putting out the fires.

One night, we were in this same type of deployment: two cars, with four of us in each car. Sergeant Bill Jordan from West Los Angeles AI was with us. We were sitting on top of a hill on a residential street. Both cars were back-to-back with the lights out, and the road went down to a major street. At one point, a car turned onto the street where we were, lights out, coming up the hill right at us. Frank Primo stepped out and shined his flashlight at the car to get it to stop. It kept coming. This car was refusing to stop. Primo jumped out of the way of the car, and we unloaded on it. Everybody was just letting it fly. They turned onto the side street from us, which was a dead end. They stopped, and three women and a man jumped out: a pimp and three prostitutes. They hit this vacant lot like a covey of quail. They were all over the place, and we were chasing them. I chased one of the women. She jettisoned her high heels, but I caught up with her and grabbed her hair—but it came off. It was a wig. She stopped, looked at me, and said, "You blue-eyed devil! Give me back my rug."

I said, "Shut up. Let's go."

We took them into custody and booked them.

The next night, we were driving down one main street, and a car came out of nowhere. We could hear him hit the passing gear, going to blow right through the barricades at this intersection. Well, there was a military deuce and a half with a .50-caliber machine gun sitting perpendicular to the road. That .50 caliber opened up on that car and cut the top right off, decapitating three people in the car. It was the damndest thing I had ever seen. As the riots settled down, I went back to West Los Angeles, but we still worked twelve-hour shifts for a while.

Right after the first of the year in January '66, I was working a traffic car on day watch. I pulled to the side of the road at Eighteenth Street and La Cienega to do some paperwork. It was early in the morning, and there was nothing going on. All of a sudden, there was a radio broadcast: "All units in the vicinity and 8A1, possible 211 in progress at 1801 South La Cienega." There was a robbery, and I was right there. Across the street was an A&P Market—a big one. There was a guy in a butcher's smock on the north side of the building, waving at me, trying to get my attention. I told Communications I was there. This guy said, "We have some guys in the receiving room. We have an alarm code, and the code tells me that we're being held up." He said, "But those guys are always screwing around. I can't tell whether this is a real deal or not."

I said, "Okay, I'll check it out."

The A&P Market had not opened yet. I ran around the corner to the receiving door, where they took deliveries. As soon as I left, the guy I had just talked to entered my car and said on the mic, "I think this officer needs some help." The RTO asked him to identify himself, and he said, "I'm here at 1801 South La Cienega, and there's a policeman here going around the corner, and you better get some help out here because he's all alone." I heard the Communications tapes later.

It turned out there were about ten delivery guys and butchers in the receiving room. Two suspects were holding them at gunpoint. I opened the receiving door as slowly and as quietly as I could. I then heard the two suspects yelling at the guys. "Where the hell's the money? Get the damn money." The two suspects were facing away from me.

I thought to myself, *Well, dummy, this is what you get paid to do. If you're going to eat it, now's the time—let's go.* Just like that. We didn't have any armor vests in those days. I crept up behind the suspects to a stack of canned goods that stood about my height. I assumed a barricade position, and the suspects were about twelve feet away. The one suspect had a .9 millimeter, and the other had a .45. I could see both guns. I zeroed in on the suspect on the left and screamed, "Police! Drop those damn guns or you're dead." I just started yelling and screaming. The suspect I had zeroed in on put his gun down on the table and raised his hands. Simultaneously, the other guy looked at me and then ran straight through the double doors into the market. He kept his gun. Then the butchers let the first suspect have it—*boom, boom.* I mean, they were just dotting his i's.

I told them, "All right, all right. When you're done with that, handcuff him," and I gave them my handcuffs. Then I did the only thing I could do: going through those doors, I made myself as low profile as I could. I hit the two doors on my stomach and rolled over a little bit. I listened and heard the second suspect running down to the other end of the market.

He went behind the deli counter and yelled at the janitor, "Give me the keys! I got to get outta here."

As soon as I got to the deli, I turned to the right, and there he was. He had the magazine of his gun in one hand and the gun in the other. But he could have had a round chambered, so I wasn't taking any chances. I came around the corner and said, "I'm going to give you one chance— that's it. That gun and that clip had better hit the ground, because if they don't, I'm gonna kill you right now." He dropped both, and the janitor took off. I told the suspect, "Lean against the counter." I couldn't think of anything else to do to get him under control. I had given my handcuffs to the butchers, so I took my big old six-inch Colt and hit him right behind the ear with that thing as hard as I could and knocked him out. I picked up his gun and put it in my pocket. By this time, Frank Delora, a motor cop, had shown up, and then some Wilshire units came.

When I got back to the West LA station, the press was there. The press had told my father, who was working, and he had come over to the station. I told him what had happened, and he said, "Dang, that's something." They took a picture of my dad and me with the suspects' guns and gave it to me. It was a remarkable day. I was later awarded the Medal of Valor.

In '66, I went to motors. My dad was not happy with me joining the LAPD, but going on motors was a foregone conclusion. That was the only thing I wanted to do. Seeing my father riding his CHP motorcycle every day and helping him polish it, I just really wanted to be a motor cop. He was all for it. After motor school, I was sent to Central Traffic Division. I rode the freeways for about six months, watching these guys splitting traffic, and I thought, *That's dangerous.* It didn't take long to figure it out how to do it, and soon I was doing the same thing. I had to in order to get to radio calls.

Pete Haynes with his father and recovered weapons

Pete Haynes awarded Medal of Valor by Chief Thad Brown, 1966

One night, we were chasing a stolen car on the freeway. The driver got off the freeway, and then we were on Figueroa. He crashed, and he took off on foot, running. Keep in mind that I hadn't done any running since the academy. I jumped off the motorcycle and chased him on foot instead of chasing him on my motorcycle, as I should have. I had all my gear on, and I was in motor boots. I got about one hundred yards and thought, *I'm gonna die.* I didn't see this guy anymore, so I stopped to catch my breath. As I was leaning over, I saw him underneath a car. "Get outta there," I said. We snapped him up. He was actually in worse shape than I was.

One night, my partner, Jack Velasco, and I were westbound on the Santa Monica Freeway, and we saw brake lights maybe a half to three quarters of a mile ahead. About the same time, a car full of kids passed us in the same direction; they were just laughing and having a good time. There were cars stopped ahead, and the kids crashed right into the stopped cars. As Jack was helping the kids, I laid out a flare pattern to warn oncoming cars of the accident. As I was walking back, I used one lit flare instead of my flashlight to stop traffic. Suddenly, there came a car, out of control, probably fifty to seventy-five yards from the accident scene. The driver jammed on the brakes and locked them up, and the car started spinning. All I could do was reach up and grab ahold of the chain-link fence. The car went by me and hit my holster. It spun around some more and took out more chain-link fence. I was close to getting it that night.

Santa Monica College was looking for instructors for a Kawasaki motorcycle training program. I thought to myself, *A little extra money wouldn't hurt.*

After my interview, the dean said, "Haynes, you have the job." Kawasaki had their idea of what needed to be done as far as motorcycle training, and I had everything I had learned at LAPD. But I was told to go to another motorcycle school at Long Beach City College before I started instructing. Richard Green, the instructor, was writing his PhD thesis on motorcycle braking. I had been taught at the LAPD motor school to stay off the front brake. If a rider used just his front brake, he was going over the handlebars. Green taught us to use the front and rear brakes in combination to stop the motorcycle more effectively. Green told me his theory, and I thought he really had something. He said we needed a balance between the front brake and the rear brake when stopping. Because of the inertia in braking, the weight being pushed forward was more on the front wheel and less on the rear. When that happened and the driver only applied the rear brake, he locked up easier and slid the motorcycle. I started teaching his technique at the Santa Monica class.

Traffic Coordination Section, Selective Enforcement Unit, had an opening, and I applied. They handled commercial enforcement of trucks, motor schools, and VIP details. During my interview, the lieutenant asked me, "What can you bring to the table?" I told him about the braking technique I had learned, and he said, "You actually can do this—cut the stopping distance of these motorcycles between half and two-thirds compared to that of a locked rear wheel?" I told him I was teaching and demonstrating the technique in my class at Santa Monica College. He said, "All right. You're going to show my four instructors what you just told me."

Here were four old-timers—each old enough to be my father—sitting there, and I told them what I was going to show them. Each said, "Baloney. You're going to kill yourself."

The lieutenant said to them, "You guys aren't averse to proving it?" Now he was putting them on the defensive. He told them to get their motorcycles up to forty-five miles an hour and to stop the motorcycles as quickly as they could, any way they could. Every one of them, without exception, locked the rear wheel and just kept right on sliding, and we measured the amount of distance for their locked-rear-wheel skids. Then it was my turn. I came down the track at forty-five miles an hour. I disengaged the clutch, applied both brakes, and cut the stopping distance in almost a half to two-thirds compared to the distances of the other four. They made me do it at least fifteen times in a row. Finally, the lieutenant said, "I've heard enough, and I've seen enough. You four will learn what he knows. He will be in charge of braking at the next motor school." This was in '73. I taught the technique to all of the motor cops who came through the motor school while I was there. After I left, Jack Dugan, the instructor who replaced me, and Wally Carr, the instructor who replaced him, both taught the braking technique.

At the Selective Enforcement Unit, we did VIP security details. When Ronald Reagan was running for president against Jimmy Carter, on election night, he was in West Los Angeles. We were supposed to be at the Century Plaza Hotel at 9:00 p.m. It was 6:00 p.m., and we were on standby at a fire station, when we got the call to respond to his residence. We were told the election had been a landslide. We picked him up, and the motorcade was on its way to the hotel. At one intersection, I had the traffic stopped, and President Reagan, the Secret Service, and SWAT all went by. I was on my motor, starting to follow the motorcade, when someone on the radio said something about a motorcycle behind us. I turned and saw a guy starting to pass me, so I kicked the cow—the Harley—in the ass and hauled over to him. "What the hell are you doing?" I said.

"I'm with the press crew."

"I don't care who you are—you're not going anywhere with this motorcade," I said, and then out came the automatic weapons from SWAT. If he had passed me, he would have been a goner—make no mistake.

He said again, "I'm with the press." He started slowing down, and I ran him into the curb.

I said, "That's it—you're done. You stay right here; otherwise, you may be eating lead."

I think the most memorable VIP detail was for the premier of Israel, Golda Meier. I couldn't believe this little woman who looked as if she were about five feet tall was running a country that was under siege most of the time. When she was ready to leave Los Angeles, we all lined up, and she shook each officer's hand. She came to me and looked at me. She said, "Haynes. Is that Jewish?"

I said, "No, ma'am."

She said, "That's all right. How would you like to be a lieutenant in my army?"

I said, "Thank you very much, ma'am, but I think I'll pass." It was a nice compliment.

At motor school, besides braking, I also taught motorcycle survival training and defensive driving tactics. I used to yell at my students about a couple things. One was taking their helmets off when they stopped someone. I told them, "If I ever see one of you take your helmet off in front of a person while you're giving them a ticket, you're gonna be in deep trouble." I also knew that when they were in front of a big storefront window, they'd look at themselves in their boots and uniforms and say, "Look at that!" I would say, "How do I know you're going to do that? Because I was one of you!" And I was. For twenty-five years, I was a cop, and for most of that, I was a motor cop. The old man was disappointed because I didn't go to the Highway Patrol, but he was happy I was a motor cop, and for me, that made it all worthwhile.

Pete Haynes: "How do I know you're going to do that? Because I was one of you!"

Richard Szabo

Birthplace: Lorraine, Ohio
Career: 1964–1994
Rank at Retirement: Lieutenant II
Divisions: Foothill, Accident Investigation, University, Devonshire, Wilshire, Juvenile Narcotics, Narcotics, Van Nuys, Robbery-Homicide, Major Crimes, Public Disorder and Intelligence

I was working at the Van Nuys General Motors plant and living in San Fernando when a friend of mine suggested I become a reserve police officer for the San Fernando Police Department, and I did. I realized I liked police work, so I applied to the best police department, the LAPD. I had problems getting through the screening process though. I grew up in a tough Pacoima neighborhood and frequently got into fights with the *vatos*, which eventually got me expelled halfway through my senior year in spite of good grades and three varsity letters in sports. After high school, I joined the Marine Corps for three years, and that changed my life. It took awhile, but I finally entered the academy in April '64.

One of my classmates was George Aliano, who became a partner at various points in our careers and a lifelong friend. After graduation, George and I went to Foothill Division for our probation. I now patrolled the streets I had grown up on, occasionally encountering people who knew me from the neighborhood. When our probation ended, George was transferred to West Valley Division. I went to Accident Investigation two weeks before the Watts riots. One of my first partners at AI was Stan Kensic, a great partner, and our area was Seventy-Seventh Division.

Richard Szabo

During the '65 riots, we were shocked to see cars overturned in the streets, buildings on fire, and mobs throwing rocks, bricks, and all types of things at police cars. We responded to a fire department help call at 108th and Avalon. Along with other officers, we assisted the firemen in getting out, leaving the building to burn. The other officers also got out, but Stan and I were trapped by the rioters, causing us to initiate our own help call. A photographer in the crowd took a picture of Stan on the side of our car, aiming his revolver at the crowd while I was trying to get in the car with a shotgun in my hand. The photo later appeared in the one-time issue of *Anarchy Los Angeles* magazine.

Stan and I got away from the crowd, and a short time later, I sustained a serious injury to my left hand while in foot pursuit of an armed suspect. He came out of a pawn shop and put a handgun into his waistband. I chased him over several fences and injured my hand on one of the fences. He stopped when I fired a warning shot into a tree next to him, and we took him into custody. He got rid of the gun during the foot pursuit, and we never found it. Stan took me to Oak Park Receiving Hospital near Manchester and Broadway. The hospital was under siege, but we managed to get in, and my hand was stitched up and bandaged. We agreed to stay at the hospital until further help

Richard Szabo, left, and Stan Kensic: "Stan and I were trapped by rioters causing us to initiate our own help call."

arrived. The hospital was full of injured people waiting for treatment, and incredibly, a man with multiple gun-shot wounds was calmly sitting on a bench, waiting to be treated. I was able to continue working with the bandaged hand. For the next few hours, we ran from one call to another. We were no longer able to arrest looters because of a lack of jail space and transportation. If the suspects had taken bottles of liquor, we smashed the liquor bottles against the walls of buildings. Later, we responded to the Watts substation, where several officers were trapped by rioters. It seemed like it took forever to get there through the mobs, smoke from the burning buildings, and blocked streets, but we finally got to the substation. Along with other officers, we got the trapped officers out. The entire business district of Watts burned to the ground; only the train station was left standing. A portion of 103rd Street became known as "Charcoal Alley."

After the riots, George put in for a transfer and joined me at AI. We became partners assigned to the Seventy-Seventh morning watch car. At this time, Seventy-Seventh was volatile, to say the least. The

Richard Szabo and George Aliano

street thugs were trying to start another riot at every excuse. Sergeant Stanley Uno from Seventy-Seventh had a squad of officers tasked with responding to assistance and help calls. Sergeant Uno and his squad rescued George and me on more than one occasion. Once, while arresting a guy for drunk driving, we had to be rescued by Sergeant Uno while a mob stole our arrestee's car. Sergeant Uno was a really tough guy. Several times, we were surrounded by angry mobs, and one time, George was shot at while measuring the street at a traffic-accident scene.

I rotated out of AI to University Division in September '66. I worked with Bud Graves, a great street cop who later went to SWAT. One rainy night, we stopped two guys who we would later learn were armed parolees out committing robberies. As we approached their car, the driver jumped out, leaving his door open. He held his hands out extended and began talking rapidly. I could see Bud moving to try to see past him into the car, but the suspect moved each time to block Bud's view. Unable to see inside because of the fogged windows, I jerked the passenger door open and saw the second suspect prone on the front seat with his arm extended out the driver's side, as if he were lining up a shot on Bud, but I couldn't see the gun. I yelled, "Drop it!" He dropped a gun and immediately backed out with his hands up. We recovered a loaded gun from his position and another in the glove box, along with ski masks and money.

In June '67, President Lyndon Johnson was appearing at the Century Plaza Hotel for a fundraiser, and a coalition of antiwar groups staged a protest. There were at least ten thousand protestors there, and University and Seventy-Seventh Division officers were posted directly in front of the hotel. We were taunted and pelted by the protestors until we were ordered to disperse them. We drove them away from the hotel with our batons.

After the Watts riots, the SWAT unit was formed, although it was not officially called SWAT then. The unit consisted of fifteen four-man teams. Bob Smitson picked Pat McKinley, Terry Speer, and me to complete his team. In those days, it was a part-time assignment, and we did a lot of training at Camp Pendleton. We responded to a few callouts, but the big test came with the raid on two Black Panther locations on December 8, 1969. By then, I had been promoted to detective and transferred to Devonshire detectives, but I was still part of the four-man team. Pat had taken over as the leader of the team, and Bob Burke joined the team. We were assigned to the group hitting the Panther headquarters at Forty-First and Central. The field commander was Inspector Charlie Reese. According to the plan, a team would capture the lookout on the roof with cover from teams posted across the street. Sergeant Dave McGill's team and another led by Sergeant Ed Williams were to ram the two front doors and gain access. Our team would then join them and enter to sweep the building. We watched the two teams ram the doors. After a few seconds, a deafening fusillade of gunfire erupted from inside the building, and the teams on the roofs began returning fire from across the street

All the burglar alarms on the block went off when the Panthers lobbed a hand grenade or pipe bomb into the street. We saw four officers down on the sidewalk. McGill grabbed our team and led us to the alley behind the building. We didn't know what he had in mind, but we followed him down the alley. The Panthers were shooting wildly across the alley through gun ports at the rear of the building, and our teams in the rear were returning fire. Bullets were flying over our heads from both directions. McGill was trying to gain a position to approach the downed officers from the south. But by the time we reached our objective, five officers who miraculously had not been hit dragged the wounded officers out of the kill zone. Cal Drake had been shot in the foot, Dick Wuerfel had been shot in the leg, and Ed Williams had several gunshot wounds to the chest area. They were all taken to the hospital. Jim Segars and Gene Trinkler had been hit in the chest with shotgun blasts, but both were protected by armored vests.

McGill then laid out a plan to chop through the interior walls of the adjoining businesses to gain access to the common wall with the Panthers' building. At the common wall, we would use a shape charge to blast a hole and gain access. We began chopping through the walls while rounds of tear gas were being fired into the building. The fire department provided a plastic shape charge, and Pat took it onto the roof and set it off while the Panthers shot at him through the ceiling. The explosion only resulted in venting tear gas. After approval from Washington, DC, we received fragmentation hand grenades from Fort McArthur. Although I'd had plenty of training with hand grenades, it felt strange to have them while in a police uniform.

The siege lasted for more than four hours, but the Panthers finally surrendered. Three of the eleven Panthers had been wounded. Amazingly, no one was killed. I was part of the team that entered to clear the building. One officer took one of the Panthers in at the point of a shotgun in case anyone was still inside, but the officer was overcome by the gas. I was still able to function, took over, and completed the search with the suspect in front of my shotgun. He was trembling and yelling, "If there is anyone in here, please come out!" He knew he would be the first one to die if anyone was waiting in ambush. There were so many empty shell casings on the floor that we had to shuffle to walk. When it was over, we debriefed at the Georgia Street station. Some of the guys couldn't stand to be near us because of the irritating effect of the tear gas that had permeated our uniforms.

My last callout with SWAT was September 1970, during the riot in East Los Angeles. Our SWAT team was assigned to protect the command post at the Evergreen Playground. We were positioned on the roof of a lunch pavilion with a group of Metro officers below us. We matched quarters to see who was to go down for the coffee, and I lost. When I dropped off the edge of the roof, my wedding ring dug into the wood, and my left ring finger was shredded off the bone. Wearing my ring was a careless mistake on my part. Two of the Metro officers took me on a harrowing Code 3 ride to Central Receiving Hospital, where my finger was amputated the next day. The injury never prevented me from doing my job during the rest of my career. In '71, SWAT became part of Metro Division, and I continued my career as a detective.

In November '68, I was selected for a detective position in Devonshire, a brand-new division working for Lieutenant Gene Rock as well as Lieutenant Lynn Selby, a World War II veteran who had served as a corpsman on Iwo Jima. I also worked with an old-timer, Detective Art Mollner. Art had been a teammate of Jackie Robinson on an AAU basketball team. Art had a gold medal from the 1936 Olympics in Berlin as a member of the US basketball team and had seen Adolf Hitler close up and in person. Art had joined the department in 1943 and never worked a day in uniform his entire career. He seemed to know everyone. When he spoke, he would get up close and glance over his shoulder as if to see if someone were listening, giving you the impression you were about to hear a great secret. I learned a lot about the department's history from Art.

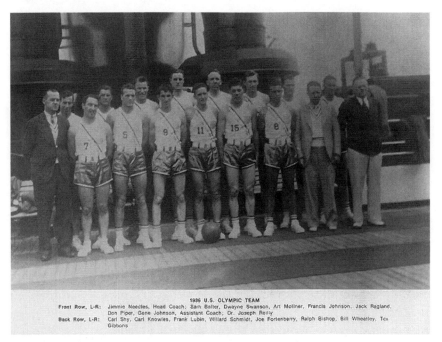

1936 U.S. OLYMPIC TEAM
Front Row, L-R: Jimmie Needles, Head Coach; Sam Balter, Dwayne Swanson, Art Mollner, Francis Johnson, Jack Ragland, Don Piper, Gene Johnson, Assistant Coach; Dr. Joseph Reilly
Back Row, L-R: Carl Shy, Carl Knowles, Frank Lubin, Willard Schmidt, Joe Fortenberry, Ralph Bishop, Bill Wheatley, Tex Gibbons

Art Mollner, #9, U.S. Olympic basketball team, 1936

My first assignment was the Juvenile Sex Crimes Detail. During the first part of 1969, I was assigned a forcible rape case of a sixteen-year-old girl. The suspect turned out to be Charlie Manson. I remember how difficult it was to assemble a photo lineup with his mug shot; he had those bugged-out eyes and that wild hair. I got a positive identification on Manson, but the girl and her mother were reluctant to proceed. I managed to convince them to proceed, only to find out later that the Spahn Ranch, where the rape had occurred, was in the Malibu sheriff's territory. I turned the case over to the sheriff, but it was never filed. Later, during the Tate-LaBianca murder case preparation, I was called to assist in locating some juvenile females I had tracked down during my rape investigation.

Around April '69, I was assigned to Devonshire Homicide to replace Charlie Collins, who had been transferred to the task force working on the Robert Kennedy assassination. I handled two cases—the first I inherited from Charlie. Fifteen-year-old Gary Rocha had been found in his home dead from a gunshot wound to his head. The second case I handled from the start at the crime scene. Thirteen-year-old Donald Allen Todd from Sylmar was found under a wooden bridge in a remote section of Granada Hills, clad only in a T-shirt—an apparent sex crime. He died of bullet wounds to the head and heart. Both homicides were still unsolved when I left Devonshire to attend sergeant school in March 1970.

While in sergeant school, I was called out and sent to Foothill Division. Mack Ray Edwards had confessed to Foothill detectives that he had killed six children dating back to 1953. Two of the children were Gary Rocha and Donald Todd. The day he surrendered himself, he had enticed a sixteen-year-old neighbor boy to help him kidnap three young sisters from the neighborhood. They tied the girls up and took them to Bouquet Canyon. Edwards intended to sexually assault all four and then kill them. The girls knew who he was, and one of them managed to escape and hide in the brush. Knowing he had been identified, he released the three remaining kids and walked into Foothill station, laid his gun on the counter, and told the desk officer he wanted to confess to some murders. He was convicted and received the death penalty. During the penalty portion of the trial, he demanded that the jury recommend the death penalty. In October 1971, he hung himself in his death-row cell at San Quentin.

George and I were both promoted to sergeant at the same time. He was assigned to West LA Division, and I went to Wilshire, a neighboring division. We used to meet on the border for Code 7. Bob Smitson, now a lieutenant, was my watch commander. He was always an advocate of self-defense. He had mattresses wrapped around the pillars in the roll-call room and had us practice kicks. This paid off for me when I encountered a big unarmed suspect by myself at the end of a vehicle pursuit. The suspect refused my orders at gunpoint and came at me. I didn't want to shoot him, because I could see he was unarmed, but I could also see he was way too big for me. I had my gun in my hand, but I was afraid he would take my gun away in a fight. I considered for a second throwing it away. When he got close, I tucked my gun into my side and kicked him, just as we had been practicing. I landed the kick perfectly in the middle of his chest, knocking him back hard onto the police car, where the back of his head struck the red light on the roof. He bounced off the car and hit the pavement on his face, smashing his nose. He was dazed long enough for me to handcuff him. I gained new stature with the responding officers when they saw the size of the suspect I had subdued. I never told them I had considered throwing my gun away.

In February '71, George and I left patrol and went to Narcotics Division. We worked Juvenile Narcotics out of the old Hollywood station for the next eight months until we transferred to the Devonshire Narcotics Unit, where we worked the next year together as partners in street narcotics enforcement.

In October '72, I went on loan to the US Department of Justice to participate in a new federal narcotics task force. We worked out of the old Federal Building downtown. My partner was Bill Welch. Intelligent and articulate, Bill was a court-qualified narcotics expert on heroin. There was a "farmer's market" of heroin dealers on Kalisher Street in San Fernando. I went undercover and started buying heroin from the dealers on the street. Many of the dealers knew I belonged in the area but didn't know I was a police officer. After each buy, we would obtain a secret indictment. I was finally burned after making twenty-one buys when a crook on the street recognized me as a cop. Bill assumed the undercover role, and we made ten more buys. We then served thirty-one arrest warrants, rounded up the suspects, and issued federal grand jury subpoenas to everyone else involved in heroin traffic on Kalisher.

The effect on the heroin trade there was dramatic. We got twenty-seven convictions for hand-to-hand sales of heroin with sentences of five, ten, or fifteen years to life, depending on their prior records.

I left the task force and transferred to Van Nuys detectives, where I worked Robbery with Sergeant Kenny Brondell. Kenny was one of the nicest guys I've ever met in the department—a real gentleman. He had been a pitcher for the New York Giants in 1944, playing with the great Mel Ott, among others. I got as many baseball stories out of him as I could. He was also a dance instructor at Arthur Murray's dance studio. Years later, after I had made lieutenant and Kenny had retired, I was visiting my father, who was dying of cancer at the VA hospital. My father told me an old partner of mine had come to visit him. Kenny had heard my father was there, so he'd stopped in and told him stories about how good a cop I was. That was typical of him and something I will never forget. Sadly, in '94, Kenny's daughter, Christy Hamilton, with only three months on the department, was shot and killed in Devonshire Division. Kenny passed away in 2004.

Kenny Brondell

In '74, I got a call from Gene Rock, now a captain at Robbery-Homicide Division. He asked me if I wanted to come to the division, and of course, I jumped at the chance. I was assigned to Robbery for a couple of months and then switched to Homicide. Frank Tomlinson asked for me as a partner because he was working on a narcotics-related homicide and I had narcotics experience. This was the beginning of a great five-year partnership. Frank rarely showed emotion and never used profanity, but if you were a criminal, you definitely did not want Frank coming after you. He was the most tenacious investigator I have ever known. He had pressed the suspect in this narcotics homicide case so hard that the suspect put out a ten-thousand-dollar contract on him with a ten-thousand-dollar bonus if done within a week. This information was verified by two independent, reliable sources for OCID. Everyone on the street was afraid of the suspect because he bragged that he worked for an organized crime boss in San Diego. We resolved the contract problem by going to San Diego and interviewing the crime boss to verify this association. He asked for—and we provided him with—everything we knew about our suspect, including a photo. The meeting immediately turned the tables on our suspect, and within a week, he fled the country.

We had a triple-murder case and got an extradition warrant issued on the suspect, who was in the state prison in Maryland. The suspect was a Muslim who hated whites, but ironically, all five of his victims were black. He was serving life plus twenty years for the robbery and murder of a Baltimore doctor. He later escaped from prison and murdered a witness who had testified against him. He was recaptured, only to escape again and hitch a ride with three young burglars on their way to Los Angeles to fence stolen musical instruments. In Los Angeles, he executed the three in their sleep to steal $2,400 they had obtained from selling the instruments. He returned to Baltimore and was recaptured after a shoot-out with drug dealers he was trying to rip off. He was a big, strong man who was considered an escape risk and too dangerous to put on a commercial airline. We brought him back to Los Angeles by train in waist and leg chains anchored to the floor of our compartment with a logging chain. Our suspect was convicted and received three life sentences to run consecutively to his life, plus twenty year sentence in Maryland, assuring he would never get out of prison. After sentencing, the district attorney insisted we return him to Maryland by commercial airline. Against our wishes, we were directed to transport him in waist chains concealed by a box of his personal belongings to be held on his lap. The pilot had taxied the aircraft almost to takeoff, when the suspect began cursing and rattling his chains, terrorizing the passengers. We were asked to leave the plane, and we returned him to the Parker Center jail. Unfortunately, he was allowed to make phone calls while in jail. We suspected that he had set up an opportunity to escape with help from his Muslim associates on the four-day train ride. We delayed the trip and then removed him from his cell without prior notice and took two Metro officers with us for additional security. We made it to Baltimore with no trouble. One year later, he was stabbed to death in prison.

In November 1977, the bodies of twelve- and fourteen-year-old Dolly Cepeda and Sonja Johnson were found dumped on a hillside in Elysian Park, near Dodger Stadium. Frank and I were assigned both cases, and ultimately, these cases became part of the Hillside Strangler Task Force under Lieutenant Ed Henderson. In January 1979, the suspects, Kenneth Bianchi and Angelo Buono, were arrested in the state of Washington, and the task force we were part of ended.

In June '79, I was promoted to lieutenant. I did a year as the watch commander at Van Nuys Division, and in July '80, I transferred to PDID, Public Disorder Intelligence Division. I later went to Administrative Narcotics Division, but before I left PDID, I had a close call with a professional hotel burglar.

In May '83, I was attending a conference in Sacramento with Richard Meraz, also from PDID. While sitting at the swimming pool with Richard and some other detective attendees, I decided to go back to my room. I walked in on a burglar who was busy ransacking the room. I chased him into the parking lot, not knowing he had my gun. He knew he couldn't get into his car without me catching him, so he stopped, spun around, and pointed the gun directly at my chest from about six feet. I looked at the gun and thought about how small the bullet was that was aimed at my heart. I turned my right shoulder to protect my heart and then dove behind a parked car. He came around the car to get a clear shot, while I maneuvered to keep the car between us. He never fired a shot. The suspect kept the gun pointed at me as he walked backward toward his car. I made a break for it and ran to a nearby building. I yelled for Richard, and he and four of the guys came running. The suspect got in his car and was driving away as one of the guys ran for his car keys

David Szabo

and a gun. Now we had six barefoot cops in bathing suits with only one gun crammed into a small car, racing around looking for the long-gone suspect. Richard and I lost all of our money, badges, identification, and credit cards. But we were the hit of the night at the closing banquet, enduring an endless string of jokes. Strangely, I wasn't upset at all. I was just glad to be there. I had gotten the license number, but the car turned out to be stolen. My gun and our badges were never recovered.

I retired on July 5, 1994. Like so many others in our profession, my marriage didn't survive, but I don't blame the job. My wife and I grew apart through the years, and after the children had grown, we divorced. In 1988, I remarried a beautiful woman. My former partner, Frank Tomlinson, officiated at our wedding. Looking back on my career, I feel fortunate to have worked so many highly selective assignments and to have witnessed so much LAPD history. What really stands out is the quality of the people I worked with. Few professions can produce people of such caliber. In 1972, my brother, David, ten years my junior, joined the department. He was a marine combat veteran of Vietnam with two Purple Hearts. He served thirty-two years and retired as a homicide detective. Unfortunately, we never had the opportunity to work together.

Charles "Kip" Meyerhoff

Birthplace: Nyack, New York
Career: 1964–1985
Rank at Retirement: Sergeant II
Divisions: West Valley, Van Nuys, Central, Wilshire

When I left the army, my wife and I fell in love with California, and we moved to Los Angeles in 1961. I had some nice jobs, and then I was recalled into the army. Later, I got out of the service on a hardship discharge with the birth of my third child. I returned to the company I had been working for, but they were taken over by another company, and ultimately, I was without work. I was trying to decide what I wanted to do when I read in the newspaper that the city was hiring policemen and firefighters. On my way to sign up at city hall, I thought of a policeman I had known when I was a kid; he had gone out of his way on a number of occasions to look out for me. He had set a good example of his profession. At city hall, as I was going down the hallway, the fire department was on the left, and the police department was on the right. I went right and started the process.

My father was upset that I was living on the West Coast, that I was not going to partake in the family business, and that I was married to an Italian. My father owned a hotel in New York, where I had grown up. He had gotten the hotel by winning a taxi company in a card game and then, in the vernacular of a gambler, parlayed the taxi company into a partnership in a hotel. My relationship with my father was, probably the best way to put it, strained. There was so much about us that was alike. He was a thick-headed Dutchman; I was half Dutch and half Irish. We didn't always see eye to eye.

Kip Meyerhoff

While waiting for my academy class to begin, I received a phone call from a man with the Federal Bureau of Narcotics. He said, "We've got a job for you. We want you to come back here. We'll have a guy meet you in Los Angeles." I told him I didn't see myself back on the East Coast. He told me that I should think about it, and he mentioned that my father had told him about me. I told him I'd thought his call was based on my military service. He said, "No, I talked to your father."

I said, "Thanks, but no thanks." That call made me dig in my heels and really decide that the police department was where I was going to work.

I entered the academy in August '64. Fortunately, because of my military training, the academy was not difficult for me. Each day, one of us was singled out for a turn in the barrel, and on this one day, Bob Smitson chose me. I had to lead everyone in PT. When we were doing push-ups, I started counting backward. I started laughing, and the whole class broke up. The instructors were laughing too, but of course, they couldn't really show it. After that day, the academy became easier. I had learned as a kid that humor was a good thing. It can take the edge off at times.

When I graduated from the academy, I was assigned to West Valley Division. One night, I was working with a guy who had to have been a hundred years old. We got a burglary call. We deployed on the building, and these safe burglars were coming out a door on his side of the building. I heard two shots. The only radios we had were in the cars, so I ran back to the car and put out a help call. Then I didn't know whether I should check on my partner or stay on my side of the building. I decided to check on him. He had the suspects proned out on the ground. He had put two rounds into the building to make them freeze. We hooked them up and booked them for burglary with explosives.

About four months later, I was working with a different policeman, and I was just off probation. There was another burglary alarm. At the time, we were getting a lot of roof burglars in an industrial area. We got there, and I went up onto the roof. I was going along flashing my light, and I could hear the police radio because we had left the doors open. I looked over the side and saw two guys with a pile of stuff. I yelled, "Freeze. Police."

They were off like rabbits. I remembered that my last partner had put two rounds in the wall. So I cranked two into the ground, and one suspect hit the dirt and said, "Don't shoot. I give up. I give up." The other guy just kept running and cleared the fence.

My partner was out front, and he got on the radio: "Shots fired. Officer needs help."

We took the one guy into custody, and I later received an admonishment for capping off the rounds. At the time, the only thing I could think about was the warning shots that my other partner had fired on that other incident. It turned out they weren't burglars; they were stealing scrap metal.

In '65, when the Watts riots started, I was on a bus headed to Seventy-Seventh for three days. The three days were a blur. We were getting shot at one day and were pulling people out of burning buildings the next day. What I remember the most was at Parker Center—Two-Gun Johnny Powers prancing back and forth on the auditorium stage. He had his hands on his guns, and he was telling us that we were not going to put up with this and that we were going to stop this. Of course, five days later, the whole city burned down. Many believed the resultant scrutiny after the riots was what killed Chief Parker. The scrutiny was brutal.

Kip Meyerhoff, third from right: Watts riots, 1965

I had been at West Valley for about eleven months, and I wheeled to Van Nuys Division. At Van Nuys, they had just started deploying one-man units on night watch. We were like a flock of bees. One policeman would pull somebody over, and two other policemen would show up to back him up. It was aggressive police work, and I really enjoyed it. The guys were all attuned to it. Because I was working the night watch, I would spend most of my days in court because of all the arrests.

One day, as I was getting out of court, I decided to wait for the traffic to die down. I went to a local bar that was a cop hangout. In the bar was Roland LaStarza. Most people knew him as an actor, but I knew him because of my father. Roland had been a boxer. In fact, he had fought Rocky Marciano for the title in 1953. Of course, he'd had his brains beaten out.

Growing up, we had a lot of fighters around. They were like part of the furniture. I struck up a conversation with Roland, and then I took him over to Van Nuys and gave him a tour of the station. We finished the tour and went back to the bar. Some guy in the corner of the bar started chipping at Roland. Roland went over and told the guy to hold it down, that his friend was a cop and he didn't want to be embarrassed in front of his friend. Roland came back over to where I was and sat down. The guy started in again, but now he knew who I was, and he

Roland LaStarza

started in on me. "What are you—undercover? Are you spying on us? Are you vice?" Then he said, "Your father never worked a day in his life."

This was how I was raised: I went over to him and said, "All right, shut up or stand up." He stood up, and I clocked him. I just knocked him out.

Some gal started screaming, "You killed him!"

Roland said to me, "Get out of here. I'll take care of this." I returned to the station, got in my car, and went home.

Of course, there was a police report. This guy had all kinds of injuries, and there was a personnel complaint. I was called into the captain's office. The captain was an old-timer with at least thirty years on the job. Two months previously, he had told me I reminded him of Jack Dempsey, the boxer. I'd said back then, "Did you know Jack Dempsey?"

He'd said, "I saw him once when I was a kid."

I met with him over this personnel complaint, and he wanted to hear the story. After I finished, he said, "Look, Meyerhoff. Just because I told you that you look like Jack Dempsey doesn't mean you're supposed to go around hitting people like Jack Dempsey."

I figured I was fired and would have to go home and tell my wife that I had lost my job because I'd punched some guy out. The guy turned out to be a local felon. I got a twenty-day suspension. In those days, when officers were suspended, they turned in their badges and guns downtown at Internal Affairs. Marvin Iannone, the captain of Internal Affairs, told me I'd had the right idea but the wrong technique. When I came back from the suspension, there was a new captain. He gave me a stern lecture and said, "By the way, you're on the next transfer to Central Division."

At Central, I had a great time working with these great old cops, all of them legends. I worked with Farrel Williamson for about eighteen months. Farrel and I worked a Z-car. A new lieutenant came in and thought Farrel and I had been working too long together as partners, so he split us up. We had done a lot of good police work together.

Then I worked a footbeat on Main Street with Marion Hoover. The first thing Marion said was "Hey, you got to keep up with me."

I had this old guy telling me I had to keep up with him. Well, he worked my butt off. He'd go and go, and he'd see things that you wouldn't believe. He had an eagle eye, but it was more as if he were an eagle flying over. Hoover was finding guys with guns and all kinds of stuff. Other footbeat guys were basically getting drunks and throwing everybody on the drunk wagon. We were out there making some big-time arrests. At first, he treated me as if I were just out of the academy, but as I got to know him, he opened up a little bit. By then, I was a five-year policeman. He started telling me these different stories, about this guy he had killed and that guy he had killed and about the guy he'd killed who'd had a gun to his head—all these stories. At first, I thought, *This is all bull.* I'll be damned if it wasn't all true. He had killed seven people at that point. After a while, we were just as I had been with Farrel—we instinctively knew what the other was doing. I had that relationship with Marion. I wasn't afraid to throw caution to the wind a little bit, because I knew he was my backup.

On Main Street, there was an all-night theater where the winos used to go to sleep. It was like a fifty-cent ticket to get in. There was a class of people who would prey on them, victimize them. They would take a blade, maybe two to three inches long, shake a guy down, and take his wallet, or they would slash his pants or coat pocket if he was

Marion Hoover: ". . . he'd see things that you wouldn't believe. He had an eagle eye, but it was more as if he were an eagle flying over."

asleep and take his money. One time, we went into this theater, and I felt as if I wanted to take a shower just walking through there. Marion said, "Watch that one over there." We watched and saw a guy bending down and cutting a guy's pocket to get his wallet. Marion grabbed the guy, and the guy instinctively came around and cut Marion's jacket. Marion had just bought this beautiful Eisenhower jacket. He was one of the first guys to have one. He loved that jacket, and this guy had cut it. The guy didn't go peacefully. We were at the detective headquarters desk to get booking approval, it was eleven o'clock at night, and they started in on Marion. The desk sergeant said, "What are you wearing that rag for?" They were just giving him the business. He started really getting mad. I mean, he was really mad. That jacket was his pride and joy.

I said, "Hey, Marion, I'll tell you what. I'll book this guy. You write the reports," because he looked as if he were going to kill the guy.

Then an old detective said to the suspect, "You're going to be number eight."

And the guy said, "Number eight?"

That's my favorite Marion Hoover story. Years later, Marion's daughter, Jeannie Hoover, worked for me at Wilshire Division, as did a half dozen or more progeny of cops I worked with along the way. I always feared something bad happening to any of them and having to tell their fathers.

One time, I was working a beggar detail, a plainclothes detail on Main Street between Fifth and Sixth Streets when two guys tried to rob me. The street sweepers would fill up with water at the fire hydrants, and they used these big brass wrenches to open the fire hydrants. I was standing near a hydrant when this guy said, "All right, man. Give us your money."

I didn't know where my partner was, but I hit the one guy. My partner then came up and got the other guy down, but the first guy grabbed the wrench off the hydrant, and he was going to hit me with the wrench. I pulled out my gun and said, "Now I'm going to kill you," and the guy took off.

There was a coffee spot across Main Street about a block away, and there were two black-and-white police cars there. The policemen were drinking coffee. This guy ran toward them screaming, "Help! Help!" I can't remember the policeman's name, but they called him "Headlamp." He was the first guy with a shaved head on the police department. He saw this guy coming, and he saw me chasing him, so he Mickey Mantled the guy. The guy's feet kept going, but the rest of him went down.

We took the two to detective headquarters, and the desk sergeant said, "Come on—you guys are making this stuff up."

I said, "That's what happened. Here's the wrench," and we booked them.

I decided to take the sergeant test. I passed the written and got an oral interview. I went to the interview all jazzed. The first question they asked—"Okay, how come somebody with such a high IQ is on the Los Angeles Police Department?"

I thought, *Well, this is an icebreaker.* I smiled at the captain and said, "Geez, I hope you're not going to hold it against me." It just went downhill from there. Of course they asked about the twenty-day suspension.

The candidates were all waiting for the list to get published, and I thought I'd be in the top hundred. I was not on the list. Garvin Reece, the footbeat sergeant, said, "What happened?"

"I don't know," I said.

A year later, I took the sergeant test again, and this time, I didn't study, but I scored pretty high on the written. I didn't prepare much because I didn't expect much. I was just going through the motions. I figured I was going to have to wait, do my penance, and stay clean. I went in for the oral interview, and one of the board members, a captain, said, "How're you doing, Kip?" It was somebody I had not worked with before, and he called me Kip. I gave them my spiel, and I told them what I'd been doing. Then it came time to talk about the suspension. I told them the Iannone story—that I had felt like a horse's ass but while turning in my gun and my badge, Iannone had told me I'd had the right idea but the wrong technique and that had made me feel better. They started laughing. It was great, and I knew I was going to be a sergeant. The Iannone story stands out as an interpretation of how you look at the situation and how to treat people. That's important when you get somebody who's beaten up and feeling low. I think the Iannone story was the reason I made sergeant.

In '72, I made sergeant and went to Wilshire Division. In '76, I was on my deathbed. I had gone from 210 pounds to 159 pounds and was passing blood and getting transfusions. Nobody knew what was wrong with me. At the same time, a friend of mine, Dick Stines, a retired New York detective, had a heart attack and was in a hospital intensive care unit recovering. Dick told his doctor in his typical New York fashion, "You think I'm bad? You ought to see my buddy Kip." Dick told his doctor my symptoms. The doctor told Dick he thought he knew what was wrong with me. He had been an intern for Dr. Burrill Crohn, whom Crohn's disease was named after. Nobody in Los Angeles had heard of it. So they started me on intravenous steroids for three days, and the morning of the second day, I knew I was going to make it. I was off work for four months. When I went back to work, I was about 170 pounds. I'd had a drinking problem up to that time. Even though I had lost so much weight, I thought I could probably still drink. I really didn't want to admit to myself that I was an alcoholic. I wanted to test it one more time. When I got home, I had a fit of anger. I broke up furniture in the house, and my son stopped me.

A lieutenant showed up, and he shared with me that he was in an Alcoholics Anonymous program called Fifth Step. I recovered and became a counselor for people in the police department with drinking problems.

In September '79, I was the assistant watch commander at Wilshire the night David Kubly was killed. David was working a report car by himself on a hot night. He removed his armored vest and wound up with a bullet. We were pretty sure the suspect was contained in the perimeter. Lieutenant Gary Reichling, the watch commander, went to the scene, and I stayed at Wilshire, making notifications. The command staff was questioning the amount of personnel deployed at the scene, and I was sitting there fielding these questions. But our decisions were made, and the decisions paid off. How do you measure that? If you're dying, you want to know they're trying to get the son of a bitch who killed you. I gained a lot of admiration for the men I worked with that evening.

One day, an officer at Wilshire went onto the station rooftop and committed suicide. The week before, Captain Joe De Ladurantely had called me and said, "I need you in here right now."

I went in, and the officer was in there crying. It turned out he had ulcerative colitis. I said, "Well, there are all kinds of treatments for that." I told him about the medications and the treatments and told him that everything was going to be fine.

He said, "I can't live like this." I thought he was talking about his illness. When you think you know everything, you don't know anything. We didn't realize the gravity of the officer's fragile state of mind. I'm saying that in hindsight now. I showed up to work that afternoon when he killed himself. It was chaos. It made me think there's more that can be done about these guys who are in trouble. Behavioral Science Services Division was in its infancy then. Captain De Ladurantely set up training sessions in Wilshire that eventually resulted in the development of the Crisis Intervention Program, a standard training program for supervisors. It was a positive outcome to a tragic event.

Capt. Joe De Ladurantely

As a sergeant, I sat on at least two hundred interviews for new hires. I think that was probably some of the best work I ever did on the police department. I knew what to ask. We were getting some people who were prepared and some who were not. But just because they weren't prepared did not mean that they didn't have the qualities that the police department could use. If we peeled back the veneer, we could see whom we would want to work with. Two of them worked for me later at Wilshire. I initially did have a thing about females being on the job. I thought some could do the physical stuff, but on the whole, I didn't think they could. I did some introspection, and I was the first to assign two women to work in a police car together. I was questioned about it that night, and I responded, "Their badges say 'police officer.'" They made it to end of watch.

My father insisted that I meet everybody, and I'm talking about everybody—politicians, big-time crooks, all the swells, the upper class, the people who thought they were wonderful when they were nothing. My parents would go to the best restaurants, and they'd drag me along. Because of that, I had a good grasp on dealing with people. I never had a problem dealing with anybody—angry people, happy people, dramatic people. It was never an issue for me. It allowed me to exert influence without exerting pressure. I always believed in willing compliance. The people who work for you should be doing it because they want to do it. You get better results than if they're doing it

Sgt. Kip Meyerhoff, third row, far right: Wilshire Division PM Watch, 1985

because they have to do it or because you're going to put a foot in their ass (although I was not opposed to putting a foot in their ass if they really needed it). There was no general rule that you hit them all with the same brush. That was how I supervised, but I got there through a bunch of incidents that occurred in my life. I was treated well by 99 percent of the people I came in contact with during my career. In return, I always hoped that I had made a difference, that I had shown others how to treat people in a good way. That was what I was all about. I've always felt that was my job, because that was what I was taught.

Terry Speer

Birthplace: Buffalo, New York
Career: 1964–1989
Rank at Retirement: Police Officer III
Divisions: Newton, University, Training, Devonshire

G ary Cooper, when asked to read a new movie script, would say, "Just make me the good guy." I grew up in an era of playing cowboys. I always wanted to be the good guy, never the bad guy. When I went to the movies, I always identified with the hero, never the villain. My heroes weren't perfect, but their characters were clearly defined, and there was no question about their morals. They were willing to put themselves in harm's way when defending the principles they believed in. They fought for those who were unable to fight for themselves. The guy in the white hat was my man.

When I was a teen, I read a news article about a young woman being assaulted on the steps of a tenement building in New York City. When she screamed for help, no one came to her rescue. Instead, it was reported that people shut their windows to avoid hearing her. This made me angry. It was then that I began to think seriously about a career in law enforcement. But that wasn't the only reason. I wanted a job with action, a job where every day wasn't the same. My dad was a steady nine-to-fiver. He put bread on the table, and I thank the Lord for him. But I wanted a more exciting way to make a living. I hated school and the humdrum of everyday life. I wanted adventure.

I got out of the army in '62 and returned to my hometown of Buffalo, New York. I immediately began looking for a job in law enforcement, but many agencies wanted applicants to be five foot ten or, in some cases, six feet tall. I was just under five foot nine. Then a friend told me that LAPD was hiring and that the height limit was only

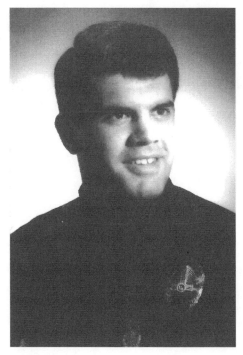

Terry Speer

five feet eight. So I packed up what clothes I had and $300 in cash, jumped in my beat-up '57 Plymouth, and followed Route 66 to Southern California. LAPD hired me in August 1964.

In the academy, we went on ride alongs, and the first cop I ever worked with was Marion Hoover. Nobody had been in as many gunfights and shootings as he had. I can still remember how disappointed I was that night for two reasons. First, the night went by so fast, and secondly, we didn't get involved in anything exciting. I discovered that police work could be routine, like anything else.

My first assignment was Newton Division. I got in my first shooting while working Newton. The suspect was a fleeing burglar who had jumped a fence and was out of my reach. I didn't think about it; I drew my gun and fired. The combat range was still fresh in my mind, and for me, at that moment, the target turned. I found out later the bullet passed through his groin and exited his right buttock. He never even broke stride. He kept running and was later found hiding in some bushes. He didn't even know he had been shot. Years later, when I was teaching officer survival to recruits in the academy, I told them we had a policy that said we shoot to stop, not to kill. Unfortunately, we used ammunition that could not carry out our policy. It was absolutely void of stopping power.

Before I left Newton, the Watts riots occurred in '65. The rioters created havoc not only for residents in South Los Angeles but also for a completely unprepared police department. We faced a crisis that was unprecedented in Los Angeles, and it was chaotic. Cops brought their own personal weapons from home, everybody wore a helmet, and we all carried shotguns. We patrolled the streets four men to a car at first. For a brief time, there was anarchy in some parts of the city. The riots started with a simple traffic stop. People gathered, and violence erupted and then spread like a forest fire out of control. No one on the department had been trained on how to handle this kind of emergency. Our reaction was a knee-jerk one: we met violence with violence. Except for some isolated incidents, I believe we handled the situation as well as might have been expected.

After the riots, I went to University Division. Two good things happened to me at University Division. The first was working with Tony Affree. He was a hardworking, sharp, no-nonsense cop. He loved to put crooks in jail, and most of the time, I followed his lead. He had a gift for sniffing out the bad guys. One night, we spotted a clean-looking black Chrysler turning north onto Denker Avenue from Santa Barbara Boulevard. Several kids were in the car. "Stolen car" was all Tony said as he simultaneously stomped on the accelerator.

We were driving a new Plymouth with a V-8 engine—a pretty good car in the late '60s. But it was no contest. The car we were in pursuit of was a Chrysler 300 that had just been tuned up. Within seconds, its taillights turned into a fading glow in the distance. However, the kid driving had more car than he knew how to handle, and possibly he didn't know Denker ended at Exposition Boulevard. He tried to make the turn, but instead, he went straight across Exposition and smashed into a house on the north side of the street. He hit it with such force that the body of the car sheared off one side of the house. When we got there, half the house was collapsing on the car, and dust and debris were billowing up all around it. To make matters worse, somewhere in what was left of the house, we could hear a woman screaming hysterically. Then, as we were making our approach, the dome light in

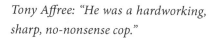
Tony Affree: "He was a hardworking, sharp, no-nonsense cop."

the car came on, and one of the suspects got out of the car. We affected an arrest of all the occupants. As it turned out, the suspects were joyriding. Thankfully, no one died, but they well could have. The city rebuilt the woman's house, and for a while, it was known as the house Affree and Speer built.

The other good thing was working for Sergeant Bob Smitson in a plainclothes crime-suppression unit called the SOS squad. No one could have asked for a better man to work for than Smitson. He was fair and trustworthy, and he had a great sense of humor. He was fiercely loyal to his men, just as we were to him. To this day, I look back on my time in SOS with profound affection.

In SOS, one of our jobs was to patrol areas that had identified patterns of crime. It was during one of these patrols that I saw a policeman die. My partner, Gerald Woempner, and I heard a patrol unit get a call of a disturbance involving a man with a gun. When we got there, we saw a uniformed officer moving along the side of an apartment building. He was moving slowly, carrying a department shotgun. As we got out of our car, we heard a *pop* and saw the officer, Gary Murakami, slump to the ground. My partner, who was senior to me, yelled at me to cover him. He and other officers pulled Gary to safety. Gary's wounds proved fatal, as he died on the operating table two hours later. At the funeral, his little son carried the American flag to his mother. I was struck by the fact that the son was so young and unable to fully grasp the enormity of what was happening and that he would never see his father again. Gary had just graduated from the academy the previous Friday. The suspect was killed. This was September '68.

Another time, we rolled on a rape in progress. We got there a few minutes after two other units had gotten there. We ran up the stairs to the second floor of an apartment building. Suddenly, a shot rang out, and by the time we got there, a uniformed officer was lying on the floor, shot in the leg, bleeding. The first officer on the scene did something that should never be done—he carried a shotgun into a small, enclosed room. As he entered, the suspect was on top of a girl. When the officer brought the shotgun to bear on the suspect, the man was able to grab the barrel, and a struggle ensued while the officer's finger was on the trigger. The gun fired, and a nearby officer took a load of buckshot in his leg. His screams of pain as he lay on the floor were not something one forgets. The wounded officer later had a plate put in his leg but returned to the job. When I became an instructor at the academy, I used that incident to illustrate the potential danger in the use of shotguns in confined areas.

Late one night, close to end of watch, three of us were working in a plain car. Bob Stemples was driving, Eddie Brown was the front passenger, and I sat in the back. We saw four young men in a late-model car sit through the green phase of a tri-light signal. They kept turning their heads and looking back at us. We hit them with our spotlight and ordered them to pull over to the curb. They complied, but as soon as their car stopped, the passenger door flew open, and one of them jumped out with a shotgun in his hand. The suspect, my partners, and I all fired simultaneously. I emptied my service revolver, threw it down on the seat of our car, and grabbed a shotgun. By this time, the suspect had thrown himself back into his car. I sprinted to the back of their car and blew the back window out with a blast from my shotgun just as they accelerated away from us. Eddie yelled for me to get in the car, and we went in pursuit.

They turned onto Exposition with us right behind them. They turned left, went onto a front yard, and struck a house. As they did, the car rocked to a stop, and one of the suspects leaped out from the passenger side. He ran toward an alley, and I went after him. The alley behind the house was narrow and lined with garages. Each garage was separated by an open space where the homeowner set his garbage cans. I flattened myself against the garage door closest to me. I was holding the shotgun in a port-arms position. I slid along the front of the garage door until I came to the first opening. I quickly lowered the barrel and shoved it into the opening. No one was there. As I came to the end of the second garage, the suspect suddenly loomed up out of the shadows and stepped toward me. I whirled and fired. The suspect fell. I stayed with him until medical help arrived. He lived, only to be killed sometime later by a gang member.

I became a marksman in the late '60s on a four-man team from University that—along with teams from other divisions—made up SWAT. Bob Burke, Rich Szabo, Patrick McKinley, and I comprised a team led by Smitson. In those days, SWAT was still a secret. Chief Tom Reddin denied SWAT's existence. A teletype was sent to our division of assignment, which said essentially, "Bring your lunch to a particular place at a particular time," which meant bring your rifle.

SWAT was voluntary and part-time, and there was no overtime pay for the extra hours we worked. Nor did we get hazardous-duty pay for the potential dangers we faced. In addition, we had to buy all of our own equipment. Because of the Vietnam War, there were many army-surplus stores, and we frequented them, buying the gear we needed. The only break we got for these out-of-pocket expenses was the tax write-off. I never heard any complaints. We were proud and privileged to be a part of something special, and no cost was too great.

The most critical SWAT operation that I experienced was the execution of search warrants at the Black Panthers' headquarters on Central Avenue at Forty-First Street in December '69. Smitson and I had transferred to the academy as instructors, but we were still part of SWAT. At the briefing before the operation, my team—Pat McKinley, Rich Szabo, and Bob Burke—was assigned as the entry team, hence we wore flak vests. However, when we got there, our assignment was changed, and another team was given the entry task. When the front door was forced open, I saw officers driven back by gunfire. Several officers were hit. It became a standoff, and officers across from the front

l to r: Terry Speer, Bob Burke, Pat McKinley, and Willie Gough, kneeling: SWAT team members, 1970

of the headquarters were exchanging fire with the Panthers. Rich went with another team of SWAT officers, knocking man-sized holes in the interior walls of businesses to reach the common wall with the Panther headquarters building. Pat went up on the roof, and Bob and I stayed in the alley next to the back of the building to cover everyone else. Hours later, the Panthers thrust something white out of an opening in the front of their location and surrendered.

My academy days represent the larger part of my career with LAPD. I was given the opportunity to be assigned to the academy as a physical-training and self-defense instructor in spring '69. I remained in that capacity until December '82. For me personally, my time at the academy was a little slice of heaven. From the time I was in the ninth grade in high school, I had been obsessed with running and working out. Now I was going to be paid for what I thoroughly enjoyed doing. I will be forever thankful to the Lord and to Smitson for the opportunity. Teaching recruits, leading them in PT and runs through the hills of Elysian Park, instructing them regarding survival in a shoot-out, and even teaching a class in nutrition and first aid—all of it made my time there good years I'll never forget.

There was a term used by the recruits—"Black Friday," as the recruits themselves identified it—that came about quite by accident. In the early '70s, one of the classes conducted themselves with a less-than-respectful attitude during one of their academic classes, and it was suggested that a little extra PT would be therapeutic for the entire class. We spent a little less than an hour on self-defense and the remaining two and a half hours on PT and running. It happened to be on a Friday. The class got the message, and Monday morning, they came to their first class with an adjusted attitude that put them in good standing for the rest of their training at the academy. Shortly thereafter, one of our supervisors overheard a member of this class who had been disciplined talking with a recruit of a new class. The new recruit was complaining about the PT, to which the other recruit replied, "You think that's bad? This Friday will be Black Friday for you—they're going to work you." Black Friday became a tradition for the next decade. This sounds ominous, but it really wasn't. No one ever touched a recruit or hurt him. No one used profanity or foul language. We worked them hard, but it was a clean hard. We never asked of them more than we were able to do ourselves. We made these young recruits work for the privilege of wearing a badge and carrying a gun and, at the same time, reminded them of the responsibility they carried along with the authority that those privileges represented. Nothing would be given to them. Being a cop was not a right; it was an honor and a privilege, and only a few—and the very best—would be given that honor. On graduation day, they could take pride in the fact that they had earned the right to be there. No one had given it to them.

At the end of the recruits' training, I taught an officer survival class in which I emphasized the dangers they potentially faced, including failing to prepare themselves for the possibility of a shoot-out, which could result in the death of a suspect. Their own death was a real possibility if they responded too slowly due to the failure to prepare themselves mentally, emotionally, and morally for such an eventuality.

A high-ranking officer on the department once asked me if I thought that our stress training, which he opposed, really changed anybody. I said, "No. That isn't why I believe our approach is important to maintain. We are giving young men a badge and a gun and, with these items, life-and-death responsibilities. I believe that we should discover as much as possible, in a controlled environment, if they can

Terry Speer, right: "We made these young recruits work for the privilege of wearing a badge and carrying a gun . . ."

handle stress without giving up or falling apart. Our purpose is not to change them to any great degree but to find out what's inside of them—what they brought with them, good or bad. Putting them under some stress is the only way we will ever find out."

A growing number of command staff personnel did not see stress training as being in the best interest of the department's image. I personally believe some saw us as mean-spirited and arbitrary in our application of discipline. They wanted more control over us, but short of transferring us out of the division without cause, they didn't quite know how to get that control. In fact, I was surprised that other like-minded instructors and I lasted as long as we did. Times were changing, and it was inevitable that our approach to training would one day be done away with.

From time to time, LAPD would have a policewomen's class. They were trained separately from the men and were not trained to work patrol. The time came when we were told that women would be trained alongside men and would be instructed and disciplined in exactly the same way. When they graduated from the academy, they would be assigned to patrol cars just as men were. The first women in this program came to the academy in '73. Most of the females had good attitudes and tried hard. We treated female recruits just like we did the male recruits; we didn't cut them the slightest bit of slack. We had a self-defense test that recruits had to pass before they could graduate. It soon became apparent that despite three months of training, a significant number of women were not going to pass. We were then told that if a recruit—male or female—failed the self-defense test the first time, he or she was to be remediated and given a second chance. If the person failed it the second time, he or she would be terminated. Some recruits did pass the test the second time around, but not enough of them to satisfy Personnel and Training Bureau. So a third attempt was authorized, but without much success. The time finally came when the self-defense test was eliminated as a deselector. Opposition to our quasi-military approach to training, with its emphasis on physical performance and strong discipline, was growing. This meant that for me and the men and women in our PT unit, our days were numbered. According to the rumors we heard, we were considered "dinosaurs." Change was in the wind, and deep inside, I knew it was only a matter of time before those of us who couldn't or wouldn't change would be forced out of the division.

Some other things happened to deepen my suspicions. For years, the upper-body control hold—commonly referred to as the "choke hold"—was the staple of our self-defense program. Officers might eventually forget all the other self-defense maneuvers we taught them, but not the choke hold. It was easy to learn, remember, and apply. Most importantly, even for the least physically fit officer, it worked. Then along came a drug called PCP. PCP strongly reduces pain perception, produces severe anxiety and delusions, and increases the heart rate significantly. It appeared as a street drug around 1967. The problem for the officers was that suspects became extremely violent when under the influence of PCP and were impervious to pain. However, in some cases, the upper-body control holds, which cut off the air supply, did subdue these artificially hyped-up suspects. Unfortunately, some of them died when their hearts gave out as the holds were applied. This, in turn, caused an outpouring of anger toward the department. The upper-body control holds were targeted instead of the drug. The severe threat to officers by these temporarily psychotic, super-strong suspects was largely ignored.

Subsequently, the US Supreme Court ruled the holds constitutional, and we were elated. Dismay quickly followed when Chief Gates came forth with a policy change that said that officers could only apply these holds when they perceived their lives to be in danger. This meant an increase in the use of batons on combative suspects, which, in our view, would be much less humane. But politics are politics, and in the final analysis, that was really all that mattered. Following that decision, chemical sprays, nets, and instruments that stunned suspects using electrical jolts were tested. What really saved the day for the street cops was that suspects opted for other drugs, and eventually, there was a decrease in the use of PCP.

Not long after all the furor over the use of upper-body control holds died down, Sergeant Ken Dionne, our supervisor, was ordered by our captain to tell us that we would no longer be able to discipline recruits or train them in the traditional manner we had been taught. If we did not feel we could abide by the new rules, we would be transferred to the division of our choice. Eleven men and one woman agreed to leave, including Sergeant Dionne. We left en masse—twelve of us all at once. It was the only time I ever made the front page of the *LA Times*.

I spent the next seven years in Devonshire Division detectives. At Devonshire, I worked for Sandi Palmer. In '69, she came to the academy to be a policewoman. She had worked the chief's office as a secretary, and initially, we thought she, among others, would not have the character to be there. Well, she proved us wrong. She definitely showed toughness. She put up with a lot and did it cheerfully, and I have to admit, she impressed me. At Devonshire, she never once demonstrated the slightest animosity toward me. If there was any woman who went through the academy who would have had a right to, it would have been her. Sandi treated me politely, courteously, and professionally. She didn't use her rank to get back at me. I look back on it now and realize that everybody griped and complained about something. At the academy, she never once uttered a complaint about anything.

I finally retired in August 1989. I had been ordained in 1975 and went into the ministry. I pastored at a church for the next eighteen years. Police work is a stressful occupation. When I was an instructor in the academy, my hope and prayer for every class was that the students appreciated the awesome life-and-death responsibilities they carried with them. Over the years, I have been a witness to some significant changes in the department. What has not changed, though, is the overall caliber of the individual who earns the right to

Sandra Palmer

wear the uniform and the badge. Like my western heroes, the men and women of the department have been and continue to be willing to put themselves in harm's way in defending the principles they believe in. They fight for those unable to fight for themselves. In the spirit of Gary Cooper, I say, "Make them the good guys."

Larry Graham

Birthplace: Los Angeles, California
Career: 1966–1992
Rank at Retirement: Sergeant II
Divisions: Seventy-Seventh Street, Parking and Intersection Control, Central,
    Harbor, Metropolitan, Jail, Hollywood

I was looking for a job, and a friend of mine told me about LAPD. I met with his friend Rudy De Leon, a lieutenant in Hollenbeck Division, and he made the police department sound pretty good to me. I applied, passed the tests, and entered the academy in '66. Right before the academy, though, I received my draft notice. I was told I had two weeks to make a choice of service. My dad had been in World War II in the navy, and he said, "I can get you in the navy reserves."

I talked to the navy and said, "Just let me finish the academy." They told me that was okay, and I signed up.

To me, the academy was when I forged my direction. We had great instructors: Bob Smitson, Tom Dickson, Robert Koga, Wayne Songer, and Bob Burke. They didn't take any garbage. They weren't abusive, but they were tough. They just scared the living bejesus out of us on a daily basis, and Bob Burke ran us to death throughout Elysian Park. The academics, at first, were tough because I really didn't know how to study. That may sound funny because I was a high school graduate and college educated, but I didn't know how to study. If they called a cadet out of a classroom and told him to bring his hat and books, that was it. Well, they called me, but they didn't tell me to bring my hat and books. They asked me how I was studying, and I said, "Well, I go home, I read for hours, and I read everything."

They said, "No, no, no. Just read what we talk to you about that day."

So from that point on, I did what they said, and I made it through the academics. We did nighttime training one night, and I was one of the investigating officers. All of a sudden, the instructor pulled out a gun and was going to shoot us. I spun him around, put him in a choke hold, and took him down to the ground. The gun went flying. He thought what I'd done was great, so I was okay for another day in the academy.

After we graduated, I went to Seventy-Seventh. Unfortunately, after less than a month in the field, I was told, "Okay, time for Uncle Sam." I went into the navy and did one tour off the coast of Vietnam. I got a three-month early out, and I went back to Seventy-Seventh. Some of my classmates were now two-year veterans. I was still a rookie.

I was assigned to the Watts substation. The substation was a two-man post. One day, my partner told me there was a robbery silent alarm going off at the Department of Water and Power office about halfway down the block from the substation. At the time, people could make their monthly payments at the DWP offices, but the offices were being robbed all over the city. My partner grabbed a shotgun, and as we got there, he told me to take the back door. I went to what I thought was the back door, and he went to the front. He ran right in but didn't see the suspect, and the suspect slapped the shotgun away from him, causing a round to go off. The round went through the wall and into a barbershop next door. All the patrons in the barbershop went running out the back door. Well, the back door was right where I was. I heard the shotgun round and saw these guys run out the back door, and I drew down on them. Now they were more terrified of me, and they ran back inside. The suspect got away. What we didn't know at the time was that Metro had a roving stakeout on the DWP offices. They were there within a minute, and I guess we got in their way. About two months later, the suspect was killed pulling another robbery. We got chastised for leaving the substation unattended. I'd had maybe a month on since I'd come back from the military, and already I was being reprimanded for doing something wrong.

Ivano Franceschini

I went to the field, and I worked with Ivano Franceschini. Any mistake a rookie could make, I was making it. Back then, our ammo pouches were designed for the loose rounds inside to fall into our hands. We went to a radio call, and I guess I hit that, and all my ammo fell on the porch. I was trying to pick up the ammo, and Ivano just kind of laughed. Slowly but surely, he made me into a halfway decent cop.

Our lieutenant, Jim Hillman, was a great lieutenant—he was personable, approachable, and professional, and he kept everything running smoothly. One time, Ivano and I had arrested a female. We booked her at SBI, the Sybil Brand Institute, a jail facility for women. Once you booked your arrestee at SBI, you had to get the arrest report approved at Central Division in Parker Center. A sergeant who had worked Seventy-Seventh had evidently not done a good job and had been asked to leave. He was now working Central Division. We handed him our arrest report, and he said it wasn't good enough. He tore it up and said to rewrite it. We wrote it again, and he said that one wasn't good enough—he told us to do it over. Ivano, thinking ahead, had made a copy of the second one before we had given it to this sergeant. We rewrote it a third, maybe a fourth time, and by the time we were finished, we were probably an hour and a half to two hours late getting back to Seventy-Seventh. Lieutenant Hillman chastised us for taking so long and asked us what we had been doing. We showed him the second arrest report and asked him what he thought of it. He thought it was a good report and asked us why. We told him that we had spent the last hour and a half trying to get a report approved by this one sergeant. Lieutenant Hillman looked on the report at the name of the supervisor and told us to go back to work. We heard him get on the phone and call up the watch commander at Central. He immediately reamed this lieutenant out for having a sergeant hold up any of his people from being in the street for a report that should have been approved when it was first presented. The lieutenant from Central said it would never happen again. Jim Hillman was a good man, and he was always there for us.

One of the legends in Seventy-Seventh was Bill "Cigar" Davis. Bill was probably six foot five. He worked the Watts car. When the election was held for mayor of Los Angeles, people in Watts voted for Bill on write-in ballots because they liked him so much. He was tough but fair. One of my classmates was working with Bill one time, not doing his job or paying attention. Bill left him on 103rd Street and drove back to the station. He told the watch commander, "I don't want him. If you want him, he's at 103rd and Lou Dillon." I never got a chance to work with him, but he was a hell of a teacher. Nobody ever said a negative thing about him.

After Seventy-Seventh, I spent three months at PIC. One day, I was working my intersection and was giving directions to somebody when I felt a bump on my right hip. I looked down and saw a hand on my gun, and my gun was coming out of my holster. There was a guy behind me, trying to take my gun. We wrestled and fought for the gun until I got it away from him and handcuffed him. He told me he wanted to commit suicide and had planned on using my gun to do it. When he was being taken away, I told him, "Next time you want to commit suicide, use somebody else's gun."

It was driving me nuts directing traffic—smelling the smoke and inhaling the smog every day. I went to Personnel and said, "Transfer me anywhere." They did—I was transferred right next door to Central Patrol. I either walked a footbeat or drove the old B-wagons. The B-wagons resembled bread trucks, and our job was to pick up the drunks. I guess that was the first time that I saw the diversity of the drunks. They were not all just down-and-out winos. There was one—a doctor—who was just stressed out. One day, we were putting this other drunk into the line, and one of the sergeants recognized him as an old partner. He got him some food and cleaned him up. You sure saw how the stress in life could affect people differently.

I worked Central for three months and then transferred into Metro Division in October 1970. I had no idea how working Metro would change my life. The officers and supervisors assigned to Metro were the best of the best. I'm not saying I was one of them, but I was lucky to have the opportunity to work there.

Metro was housed at the old Georgia Street station and was divided into platoons. I worked the south-end platoon. We had to call in every day or the day before to find out what our assignments were, because they were always changing. We had plain cars and no radios in the car. We wrote no logs. We just went out and made arrests. At end of watch, we'd call in on a Gamewell and give them our recap: a felony arrest, two misdemeanor arrests, or nothing.

While I was at Metro, they started to form the Special Weapons and Tactics Team, and my partner, Bill Arnado, wanted to try for it. I had no idea what I was going to do in SWAT, but I applied for it because I was working with Bill and he was a good partner. We both made it.

We wore World War II flak jackets that probably wouldn't have stopped a .22 and no helmets. We did all our own training. There was no book on SWAT. SWAT was a new idea. In the military, they would throw a couple of hand grenades into a building, go in, and take out whoever was alive. Well, in the city, you couldn't do that. We learned something new every day, and after every callout, we critiqued what we had done and how we could improve. We were learning by the seat of our pants. We came up with all kinds of ideas—some good, some not so good.

One time, we were trying to figure out different ways to make an entry. We tried putting the shotgun man in the middle of the front door, lying down and facing the door. Somebody would kick the door open, and there he was, sitting there looking inside. As time went by, and with different input from different people, we came up with better ideas and started formulating how to implement them. We probably had two or three ways of handling every type of situation. Overall, it came down to a lot of hard training and trying to figure out what we

Larry Graham

were supposed to do and how to do it. I worked my way from shotgun to observer for the long rifle to a scout, and my last nine years, I was a team leader.

We trained constantly. One day, Jim Dahl and I were at Camp Pendleton to practice extractions. They figured if we were on top of a building in a shoot-out and they needed to pull us off the building, they were going to bring a helicopter in, hook us up, and extract us from the building. We put harnesses on, and they were supposed to be in the back of our thighs. Well, I had it in the crotch. The helicopter came in, hooked us up, and took us up nine hundred feet. We were hooked up on a single rope. As we were going up, I started to black out because I didn't have the harness on right. I told Jimmy that I was blacking out. He was maybe a foot above me. I tried to grab the rope and pull up to take the pressure off. They took us down, and we finally landed. They saw my harness and said, "Oh, this is supposed to be behind your thighs."

"Oh, you mean like this?" I said, and I adjusted it.

"Yeah, take it away." And they took us right back up nine hundred feet.

"Sweet Jesus."

When we were done, Chuck Perriguey, the pilot, said, "Well, you know, on extraction, if anything happens to the helicopter and we start to go down, we're going to have to cut the rope."

"What do you mean you're going to cut the rope?"

"The helicopter's worth X number of dollars. We got to save the helicopter."

I looked at Chuck and said, "You better hope I die, because if I live, I'm going to come looking for you for cutting the rope on me." The pilots were all ex-Vietnam pilots, and they were good.

On one callout, there was a consulate downtown, and the suspect was barricaded in the building with a victim. We didn't know it at the time, but he had poured gasoline all over the interior, and he was going to torch the inside. My lieutenant said to me, "We want you to get on the outside of the building and rappel down. When we tell you, if we have to, we want you to shoot through the glass and shoot the suspect." We learned later about the gasoline. The fire department told me that with all that gas in there, the explosion would have come right back into my face.

There are incidents that stand out because they were funny or because of screwups, or ones that were sheer tragedies. We had one callout that was inside a market, and unfortunately, the shooter was so mentally screwed up that he wasn't listening to anything the crisis negotiator said. He had the store intercom on, and from anywhere in the market, we heard the victim pleading for his life. Then we heard him being shot and killed and the suspect committing suicide. Moments like that live with you.

Most of the time, the suspects were talked out of a situation, but sometimes they were not. One time, some psycho walked out on his porch and started shooting kids on the school grounds across the street from his house. We evacuated the school and all the people from the houses nearby, and we scouted the best way to get up to his house. It was a two-story apartment house with one staircase. We finally got up to his place, only to find out that he had shot himself. Why people kill innocent victims and then commit suicide, I have absolutely no idea.

We had another callout where a little old lady was shooting rounds out of her place. We didn't know why she was upset. Jim Dahl and I and a couple others crawled up a wooden staircase to get up to this lady's apartment. It was dark, and there were no lights on inside of her apartment. Jim and I reached a place right under her kitchen window. We thought we were being quiet and nobody would hear us. All of a sudden, we heard this little old lady's voice go, "Get off my porch!" We flew down the stairs, and next thing we knew, she opened up and was shooting rounds everywhere. She must have shot thirty or forty rounds. I think Jim and I fell backward down those stairs more than anything. I'll never forget her words: "Get off my porch!"

My last nine years as a policeman in Metro, I worked with Steve Stear. Of all the great partners I worked with, Steve Stear was the best. We didn't have to say anything to each other. We just started reading each other's mind. I could say something and he would finish the thought, or he'd think of something and I'd say it. We did a lot of stakeouts together.

At the end of '74 and into '75, we were doing stakeouts for the Skid Row Slasher murders. We would get dressed up as bums—wear funky, dirty, gnarly clothes—and go into the downtown Skid Row area. We'd lie in the alleyways, waiting for the suspect to come around. Nobody knew who he was or what he looked like. We were literally waiting in the middle of the night to have some guy come try to slit our throats in order to catch him. One night, Steve and I were lying in an alleyway. Two American Indians were walking down the alley and were talking about killing somebody. As we were sitting there, they walked by us. Well, about half an hour later, they came back, and they were still talking about killing somebody. They never approached me, but they approached Steve as he pretended to be asleep. One of them said to him, "Hey, you got to get out of here or the Slasher is going to kill you." Steve was lying on a slight incline, and they started to shake him. While one of the guys kept trying to wake him up, the other guy stood above Steve on the incline and started urinating. God bless Steve—this urine was going right next to his head, along the side of his body, and into the middle of the alley. Finally, they decided they couldn't wake Steve up, so they left him alone and kept walking. He couldn't move because he was waiting to see if one—or both—of these guys was the Slasher. We didn't know if the Slasher had a partner. These two had been talking about killing somebody, so they could have actually been the suspects. Steve was waiting for them to make a furtive movement toward him, and then we would have taken action. He did not want to

Larry Graham and Steve Stear, at door, take robbery suspect into custody: "Of all the great partners I worked with, Steve Stear was the best."

break character and get up and say something. He used a lot more restraint than I ever could have. Eventually, the suspect was caught. But that stakeout went weeks on end, lying out in the middle of the alleyways, sitting on rooftops, and working holidays, including Christmas Eve. And everybody thought LAPD was glamorous.

When I first went to Metro, Lloyd Woller was a sergeant there. Lloyd was a former marine and had won the department's Medal of Valor for saving the life of a disabled motorist. He was on the freeway going home one night, and he stopped to help a disabled motorist. Somebody drove right at them, hit him, and kept going as he kept the motorist from also being hit by the car. Lloyd's leg was so damaged that he had to wear a metal brace for the rest of his career. As a former marine, he was a gruff individual, and he scared the hell out of us. But he had a heart of gold. He made lieutenant and later retired. He moved to Grass Valley, and in 1984, he passed away. The family requested an LAPD honor guard, which he had wanted, but the powers that be at the time said, "No, we can't send an honor guard up to Grass Valley for an old retired lieutenant." So four of us—Jack Hoar, Scotty Landsman, Randy Frederickson, and I—were able to borrow the honor guard equipment and flags, and we went to Grass Valley to be his honor guard. We had never been part of an honor guard before. His wife sent a letter thanking us for doing that. It was a shame that some within the department didn't care more for the people who made the department what it was.

I made sergeant out of Metro and went to Hollywood Division. One night, I responded to a call of a man with a gun. It was a male doctor who'd had an operation and become a female. He was also a gun collector and had a room full of never-out-of-the-box, brand-new guns, and his apartment was full of black powder. He came out of the place wearing bikini panties and an open robe, with breasts and a face like a Mac truck that should have never been a female to begin with. We took the guy into custody, and we spent hours booking forty or fifty guns that he had in this house. Afterward, he accused me of sexually molesting him in the station holding tank and accused a female officer of being at some sexual party he had attended earlier. He filed a lawsuit to get his weapons back after he had some disagreement with the detectives over the release of his weapons. I went to the city attorney hearing on the lawsuit. There was a young city attorney, and all she saw was the guy's female name. She looked at me as if I were dirt, as if I were guilty. She didn't give me the time of day until the doctor walked in. She took one look at the doctor, who was about six foot two and 230 pounds, and she looked at me and just started shaking her head. She came around to my viewpoint. When the doctor found out I had nothing to do with releasing the weapons, he dropped the molesting allegations. Hollywood was a strange place to work.

On the wheel, I went to Jail Division in Van Nuys and right back to Hollywood about a year later. In Hollywood, I worked both the uniform and plainclothes side of Hollywood Vice. The big problem in Hollywood was prostitution. The Hollywood area was part of a circuit—a triangle that the prostitutes followed. They worked San Diego, Los Angeles, and Seattle and then over to Hawaii and back around. In fact, we had a couple of vice officers go over to Hawaii on vacation. They happened to be walking by a street corner where some Hawaiian police officers were talking to a young lady. The vice officers recognized her as she gave the officers a false name. One of our officers heard her and said, "That's not her name. Her name is so-and-so, and we arrested her in Hollywood." The officers checked the name our guys had told them and found out she had multiple warrants. Small world.

*Wilson Wong, Mary Grace Rivera, Sgt. Larry Graham, Jim
Marshall, and Paul Hinton: Hollywood Vice, 1992*

The last year in Hollywood was the toughest year I ever had on the
job. I was just burned out. It was time to go. My time on the job was
great, and as I said, when I went into the academy, my direction was
forged. By being on the job, I became a better person. I learned to work
hard, I was dedicated, and I worked with and shared in experiences
with some of the finest people I've ever known, some of whom have
become lifelong friends.

Throughout most of my career in the department, I was involved
in sports. I played baseball my entire life, and I was fairly good. I
was on the department team, and we traveled all over the United
States. I did that for fifteen or sixteen years, primarily as a pitcher.
In my generation, everybody had a nickname. Mine was "Pig Pen."
I picked up the nickname when I was playing baseball for Seventy-
Seventh Division. We were playing a game against Newton Division,
and the game went about eighteen innings. As the catcher, I was
wearing shin guards, a chest protector, and a mask. It was about
ninety degrees. I caught the whole game, and by the end of it, the
chest protector was off and the shin protectors were off—it was
just too hot to keep wearing them. I was dirty, and I was sweaty.
Mike Gesselman said, "You look like Pig Pen in the cartoons." The
nickname just stuck. I also played on the Metro Division football
team.

*Larry Graham, front row, second from right: Metropolitan
Division football team, 1972*

One of my hobbies I got into years ago is stained-glass art. In
fact, I originally got into it by watching Mike Albanese do it. I created
two stained-glass windows—one that was placed in the Hollywood
Division station sergeants' room, which read "Sergeants' Room," and
one at the Van Nuys jail that read "You hook 'em. We book 'em." As
far as I know, both stained-glass pieces are still there. It gave me great
pleasure to be able to do something for the people I worked with on the
job.

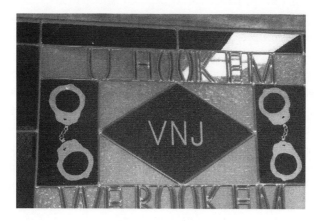

James Dahl

Birthplace: Los Angeles, California
Career: 1966–1994
Rank at Retirement: Sergeant II
Divisions: Wilshire, Highland Park, Central, West Bureau CRASH, Metropolitan

In 1966, I was a delivery driver for Coca-Cola, and with the birth of our first child, my wife agreed with me when I said, "I can't be doing this all my life." We read in the paper that LAPD was advertising for police officers. They needed them badly. "Okay, let me go take a shot at this," I said. I was only twenty years old, but I was turning twenty-one in September. I passed the test, they gave me a quick physical, and it seemed like within weeks, I was on the fast track to becoming a police officer. By October '66, I was in the academy. It was quick. They really did need officers.

In the academy, everything was spit and polish. I'd come home at night exhausted and still have more to study. My wife ironed my uniform every night while I polished my shoes and gear. We worked as a team. I know I was terrible at trying to be a decent father with changing diapers and everything. But I was dealing with the stress of the instructors and having to pass exams. There was added stress knowing that the sergeant was calling fellow classmates out of class and they were gone. I just wanted to not be noticed, to just get through.

Over Christmas break, for about a week or so, they sent us out to help direct traffic around some of the big shopping centers. When you had young guys who were still in the academy trying to direct traffic, what you were doing was just causing havoc with the traffic. We were making traffic jams everywhere. When we came back to the academy, everyone tried to relate their stories as far as being a big cop out on the

Jim Dahl

street. There were three of us assigned to a particular mall, and our story was that we had chased a shoplifter but that he had gotten away.

I graduated in the middle of my class and was assigned to Wilshire Division. It was my first division, and that was an intimidation factor right there. But I had an added factor to my probationary experience. My father-in-law worked as a clerk of the court. He was talking with a reporter from the *Los Angeles Times* newspaper who told him he wanted to do an exposé on a graduating police officer going to his first division. My father-in-law gave the reporter my name. So this reporter followed me around as I was working with these veteran officers. All these veterans were just shaking their heads. The reporter was trying to get a view from a young rookie out on the street. I probably looked like a fool, but the article made the paper.

All the veterans were on morning watch. They did a lot of police work, and they didn't take any guff from anybody. One time, we went in pursuit of a car thief. We got him pulled over, and he had a gun.

Jim Dahl, far right: stolen vehicle suspects in custody, Wilshire Division

It was the first time I'd had a suspect with a gun. It got my adrenaline going, being confronted with the reality that there were some bad guys out there with weapons. Only a few years prior to that, two detectives, Charles Monaghan and Robert Endler, had been killed at a Sears next door to Wilshire station, so I was aware of the seriousness of guys with guns.

Toward the end of my probation, I was working by myself, and I got involved in a beef for excessive force. That was the first time I'd had a complaint, and I was penalized three days. I was devastated and feeling sorry for myself. About that same time, I wheeled to Highland Park Division. I had been raised in the Highland Park area, so I was pretty familiar with the whole area. Eventually, I forgot about the beef and concentrated on doing my job. I started getting more and more respect from the command staff, and the captain assigned me to a basic car. Chief Ed Davis had just implemented the basic car plan, part of his team policing program. I was assigned as one of the lead officers in the El Sereno area. It gave me a lot of responsibility, and I was involved with the community. The team policing concept was pretty good, and I think the community really liked it.

Highland Park was a good place to work, but I was looking for more experience and more adventure, so I applied to Metro Division. Metro was hard for an officer to get into if he didn't know anybody. In those days, they'd put your picture up on a wall. If it was turned upside down, that was a rejection, and it didn't take much to get rejected. But I was accepted and went to Metro in '72. At Metro, I was working with experienced officers—the best of the best in the department.

We did various types of stakeouts, and it was important to not do anything to jeopardize the stakeout. We were working a stakeout on the Westside Rapist case. There were about thirty guys on the stakeout, and we were all over West Los Angeles. On one of the nights, my partner and I were hiding in the bushes along a wall near a Mormon temple. It was about two o'clock in the morning, and we were fighting to keep awake. The sprinkler system came on, and we sat there soaking wet, but we couldn't move, because we'd give away our position if we did. The rapist was never caught.

In '74, we got a call from Metro to respond to Fifty-Fourth and Compton Avenue. It was the Symbionese Liberation Army shoot-out. I was there near the end of the incident, stationed on the outside perimeter. Our job was to make sure that no one escaped or went in to help the suspects. Even as the house was burning, rounds were being fired from inside the house. After a while, it became obvious that it was a done deal.

About six months later, I transferred to SWAT. This was like being elevated from being in a great group to a super-great group. I mean, these guys were good. I never thought I'd have a chance to get into SWAT, but the opportunity came along, and I was accepted. SWAT was involved in things like dignitary protection and taking down barricaded suspects. My partner was Larry Simms, a gung-ho guy. At the time, we lived close to each other, and we used to run to each other's house. Our chemistry was great. He was a team leader, and he showed me from the get-go how to do basic entries and other tactical things. He made me a shotgun man. The shotgun man was usually one of the first element members through an entry point, so the pucker factor was always there for any kind of barricaded situation.

One time, we had a barricaded suspect with a child inside. The suspect was ripping out the child's fingernails. We made our entry and took him into custody. It just made us sick what he had done to that child.

We had another barricaded suspect at a high-rise hotel by the airport. The suspect was holding his girlfriend hostage in the bathroom of a hotel room. The negotiator was trying to talk the suspect out by saying "Let your girlfriend go"—that type of thing— and it went on for hours. As soon as the next shift replaced us at our positions, the suspect came out with a gun to the girl's head. An officer fired a shot, putting the suspect down, and the girl was unharmed.

After a couple of years, I made team leader. One time, I had to assign my personnel to go into a room where a guy had already killed a gal, but we knew he wasn't going to give himself up. When the door opened, I was off to the side of the door, and my entry team started going through. They saw the gun coming up, and they had to put him down. The responsibility of being a team leader was mind-boggling. Team leaders were tasked with setting up the tactics to make sure that their fellow officers were as safe as possible. Obviously, they knew what to do based on their training, but I was always thinking, *Am I setting up the right plan for this particular entry?* There was a lot of pressure on a team leader. On that particular incident, it worked out.

In 1984, before the Olympics, some Metro personnel went to Europe to train with some of the commando teams there. When they came back, we trained in some of the techniques they had learned. One technique was fast-roping. With fast-roping, we were basically coming in on helicopters, and as we approached the target spot, the crew chief threw out a big rope that was about two inches in diameter. When we were about fifty feet off the ground, our squad slid down the rope. We were essentially coming down on top of each other, but we were down in nothing flat. When we first started to learn the technique, the officers would be crashing on top of each other, and we looked like a bunch of buffoons. After a while, we got our technique down, and it worked great. In the early days, we used to rappel out of the helicopter. We had to have four guys going off at the same time to keep the ship balanced. It was a Huey—a Vietnam-era helicopter—so if the engine started coughing, it was just going to go down. In fact, the crew chief told us that. He said, "If this thing starts coughing on us, we're going to cut the ropes with an ax. You guys are expendable." It made me think of the possibilities.

SWAT Fast-Roping Technique

There were a couple of close calls in our training where we just thanked God that it wasn't our time. We were doing a training session on a fifty-story high-rise building. If we missed the roof, we were dead. When we came in, for some reason, the pilot of the helicopter didn't hold his spot and was drifting toward the edge of the building. John McCrossen was the last one on the rope, and he saw that he was drifting toward the edge of the building. There was no way to hold on to the rope, because he had too much equipment on. He was over the catwalk, and he let himself go the last ten feet and just fell down onto the catwalk—so close. Another time, we were doing a demonstration at the academy, working with the old Huey helicopter. It was in the summertime, and we were demonstrating fast-roping. I was on the rope, getting ready to go down, when the warning lights went off, and my partner grabbed me and pulled me back in. The helicopter's red warning lights meant it was losing power. We took off and needed to get lift to clear the tree line.

We had training one time moving from the top of a building over to the top of another building. The scenario was that the suspects were in one building, and we would make entry from above their location. Our job was to go up to the roof of one building with a ladder, drop the ladder across the space between the buildings, crawl across the ladder to the other roof, and work our way down to the suspects. We put the ladder across an alley to the other rooftop. We were about thirteen stories up, and we had all these drunks in the alley looking up at us as we were going across. Larry Graham got about five to ten feet across and said to me, "I ain't going across," and he started to come back. He said, "I don't care. It's not safe." We had a safety line we hooked on to, but it definitely was a pucker factor on that exercise. He had a fear of heights that day. It doesn't take much, right? Officers couldn't get any better than Larry. He was one of the top officers in the unit.

Most of our situations for SWAT included barricaded suspects. I don't know how he did this, but Sergeant Albert Preciado got us an armored personnel carrier. We painted it department colors and modified it by putting a big ram on the front. The first couple of times we used the thing, we basically took out the whole front of a house. We'd hit the house and sweep the ram back and forth a little, and the whole front of a house was gone. During one barricaded-suspect situation, once the ram was pulled out of this house, all we had to do was point to the guy and say, "Come on out." He had nothing left to hide behind.

In preparing a plan on an entry, we usually took photos to determine the best way to enter a location. One time, we were going to make entry on a house up in the Hollywood Hills. We had been told that the suspect had a .30-caliber machine gun. In looking at the photos, we noted that there was a trail behind the location in the foothills. The whole entry team, about fifteen of us, traversed this trail behind this house and neighboring backyards at about three o'clock in the morning. We were trying to be super quiet, but we had some big buffalo guys carrying rams, big armored vests, and other equipment. We made our entry from the back, breaking windows and throwing flash bangs. The whole thing went down beautifully. It was my operation, and my partner, Steve Beidle, and I had put the entry plan together. We took everybody into custody. Fortunately, there was no

.30-caliber machine gun. If there had been, somebody could have opened up on us and taken us down in nothing flat.

Sometimes things didn't go as smoothly. One time, we were in the Pacoima area, making entry into a rock-cocaine house. We were tiptoeing by the pool to get to the back door of the house. As we were getting ready to hit the back door, I heard a big splash in the pool. We looked over, and the sergeant had fallen into the pool. His radio was sparking and arcing. We tried to keep straight faces because we were in the middle of a serious situation. He managed to get himself out of the pool, and he was embarrassed. We made entry, and we got everybody out of the rock house. Afterward, we were laughing so hard.

We had so much fun in SWAT. Those were great years, but they went flying by. It became apparent after fifteen years that I could not do that forever. I think sometimes my wife and family got the short end of the stick because I was constantly being called out in the middle of the night. So I started studying to promote to sergeant.

In '85, I was in Albuquerque, training members of the Department of Energy on urban tactics. They were responsible for security of nuclear power plants, and they wanted training in current SWAT techniques. I was teaching rappelling, and one of my fellow instructors was telling me a joke at the time I was hooking up to do a demonstration. I didn't hook up right; the carabineer didn't snap. I heard it clip, but it didn't snap, and

Rick Massa, Randy Frederickson, and Jim Dahl: SWAT, 1986

I didn't look down. Once I went over, *whoosh*—down four stories. The only thing that saved me was that my hands kept me upright. I didn't fall on my back, but when I hit the ground, I swung backward and basically fractured my back. I also had a huge hematoma in my groin area. I felt so embarrassed because the accident was just due to a lack of concentration. I went to the hospital, and we thought the procedure was going well, but I ended up having a big blood clot in my groin area. When I got up to take a shower, it shifted up into my lungs, and I had a pulmonary embolism. The on-call doctor didn't respond for hours, so I was just basically dying. My blood gases were really low, and the only thing that was saving me was my conditioning from being in SWAT all those years. I was in my early forties. I was in the hospital in Albuquerque for about a month, and when I came back to Los Angeles, I spent another couple of weeks in the hospital. Metro gave me six months to get back into conditioning, and I passed the SWAT physical fitness test, but it was obvious that my body was beat up. I started studying harder to make sergeant, passed the test, and, in '88, went to Central Division.

Being a supervisor was a good learning experience for me, trying to tell these young officers who were still wet behind the ears what to do as far as tactics and how to approach the public and so forth. It was a different aspect of police work, and I was ready for it. With my SWAT background, I taught them a lot on tactics.

One night on morning watch, a patrol unit put out an assistance call. Two patrol units responded Code 3, and at one point, they collided with each other. Three of the officers were killed, and the fourth, a probationer, survived. The probationer was the only one wearing a seat belt, and it was his first day out of the academy. It was mind-boggling to lose almost half the watch in a single traffic accident. They had been responding to a fellow officer's need for assistance. That hit me pretty hard. I knew those young guys and knew how hard they worked.

A couple of years before I retired, I had an opportunity to go back to Metro in the Mounted Unit, doing police work on horseback. I thought this would be great to learn two things at once: learning how to ride and do police work on horseback. Then after I retired, if I decided to have horses, I would know how to take care of them. When I went to the riding school, it was a sight to see this big old thug on horseback. One time during training, I got bucked off and hoofed in the head.

The horses were basically given to the unit, but there was a selection process to determine which horses had the demeanor to do police work. A horse had to be able to put up with things like traffic and the sound of air brakes. We would throw firecrackers or do other distracting things to train the horses. We had to make sure they were not going to whirl on us or buck us off in the middle of the street.

I was teamed with my former partner in SWAT, Steve Beidle. He was one of the senior officers in the Mounted Unit and one of my best friends. He had also been a team leader in SWAT. Steve was one of the innovators on police tactics on horseback. He taught me how to handle horses for working patrol and making investigative stops and how to utilize a horse for working a demonstration. He showed me how to move slowly on a horse, how not to give away my moves, and how to slowly get off the horse to give me the best chance of catching someone with dope or about to commit a crime.

When we were involved in crowd control during demonstrations, sometimes those demonstrations got ugly. While we were working one demonstration near the Dorothy Chandler Pavilion, we had to make a line with our horses and keep the demonstrators back. Some of the demonstrators had squeeze bottles containing caustic chemicals, and they were trying to squeeze the bottles and shoot the chemicals into the horses' eyes. After that demonstration, we started putting shields in front of the horses' eyes. Other times, people would take a hat

Jim Dahl: Mounted Unit at scene of demonstration

pin, come up close to the horse, and stick it into the horse's neck—
the objective being to make the horse rear up and throw the officer
off. At the scene of a demonstration, we had spotters high up to watch
for these suspects, and most of the time, we were able to identify
the person and take the person into custody. We usually were pretty
successful at controlling crowds. When the demonstrators saw twelve
hundred pounds of horse coming at them or they saw the horse whirl
around with its ass end toward them, they didn't want to get stepped
on by a horse, and they usually left the location.

After twenty-seven years, I figured it was time to pull the pin. It
had been a great career as long as it had lasted, but I was done. Steve
Beidle, my last partner and close friend, had a heart attack and passed
away. When I gave his eulogy, I looked at my old partners, all with gray
hair, and it was just mind-boggling how fast the years went by. As I
think about it now, the LAPD was pretty good for me and my family.
I think back to 1966, when this young officer started the job, trying to
learn tactics and how to handle people out in the street and then slowly
working my way up, gaining experience, working with veterans, and all
that—yes, it went by pretty quickly. What a great experience.

l to r Steve Beidle, Rick Lopez, Jim Dahl, and Gil Waldron:
". . . it was just mind-boggling how fast the years went by."

James "JJ" May

Birthplace: Long Beach, California
Career: 1967–2007
Rank at Retirement: Lieutenant I
Divisions: Seventy-Seventh Street, Parking and Intersection Control, Harbor,
Public Disorder and Intelligence, Southwest, Southeast, South Bureau
CRASH, Northeast

I was working in the aerospace industry, and I didn't like the work, so I decided to pursue another career. I read in the newspaper that the LAPD was hiring and paying $640 per month. I thought being a police officer would be a good job, so I applied, went through the hiring process, and went into the academy on April 27, 1967.

Toward the end of our academy training, our class was sent to the Century City Plaza Hotel. President Lyndon Johnson was in town for a fundraiser, and there was a big protest. The department needed some additional manpower because the protest was larger than expected, and our class was the additional manpower. This was the first time we wore our blue uniforms. Once we arrived, we were directed to stand by in a subterranean room near the hotel kitchen. About an hour later, one of the squad leaders entered the room and said, "Let's go, boys."

Across from the hotel were approximately ten thousand protestors. There was a skirmish line of officers between the protestors and us. Our skirmish line was the last line of defense. When President Johnson arrived, the protestors became unruly and violent. They attempted to breach the skirmish line while swinging their signs, and the officers went into action with their old wooden batons. At one point, a couple of squads from our class were sent to reinforce the skirmish line. The protestors, though, after seeing some of their buddies getting knocked around, had no stomach for a fight and left. We had no more problems. By night's

JJ May

end, we loaded onto the buses, and Police Chief Tom Reddin took time to board each bus to thank all of the officers for their efforts that night. We only had a couple of weeks left in the academy. Our instructors were proud of us because we had stood tall that night at Century City.

After graduation, I was sent to Seventy-Seventh Street Division on night watch. My first partner was Jerry Mount. Jerry was the person who gave me my nickname, "JJ." About an hour after we left the station, we were talking, and Jerry said, "I know your first name. What's your middle name?"

I told him, "John."

Jerry told me that with my first name being James, he would call me JJ. That nickname has stuck with me ever since. No one had ever called me JJ before then.

A few weeks later, my other training officer, Sam Agrusa, decided it was time for me to drive. That night, we were on Hoover Street, approaching Manchester, when we saw a '56 Chevrolet accelerate out of a corner gas station. We thought the occupants had just committed a robbery. I pulled in behind the car, it took off, and Sam told Communications we were in pursuit. At one point, the suspect attempted to make a left turn, and as he was turning, he drove up onto

Century City protest, 1967: "The protestors, though, after seeing some of their buddies getting knocked around, had no stomach for a fight and left."

the sidewalk. I thought this was a good time to end the pursuit, so I rammed the suspect's car, causing him to lose control and run into a cement wall. Once the suspect was in custody, a sergeant approached me and said, "May, we don't ram vehicles." He walked away, and I never heard any more about it. We found out that the two suspects had only committed a forgery at the gas station.

While still on probation and working the night watch, my partner and I responded to a shooting call on Lou Dillon Street. When we arrived, the ambulance was already there, and the attendants were treating a male adult for a gunshot to his left eye. I asked him what had happened. He told me that he and his wife had gotten into an argument, and he had punched her several times. His wife had gotten a .22-caliber revolver and chased him out of the residence and around their vehicle parked in the driveway. During the chase, his wife had started shooting at him. He had counted the shots, and when she fired the sixth shot, he had told her, "Bitch, I'm going to beat your ass now." He hadn't realized that the gun was a seven-shot revolver until his wife fired the seventh round, striking him in his eye. The ambulance crew, some neighbors, and the rest of us started laughing when we heard his story. Even he chuckled after he told it.

One early morning, my partner and I responded to a help call in Newton Division. We were about six blocks away and were the first to arrive. The Newton officers had responded to a robbery call and encountered two armed suspects inside a liquor store. When we entered the store, I saw one suspect lying on the floor with a gunshot wound to his upper body and an officer standing over him. The officer told us that his partner had chased the second suspect toward the rear storage room. My partner and I ran to the back, and there was a large hole in the back wall of the liquor store. The second suspect was lying in the alley with his foot hung up on the hole in the wall. The second officer had engaged the suspect in the storage room. The officer was armed with a department Ithaca shotgun, and when he'd shot the suspect, the force of the shot had knocked the suspect through the wall. I thought, *That's the gun I want to use.*

One day, a help call came out in the Watts area. Some officers had gone in foot pursuit of a suspect. One of the officers was known as Frenchy. He chased the suspect into a storefront on 103rd Street and into a backroom. The only problem was that this was one of the headquarters for the Black Panthers. After Frenchy entered the backroom, the door shut behind him, and he found himself trapped in the room with several suspects. The cavalry arrived, the back door came down, and we got him out. At Seventy-Seventh Division, you could always depend on getting help when you were in trouble.

After probation, I was transferred to PIC, Parking and Intersection Control. I hated that assignment. When I finished my eight hours directing traffic, my back was killing me after standing in the intersection all day. One Saturday, I was standing in the middle of the intersection at Seventh and Broadway, directing traffic, when I noticed that none of the vehicles were moving or following my directions, and there were several people standing on the sidewalk, laughing. I turned around, and a drunk was standing there trying to direct traffic. I told this guy to get out of the street. He shouted back, "Fuck you." As I approached him, he came out with a pocketknife. I was standing right in

Seventh Street and Broadway: "I turned around, and a drunk was standing there trying to direct traffic."

front of him, so I slammed my hand into his shoulder, spun him around, and choked him out. I handcuffed him, dragged him over to the gutter, and called for the B-wagon. I then went back to directing traffic.

A couple years later, I was a training officer in Harbor Division. One of my favorite probationers was Jim Tatreau. One day, we were cruising an alley in San Pedro when we came upon a male adult and a thirteen-year-old male juvenile. The adult was a hype, and he was having the juvenile forge blank checks that they would cash at nearby stores. The guy's name was Archuletta. That was Jim's first arrest. Thirty years later, Jim asked me, "Remember that first guy?"

"Yeah, Archuletta."

"I can't believe you still remember his name."

I said, "Well, it wasn't often I had a redhead that worked with me."

Jim was just like me. It didn't matter what rank we were, we still had the urge to do police work. Jim was a hell of a cop and a hell of a supervisor. He had a great career and made commander. He passed away a few years ago, and I really miss him.

Jim Tatreau

I was promoted to detective and worked PDID—Public Disorder Intelligence Division—for a year and then Harbor Division narcotics. My partner was Bill Alverson, whom we called "Oaky Bill." I worked the narcotics unit for almost two years. One day, Bill and I were on surveillance at a housing development located on a hill in San Pedro. From our vantage point, we could see all the way to downtown Los Angeles. We picked up some chatter over the police radio regarding an incident that was occurring in Newton Division. We switched our radio over to a tactical frequency and learned that there was a gun battle between our SWAT unit and members of the Symbionese Liberation Army, a radical group, who were barricaded in a residence. The SLA was the group who allegedly kidnapped Patty Hearst. The battle went on for a considerable amount of time. When the officers broadcasted over the radio, we could hear the gunfire in the background. It sounded like a war. At one point, the officers broadcasted that the residence was on fire. From our location, we could see black smoke billowing into the air from the burning house. I'll always remember that.

In '75, I was promoted to sergeant and transferred to Southwest Division. I was glad to be back in a busy division. I was en route to the station to go end of watch one night when I saw a car going in the opposite direction with three guys in it. They were looking straight ahead and avoiding eye contact with me. I had a gut feeling about these guys, and as I made a U-turn, they made a quick right turn and sped off into a residential neighborhood. I pursued them for a couple of blocks until they pulled to the curb and fled on foot into the surrounding neighborhood. I put out a broadcast for assistance and set up a perimeter. Once the perimeter was set, a systematic search began. As the search was underway, I was standing near the back of the suspects' car when I heard a knocking noise from inside of the trunk. We opened the trunk and found a male adult inside. This was his car. The three suspects had carjacked him and thrown him into the trunk. I asked him why he hadn't knocked on the trunk earlier; we had been there for about twenty minutes. He told us he had heard our voices but thought we were the suspects. The guy was really scared. That night, we caught one of the suspects. The next day, the detectives told me that the suspects were responsible for numerous carjackings throughout Los Angeles. The suspects would always throw their victims into the trunk of the stolen car, and on one occasion, they had shot the victim while he was in the trunk. It was a good thing for my gut feeling, because I may have saved a life that night. With information from the guy we caught, the detectives located and arrested the other two suspects.

The new Southeast station opened up in '78. Bob Smitson, the new captain at Southeast Division, selected me to be one of his vice sergeants. One night, my partner, Bob Pritz, and I were driving eastbound on Manchester, crossing Avalon, when I saw two males run out of an alley from behind the ABC Market. It was about one o'clock in the morning, and I thought the two males were up to no good. I made a U-turn and drove south on Avalon. The two males had split up and were walking on opposite sides of the street. We decided to stop the guy who was walking on the east side of the street, because he kept looking back at us. We were the only car on the street. We stopped at the curb, and as we got out of the car, the guy, who was about fifteen feet from us, turned toward us and fired two shots from a revolver. I fell onto my back on the seat to avoid being shot and to draw my revolver. When the shots were fired, I heard what sounded like Bob's body falling on the pavement. I thought Bob had been shot. I stood up with my gun in hand, and the suspect ran across a dirt lot into an alley and then out of sight. I never did get a round off. I broadcasted a help call and ran to the other side of our car, where Bob was, and he was okay. Bob told me that when he'd heard the shots, he had hit the ground hard. We had a great response by the patrol units and quickly established a perimeter. Barney Frazier and his partner caught the suspect attempting to walk out of the perimeter. A few minutes later, one of the other patrol units arrived with a victim of an armed robbery. Our two suspects had forced our victim into the alley and had robbed him at gunpoint. The suspect who had fired at us was convicted and sentenced to seven years in prison. Years later, I received a telephone call from a detective from Robbery-Homicide Division, who told me that two weeks after the suspect had been released from prison, he had been shot and killed by another thug during an argument in a liquor store parking lot. What goes around comes around.

Eventually, I left Vice and returned to Southeast patrol as a supervisor. While assigned to the morning watch, I responded to an assistance call at 102nd and Main. One of the patrol units had been following a stolen car when the suspect had suddenly stopped and fled on foot. When I arrived, the stolen car was in the middle of the street, just east of Main Street, and the officers were a block over from me. I parked my police car behind the stolen car and activated my overhead rear emergency lights. Once I heard over the radio that the suspect was in custody, I was about to enter my car when I heard a loud, revved-up car engine behind me. I turned and saw a van bearing down on me, traveling at least sixty miles an hour. I ran toward the south side of the street to a motor home parked at the curb as the van hit the rear of my police car. The police car exploded and hit the stolen car, and both the police car and the stolen car were sent rolling across Main Street. The police car hit a stop sign and a telephone pole, and the telephone pole caught on fire. The van careened off the police car, clipped the back end of the motor home, and came to rest in the parking lot of a business just north on Main Street. Thank goodness the motor home was there. I couldn't see anything but flames ten feet in the air. My handheld radio was in the police car, and the car was engulfed in flames. I kicked in the front door of a small lock shop in order to gain access to a telephone. When the door flew open, I scared the heck out of an elderly couple who owned the lock shop. I called Communications and told them I needed help. Sergeant John Kinard, Officer Matt Jaroscak, and other officers who had been involved in the perimeter search a block away saw the wall of flame and thought I was trapped in my police car. Jaroscak ran across Main Street to see if he could pull me out. As he ran across the street, he got gasoline on his pants, and his pants caught fire. As I came out of the business, John saw me and gave me a big hug. They thought I had perished in the fire. John told me the van was on fire and the officers had broken out the van windows and pulled the two drunks out to safety. The officers received medals for their actions that night. As for me, I received a reprimand for parking my police car behind the stolen car. I was told we didn't park behind a traffic hazard. Not too long after that, at roll call one night, the officers presented me with the half-burned stop sign that my police car had hit. They also gave me a new nickname: "Nine Lives."

Detective Jan Carlson, who worked Southeast detectives, wanted to go on some ride alongs with a field supervisor to gain field experience. She was due to make lieutenant. She rode with me one night, and she got what she wished for. About an hour after we had left

JJ May's police car: "They thought I had perished in the fire."

the station, we were driving through the Jordan Downs Housing Development, and I was explaining to her what a field supervisor's responsibilities were. Jordan Downs was a hotbed for gang activity and violent crimes. We were on 102nd Street, approaching Grape Street, when I heard a gunshot. A few seconds later, I heard a second shot ring out. We then saw two young males run out from between two buildings onto the street in front of our police car. As I got out of the car, one of the guys said, "He's shooting at us." I asked them where the suspect was. He turned and stated, "There he is," and he pointed at a male adult who had just walked out from between the same two buildings that these guys had run from. He was wearing a heavy green army jacket, and he took off running across 102nd Street. I grabbed the shotgun, and I told Jan to get us some help. I paralleled the suspect as he ran across a parking lot. I yelled "Police!" and told the suspect to stop.

The suspect had a chrome-plated revolver in his right hand, and he reached around the front of his body and pointed it at me. I did not have time to shoulder the shotgun, so I brought it up to my hip and fired a shot at the suspect. The suspect stumbled and almost fell to the ground but gained his balance and continued to run. I was sure that I had hit him and was surprised that he had not gone down. I continued to chase him between two buildings and yelled again for him to stop. He swung his right arm around to under his left armpit and pointed his gun at me. This time, I stopped, shouldered the shotgun, and fired one shot. He went down immediately. As he fell onto his stomach, his gun twirled through the air and landed about seven feet in front of him. As I approached, he was attempting to crawl and get the gun. I thought, *Who is this guy—Superman?* He had been hit by numerous twelve-gauge pellets and still wanted to get his gun. His actions shocked me.

Before I knew it, I was surrounded by about a hundred people. They were on me like flies on molasses. I heard the crowd shouting, "Kill the motherfucker." I thought they were referring to me, but I soon realized that they wanted me to kill him. Jan ran through the crowd and handcuffed the suspect. Fortunately, a Highway Patrol unit and a Housing Authority Police unit were nearby, heard the shots, and came to our aid.

Hours later, I learned the suspect was extremely high on PCP. I also learned that my last shot had paralyzed him from his waist down, which still did not stop him from attempting to retrieve his gun. He had felt no pain due to the PCP. Detective Arleigh McCree, the department's firearms expert, told me I was lucky that day. Arleigh said that he had examined the suspect's firearm and discovered that the first time the suspect had pointed his weapon at me, he had pulled the trigger, but the hammer had fallen on an empty chamber. The second time the suspect had pointed his weapon at me, as he'd reached under his left armpit with his right arm, he had again pulled the trigger, but the hammer had caught part of the heavy jacket and hadn't had enough force when it struck the primer to fire. The primer had been dented only. Yeah, nine lives.

In '80, Lieutenant Sam Dacus brought me over to the South Bureau CRASH unit. The unit monitored gangs in Southwest, Southeast, Harbor, and Seventy-Seventh Divisions. Initially, I supervised a uniform squad, but later, Lieutenant Dacus and I formed a plainclothes search-warrant team. Our mission was to conduct follow-up investigations and write search warrants for gang-related crimes and dope houses operated by gang members. We became successful and effective. Over roughly a three-year period, we wrote and served, with the help of SWAT, approximately three hundred search warrants.

I was at home when I got the call that Officer Daniel Pratt had been shot and killed by gang members in Seventy-Seventh Division. I responded to the scene of the shooting at Tenth and Florence, an area claimed by the Rollin' '60s gang. Sergeant Terry Barclay, who was in charge of the command post, gave me a description and license number of the suspects' car. I searched for the car, and about ten minutes later, I found it parked at the curb in front of a residence. I notified the command post and maintained a visual on the suspects' car. Approximately thirty minutes later, SIS officers took my position. Unbeknownst to us at the time, I had just missed the suspects, who had fled to Las Vegas. They later turned themselves in and are now in prison. To honor Danny, T-shirts were made with Danny's image on the front. I still have mine.

I left the gang unit and went back to Seventy-Seventh patrol. One night, I was out on patrol when a radio call of an armed robbery at a market on Manchester and Western came out. The suspect had committed a robbery, taken the security guard's gun, and been last seen running north on Western from the market. Due to the location of the market and description of the suspect, I thought that the suspect could be a member of the Eight-Trey Gangster Crips. I decided to turn into the residential neighborhood claimed by that gang. I was getting ready to make my left turn when I observed an unmarked Metro police car with Tim Russell and Bob Hamilton. They turned onto the street that I was going to turn on, so I drove two more blocks and made my turn. At the first cross street, I made another left turn and started driving toward the street that Tim and Bob had turned on. When I reached midblock, I heard numerous gunshots and saw muzzle flashes one block north of me. I initially thought that I was being shot at, so I drove up onto the curb behind a parked vehicle for concealment, and I broadcasted, "Officer needs help. Shots fired."

A few moments later, I saw the headlights of a car traveling slowly in my direction. I took cover behind the trunk of my car. As the car drew nearer, I could see it was the unmarked police car I had seen Tim and Bob driving. I also noticed that the car had numerous bullet holes in it, but I could not see anyone inside of it. I thought that Tim and Bob had been ambushed and were down in the vehicle. I started to leave my position when I observed a police vehicle coming north toward my location. Officer Frank Montelongo was driving the police vehicle. I broadcasted over my handheld radio for Frank to hit the unmarked police vehicle head-on to stop it. He did and was successful in stopping the Metro car. I ran up to the driver's side, and there was a male black lying across the front seat. The suspect had been shot, and he was dead. A few minutes later, Tim and Bob approached us. Tim had a gunshot wound to his face, and Bob had a gunshot wound to his left forearm. They told me that they had seen the suspect and decided to stop him because he fit the description of the robbery suspect. As they'd gotten out of their police car, the suspect had engaged them in a gun battle. The suspect had then entered their police car and put it in gear to attempt to drive away, but he'd died of his gunshot wounds. He was an Eight-Trey Gangster and was the suspect from the market robbery.

Tim Russell   *Robert Hamilton*

I was at the Seventy-Seventh station finishing some paperwork when the not-guilty verdict came in for the Rodney King incident. A crowd of protestors had formed at Florence and Normandie, and when they because unruly, the officers were directed back to the station instead of requesting more manpower. I located Sergeant Nick Titiriga, the CRASH supervisor, and told him that we needed to get out to Florence and Normandie because things were getting out of hand. Nick, Officer Tom Mathews, some other officers, and I responded to the intersection. There were at least one hundred to two hundred people there. A large group of people were looting a liquor store on one corner. We received a barrage of rocks and bottles, but as we exited our police cars with our shotguns, the liquor store emptied out, and the crowd began to disperse. I told Nick to request additional units, but he told me that we had been ordered to the command post at Fifty-Fourth and Arlington. My gut feeling told me to stay, but I did not want to disobey an order. We loaded into our police cars and drove away. I had only driven a few blocks when I decided to return to the intersection. I knew it was wrong to leave, so I drove back. When we came back, the crowd was back inside, looting the liquor store again. And again, we were pelted with rocks and bottles, but as we exited our police cars, the crowd began to disperse. Within a few minutes, we were in control of the intersection. We were there for approximately ten minutes when we were again ordered to respond to the command post. I did not want to expose Nick or the other officers to any disciplinary action for disobeying a directive, so we left the scene.

When we arrived at the command post, I observed our assistant bureau commanding officer and our captain walking through the parking lot, talking to each other. I ran over to them and told them what had happened and said that if they would give me two squads of officers, I would respond back to Florence and Normandie and retake the intersection. They told me no and said to stand down.

A couple of days after the riots ended, Nick and I were told to respond to Chief Gates's office at Parker Center. We had no idea why we had been requested to go there. When we entered the chief's conference room, I observed other command staff sitting at the conference table. I noted that our captain and the assistant bureau commanding officer were not there. For the next thirty minutes or more, we told the chief what had happened that day when we responded to Florence and Normandie and when we had responded to the command post. The chief was interested in what we had to say. I told the chief that it had really bothered me that we had left the intersection that night, and I said if I'd had to do it again, I would have disobeyed orders and stayed. Chief Gates stated, "I wish you had." It was always my opinion that because of bad decisions made by others, Chief Gates suffered the wrath of the media and politicians. I really felt sorry for him because to me, he was a great chief of police.

My last arrest during my forty-year career occurred when I was a lieutenant. I was assigned to Southeast Division, supervising the Crime Intelligence Team. Southeast Division was having a major problem on day watch with residential burglaries in one corner of the division. I assigned the Bicycle Unit and Special Problems Unit to this area, but they had no luck, and the burglaries continued. One day, Officer Jude Washington and I drove out to the area. We were in the area for about twenty minutes when we saw an older male walking down the street, carrying a pillowcase that obviously had stuff in it. We followed the suspect for about five minutes and stopped him for a traffic violation. We discovered that the items he had in the pillowcase were parts of a broken piggy bank, money, and electronic

Lt. JJ May

game items, common items taken during burglaries. While we were talking to him, we heard a radio broadcast of a burglary a few blocks from our location. We went to the location and determined that the items in the suspect's pillowcase had been stolen from the place of the burglary. We placed him under arrest. The suspect pleaded guilty during trial and was sentenced to prison for a long time. He was over fifty years old, was a heroin user, and had AIDS. The detectives were able to connect him to fifty burglaries. That was a good way to end my career. I could go on forever with the stories, but suffice to say, it was a great career of good times and experiences and of being a part of the LAPD family.

Patricia "Patty" Fogerson

Birthplace: Los Angeles, California
Career: 1969–1994
Rank at Retirement: Detective III
Divisions: Wilshire, Jail, Juvenile, Highland Park, Internal Affairs, Seventy-
    Seventh Street, Public Affairs, Personnel, Devonshire, Training, North
    Hollywood, Hollywood, Bunco-Forgery

On Friday, I graduated from high school, and on Monday, I started working for the telephone company. One day on the way to work, I saw a little kid, about three years old, walking down the street by himself. I stopped, and I was able to find out where he lived. I knocked on the door of his house, and the mother had been asleep. I got to work, and I said, "I was late because this kid was walking down the street."

My supervisor said, "Well, that's mildly interesting. We're going to dock your pay."

Another day, I was driving to work, and I saw smoke up on a hill. I drove up into this hilly area and found the source of the smoke—it was just roofers. My pay was docked that day too. I was always doing things like that, which really wasn't any of my business, but I felt compelled to get involved.

Several years later, I became a service representative with the telephone company. There was a training school that the representatives took turns attending, and I was up next. It was important to me because it was a step toward promotion. Another girl went instead of me. I found out later the director was having an affair with the girl he sent. So I gave the telephone company two weeks' notice and resigned. A lady I worked with said, "Why don't you be a policewoman?" It wasn't the first time I had thought about police work. During the Watts riots in '65, I just couldn't believe that people would

Patty Fogerson, back row, far left: policewomen academy class, 1969

treat others that way, and I had wanted to help. My husband at the time had said that I couldn't join the police department, and I accepted his decision. Now I was divorced, and my son was three years old. I took the test, went through the application process, and was hired as a policewoman.

In February '69, I was in the academy, and Sergeant Gustie Bell was the first policewoman I ever saw. She was our class coordinator along with Sergeant Patty Smith. I liked Gustie because she was personable and had common sense. She was a good image for the job, had fun with the class, and sincerely cared about us all getting through.

In the academy, I was pretty quiet, but I got in trouble when we were on this one run. I commented, "Here I come to save the day!"

Everyone stopped, and Bob Smitson, our PT instructor, said, "Who said that?"

Under my breath, I said, "Mighty Mouse."

"Oh, Mighty Mouse. Which one of you is Mighty Mouse?"

Nobody said anything. Finally, I said, "I'm Mighty Mouse." Yeah, I copped out on myself. I was a "burpee queen" for a while after that, but I learned to keep my mouth shut.

"Sergeant Gustie Bell was the first policewoman I ever saw."

After I graduated, my first assignment was working the Wilshire Division front desk; then I was transferred to Jail Division, where I learned how to search prisoners and defend myself. I was there a short time and then transferred to Highland Park Division. I worked sex crimes with Detective Rita Knecht. I learned an awful lot from Rita. When I finished probation, I stayed at Highland Park and worked the front desk. If I had questions, I used to call Sergeant Lomie Hall, who was working the detective desk at the time. She was pleasant, helpful, and informative and answered whatever questions I had. She also trained student workers. She always looked out for us. She told me one time, "If you go out with the guys from work, never let them see you drunk." I always remembered that.

While at Highland Park, I saw my first dead body. I went to the location with the detectives. The man had taken sleeping pills and had written a letter to his family. It was not bloody or anything, but the man was in bed, and his mouth was wide open. My big thing was *Am I going to cry? Am I going to throw up? Or am I going to pass out? What am I going to do here?* You don't know what your reaction is going to be when you see a dead body. Fortunately, I didn't do any of those things.

Ad Vice was investigating a modeling agency for prostitution activities, and I was loaned to Ad Vice to work undercover posing as a model. I was dressed in a hippie look, and I had a wire on, with my fellow investigators listening in on the conversation. I handed the guy my business card, which read "Marvin's Models."

The guy said, "Marvin's Models? They're a bunch of cops."

I said, "You're kidding me!" I started laughing because I got scared.

He said, "You're not a cop, are you?"

"No, I'm not a cop."

"Well, we're going to have to make sure. You're going to have to take your clothes off."

I said, "I can't, because it's my time of the month, and I'm sunburned," which I was, and I kept peeling off my skin.

"Well, you got to take off your clothes."

"Ah, I don't need to take off my clothes. You can see what I look like." I was going on and on, but I kept laughing when they would say things to me.

"You don't have to worry about it if it is your time of the month. We'll just shoot around it," the guy said finally, and they made some crude remarks. Well, the crude remarks they made embarrassed me because I knew the detectives were listening, so I laughed again. These guys thought I was stoned because I was laughing so much. Finally, they gave me a violation.

Because I acted embarrassed by what they were saying, this one guy said, "Well, this guy's gay. You don't care if he's gay, do you, and have sex with him?"

I said, "No, I don't care. Every cat to his own sandbox."

They started laughing at that, and I went out the door and signaled, and the arrests were made. I went back to the van, where the detectives were listening in on the conversation. They just roared laughing over that. It was a good case.

At Highland Park, I worked the Youth Services program and started the Ladies Assisting Cops Enthusiastically program, or LACE. It was a women's booster organization. I wanted a feminine-sounding name yet one that would tell what the girls did, so I came up with LACE. That organization still exists. I also started the Law

Enforcement Explorer Girls, and we called them LEEGS, so we had LACE and LEEGS. You probably couldn't do that nowadays.

I was loaned to Seventy-Seventh Division to take over their Youth Services program. I was used to ten or fifteen girls in my youth group at Highland Park. At the first meeting at Seventy-Seventh, when I walked in, there were thirty kids there. It was a ruckus with no discipline—nothing. They were all yelling, screaming, and carrying on. My aunt taught me how to whistle like a guy, so I whistled, and they all turned around and looked. I said, "Sit down!" and they did. I started with thirty, and by the time I had screened out the ones who were not serious about it, I had fifteen to twenty good girls. I got a little bit of heat from the community because this so-called white chick had come in and taken over. Some said, "She's prejudiced, and she didn't want the black kids."

Then one day, I was at a meeting with Mrs. Estelle Van Meter, an elderly black community activist who lived in Seventy-Seventh Division. She was running the meeting. This was in the days of short skirts, and I went to the meeting wearing a miniskirt. That was the style. She was sitting in a chair, and she looked me over and said, "How old are you?"

"I'm twenty-eight. How old are you?" Stupid, stupid thing to say. I came on the job when I was twenty-four years old, and people mature as they gain experience. That moment was part of my growing up. Once she saw that I was a disciplinarian and had turned out some pretty good girls, she was my backup after that. She'd tell people, "Leave her alone; she's doing a good job." Whether you were the captain or an officer, it was good to have Mrs. Van Meter on your side.

The deputy chief in charge of Personnel and Training Bureau thought there were not enough women in the police officer program. I was now working recruitment, and he told me, "I want you to recruit women who are already on the job to return to the academy in a modified program to become police officers." He said the women would not have to do the same program as the men. I recruited seventeen women from the department for the modified program. We later discovered the program was not going to be as modified as was first offered. Some of the women were established in their positions and decided to not participate. Eventually, four of us entered the program: me, Jeannie Eisentraut, Barbara Blodgett, and Kissy Mixen—all policewomen.

My academy class was January 1975. We did everything the same as the men. As part of the modified program, we were allowed to keep our policewoman badges, retain our ranks, and wear blue uniforms, not the khaki uniforms worn by the recruits. However, one day while we were still in the academy, a captain looked at our badges and asked why we hadn't changed to police-officer badges. We said we had an agreement with the deputy chief. A few days later, we were told we were going to be issued police-officer badges. We said, "No, we have an agreement with the deputy chief."

"He doesn't remember that agreement."

So we had to change badges.

After graduation from the academy, I went to Devonshire Division. I was the first female to work Devonshire as a police officer. The officers knew that I had been a policewoman. I went to day watch because, at least in Devonshire Division, women were not allowed to work nights. At first, the guys were protective. One of my partners said, "Do I open the door for you?"

Jeannie Eisentraut, Barbara Blodgett, Patty Fogerson, Julie Short, and Suni Cookson: academy graduation, 1975

"No, you don't open the door for me," I said.

My first training officer, Jim Murphy, was a P3, and there I was with P3 stripes on, the same as him. He was a good old-fashioned training officer who took pride in training. He was okay with my time on the job and had no problem with my rank.

Later, I went to Hollywood Division as a detective trainee and worked sex crimes. One day, some women from the Commission on the Status of Women came into the station to see how we were treating rape victims. I happened to have a victim who didn't know where she had been raped, and I was going to take her out to try to find the location where it had happened. The women from the commission went with us. After a while, we found the house, and it happened to be in Rampart Division, the division that later handled the case. On that same day, I got a call asking for a crisis negotiator, a job for which I had been trained. I dropped off the women from the commission at the station and responded to the crisis situation, a jumper. When I arrived, it was just like in the *Superman* movies—the crowd was all looking up. After I was given a briefing, I started to talk to the jumper, but there was some guy across the way in another building yelling, "Jump! Jump. You don't have any guts if you don't jump."

I said, "Get him out of there."

They got the guy who was yelling, and I again started talking to this jumper. Apparently, it was on the news, and this jumper had some connection with the boxer Muhammad Ali. Muhammad Ali lived near there, and he came to the scene. I was ordered to let Ali talk to the jumper, which he did, and he talked the guy out of jumping. The police management at the scene were so caught up in Muhammad Ali being there and Ali being the hero, they let him take the jumper in his Rolls-Royce and leave. Later on, I heard Ali had bought the guy a car and tried to help him. But the guy was nuts and wrapped the car around a telephone pole. He really needed medical attention. That was the only crisis negotiation I was called out on, but it was a good experience for me.

There was one case I handled at Hollywood in which I became personally involved. A young girl went to a teenage club where teenagers could go in and drink nonalcoholic beverages and dance just like at a regular adult nightclub. She went with a girlfriend, but when the girlfriend wanted to leave, the girlfriend couldn't find her. The next morning, the girl had not come home, her car was still in the parking lot of the club, and her parents reported her missing. On the missing report, she was listed as five foot nine with blonde hair. I got involved with it because I had responded to the hospital where an unconscious, badly beaten-up young female was being treated. She had been left for dead behind a building not far from the same club the missing girl had gone to. She was listed as five foot six. She had so much blood in her hair that they didn't know what color her hair was, so her hair was listed as red. It was believed she had been sexually assaulted. When she regained consciousness, she didn't know who she was and had no memory of what had happened. I now had a victim in the hospital, and I didn't know who she was.

I checked the missing person's reports and came up with the report for the girl from the club. I talked to the parents, and they offered that their daughter had a freckle on the inside of her finger. I checked my victim, and she had a freckle on the inside of her finger; it was the missing girl. Now I had her identified, but she did not know her parents. They eventually put her in a home. Four months later, when she woke up one morning, part of her memory was back. The swelling in her brain had gone down. She recognized her parents but had no recollection of the night she was reported missing or of being raped. We never developed a solid lead on the case. As time passed, the parents would call and tell me how their daughter was doing. Her parents both had professional positions, but they had to make adjustments to take care of their daughter. Her sister also moved out from New York to help care for her. I kept in touch, and they sent me Christmas cards and things like that. The family later moved to Santa Barbara.

One day about seven years later, I got a call from a detective with the Santa Barbara Police Department. He asked, "Do you remember this particular person's case?"

"Yes, I do."

"Can you tell me anything about it?"

I told him everything I knew.

"Well, we have a head and the left arm of a woman up here that we believe is that girl." He said, "Can you tell me anything that can identify her?"

"Well, she has a freckle on the inside of her left finger."

It was her. What had happened was she had been thin and beautiful. She had always felt guilty about the fact that she could never identify anybody from the rape or remember what had happened to her. Because of the guilt, she had become heavy and had to go to therapy for being overweight. She had never really recovered. Her mother had gotten her a job, but the job was somewhat mundane. She had responded to an ad for a job as a nanny and met someone in the parking lot of a supermarket. She was never seen again until they found her body parts. I went to the funeral. It was tragic. I kept in contact with the Santa Barbara detectives, and one day, a woman called them and reported that her boyfriend had threatened to chop her up "like I did that other girl." Long story short, the detectives thought this boyfriend was the one who had killed her, but they couldn't prove anything.

After a while, I wanted a change from working sex crimes, and I started working the Robbery table. I was the first woman to work Robbery at Hollywood. I loved the job because I didn't have to worry about what the victims were wearing when they were robbed.

During the '84 Olympics, I worked a pickpocket detail out of Forgery Division, where I was now assigned as a detective trainee. We were taught to look for people who were looking down and not up, anything unusual and out of the ordinary. We didn't make any arrests of pickpockets, but we did arrest the so-called Olympic flasher. There were many people at the tables where Olympic pins were being sold. The people were four and five deep at these tables, all trying to get close. I saw a guy moving around, but he was moving differently from everybody else. I got closer and saw what he was doing. He had his penis out, and he was rubbing it against a lady who was looking at pins. She had no clue. He was drunk. I grabbed him and started to pull him out of the crowd. All of a sudden, people surrounded us and were yelling, "Leave him alone!"

I yelled, "He's exposing himself!"

And they said, "Whoa."

We also arrested scalpers. My partner and I were talking, and a guy motioned to us and said, "Come here. Come over here away from the cops." We went over to him, and he warned us there were police around. "I've got these tickets. I have one ticket to the closing ceremony, so you can take turns coming and going." He was asking for $300.

My partner said to me, "Shall we do it?"

"I don't know. What do you think, honey?"

"Well, I don't know."

"Oh, honey, I think we should."

"Okay."

We reached into our pockets, badged him, and made the arrest. We didn't arrest any pickpockets, but we did arrest a lot of scalpers.

Sergeant Frank Whitman called me and offered me a job to teach at the academy. I accepted, and I taught report writing. After I had been at the academy for a while, Frank put me in charge of a recruit class. I felt so honored that he had felt I could be a drill instructor. I had to bite my tongue to keep from crying. I didn't cry, but he could tell I was welling up, and I think to save me and to give me a little space, he said, "Okay, Fogerson, now get out of here."

Frank was great. With him, one day was one day. We could get in trouble one day, and the next day was a clean slate—everything was fine—which I think is an important lesson. I had two classes: March '87, "Fogerson's First and Finest," and July '87. I was the first female drill instructor at the academy for classes with male recruits. That was a great job.

On the first day when a class started, the recruits typically milled around, waiting. The instructors looked forward to it because we would hope that they'd be milling around, and we'd come in and start yelling at them.

"What are you doing standing around here?"

"Get on that black line."

"Pick up your things."

"Why are you wearing a pink shirt? Are you a girl?"

The things we would say to those people. My second class, though, had gotten the word on what to do, and they were all lined up on the black line when we walked in. To mess with them, we made them go to another black line. They were also lined up tallest to the shortest, and we had them do the opposite—the shortest to the tallest. There was one woman in the class: Patricia Ferguson. I said, "See what my name is?

"Yes, ma'am."

"You have four words to remember on this department and your entire career: 'I'm not Pat Fogerson.' You keep that in mind."

She had a really good career, and every time we'd see each other, we'd laugh. I had another gal who was small in stature. There was a five-foot-four minimum-height requirement at that time. I wasn't so sure this gal was that height. I asked her, "How tall are you?"

Sgt. Frank Whitman: "With him, one day was one day."

She said, "Five foot four, ma'am."

I said, "No, you're not." And she copped out. I said, "You must have passed your physical."

"Yes, ma'am."

"Okay, from now on, when people ask you how tall you are, you say, 'I'm six feet on the inside.'"

To this day, whenever I see her, she says, "I'm six feet on the inside." I'm always pleased when I later meet officers again and they remember something I did that meant a lot to them from their academy experience. It also gave me a lot of pride seeing them graduate. It was my biggest accomplishment when I finally got these kids—I called them kids—through the academy.

In '89, I made sergeant and went back to Hollywood Division. I liked being a sergeant, and the adjustment wasn't too difficult. One time, a radio call came out involving a man with a possible gun. I was around the corner from the call, and I saw flashing red lights and heard sirens coming my way. The officers weren't supposed to use their emergency equipment. Of course, they turned the equipment off by the time they got to me. We handled the call, and there was no gun. Afterward, I said to them, "Did you see that fire truck go by just as you guys were coming up?"

"What fire truck?"

"You know, the fire truck that had all the red lights and sirens on that came by just about the same time you did." They got the message.

My concern was always about overdriving. One kid from one of the classes I had put through the academy was one of the three officers killed in Central Division when his police car and another police car were responding to a backup request and collided with each other. That was my big push to not overdrive.

When I made detective, I went to Bunco-Forgery Division. Because of my sex-crime investigative experience, I was loaned to Robbery-Homicide for the investigation of Brandon Tholmer, a serial rapist and murderer of elderly ladies. He would stalk his victims, go into their houses, rape them, and then bludgeon or stab them to death. There were a series of murders, rapes, and robberies by this guy. Before we identified Tholmer, we had reviewed three years of crime reports with similarities in MOs. Ultimately, the investigation narrowed down to Tholmer. SIS followed him and caught him looking in the window of an elderly lady's house. He was convicted and is now serving life terms for four of the murders. This was in the early '80s. He was also suspected of being the West Side Rapist from the late '70s, but it could not be proven.

I participated in the Police Olympics from 1969 to 1979. I ran the 100, the 220, the 440, and several long-distance events. I had no prior running experience, with the exception of running to the goal posts as a cheerleader in high school. When our team scored a touchdown, the cheerleaders would run to the goal posts and bow down. I always

CALIFORNIA POLICE ATHLETIC FEDERATION
Fourth Police Olympics
1970

R E S U L T S   Long Beach, California

-13-

TRACK and FIELD - WOMEN

100 Yard Dash				220 Yard Dash		
1 - P. FORGERSON	12.9	L.A.P.D.		1 - P. FORGERSON	30.3	L.A.P.D.
2 - L. WOOD	13.2	L.A.S.O.		2 - E. COOKS	32.3	L.A.S.O.
3 - J. CABE	13.9	L.A.S.O.		3 - L. WOOD	32.6	L.A.S.O.
4 - L. ETRUCKUS	14.7	L.A.S.O.		4 - I. D'ALBERO	33.9	L.A.S.O.
5 - N. BAILEY	14.8	King City P.D.		5 - N. BAILEY	34.8	King City P.D.

440 Yard Dash				Long Jump		
1 - P. FORGERSON	10.74	L.A.P.D.		1 - L. WOOD	12'6-3/4"	L.A.S.O.
2 - J. CABE	11.46	L.A.S.O.		2 - P. FORGERSON	12'1-3/4"	L.A.P.D.
3 - I. D'ALBERO	11.95	L.A.S.O.		3 - J. CABE	12'1-1/2"	L.A.S.O.
				4 - N. BAILEY	11'1-1/4"	King City P.D.

beat the boy cheerleaders. My running career started in '69, when I
worked out with Officer David Wheeler, who was training to compete
in the decathlon. Bob Burke saw me running with Dave. Bob needed
a women's team for the Police Olympics, talked me into going out for
the team, and became my personal coach. I didn't know it at first, but
I *was* the team. Bob trained me for all of the events—the 100, 220, 440,
and mile, as well as the long jump. In 1970, at the Police Olympics in
Long Beach, I won gold medals for all of the events, with the exception
of the long jump, in which I took second. In '71, I won all the female
track events at the Police Olympics in San Diego. That same year, I
competed in the International Competition in Tulsa, Oklahoma. I won
all of the women's track events except for the hundred-yard dash. As
time went on, there were more women on the team, and we were able
to run in the relays as well. I competed for ten years. I was also the first
female on the Los Angeles Police Revolver and Athletic Club board of
directors. Not bad for a high school cheerleader.

*Los Angeles Police Revolver and Athletic Club Board of
Directors,1984: Standing l to r: Bob Smitson, Frank Kanne,
William Burke, Lorne Kramer, Michael Albanese, Patrick
Connelly. Sitting l to r: Chuck Foote, Larry Moore, Patrick
McKinley, Dick Newell, Patty Fogerson*

I also ran in the first Death Valley Race for law enforcement, which later became the Baker to Vegas Relay race. I continued to run in those races for several years, and I was honored by being the captain of the team. I ran in the first Los Angeles Marathon, and I have competed in two more marathons since then. I still compete in local 5K races in the "old lady" category.

In March '94, I retired. My world changed when I joined the police department, and I learned a lot about life. I have friendships from my time on the job that continue to this day. I am the past president of the Los Angeles Policewomen's Association, and I still socialize with the Legendary Ladies, an organization of retired policewomen, and with the Los Angeles Police Officers and Associates Organization. Like taking that kid home or finding the smoke on the hill, I'm still involved, and I have no worries about getting my pay docked!

Richard "Dick" Eyster

Birthplace: Los Angeles, California
Career: 1969–1999
Rank at Retirement: Sergeant II + III
Divisions: West Valley, Press Relations Section, Wilshire, Internal Affairs, Air
   Support, Training

In 1968, I was an engineering major at San Fernando Valley State College in Northridge. I wanted to get my degree and go into the air force. My friend Dave Buck and I wanted to be fighter pilots after college. I signed up for my fifteen units to keep myself out of the military draft so that I could finish school. Sometimes planning never works out in life. There was a printing error in the catalogue of classes, and I ended up with fourteen units. Dave was in the same situation, and we knew we would be drafted. We both looked at the police department for an occupational deferment so that we could finish college. We applied and entered the academy in March 1969. Three weeks after I was in the academy, I received my draft notice. I went down to the recruiting center, totally expecting to end up in their choice of whatever service they wanted to put me in. I spoke with a colonel, and I showed him my badge. He said, "You're an LA police officer. You stay and fight the war going on here. I can get all the people I need," and he kicked me loose.

We started with sixty people in my academy class, and we graduated thirty-six. If a recruit failed one test back then, he was out. Nowadays, they help people and provide remediation so that they don't have to go through the whole hiring process again. It was during my time in the academy that Neil Armstrong and Buzz Aldrin landed on the moon. I was an aviation fan with a private pilot's license, so for me, their feat was special.

Dick Eyster, back row, far right: academy class, 1969

On our month out in the field, I was sent to Devonshire Division. On my first day, I was assigned to a traffic car. My partner said to me, "Kid, we probably won't even get a traffic-accident investigation today."

We were about ten minutes out of the Devonshire station when, all of a sudden, it sounded as if our front window exploded. A sniper in some bushes had shot out our front window. I found out that a person can actually get under the glued-down floor mat pretty easily! We put out a help call. Neither of us was hurt. The window had been hit, but the round had glanced off. The suspect wasn't caught, but we found some .22-caliber spent rounds. He'd probably been shooting at cars and happened to hit ours. I thought, *If this is Devonshire and nothing happens, what is Seventy-Seventh like?* After we graduated, Dave Buck and I were both assigned to West Valley Division.

One night, my partner and I were cruising a residential area. I was the passenger. I looked over to one house and saw a big, round bush and the barrel of a rifle pointing out of it. We were going slowly, and the barrel was following us, as if it were tracking us. I yelled to my partner, "There's somebody with a gun in the bush."

We stopped and drew our weapons. We couldn't really see who was behind the bush, but we yelled for the person to throw the gun out.

Dick Eyster and Dave Buck

Finally, the person threw the gun out, and a ten-year-old kid stood up. It was a pellet gun. We knocked on the door of his house, and his mom was there. We told his mom what had happened. She told us she was really upset with her husband for getting the gun in the first place. She took the barrel, and she just beat the heck out of this pellet gun on the concrete steps. She said, "With what's left, I'm going to start on my husband tonight."

In '69, while I was at West Valley, I got my first ride in the Bell 47 police helicopter as an observer. At that time, they were testing the helicopter to see if it was effective in reducing crime. That was the day of the parking-lot observer. The observers were only at West Valley and Southwest Divisions. The pilot would fly in, and he'd pick up the observer in the station parking lot. Lieutenant Frank Mullins knew I had a private pilot's license and wouldn't get airsick. One day, he called me into the station and said, "The observer's in court, and we need someone to go in the helicopter. Take a baseball cap, a notepad, your map book, and a couple of pencils, and when they land here, the pilot will tell you what to do."

Bell 47 helicopter, LAPD

There were no doors on the helicopter; we just hopped in. I had my binoculars around my neck and tried not to drop my map book out the door. That was my first experience in the helicopter. Fortunately, I had grown up in the San Fernando Valley, and I knew the area. We went to a couple of calls, and I directed the police cars in. After a while, the pilot said, "Hey, you're good. You know your way around." So they put in a good word with the lieutenant, and anytime they needed a relief observer, I got to do it. For most of 1970, I was the relief for the observer, Barry Bowman.

In January '71, I became a training officer at West Valley, and in '72, I was assigned to the chief's office in press relations. I was the backup driver and bodyguard for Chief Ed Davis. There was no formal training other than learning how to drive a big Chrysler and a big Oldsmobile. When I wasn't driving him around, I worked in the press relations office. On the day of the Symbionese Liberation Army shoot-out, Lieutenant Dan Cook, who was in charge of press relations, and Commander Pete Hagen went down to Fifty-Fourth and Compton, where the shooting took place and the house burned. I had the office to myself, answering five phones, including some calls from as far away as Italy. The interest was in Patty Hearst, who had been kidnapped by the SLA group. It was call after call after call, and the closest I got to the scene was looking out the window of Parker Center on the sixth floor and seeing the smoke coming up from the burning house.

Chief Davis was intelligent and a nice person, and I got along with him quite well. Once in a while, he would say things that generated some controversy in the news media, including the use of a submarine. I asked him, "Why did you tell them we could use a submarine?"

He said he was throwing stuff out to get attention that we needed drug interdiction on the high seas because drugs were coming in through the harbor or being dropped off at the beaches. He said, "Yeah. If the military gave us a submarine, I'd find a use for it to help the city." The news media turned his statements into having a submarine to spy on the drunks in MacArthur Park. He also said, and I'm paraphrasing, "Hang them on the gallows at the airport if you catch these terrorists," in reference to hijackers. But what the media didn't add was this part: "We would hang them with due process." The media forgot the "due process" part. They made him out to be "Crazy Ed." He didn't mind. He just wanted to get matters of attention out to the public, so he put up with the media.

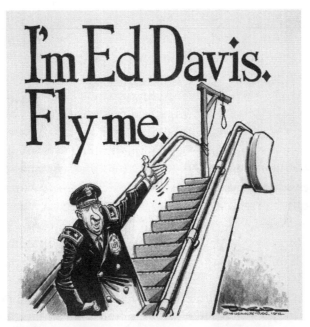

LA Times cartoonist Paul Conrad's drawing of Chief Ed Davis: "He also said, and I'm paraphrasing, 'Hang them on the gallows at the airport if you catch these terrorists,' in reference to hijackers."

When I was promoted to sergeant, I was assigned to Wilshire Division. Wilshire certainly was a much busier division than West Valley. I learned a lot from the senior officers. I've always been a person who had a philosophy of not micromanaging. If I saw something that I knew was going sideways, I'd jump in and help, but I didn't get in the way of people doing their work. Anybody who's ever been in the police department knows there are times when you have the world on your shoulders. You don't need some sergeant yapping in your ear a bunch of nonsense.

Probably the biggest thing that happened to me at Wilshire was a bank robbery at the Bank of America at First and Larchmont. That was July 12, 1976. Steve La Roche had just been in a pursuit of a purse snatcher. There had been a big accident at the end of the pursuit, and I was handling that. When we finished, we went back to the station. As we were both pulling into the parking lot of the station, we heard a robbery call at the Bank of America. Jim Copeland and Ray Hernandez, in uniform, responded to the bank. As Steve and I were walking into Wilshire station, the front desk officer put a message out over the public-address system: "Bank of America—shots fired."

Everybody jumped in their cars and went to First and Larchmont. Steve and another officer jumped in my car, and we responded. I stopped a block short because I was the first supervisor at the scene, and I was going to set up things. We had an air unit overhead. The pilot was Lieutenant Cliff Owens, and the observer was Officer George Lafferty. They were trying to get somebody to come up to the bank and block a driveway. The other driveway had already been blocked. The suspects were exiting the bank with hostages and getting in their car—two suspects and three female hostages. I told the air unit I would block the driveway. Steve and the other officer were already out of the car, working their way up to the bank. As I was pulling up, the suspects' car came out of the driveway right in front of me, and the chase was on. The pursuit went for quite a few miles, shots being fired by the suspects the whole time. There was a suspect in the backseat, and a female hostage was on either side of him. The other suspect was driving, and the third female hostage was in the front passenger seat. The suspects had several guns and a shotgun. The guy in the backseat blew his back window out so that he could shoot at me. He probably fired thirty or forty rounds at me throughout the course of the pursuit. Fortunately, only buckshot hit the car and kind of bounced off. They never got a direct hit. Some of the other police cars following were hit though.

At one point, another sergeant came off of a side street and cut in between the suspects and me. The front window of his car got hit by probably a .357 round, and he went a little ways and was then out of the pursuit. I was back as the primary. On Wilshire, near Detroit, the suspect suddenly veered over the center divider. By the time I could try to turn, traffic had surrounded me, and I couldn't get over the divider.

I was disengaged from the pursuit at that point, but I went up La Brea, paralleling it. The pursuit terminated on Beverly at Irving, where there was a shoot-out. One suspect was killed, and one of the hostages—a seventy-eight-year-old lady—was hit in the forehead with a fragment of a .38 round and died also. I'll never forget her name: Osee Newfield. The other two hostages—a forty-five-year-old bank teller and a sixteen-year-old who had been in the bank to open up an account—were all right. The second suspect was captured. A lot of people did some brave things. I've never had that many rounds fired at me before or since. Because they had hostages, we kept going and did what we needed to do—it was part of our work.

I was in court for the one suspect who had survived. I was speaking with one of the bank tellers, a male in his early twenties, who said he couldn't believe how vicious the bank robbers were. The robbers had told a male customer in the bank to drive the getaway car, and he'd said no. They had put a gun to his face and pulled the trigger, but he had put both of his hands up and diverted the bullet from his face. His hands had been injured. Both suspects had previously gone to prison for bank robbery and had been out six weeks and were back at it. Obviously, they hadn't gotten enough time. That was probably the hairiest caper I was involved in, certainly at Wilshire and probably the whole time on the job. Everybody has one at some point.

After Wilshire, I went to Internal Affairs for about eighteen months. That was the most stressful job during my career. Along with Sergeant Terry Cunningham, we started the Benefit Abuse Team. The focus of the team was employees who were suspected of abusing their benefits. We did a lot of surveillance work and were able to show in most cases that the officers had not abused their benefits and that the allegations stemmed from a family dispute or something similar. One time, I needed to scout for an upcoming surveillance. I was up in the

Dick Eyster, pilot, left: LAPD Jet Ranger helicopter

helicopter, and Barry Bowman from West Valley, way back when, was now a pilot at Air Support Division. He said, "There are a couple sergeant openings coming up in the next year or so."

When we got back from scouting an area for surveillance, I went in and talked to the captain. He said, "Well, you need a commercial license," which I did not have. He said, "If you get that, we can talk."

The commercial license could be fixed wing; it didn't have to be helicopter. They just wanted a commercial rating to show that pilots had experience. I talked to my wife about it and told her it was something I wanted to do—have a flying career. She agreed and was supportive. I spent a lot of money in a quick period of time for the commercial rating. I drained our savings down to the last hundred dollars to get the hours of flying time, but I got it. I interviewed with the captain and got a supervisor pilot position in the summer of '79.

My training started on the Bell 47. It was the bubble type and had pretty old technology, but if a pilot could learn to handle those, he was good. Then I progressed to the Jet Ranger. In 1988, the department got rid of the last Bell 47s and brought in the new AStars built by Aerospatiale. They were faster and had bigger windows than the Jet Rangers, and they had an environmental-control unit—in other words, air-conditioning. The Jet Ranger was lovingly referred to as the "Sweat Ranger." You could literally lose five pounds on a two-hour flight in the heat. There was no good way to get air inside of it. There were a couple of vents, but the air blew down onto our boots. With the rest of our equipment and our gloves and helmets, it got pretty hot.

One night, we were in the new AStar helicopter, ready to head back to the heliport. Officer Mel Stevenson was my observer, and we had a Crime Watch photographer on a ride along in the backseat. While over Southwest Division, we heard a radio call involving a gang in Newton Division. We were just hauling toward the call when Mel said, "Hey, Sarge, I think the call is a little behind us now." As I reached down, my glove hit the hydraulic switch and turned off the hydraulics. Instantly when that happened, an obnoxious warning horn went off that was very loud, and a light on the emergency-indicator panel came on. The helicopter violently jerked to the right, and it was basically like driving a big rig without any power steering. The helicopter inverted. It was the only time that I have every flown a helicopter upside down. I was able to get it back upright as we pulled out maybe fifty feet above the trees and telephone poles. That was just an inadvertent thing that happened with the hydraulic switch. Aerospatiale has since redesigned the craft differently so that this type of dangerous situation won't happen again. The photographer in the backseat had been a photographer in Vietnam and had been in a few helicopters that were shot down. He wasn't upset by it at all.

I was in charge of our surveillance section for probably seven of the fifteen years that I worked air support. One particular instance, kind of comical, could have had a bad outcome but didn't. We were at about thirty-five hundred feet over North Hollywood one late afternoon. I had a detective from SIS with me. He was on the binoculars and directing his ground units, who were following some robbery suspects. We were a little bit south and west of Burbank Airport. Well, every afternoon, when the shuttle flights left Burbank, they headed south, turned west, and climbed right to the level where we were. We were in communications with the Burbank tower, and they told us a Southwest jet was taking off and would climb to three thousand feet and said for us to stay at thirty-five hundred feet. A five-hundred-foot separation— that was enough room. I watched the jet taking off, and the detective was looking down to the ground at the surveillance. The jet's headlights were steady, and they were just getting bigger. Well, that meant it was on a direct course. If you've ever seen a picture of a deer in headlights, that was me. I figured, *When he gets up to three thousand feet, he'll level off.* He didn't. I started grabbing some air—3,600 . . . 3,700 . . . 3,800 . . .

3,900 feet—and the jet came under us by probably one hundred to two hundred feet. It was close. I had told the detective earlier, "Don't worry—it's not going to hit us," and then the jet went right under us. He never looked up; he never jerked. He was looking through the binoculars and just said, "Hey, the stewardess is serving orange juice!" He went right back to following the movements of the suspects on the ground. He never blinked. I thought, *What nerves of steel that guy has.*

In '82, I worked aerial surveillance with Internal Affairs and the district attorney's office on the Hollywood burglar scandal involving two Hollywood officers. The officers were working a burglary car and had set up some burglaries to help themselves in taking stuff. They would load up the trunk of the police car and off-load the stolen stuff into their personal cars. I had previously worked Internal Affairs, so I was asked to do the flying. For several nights during the investigation, we would be at ten thousand feet all night long. I had an SIS detective with me. That investigation started because one day, the police car with the stolen stuff was returning to the station and got in an accident, and the trunk popped open. A detective happened to go by, stopped to help with the accident, and saw the stuff. "Oh, what's all the stuff?"

"Oh, we're taking it for prints."

The detective later asked a burglary detective whether there had been hits on the prints from the items that he had seen in the police car. The burglary detective didn't know anything about it, and they started putting two and two together. Also, the two officers were selling some of the stuff that they had taken to other officers. Those two officers were arrested. One went to jail, and the other one died in a traffic accident. It was really sad when that stuff happened—when officers became criminals. It was not prevalent by any means. Some departments were wracked with corruption, but anybody who thought our department didn't go after a bad cop was wrong.

We had a helicopter crash in March '83. It was an El Niño year, and we had a tornado down on South Broadway. At Fifty-First and Broadway, a command post was set up for the aftermath of the tornado, and we had a helicopter overhead. They needed another helicopter as a relief. We were still stationed at the Glendale Heliport, and Sergeant Ron Hansen and I were there. Ron and Officer Tom Brooks, an observer, flew down there. Reserve Officer Stu Tiara was operating the camera system on the helicopter at the scene, and he was the only one who knew how to use it. He was going to transfer over to Ron's helicopter. Ron landed in the street, picked up Stu, and took off. In that awful storm, the helicopter hit a wire on takeoff, causing it to crash. All three survived the crash, but the helicopter was leaning over on its left. The blades were still turning, but they were within two feet of the ground on one side. The fuel tank split, and fuel was coming out. Stu was in the backseat and got out through the back door of the helicopter. Unfortunately, he was on the side where the blade was low. He got out with his helmet on, stood up, got hit in the head with the rotor blade, and was killed. Ron and Tom survived. Some Metro officers crawled in and got them out. It was quite a situation.

Before they crashed, my observer, Bob Cuipa, and I were responding to a report that the Stone Canyon Dam was failing. The weather was horrible, with rain and wind—just a really bad storm. While we were flying, the helicopter did a complete spin. We must have flown through a vortex, like a mini-tornado that hadn't hit the ground but was circulating. That got our attention. We checked the dam. It was full of water that was spilling over, but the dam was intact. It didn't look like there was any immediate crisis that we could tell. As we were coming back, we heard the help call down at Fifty-First and Broadway. I said to Communications, "We have a helicopter there; have them respond."

They came back and said, "It is the helicopter. They are down."

We flew down there and were overhead, and the blades to Ron's helicopter were still going. I gave instructions to Lieutenant Ken Hale from Metro on how to turn off the battery. They were worried the electricity from the helicopter lights might ignite the fuel. They were able to secure that.

Bob had been classmates with Ron, and they were really good friends. Bob wanted me to land and let him off. I said, "No, we're not putting a helicopter down at the scene of a crashed helicopter. We've got people and Fire Department Rescue there." Another helicopter at a scene like that would have done no good, only harm.

I had a friend who was a paramedic who responded to it, and when he got there, another paramedic unit was at the scene and had Stu covered up. He knew I was working that day and told me he'd had a little trepidation and had said, "I hope it's not Dick." It was just amazing how a situation like that could affect people.

At air support, we had a policy that on New Year's Eve, the air units were out of the air an hour before midnight because of the amount of

Sgt. Dick Eyster

bullets fired into the air. One New Year's Eve, we were over the projects in Southeast Division, just east of the Harbor Freeway. We were helping officers who were chasing suspects through the projects, and shots had been fired. It was a situation that we didn't want to leave. It was eleven o'clock, then eleven fifteen, and then eleven thirty. Finally, they got it situated. We had set up the perimeter, and we advised them we had to leave. We could see flaming bullets here and there, some coming toward us. And those were the ones we could see. We pulled off at about a quarter to twelve and went up the Harbor Freeway. I turned my lights out because I didn't want to illuminate us as a target. We were thinking nobody else in his right mind would be flying out there. We didn't get hit, and we made it back to the heliport. It was just incredible. On New Year's Eve, a lot of lead goes into the air.

About a year after I first got to air support, I injured my back. I herniated the disk in my lower back, and it took about ten years before it finally blew out. I had surgery to have it removed, and then I was retired for about two and a half years on a medical disability pension. I worked to get back on the job. It was an interesting process, but I made it back onto the department. I wasn't done working, and I wasn't done flying.

Terry Barclay

Birthplace: Monterey Park, California
Career: 1969–2007
Rank at Retirement: Sergeant II
Divisions: Southwest, Central, Rampart, Training, Seventy-Seventh Street,
    South Bureau CRASH, Newton

In 1965, I was working on my uncle's freight dock as a swamper. We had a truckload of lightbulbs that we were unloading off Broadway Boulevard in South Los Angeles. I heard a *pop, pop, pop*, and I thought we had dropped some of the lightbulbs. As it turned out, there was a shoot-out, and the Watts riots were starting. It just so happened that my dad was the watch commander at Newton Division. Almost thirty years later, during the 1992 riots, I was the assistant watch commander at Newton Division. That was pretty unique.

My father, Roy, came on the department in June 1950. When my brother, George, got out of the Coast Guard, he decided he also wanted to go on the LAPD. My brother was four years older than me. In 1966, he started the testing. I was about nineteen and kidded him that I would hold his hand while he went through the physical agility and everything. At that time, if you were in college or in the military, your test scores were good for three years, so I did the testing as well. George got himself an academy class date, and he started in 1966.

I ended up being drafted and went into the army. After my tour in Vietnam, I called Personnel Division, and they said, "All of your tests are in good standing." My official release date from the army was on a Friday, and I started the academy the following Monday. I got down there just in time to have my dad shave my head.

Terry Barclay

The biggest thing about the academy for me was that half the staff had worked for my dad. My dad was a lieutenant at Southwest Division, which had been University Division. Bob Smitson, Bill Henry, Terry Speer, Bill Gilstrap, and Elmer Pellegrino—all of these guys had come from Southwest, which I didn't know at the time. One day, I was on the PT field, and I was out there doing push-ups. I had already done what I could do, and now I was halfway doing some push-ups. An instructor was standing over me, saying, "Hey, Barclay, have you cheated all your life? What would your dad think of us?" That was the last thing I needed. More than once, I had my dad and my brother thrown in my face. Anytime I came up short on anything, I heard about the family history and that I wasn't upholding my end.

The last week before we graduated, they gave us our badges and our division assignments. My father was at Southwest Division. So where did they send me? Southwest Division. Again, my family connection kind of haunted me a little bit when I first got there. Like anybody else, I was nervous the first night. I didn't want them to know I was the

Roy Barclay

George Barclay

lieutenant's kid. I got there an hour and a half early, I got all dressed, and I was ready to go. I got my books and went into the roll-call room, and there was nobody there. I went to the back row to the farthest seat in one corner. I put my books on the table, sat down, and waited. The room slowly started to fill up, and as it was getting closer to roll call, there were now forty to fifty cops in there. It was a pretty good-sized roll call. Just before the lieutenant and the sergeants came in, the last person to enter the room was Tom Purrington. I didn't know it, but I was sitting in Tom Purrington's seat. He walked over, and without saying a word, he pushed my books off onto the floor. The books made a big thud, and he had everybody's attention. He looked at me and said, "You're the lieutenant's kid?"

I said, "Yes, sir."

He said, "You sit up there," and he pointed to the front row, the center seat. That was how my career started at Southwest.

On my first night, my first call was a stabbing on a bus on Crenshaw Boulevard. I walked onto the bus, and the bus driver had a knife right in the middle of his chest. He was dead behind the wheel. Of course, who did they call? My dad—he was the homicide lieutenant.

On the tenth day I was there, I shot my locker. That night was going to be my first gun inspection, and being conscientious, I got to work an hour early. I was cleaning the gun, I had it cocked, the cylinder was open, and of course, it was empty. I finally was done and thought, *Okay, it's clean,* and I reloaded it. I was standing there pointing it at my locker. There was nobody else in the locker room. I just slammed the cylinder. When I slammed the cylinder, the hammer fell, and the gun discharged right into my locker. The bullet put a little hole in the locker door, but it didn't do any other damage. I was standing there shaking. Out of the corner of my eye, I saw a sergeant. The sergeant said, "Hey, kid, when you quit shaking, come on downstairs, and we'll write that up." Aside from the embarrassment to my father, I took two relinquished days off for my accidental discharge.

One night, about a week after I shot my locker, I was working with Matt Cunningham, who had twenty-five years on the job and had been born and raised in Southwest Division. We were driving down a residential street, and a guy came stumbling out from between two cars. We could see blood trickling down the side of his head. He pointed to two suspects and said, "They just robbed me."

Matt told him to stay there. The suspects were about twenty yards in front of us, and they saw us and started running. Matt told me, "You go get them, and I'll drive the car around."

Well, there was an alleyway right there. I jumped out of the car; they were running and turned into this alley. Both had big trench coats on. I did not excel in running, but I was gaining ground on these guys. All of a sudden, I saw the front one turn, drop down on one knee, and pull out a chrome-plated double-barreled sawed-off shotgun. I dove for the other side of the alley, and by the time I hit the ground, my gun was empty. I had fired all six and then pulled out my backup gun. The second guy had gone down on his belly. The front guy threw the shotgun down and said, "It's not loaded." They were prone in the alley, and there came Matt. He heard the shots and nearly ran over them while sliding to a stop. Needless to say, I had missed with all six, but I had made a great pattern in a garage door behind them. We found the victim; they had just robbed him and butt stroked him with the sawed-off shotgun, which had caused the bleeding. The sergeant came out, and since there were no hits, he took a couple of pictures and said, "Okay, you guys—that's it." So they went to jail; we were told, "Good arrest"; and that was the end of it.

The next month, I was working with Pat Dammeier. Pat was one of the most aggressive street cops, and his thing was narcotics. Pat went on to be a big dope cop. It was nothing for him to stop ten cars in an hour. We were going down a street, and he saw a guy that he knew was a doper. He said, "We're going to stop him."

We got out of the car, the guy resisted, and I choked him out. The bar arm was the tool of choice in those days. If anybody resisted, we just choked him out. I had so much confidence in it. I could take somebody who was a whole lot bigger than me, and I could control him in no time with the choke hold. I put the handcuffs on him, and we picked him up and put him in the backseat of the car. He had a baggie of reds in his pocket. We got to the station, and I was sitting in the backseat, and I said, "Okay, get out." And he just slumped over. He was dead. I was scared to death. Pat and I were split up; I was taken to a little room, and Pat was somewhere else. I was sitting in this little room, thinking, *I want to call my dad. I'm going to be fired. I just choked this man to death.*

We found out that the guy had swallowed another bag of reds, and they had been in his throat at the time I choked him. That was what had killed him. I came back the next night, and I was working 3A81 again. There was nothing more to it. There's a side story: Maybe five years later, I was a squad adviser at the academy. I took the recruits to the city morgue for a tour. We sat down in a room for a slide presentation. All of a sudden, they put up on the projection screen a picture of a suspect lying there with his esophagus sliced opened and a bag of reds stuck in his throat. It was the guy I had choked five years earlier. Some things come back to haunt you.

There was a big push for station security because some radical groups had made threats against the police department. So every police station had 24-7 station security. One night on morning watch, I was assigned station security, stationed at the back gate. It was two o'clock in the morning, and my dad was in on a homicide and had just finished. He came by where I was standing and said, "Good night. I am going home. I'll see you in the morning." He was a workaholic. He got up the next morning at six o'clock and made his way back to work. While driving on the freeway, he had chest pains. He pulled over, and when he started feeling better, he drove to work.

I was still standing at the back gate when he drove in. He stopped and was white as a ghost. He said, "I'm not feeling well. I think I might have had a heart attack."

I said, "Scoot over." I got on the radio and notified the watch commander, saying, "You don't have any security at the back gate," and I told him I was en route to Central Receiving Hospital. That was the last day my dad worked.

I had some classmates at Central Division. They had not worked the field because of working station security, and there were only a couple of months left on our probation. So a personnel swap was made, and I went from Southwest to Central.

One of my first assignments was with Harry Lee, walking the East Fifth Street footbeat. Harry had maybe twenty-five years on, and he had been walking a footbeat his whole time. Harry showed me that when officers mean business, they take care of business. He said, "Don't do things halfway." We were on Fifth Street, and on one of the side streets, there was a group of drunks. Most drunks, when they saw Harry coming, would scatter. Harry had me search one drunk, and the guy tried to hit me with a wine bottle. Harry had fists that were about twice the size of mine. He punched this guy, and I didn't think he was ever going to get up. I thought Harry had done him right there. Harry explained to me, "You have to earn your respect out here, and you don't allow anyone to take advantage of you, challenge you, or even come close." I figured it out: if Harry was on the east side of the street, everybody else went to the west side. There was nobody on the same side of the street as him.

Marion D. Hoover was the biggest character around. He had a reputation, and everybody knew it. Marion drove a red Cadillac Eldorado convertible that had a personalized license plate on it: MDH9. And if anyone asked him what the nine stood for, he would say, "Do you want to be number ten?" He had shot and killed nine people. He was a Distinguished Expert, and the top flat edge of his Distinguished Expert shooting medal was all inlaid with diamonds. He had the old eight-point hat, and he would wear it cocked to one side. He never wore it properly, straight on. And he didn't walk a footbeat; he *strutted* a footbeat.

One day, I was working one of the station security posts at the front door to Parker Center with Marion. One of the staff officers walked in,

Harry Lee: "Harry explained to me, 'You have to earn your respect out here, and you don't allow anyone to take advantage of you, challenge you, or even come close.'"

looked down, and saw Marion. I didn't know if they'd had any prior relationship or contact with each other. But this staff officer said to Marion, "Your hat is on crooked." Marion didn't respond right away; he just kind of looked at him. Then he reached up without saying a word, grabbed his hat, which was tilted all the way over to the right, and tilted it all the way over to the left.

Marion said, "Thank you, sir." The staff officer just walked off; he didn't know what to do. But that was Marion.

Just before I left Central, I was working morning watch with Stu Foreman; we were just a couple of young policemen. It was about one thirty in the morning, and we were headed down North Spring. At North Spring Street and Ord, we heard a gunshot. I mean, it was right next to us. Stu was driving, and he made a turn into the middle of the intersection. We were looking straight on through the front door into Johnny's Liquor store. We saw a kid holding an automatic, and he had a Chinaman for a hostage. There was a second suspect standing off to the side, and Johnny was behind the counter. We got out of the car, and I took cover behind a telephone pole right across the street from the entrance to the liquor store. The next thing I knew, the kid shot the hostage in the back. The hostage went down. Johnny pulled out a five-shot revolver and shot at the kid with the gun. The kid backed up toward the front door. As the kid was at the door, I took one shot, and I hit the kid. Johnny fired another shot as the kid was going down. It hit the telephone pole near where I was standing. Then the second suspect came running out. He was running straight at us, and we fired again. I missed, Stu missed, and the second suspect went over a big chain-link fence into a produce area. We didn't know it at the time, but they had a getaway driver who took off in a Volkswagen. We put out a help call. I ran over to the liquor store, and Johnny wouldn't let us in. Johnny, for some reason, shut the front door and locked it. The suspect was on the floor with a gun in his hand. The Chinaman was lying there bleeding out, and Johnny had the door locked. The troops got there, and they captured the second suspect. The guy in the getaway car drove around the block and came back to see how his buddies were doing. He got stuck in traffic and ended up getting caught. Two of them had criminal records that stretched forever. They were thirty, thirty-five years old. The kid they had given the gun to was a high school football star. He was around eighteen and was just getting ready to graduate. They had given him the gun, and unfortunately, he died.

That was it for Central. Then I went to Rampart Division. The incident with the two guys in the alley at Southwest was October 1970. Johnny's Liquor store was October 1972. In October 1974, I had been at Rampart for a couple of years, and I was one of the old salts on morning watch. Phil Michaelson and I received a radio call of a man screaming at Second Street and Constance. We got there, and people told us, "He's back there; he's back there."

There was a guy screaming. Phil and I put our lights on this guy. He was standing ten yards in front of us, and he was just screaming and babbling. He had his right hand directly behind the back of his head, and we saw something over his left shoulder, but we couldn't make out what it was. The next thing, he came right over the top of his head, and he had a chrome revolver in his hand and pointed it at us. I fired six, and Phil fired five rounds. The suspect went to the ground, but he was lying there face up, holding the revolver with a firm grip just above his chest. I told Phil I was going to reload, and I stepped behind him. We had no cover. We were in the middle of this alley. I got about two rounds in my .38 revolver, and Phil said, "He's getting up."

I shut the cylinder, and we fired. Down he went, and he slumped over, but he still had the gun in his hand. We got up close, and I reached in and grabbed the gun. Well, it was a chrome-plated cap pistol. When I grabbed it, my heart sank, and I said, "Ah, shit." I tossed it over my shoulder. Of course, when the investigators got there, the suspect was here and the gun was over there; me tossing the gun over my shoulder wasn't the only issue though. The people said, "Yeah, we heard shots, and then we heard, 'Drop the gun! Drop the gun!'" It wasn't "Drop the gun" and then the shots. We had fired that first barrage, he had still lain there, we told him to drop the gun, and when he'd started to get up, we'd fired again. That was what they'd heard.

That shooting was October '74, and I was on the transfer already. The next week, I transferred to the academy. I got a job working for Eddie Watkins in the Situation Simulation Unit. We taught report writing and tactics. Eddie taught just about everything, but tactics and report writing were his thing. Eddie was a huge character and a fantastic instructor. He'd be in front of a class, and he had everybody's attention. He was good at what he did.

About the latter part of '78, though, we had a hiring lull. They told the instructional staff, "Hey, you need to go find a job." I got a position in Central Vice, and after Vice, I was promoted to PIII + I, working 1A69. It was a new car established for the northwest part of Central Division. Tim Plaster and I were regular partners. One of the most significant things for me was partnering up with Timmy, who had been at Central most of his career. Timmy was one of the most intelligent and one of the best street cops I've ever known. Timmy was six four and 240 pounds, spoke fluent Spanish, and was the spitting image of Hulk Hogan—so much so that one time, down in Mexico, he was mistaken for Hogan. So he signed a few autographs as Hulk Hogan. Timmy was powerful. He commanded respect from people, and it was readily given. We walked a footbeat on Fifth Street for a while. Like Harry Lee, Timmy would be on one side of the street, and everybody else would be on the other. They called him "Big Red." Nobody challenged "Big Red."

Tim Plaster: "They called him 'Big Red.' Nobody challenged 'Big Red.'"

From Central, I went to Seventy-Seventh as a new sergeant, and then in '85 or the first part of '86, I found my home as an assistant watch commander. That was what I did for the rest of my career. I spent four years as the AWC at Seventy-Seventh. I happened to be the watch commander the night Danny Pratt was shot and killed. Scott LaChasse was the captain, and Matthew Hunt was the bureau commander. They decided early on in '87 or '88 that they wanted a street crimes unit, a robbery apprehension detail. Bob Green and Ken Kessner were selected as the sergeants. Both had worked Metro and SWAT, and they were terrific trainers and tacticians. Green was tasked with putting this unit together. He said to me, "This is what we're going to do." I was the watch commander at the time because we had no lieutenants. I told him that in 10 percent of the robberies in Seventy-Seventh, the suspect just walked up and either cut or shot somebody and didn't say a word. I told him there was no way I was going to front a cop with those kinds of odds and that I wouldn't have any part of it.

The unit had been operational for about six weeks, and they'd had some limited success. They only operated in Seventy-Seventh, and when they were not doing an operation, they worked as a special problems unit. On the night Danny was shot, they were doing just that. We had a liquor store that was constantly getting broken into. They staked out the liquor store to try to capture some burglars. Danny and his partner were sitting near the location when they heard gunshots coming from a block behind them. It was a drive-by shooting at a gang party.

Danny and his partner were in plainclothes and in a plain car. They saw the drive-by suspect's vehicle and followed it. I was the watch commander, and I was sitting in the office with Bob Green. As soon as I heard them say they were following this car, I don't know if the hair on the back of my neck stood up or what, but I went and got in my car. Danny's partner was driving, and they followed the suspects to a doughnut shop on Florence. That was when the suspects realized who was behind them or that somebody was following them. Either way, shots were fired. The officers put out a help call. The suspects continued westbound on Florence, and at Crenshaw, when the officers pulled into a carwash on the south side of the corner, the suspects made a U-turn and came back toward the carwash. One of the suspects had an AK, he opened up, and Danny caught one right in the face.

That was one hell of a crime scene. The whole area was locked down, including the original crime scene at the gang party. I had Bob go to the hospital with Danny. I think I had twelve sergeants out there from Seventy-Seventh, Southeast, Southwest—from everywhere. Each one said, "Tell me what you need." We had a partial description of the car. Sergeant JJ May found the car parked a mile or so away. Of course, the suspects were long gone. We held that crime scene until the following morning. It's hard to say that you were proud of the way that you handled something, but given the circumstances, I was. But I was especially proud of the way everyone had responded to the most difficult situation a policeman could encounter. The suspects were later convicted.

One of the most fortunate contacts I ever made while I was at Seventy-Seventh was with Lieutenant Jim Tatreau. Jim was at South Bureau CRASH. He called and asked me if I would be interested in a sergeant position that had just opened up. "Maybe," I said.

Then he let me know what the position really was: the OIC of the RAD detail, the Robbery Apprehension Detail—the detail I absolutely did not want a part of because of the risk. We came to a meeting of the minds, and I told him, "Yeah, I'll take the job." I was the night-watch commander, and JJ May was the day-watch commander. He had the Warrant Unit and the regular gang unit. I

Capt. Jim Tatreau

had about forty cops, but they were the RAD detail, although we did some gang suppression. Bob Green and Ken Kessner were still in the unit. It turned out to be absolutely the best, most satisfying job I had ever worked in my entire career. We refined the detail, put tight parameters on it, and did extensive training before putting any cops on the street. We operated bureau-wide. Over a year's time, we did about 500 operations, made about 120 arrests, and had a 95 percent filing rate and a 100 percent conviction rate. We were in three shootings.

One time, we were set up at a gas station. As we were positioning everybody, one of our officers said, "I got three suspects in a car, and they are putting on ski masks, and it looks like they're getting ready to rob the gas station."

I had cover officers who were in the gas station, and I had one of them get our UC—our undercover officer—out. She was our primary concern. These suspects were parked in a back alley. They put their ski masks on, and they started to walk over to the gas station. We had black-and-white chase cars, and one of the suspects saw one of the black-and-whites. He came back and told his buddies, and they took their ski masks off and started to walk away. My cover officers were right there, popped up, and took them into custody. The suspects didn't know what hit them. We got three ex-cons on gun charges.

Another time, we were set up at Ninety-Seventh and Compton. It was two o'clock in the morning, and we were getting ready to shut down. I was getting ready to call it when Bob Green said, "There's a Mercedes coming around, and it's the third time."

So we waited. Sure enough, the Mercedes pulled up and stopped. There were two males and a female inside. The female and one of the males got out. The male walked over to our UC and said, "Bitch, what are you doing in my neighborhood?"

"Well, I'm just—"

"You have no business in my neighborhood." He then pulled out what the UC thought was a gun.

She signaled to us by saying, "Don't shoot me; don't shoot me," which meant he had a gun.

I told my people, "Okay, he's got a gun. Let's move in."

He grabbed her purse, pushed her back, and turned. The cover officers fired, I fired, and we put him down. The guy in the car panicked and took off. He hit a parked car, and he was pushing the parked car down the street. The chase units captured him. The first suspect died, and the female and the suspect in the car got fifteen years in prison.

Jim Tatreau eventually made captain and went to Newton Division. He called me and asked me to come to Newton as an assistant watch commander. I went to Newton in '91.

Two gang cops—Jerry Ballesteros and Ray Mendoza—picked up a gang member at Seventieth and Broadway and headed back to the station. When they got to Fifty-Fourth and Main, they made a right turn, and as they were going down the street, a group of gangsters— about seven of them—was standing there. One opened up on them. The gang member in their car took a round, but he didn't die. Ray was shot in the leg through the door. Jerry was returning fire, and he was shot in the hand. They put out a help call. I was the watch commander and responded. A perimeter was set up, and SWAT was on their way. We captured four suspects but not the primary shooter. Somehow he had gotten out of there. About six weeks later, Sergeant John Paige, the Newton Gang Unit supervisor, received information from Robbery-Homicide Division that the suspect may have a girlfriend in an apartment in the city of Hawthorne. They asked him to do a door knock to see whether there was anything to it. John came to me because I was the night-watch commander and told me that he was going to Hawthorne with two units. I said, "Why don't you take everybody?"

He said, "Okay."

He deployed on the location, and they did a door knock. The suspect jumped out the back window with a gun in each hand. He was shooting, and they end up killing him. "Take everybody" had paid off.

It was at Central Division that I met my mentor, the person I modeled myself after as a supervisor: Luther McCormick. He was a sergeant and he knew everything. You could not ask him a question that he did not have an answer to. His sole purpose, his absolute sole purpose sitting there as the assistant watch commander, was to take care of the cops. When I was on the transfer to Rampart Division, I was eligible to take the PIII test. He went out of his way to put together a book of all his study material, and he gave it to me. I never approached him about it. He said, "You're going to need this. Take this with you"— for no other reason than to make sure that I did well. That impressed me. And that was what I tried to do—take care of the cops.

Gordon "Gordy" Campbell

Birthplace: Vancouver, British Columbia, Canada
Career: 1970–1999
Rank at Retirement: Sergeant II
Divisions: North Hollywood, Rampart, Detective Headquarters, Wilshire, Jail, Hollywood

In Canada, my dad worked for a bank, and his banking career eventually led us to California. By that time, I was sixteen years old. I decided then that I wanted to be a police officer. We lived in Glendale, and while I was still in high school, my dad arranged an interview with the police chief of the Glendale Police Department. After the interview, the job still sounded great.

Although I was a Canadian citizen, I was subject to the draft. I joined the army and was assigned to the military police. That gave me a chance to see what police work was like. After coming back from South Korea, the army sent me to Georgia, and I became a drill sergeant. Toward the end of my commitment with the army, I still wanted to be a policeman. There was an agreement between the military and municipal police departments that if someone was scheduled to enter a police academy, he could get a three-month early out of the army. I was due to get out of the army in July, and I had a tentative date to go into the academy three months earlier than that. Well, I broke my foot. Nothing heroic—I tripped on a curb and broke my foot. There went my three-month early out. I had monthly foot examinations, and at the end of October, I was told on a Friday, "Okay, your foot's healed. You start on Monday." Needless to say, I wasn't in great running shape when I entered the academy in November '70.

The academy was five months long—three months in the academy, one month in the field, and back to the academy for the last month. On the month out, the San Fernando earthquake hit, and I experienced my first twelve-hour shifts. It wasn't really exciting, because we were just patrolling for looters in areas where people had been evacuated. One of my classmates, though, got into a shooting with a guy who had a gun and killed him. After hearing his story, I thought, *Wow! Is this what it will be like out there in the streets?*

I met my future wife about a month before we graduated. We really hit it off, and I invited her to the graduation. What I didn't know was that her father had a connection at the academy, and he had me checked out to see what kind of guy I was. I had no idea at the time he had done that. I ended up graduating number one in my class, and what was funny was that he knew it before I did, and he didn't tell anybody. We were married after I finished probation.

After the academy, I went to North Hollywood Division. On New Year's Eve, my partner and I were driving down Lankershim Boulevard, just a few blocks from the police station. We saw a drunk woman stumbling all over the place. It was two o'clock in the morning, and we couldn't leave her out like that. We put her in the backseat of the police car, and on the way to the station, she said, "Do you know Gordon Campbell?"

My partner looked over at me and asked, "Do you know her?"

"No. I have no idea who she is."

She then said, "He's on the police department."

We got to the station, we talked to her a bit more, and it turned out she was my dad's secretary! We asked her if there was somebody who could come pick her up and take her home, and she said, "Nope. Nobody."

I called my dad, woke him up in the middle of the night, and said, "Dad, I've got your secretary down here, and she's drunk as a skunk. You need to come and get her." I also said, "Dad, I'm on probation, and I don't need my name mentioned to the sergeants that this drunk woman knows me."

He came down, and we released her to him.

My wife was a nurse working at Queen of Angels Hospital in Rampart Division. At the time, officers did not rotate out of a division at the end of their probation. My wife found out an officer at Rampart wanted to come to North Hollywood. He and I did a switch. Rampart was a whole different culture and much more active. It was a good place to work, and I was there for about ten years, mostly on morning watch.

One night, my partner and I got a robbery call at a motel. According to the call, the suspect was gone, and it was just a crime report. It was a two-story motel, built partly on wooden stilts, with an open space underneath. We knocked on the door, and a female asked who was there. We replied, "Police officers."

There was a side window, and the next thing we knew, a guy jumped through it, busted the glass, and took off. We chased him, believing he was our robbery suspect. He ran down the stairs and into the open area under the motel. It was dark, and he was trying to hide. We were a little behind him, but we knew he was in there. We found him and he fought with us, but we were at a disadvantage with our guns out. We were tussling with him, and my partner accidentally fired a round. The guy stopped, and we took him into custody. We were walking back to the police car, and he started moaning. We didn't know it right away, but he had been hit in the wrist from the round fired. We booked the guy for robbery. My partner was penalized for an

Rampart Division police station

accidental discharge. We had just screwed up. When we'd gone into that space, we hadn't known if the guy was armed or not. You really don't want to approach a suspect to make an arrest with your gun out. It was a learning experience for both of us.

One time, we received a call of a suicide. We got there, and the gentleman who had called us said, "He just killed himself." We walked into this room, and the guy had taken a shotgun, put it in his mouth, and blown the whole top of his head off. There was a lot of blood and brain matter scattered all over the place. We called for the detectives and the coroner. The coroner had gloves on, and he held a brown paper bag, like a lunch bag. He was picking up all the pieces all over the room and putting them in this bag. Nothing fancy, no sealed envelope—just a brown paper bag. And he was going about his business. Those kinds of things stay with you.

There was an officer at Rampart who had a drinking problem. When he got off duty, he'd buy himself a six-pack of beer, go home, and drink. The reason for it: he had come home one day and found his wife in bed with another man. He'd developed a drinking problem over that and, I think, a death wish. One day, he was riding his motorcycle and crashed. The injuries were such that he was put on life support, and the doctors waited for the family to get there. My wife, a nurse at the hospital, knew most of the Rampart officers, and she knew him. My wife was on duty that night and was there when the family arrived. The family had the life support turned off, and the officer died. My wife was pretty shaken up over it, and Lieutenant Rick Batson from Rampart was there. He sent for me and had me take her home. Lieutenant Batson was a thoughtful man. Although it's partly a story about my wife, it really is a story about Rick Batson and what kind of person he was.

In 1973, the first female police officers were hired to work patrol. That was a new experience, and I have to say, I admired those women. They took a lot of harassment from male officers. In the beginning, I was of the same opinion—that the females did not belong in patrol. But I worked with some of them, and my opinion changed. Some were good. I was a training officer for Donita Van Gelder, a female probationer. She was a good probationary officer and really wanted to learn. I thought she'd make a good police officer. She had the right personality, and she was a hard worker. One of the biggest things that

POLICE WORK, A MANS JOB!
A CAREER WITH A FUTURE

 1969-70

⬇ DAILY TESTING

WRITTEN TESTS

Mon.	Hollenbeck Div.	7 p.m.
"	Van Nuys Div.	"
Tues.	Harbor Div.	7 p.m.
"	Wilshire Div.	"
Wed.	West Los Angeles Div.	7 p.m.
"	77th Street Div.	"
Sat.*	City Hall South	8:30 a.m.

INTERVIEWS

Mon.	West L.A. Div.	7 p.m. - 9 p.m.
"	77th Street Div.	7 p.m. - 9 p.m.
Tues.	City Hall	8:30 a.m. - 4 p.m.
Wed.	Hollenbeck Div.	7 p.m. - 9 p.m.
"	Van Nuys Div.	7 p.m. - 9 p.m.
Thurs.	Harbor Div.	7 p.m. - 9 p.m.
"	Wilshire Div.	7 p.m. - 9 p.m.
"	Van Nuys Div.	7 p.m. - 9 p.m.
Sat.*	City Hall South	10 a.m. - 1 p.m.

FACILITY

Harbor Div.	2175 Wilmington-San Pedro Rd.
Hollenbeck Div.	2111 E. First St.
Van Nuys Div.	6240 Sylmar Ave.
West L.A. Div.	1653 Purdue Ave.
Wilshire Div.	4526 W. Pico Blvd.
77th St. Div.	235 W. 77th St.
City Hall South	111 E. First St.

A written test is also given Tuesday through Thursday at 12:30 p.m., and Friday at 8:30 a.m., by the State Department of Employment, 141 W. Venice Blvd. Call 744-2415 for an appointment.

* - You may take both the written test and the interview on Saturday. If you intend to take advantage of this opportunity, you should wear a coat and tie to the testing session.

⬇ SALARIES

POLICEMAN SALARY RANGE

First Year	$755
Second Year	797
Third Year	842
Fourth Year	889

SALARY BONUSES

Motorcycle Officer	$ 86
Helicopter Pilot - 24 3/4% bonus	

Marksmanship Bonus

Marksman	2
Sharpshooter	4
Expert	8
Distinguished Expert	16

Longevity Pay

10 Years	25.50
15 Years	51.00
20 Years	77.00

PROMOTIONAL SALARIES

Sergeant	$ 940 - 1048
Lieutenant	1107 - 1236
Captain	1306 - 1458
Inspector	1627 - 1816
Deputy Chief	2027 - 2263

⬇ WEIGHT SCALE

Height (Inches)	Weight Min	Weight Max	Height (Inches)	Weight Min	Weight Max
68	140	173	75	169	215
69	145	179	76	172	221
70	149	185	77	176	227
71	154	191	78	178	233
72	158	197	79	180	239
73	162	203	79 3/4	182	245
74	165	209			

Donita Van Gelder

most male officers were worried about was how the female officers were going to do in a fight. When we got in a fight with a suspect, Donita was right in there. She was willing to do whatever it took to subdue him. I was really impressed with her, and her performance was reassuring.

Tim Cooper and I were partners for a long time. He later went to Metro and finished his career at the bomb squad. One night, Tim and I were working, and I was driving. We had handled a call, and when we got back in the car, Tim had left his hat on top of the car. It fell off as we started to leave, but when I backed up for Tim to retrieve it, I accidentally ran over it. Not a big deal—running over the hat—but now the cap piece was damaged. Well, the cap piece on his hat was labeled "Policeman." This was at a time when the department was changing the badges and cap pieces to "Police Officer." There were no more "Policeman" cap pieces, and he was given a "Police Officer" cap piece. He got razzed by everybody because we had been on long enough, and we were proud of wearing a badge that said "Policeman." He never forgave me for running over his hat.

Tim Cooper

In '82, I got a spot in Rampart Vice. My partner was Kevin Giberson, and we worked primarily bookmakers. We knew of a house where a guy was doing bookmaking, but we heard he was using flash paper to record his bets. We watched the house for a while and observed all the betters with their racing forms coming and going. We couldn't knock at the door, because he could easily destroy the evidence. The question was, how could we get in there and arrest him? We finally came up with an idea. There was an older reserve officer who worked Rampart. The plan was for him to use a crutch or a cane and knock on the front door of this house. When the bookmaker answered, the reserve officer would collapse, faking a medical problem. Then we would be in a position to rush the door while the bookmaker was busy with the "medical emergency." That was exactly what happened, and it worked out perfectly. The reserve officer knocked on the door, the bookmaker answered, and the officer fell to the ground. We came running up, and we recovered all the evidence and got this guy for bookmaking. It was a tough case, but sometimes you had to be creative.

MacArthur Park had a lot of homosexual activity involving lewd conduct. At nighttime, the men would loiter around the public restrooms and wait until they thought there was someone willing to

MacArthur Park

participate in a sexual act in the restroom. Because the restrooms were for the public, it made it our job to take enforcement action. I found it uncomfortable going into the park restrooms. What we were trying to do was get a violation, but the violation consisted of the suspect either propositioning us to engage in a sexual act or committing a lewd act in our presence. It was difficult for you as an officer because people would go to use the restrooms and they see you hanging around maybe thinking you were one of the perverts. I was just there doing my job, but people didn't know that. One time, we arrested an adult for lewd conduct, and there was a sixteen-year-old kid standing at the urinal. Well, it turned out he was masturbating too. We arrested the kid and booked them both. A couple days later, I got a call from the kid's guardian. The guardian questioned if we had the story right; the kid claimed he hadn't been doing anything. Naturally, that was what the kid was going to say. I said, "This was what he was doing. We're not going to arrest a young kid just because. I've already got one suspect in custody; we didn't need anybody else." What the guardian wanted was for us to change our story.

When I made detective, I went to Detective Headquarters Division, working the K-car. The K-car handled dead-body investigations other

Gordy Campbell

than murders in the off hours. One time, Southwest Division detectives asked me to handle a case to determine if it was murder, because they were swamped with murder investigations. An old woman had died, there had been no forced entry, and it didn't look suspicious. She had been dead for a few days, so she was all bloated, and bugs were everywhere. The patrol officers were glad to see me show up. Another time, I handled a suicide-by-hanging investigation. While his family was in another room, this young man went in the bathroom and hung himself from the shower-curtain bar over the tub. He was in his early twenties. He wrapped a cord around his neck and just let himself hang. I'm not sure how the bar supported his weight. I was called because we needed to determine if somebody had hung him or if he had done it to himself. It turned out he had been depressed and had essentially said, "What the hell," and hanged himself.

Six months later, I made sergeant and went to Wilshire Division. I was fortunate at Wilshire because one of my old partners from Rampart, Gene Lewis, was a sergeant there, and he helped me adapt to my new role as a supervisor. When it was time for me to transfer from Wilshire, I put in for three patrol divisions, but I was sent to Jail

Division. I was pretty grim about working the jail. At roll call, I was presented a bouquet of flowers in sympathy for going to Jail Division. My wife was behind that.

In all my time in patrol, I never used a Taser. At the jail, I used the Taser a few times. One time, officers were trying to book an arrestee, and he started fighting. I zapped him, and he went right down. It was effective. I was impressed, especially when we didn't have any other weapons inside the jail. On weekends, sometimes we would have from 50 to 150 prisoners filling up one room by breakfast time. If they had decided to act up or riot, it was just two or three detention officers, me, and the Taser. Luckily, it never happened, but that was always a concern. It wasn't like in the movies, where at the state prisons, guards are walking around with rifles. We had nothing.

After six months, I transferred to Hollywood Division and was working as a patrol supervisor on morning watch. One night, there was a shooting-in-progress radio call. It was off Sunset Boulevard on the east end of Hollywood, and somebody had been hit. Well, just my luck—I was a one-man unit and not that far away. As I rolled up to the scene, a bunch of people pointed to the suspect and yelled to me, "That's him! That's him driving away in the car!" I broadcasted that I was following the suspect and asked for backup. He pulled over before my backup got there, so I stopped, got out, and held him at gunpoint. My first backup was a security guard. He was actually more of a hindrance than anything, but he was trying to be helpful—I'll give him that. I took the guy into custody, and the gun was in the car. The suspect and another guy had been arguing, and he'd shot and killed the guy. He could have shot at me if he'd wanted to, because it was just me until the security guard got there.

One day, there was a report of a jumper at the corner of Sunset and Vine at a tall office building. We went up to the roof, and sure enough, there was a woman threatening to jump. We called in the crisis negotiator to try to talk her down. We found out she had already tried to jump once before. She had also been previously caught walking the runways at the Los Angeles airport, trying to get hit by a plane. We spent several hours there with the negotiator, and he was finally able to talk her down, and she was taken for a mental evaluation. About a month or so later, she went right back to the same building, and this time, she jumped—no warning to anyone. It was a ten- or eleven-story building, and she landed right in front of it. I don't know what you can do for people like that.

Then I went to Hollywood Vice as a supervisor. Of course, the big problem in Hollywood was prostitution. Rae Pride and her partner, Frank Hintz, arrested a young prostitute, and they wanted to work on arresting her pimp. This gal had been a prostitute for a long time, even though she wasn't that old—about nineteen years old. They eventually arrested the pimp, and he was convicted. The officers went above and beyond in that case. They tried to help this girl by getting her a job because they thought she was salvageable. She was good for a few months but ended up going back to prostitution. She did not have a work ethic in the sense of holding a regular job. They were struggling with her even during the case. They spent a lot of time with her, trying to convince her to stay out of prostitution. I have the utmost respect for Rae and Frank for the effort they made.

One time, some uniformed officers from the PED team, the Prostitution Enforcement Detail, saw what looked like a woman in an area where all the drag queens and female impersonators hung out. They kept an eye on her and watched her pick up a filthy old drunk. They drove to a secluded area and parked on the street, and this female proceeded to give this filthy old drunk oral sex. The officers swooped in and arrested them for lewd conduct. The female turned out to be a guy, an airline pilot, who was married with a family. He lived on the East Coast. He'd fly to Los Angeles, bring his female paraphernalia, and dress up, and that was the way he got his kicks. He would go out and pick up some drunk—some grungy old guy—and give him oral sex. I've never forgotten that, because I felt so sorry for his family. I just couldn't imagine somebody like him doing something like that, but when you work vice, you see almost everything.

In the '94 earthquake, I was amazed at all the damage in Hollywood. There were a number of buildings that were red tagged, buildings that were now going to be demolished. Many officers lived near the epicenter, and their homes were totally destroyed. Yet they made arrangements and somehow came to work. I was thinking about that a few years ago when Hurricane Katrina hit New Orleans and all the officers abandoned their posts and didn't show up for work. I thought we had a situation that was as devastating as far as property loss; I don't know about the number of deaths. Yet we had our officers coming to work even though their own homes had been destroyed. They didn't know what they were going to do from one day to another, but they showed up and worked their twelve-hour shifts. They did their job.

After twenty-eight years, I retired, and Hollywood Division was my last assignment. I believe I had a good career with the police department—certainly not as exciting as some others but still full of adventure. When you work with the right people, as I was lucky enough to do, being a police officer can be a lot of fun. But you do make sacrifices: you work unusual hours with odd days off; family plans get canceled because of court, or you could not get the time off; and you see and experience the worst of human behavior. I made many arrests and put bad people in jail, but I think I was always there to help others who had nowhere else to turn for assistance. For me, being a police officer was definitely the right career choice. As I said, I had my interview with the Glendale police chief, and the job still sounded great. And it was.

Hugh O'Gara

Birthplace: Los Angeles, California
Career: 1970–2007
Rank at Retirement: Police Officer III + I
Divisions: Highland Park, Newton

One time, we were in South Park at Forty-Ninth and Avalon. There were a number of hypes in the park because there was a methadone center across the street. We came across this hype I had arrested several times before. He was a bad person, and he had overdosed. He was breathing, but he had taken so much heroin that it had slowed his body down to a point where it was shutting down and he was dying. I looked at him, and to say that I didn't wish he would just die would be a lie. But I couldn't let him go like that. We called an ambulance, and he was taken to a hospital. We cleared from the scene and went back to work. He lived and probably went on to commit more crimes.

You know, a lot of people who came on the job had wanted to be policemen since they were little kids. When I got out of high school, I had no idea what I wanted to do. It was the height of the Vietnam War, so it was either college or I was going into the Marine Corps. My older brother and sister had both gone to college, and I was expected to go too. So I started at Pasadena City College. I met with a counselor, and he said if I only knew what I wanted to do, he could direct me. He made out my schedule, and it included administration of justice. I said, "What's administration of justice?"

He said, "It's police science."

"I didn't say I wanted to be a policeman."

He said, "You just told me you didn't know what you wanted to be. Besides, you look like a policeman. That's exactly what you look like—a policeman."

Hugh O'Gara receiving diploma from Chief Ed Davis, 1970

The next semester, I took another administration of justice class. Well, I had developed an interest in that, and I graduated with an AA degree in administration of justice. I saw that LAPD waived the written test if applicants had a degree. I applied, they waived the written, I passed everything, and I was in the November 1970 class.

The academy was five months long. We did some ride alongs, and our fourth month was in the field. On my first ride along, I went to Central Traffic Division. I was there an hour early, sitting in the front row, waiting. Everyone came in, they went through their roll call, and it was as though I were not even there. Finally, the old sergeant said, "Oh yeah, we got a boot here. Who's going to take the boot out?"

I heard a few responses of "I don't want to take him out."

Then one old-timer said, "I'll take the kid out with me."

We got in the police car, and we tried to pull out of the parking lot, but we were blocked by an antiwar demonstration that had formed outside Parker Center. My training officer asked me, "Got your helmet with you?"

"Yes, sir."

"Well, put it on."

Just as I got my helmet on, Metro moved in front of us and started to move the crowd. We just fell in behind Metro. This wasn't a big thing once I'd been on the job awhile, but I was twenty-two years old. All of a sudden, I was running, stepping over bodies, and asking myself, *Is this what police work is all about?*

In the fourth month of the academy, I was assigned with detectives at Hollenbeck Division for two weeks. I worked with Joseph Wambaugh. His first book, *The New Centurions*, had just been published, so no one really knew who he was. He was a nice guy, and he treated me well, even though as a recruit, I was just a hindrance to him and his partner. They were burglary detectives, and they spent time with me and explained what they were doing.

After graduation, I went to Highland Park Division, which was renamed Northeast Division shortly after I got there. One of my training officers, Tom Marshall, was a really good training officer, and I had a lot of respect for him. I wasn't the fastest at learning or the most brilliant probationer, but Tom took the time to explain and go over things. He didn't just hope I learned something. Later in my career, I worked with Tom's son at Newton Division.

I had another training officer who was a good policeman and one I thought highly of. He made sergeant and, unfortunately, got caught up in the Hollywood Division burglary scandal. He wasn't one of the burglars, but he bought some of their stolen items. When we worked together, we did things the right way. Maybe he did because I was a

Highland Park Division police station   *Tom Marshall*

probationer—I don't know. When his name came out, I couldn't believe it. It was as if I had been stabbed in the heart. These officers were victimizing people we were supposed to protect.

Fred Miller and I got a call in El Sereno of a robbery suspect at a Tastee-Freez on Peyton Drive one night. We got there, and a couple of cars were in the parking lot, but there were no customers. We walked up to the girl behind the counter. She said, "This guy keeps coming up to my counter and asking me for all kinds of things I don't have, like hamburgers and stuff. As soon as customers come, he leaves. And as soon as the customers leave, he comes back to the window."

We were thinking he was a possible robbery suspect. We asked her where he was. She said, "I don't know where he is, but that's his car over there in the parking lot."

Fred and I approached the car. Fred was on the driver's side, and I was on the passenger side. As I approached, I could see the guy lying down in the car, hiding. I opened the car door with one hand and pulled my gun out with the other. I had just changed my holster to a western-style holster. That was what the old salts had, and I guess that was why I changed it. I got the gun halfway out of the holster and accidentally fired my weapon. The round traveled the whole length of my leg, and the doctor actually had to dig the round out between the bones. It was a miracle I didn't cripple myself. I stepped back because my first thought was *My partner's going to start shooting*, and I yelled, "I shot myself." It took Fred a moment for everything to click. I got to the back of the car, and I fell. Fred pulled the suspect out of the car. It turned out that he wasn't a robbery suspect. He was just a drunk— just a damn drunk. In the hospital, the doctor told me that there was some nerve damage, that I would probably limp for the rest of my life, and that I was not going to be a policeman anymore. I was still living at home with my parents. For two months, my younger brother would take my foot and just keep moving it and working with it, which helped the muscles. He would do it until we were both sweating. It worked because the nerves were able to regenerate, and the muscles did not atrophy. My youth and my home physical therapy from my family helped me recover, and I was able to continue my career as a policeman.

Right before I got off probation, I was working a one-man car. I was in El Sereno, and two brothers waved me down. One told me, "Hey, this guy over there"—they pointed down the street—"just pushed us up against the wall and said he was a police officer, that we had drugs, and he wanted them." The brothers had been on their way to work. The guy they were pointing to was walking off.

I made the mistake of saying, "Stop," and he took off running between the houses. I broadcasted my location, and I took off after the guy. I was running between the houses, and I couldn't see him, but at one point, I could hear him on the other side of this one house, because he was breaking branches. We actually almost ran into each other. I shoulder slammed him and choked him out. He was down, and I was catching my breath. As I was handcuffing him, a woman from across the street started yelling, "Hey, what are you doing? Why are you fighting with that guy?" A crowd started to gather. I was a long way from my police car and it didn't look really good. El Sereno was an isolated area from Highland Park. I realized no one was coming, that I must have been in a dead spot and Communications had not heard me.

A little girl came by riding on her bike, and I said, "Honey, do you live around here?"

"Yes, we live right up on the hill."

I said, "Tell your mommy to call the police and tell them a policeman needs help." She rode off.

I was now surrounded and pitifully outnumbered. The next thing I knew, I got pushed and fell into the gutter. As soon as I went down, they started putting the boots to me. I couldn't pull my gun out, because my holster was crammed up against the curb. I was not being heroic; I was just trying to cover my head. All of a sudden, I heard sirens. The little girl had come through for me. I felt fewer and fewer people kicking me. The first unit there grabbed the original suspect. He had been part of the crowd kicking me. The rest of the group ran into a house. The posse got there and pulled everybody out. A number of them were arrested—not because I could identify them but because they had blood on their shoes. I hadn't been able to see who was kicking me. They'd cracked my ribs, but I was young, and the ribs healed quickly. I was off for a few days, and then I came back to work. The suspect I'd chased was made on three robberies, each time for impersonating an officer. He had nothing to do with the other people; they just didn't like the police.

Bill Greenwell

Bill Greenwell and I worked together as partners for almost eighteen months until I transferred to Newton Division. We were good partners and close in age and time on the job. I was best man at Bill's wedding and godfather to his first child. One night, Bill and I stopped a car with two gangsters in it in El Sereno. We got the guys out of the car, and except for the fact that they were gangsters, there was nothing that really set us off. I asked the driver for his driver's license, and it was in the car. I told the driver to go get it. Not smart, but that was what I did. The driver walked back to the car, and I started talking to the passenger. Bill was up by the car. All of a sudden, I heard, "Freeze."

I saw the suspect leaning into the driver's side of the car, and I saw Bill leaning into the passenger side of the car. The guy was leaning down to grab a sawed-off shotgun. We prone them out, handcuffed them, and took them to the station. We were talking to them at the station, and the driver looked at me and said, "If your partner wasn't that close, I could've got two rounds off." It was scary, because yeah, he could've.

There was a shooting involving one of my partners, Kirk Harper. I was not working that night, but Kirk went over it with me a number of times. It weighed heavily on him. He and his partner, Jim Van Pelt, while working morning watch, got a call of a prowler by Occidental College. They got to the location, got out of the car, and approached on foot. It was on a hilly area. They saw a black guy come out from the side of a house and onto the front yard. They gave him a couple of commands, and he obeyed their commands but said nothing to them. Kirk and Jim approached him, and he karate kicked Kirk and grabbed Jim's gun. They were on a steep hill, and Kirk went rolling down the hill from the kick. He had a western-type holster, and he lost his gun. Jim grabbed the suspect to try to keep him from shooting at his partner, but Jim was shot, and he went down. The suspect also fired in Kirk's direction and then ran after Kirk. Kirk realized he didn't have his gun. He always carried a little .25 auto in his handcuff case, but at the time, the department had started getting a little testy about the guys carrying automatics, so he didn't have his backup gun. Kirk jumped up on an embankment to conceal himself from the suspect. The suspect didn't see him and returned to his car at Occidental College. A guard confronted him, unaware of what had happened to Kirk and Jim. The guard was an older gentleman and unarmed. The suspect pointed Jim's gun at the head of the guard and pulled the trigger. He was out of ammo. He jumped in his car and fled.

Several months prior to that incident, a young coed at Occidental College was brutally beaten up. Besides being a black male, there was no description of the suspect. The contents of the victim's purse were thrown onto the ground, including a pair of eyeglasses. When the detectives did a follow-up, the girl was going through her property, and it turned out the eyeglasses belonged to the suspect. The eyeglasses were prescription, and they were a weird prescription, but it didn't generate a lead. A few months later, the same suspect who'd shot Jim went into a state building and killed a state guard. He walked up behind the guard and executed him. A short time later, there was a murder of an ice-cream truck driver in Inglewood. Two Inglewood police officers were driving down the street, and they saw a suspect who was similar in description to the murder suspect they were looking for. They approached him, and he took off running. He ran down an alley, and it turned out to be a dead-end alley. As the two Inglewood officers approached him, he pulled a gun out of a shoulder holster. The Inglewood officers wrestled him, and they ended up getting the gun. It was Jim's gun. Everything was finally tied together. This suspect had killed the guard with Jim's gun, he had poor vision, and the prescription glasses found at the scene where the coed had been assaulted were his. The suspect went to prison. Shortly before I retired, he was released from prison and was placed on parole. Within a year or so, he ended up dying either of natural causes or he was killed.

Jim left the job, and Kirk was never the same after that. I remember that before that happened, Kirk had been worried about his holster. He had bought a six-inch gun, and I had a breakfront holster for a six-inch gun, which was more secure. I had given it to him, but he hadn't used it. The incident haunted him. He felt he had let his partner down. He wasn't blamed for anything that had happened, but it affected him a lot. After that, he worked the field for a short time, and then he went inside and worked detectives. I understand he did a good job in detectives. I always thought of him as a great partner.

After five years at Northeast, I transferred to Newton Division. There was a difference between Newton and Northeast—the demographics, the culture, the crime, everything. The entire five years I was at Northeast, I was probably at the scene of maybe three or four murders. In the '80s in Newton, we would have three homicide scenes at the same time. Crimes of violence I never really saw until I got to Newton.

One time, there was a shooting call on Central, just south of Forty-Sixth Street. We got there, and one guy was down; he had a bullet hole in his chest. I was not getting a lot of information from anyone, so we started handcuffing everyone. There were cards, dice, and bottles of booze, so it was obvious gambling was going on. Finally, one of the older guys said, "We were gambling, and we were drinking. He was cheating. We called him on it. He threatened me, and I shot him."

"Where's the gun?"

"It's over there."

It was pretty simple, and being the great detective, I arrested him, and we took him in. My partner was a probationer. Several months later, I got a subpoena to go to court. I didn't recognize the name, so I went to the homicide detective and told him I had a subpoena, but the name was not the person I had arrested. I asked him what had happened. He said, "The guy you arrested didn't kill the guy."

"Well, he told me he killed him, and he showed me where the gun was."

The detective told me what had happened. They were all friends, and they all knew each other. The person who'd actually shot him was one of the youngsters there. The old guy we arrested, who was maybe sixty-five years old, had told the younger guy, "You're young. Your life's ahead of you. My life's almost over. I'll take it." It was unusual for someone to accept a murder charge for someone else. It wasn't so much heroic as it was these folks' lives were pretty bleak. No one had jobs, they were alcoholics, and they just lived from day to day.

It was about eleven o'clock at night, and my partner and I received a cutting call at a boardinghouse. Two roommates were in a fight, and one of them had a knife and had cut the other across the stomach. I had seen plenty of cuttings before, but in this one, the victim's intestines were actually lying in his lap. If it had happened to me, I would have passed out just from the sight of it. It wasn't me, and I still almost passed out from the sight of it. We called for an ambulance, and he told us the suspect had fled. Sure enough, we saw the suspect walking down the street not far from the boardinghouse. We stopped him, and he has a plastic bag. He'd figured he had to move out because of the fight, so he'd thrown his clothes in a plastic bag, along with the bloody knife, and taken off. The victim lived.

One night, we were probably the second or third unit in pursuit of a stolen car. I was working with a probationer. At Fifty-Fourth Street, the two suspects crashed into the front porch of a house. Both were trapped inside the car. The car caught fire, and one of the officers, Nemo Reyes, got a hose and tried to put the fire out, which was not working really well. There was gas dripping, and the fire kept flaring up. We finally got in, and I tried to pull the passenger out. It was hard to get him out, because the dash and everything had come down on his leg. Finally, we were able to free them and get them out. We all stepped back, and the house and the car became engulfed in flames. The fire department got there and put the fire out. We arrested the suspects for the stolen car, and we were commended for saving the suspects.

Patty Fuller and I were partners for almost a year. Patty was quite a character, and she was a great partner—just a jewel of a partner. She could talk just as well as anybody else could with suspects. Patty had met an older gentleman, Clifford, at the time of his wife's death. He was in his nineties and had been a city worker. Patty and I would check on him at least once a week, and on his birthdays or at Christmas, Patty would bring him presents. He was an interesting gentleman to talk to. He talked about what had gone on in the city years before and when segregation had been the will of the land. He didn't talk negatively or with bitterness—to him, it was just the way it was. After Patty had left Newton, I came by Clifford's house one day, and there was a younger man there. He told me Clifford had passed away. That was a tough one to tell Patty.

The first day of the '92 riots, I was getting ready to go home, and Brent LaFontaine got ahold of me and said, "Hey, things are breaking loose in the field." We teamed up and went in the field. It was getting dark, and there were radio calls, one after another after another— window smashed after window smashed. We worked until about three in the morning. I didn't go home but slept at the station for a few hours and then worked the next day. That was the routine for the first three days of the riots.

During the riots, things were handled differently, and a shooting call was just one of thousands of calls. We got to the scene of one shooting call, and a guy had been shot but not seriously hurt and had been taken to the hospital. An elderly gentleman told us that the guy who had been shot lived with his elderly mother and that he was the neighborhood bully. There had been yelling and screaming, and he had been beating his mother. The elderly gentleman said he had tried to pull the son off his mother but couldn't because he was too frail. He'd gone back into his house, grabbed a gun, and told the son to stop. The son had kept beating his mother, so he'd shot him. Again, this was during the middle of the riots. The gentleman was standing there, and we had the gun. The gentleman was waiting, as if to say, "Well, what are you going to do with me?" After hearing more about this lady's rotten son, we gave the elderly gentleman his gun back. We said, "Have a good day," and we left.

Several years later, we got a shooting call at the same location. The son had recovered from the prior shooting, and he'd been shot again. There was a Mexican family living across the street from him that was dealing drugs. They had gotten into a dispute over drugs, and someone from that household had shot him. When we first saw him, we thought he was dead. All of a sudden, he rolled over, and it was just like a scene right out of a horror movie, because the side of his face was completely gone and his eyes were floating around. His whole lip was off, so talking was difficult for him. I tried to get a statement out of him, but being the true criminal, he wasn't going to give up who had shot him, even though it was the guy next door. The suspect was arrested, but the victim and all of the witnesses were drug dealers. Many crimes in Newton were righteous crimes but were hard to prosecute because people were suspects one day and victims the next.

I never worked with Marion Hoover, but I did work with his son, Greg. He was a probationer and a good one. He obviously grew up on his dad's stories. There were times I had to tell him, "No, we can't do that." Greg later went to Metro and SWAT, and I believe he was hurt and pensioned off the job. Greg's sister was on the job too, but I didn't know her.

It was two or three in the morning, and a call came out—a silent alarm at a closed liquor store on Thirty-Fifth and Central. I was the passenger in the car, and I had one eye open and one eye closed. As we arrived at the location, my partner yelled, "There he goes!" The liquor store had an accordion-type steel grating across the front of the business. The guy was sliding out from underneath it. He took off, and my partner went after him. They ran around the liquor store, and I went around the other way. I went from pretty much a dead sleep to a dead run, and I ended up running into him. We wrestled him down, and I choked him out. Normally, if you choke someone out, he or she is unconscious for thirty seconds to a minute. It's usually enough time to handcuff a suspect. As soon as I choked him out, he popped right back up and was talking crazy. We were finally able to get him handcuffed and off to jail for burglary. It was one of my first encounters with someone high on PCP.

Another time, a guy entered a front yard, and the homeowner chased him out. When the guy returned, the homeowner had armed himself with a gun. The guy came past the front gate, into the yard, and tried to enter the house. The homeowner shot, and the suspect ran off. We got there, but we didn't know about the shooting. The guy was running up and down the street, and he was obviously on PCP. He was acting like a fish out of water. We grabbed him, wrestled him to the ground, and handcuffed him. He was bleeding, and at first, we didn't think anything of the bleeding, because we could see places on him where he had scraped himself. We were waiting for the ambulance when a little guy came up and said, "He tried to break into my house." As I was getting information from him, he said, "I had to shoot him."

"What?"

He said, "I had to shoot him."

Sure enough, the suspect had a bullet hole in his chest. PCP suspects were some of the most bizarre we had to deal with.

During one of the times when we were low on supervisors, I was sent into the field as a supervisor for a couple of months. I knew the lieutenant thought he was doing me a favor by it, but I didn't care for it. It didn't matter how much time I had on the job, I was still a policeman, not a sergeant. As a policeman, I got a call, and I was there to do something, such as make an arrest or take a report. But as a field supervisor, it was the first time I actually wasn't doing anything other than standing back and observing. I would see officers handling calls, and I'd watch them. I obviously had my own way that I thought police work should be done, but I came to realize that there were many different ways of getting things done. In those few months, I actually got more from it than the policemen did. By being out there as a supervisor, I learned quite a bit.

People were always saying, "O'Gara, when are you going to take the sergeant or detective tests?" I knew their intentions were good.

I remember talking to my wife about promoting. She said, "Hey, if you're happy being a policeman, be a policeman." I was.

I stayed in patrol a long time. Patrol was where the youngest officers worked, and at one point, it almost became a generation gap. I was working with officers younger than my children. Besides police work, we didn't have anything in common. I was talking about my grandchildren, and they were talking about their next party. Over time, I noticed a difference in probationers. The first probationers I worked with had come on to be policemen, as I had. They were going to be Los Angeles police officers. That was their job. As time went on, the good probationers were talking about, after two or three years on the job, trying another law-enforcement agency, such as the FBI. Their attitudes changed to "I'll see how this works out."

Hugh O'Gara and Maria Rivas: Newton Division Officer and Detective of the Year Award recipients, 1997

When I got to Newton, I was assigned 13A61. Outside of my loans to narcotics and detectives, 13A61 was my unit, and I worked it for close to thirty years. When I retired, the officers at Newton had the unit number 13A61 retired as well. The unit number is now 13A63. I had never heard of a unit number being retired, and I was extremely honored. I'm not saying I was some great police officer, because it's not as if I did a bunch of heroic stuff, but it's a job that I dearly enjoyed doing.

I had many good times in the patrol car; some of the best times in my life were in a patrol car. But at some point, I had to say it was time to go. I think I was effective most of the time when I was out there in the field. It was a good spot for me, considering it was just blind luck how I'd come on the job.

John Hall

Birthplace: Portland, Oregon
Career: 1971–2002
Rank at Retirement: Police Officer III
Divisions: Hollywood, Metropolitan

After high school, I worked in the logging industry and attended college at night. In '67, I was drafted into the army, completed armor recon training, and served in Vietnam in the northern highlands along the border of Laos and Cambodia. Within four months, I went from private to sergeant due to the loss of people in my company. My tour ended during the '69 Tet Offensive, and I always felt guilty for having left my platoon before the bloody battles were over.

When I got home, I went back to logging, but the industry went flat. I had married and needed a job. LAPD, at the time, was advertising. We went to Los Angeles, I took the tests, and in June 1971, I entered the academy. On my month out, I went to Rampart Division. My first night in a patrol car, we went in vehicle pursuit of a stolen-car suspect. He stopped and fled on foot, I went in foot pursuit, and we caught the suspect. I also worked with the detectives. The detective I worked with had been involved in the Charles Manson investigations. During one of the trials in which Manson appeared, we went to court, and I sat in the back of the courtroom and looked at him as he turned around and gave his sickening grins back to the public. That month was my introduction to police work.

John Hall

When I graduated from the academy, I was sent to Hollywood Division. My first night, like all probationers, I arrived early and found my locker in the basement of the old station. I was organizing my equipment when two policemen came into the locker room and began changing into their uniforms. One called over to the other and said, "Who are you working with?"

"I've got to work with some damn probationer. I'm tired of having to work with these worthless slugs," he said, and he slammed his locker.

I had looked at the work schedule and knew I was the "worthless slug" he was working with that night. Other than him telling me where to stand and when to answer the radio, there was no conversation in the car between us. We had made an observation arrest and handled our calls. For me, it was an exciting night. We later became friends and worked as partners. I spent the next ten years working Hollywood, including a loan to detectives working under Russ Kuster. Long after I left Hollywood, Russ was killed in a shoot-out, but not before fatally wounding his killer. Russ was known for not leaving anything for others to clean up after him.

Hollywood Division police station

In August '75, I was working Hollywood, and one night, my partner, JJ Bryan, and I stopped at the IHOP restaurant on Sunset and Orange for dinner. We parked the police car in the parking lot right next to a large window of the restaurant. After we finished, JJ and I were paying for our meal when we received a call of a robbery in progress with armed suspects at Fountain and Highland two blocks away. We ran to our car, and as we were getting in, there was a little girl, probably about seven or eight years old, waving at us through the bay window of the restaurant. Her little brother was sitting in a high chair next to her, and her mother and father were sitting there. As we pulled the car out, unbeknownst to us, underneath the car was a pipe bomb. Fortunately, the contact pins missed going off by one-sixteenth of an inch. We believed the way JJ had jerked the police car in backing out had caused the pins to miss. Otherwise, if contact had been made, the bomb would have gone off. We, along with the little girl, her family, and many other people, would have been killed or injured. We continued to the radio call, which ended up being a phony call. Some officers who had responded with us to the phony call were flagged down by some people walking through the restaurant parking lot. They saw the pipe bomb wrapped in plastic lying on the spot where we had been parked. They told the officers, and that was how the pipe bomb was discovered. We were dragging the pin under our car. The department ordered a search of other police cars, and a second bomb was found under another police car.

It was ultimately determined that members of the Symbionese Liberation Army, the SLA, were responsible for planting the bombs. The purpose was to retaliate against LAPD for the deaths of their comrades the year before in the big SLA shoot-out with SWAT at Fifty-Fourth and Compton. Six members of the SLA had been killed, and the house had burned to the ground. In 1976, Kathleen Soliah and other members of the SLA were indicted for planting the bomb under our car. The charges were conspiracy to commit murder, possession of explosives, and attempt to ignite an explosive with intent to murder. Soliah fled before the trial started. One year after this incident, my partner, JJ, left the job on a stress pension, while I continued working, trying not to remember what could have happened that night.

In 1999, near the end of my career, our Criminal Conspiracy Section, along with the help of the FBI, captured Soliah, the last SLA suspect. She had been living in Minnesota under the name Sara Jane Olson. In 2002, she pleaded guilty. At her sentencing, this was my statement to the court:

> My name is John Hall, and I would like to start by thanking you for allowing me to address you today. I am one of the policemen that were occupying the police car under which a pipe bomb was placed in August of 1975 while my partner and I were in a restaurant eating dinner. I recall how full the restaurant was that night with men, women, and children, waiting in line to be seated to enjoy their dinners. I specifically remember walking out to our car, as I had waved to a little girl no older than seven or eight years old. She was sitting in a booth with her parents and baby brother, no more than four or five feet in front of our vehicle.
>
> It horrifies me today to think that the lives of dozens of innocent people like that child and her family would have ended in an instant had the defendant and her co-conspirators successfully carried out their terrorist act. As for myself, I would have died that evening, leaving behind my wife and three-month-old daughter. My other two children would never

have been born, nor one of my grandsons. One of my children, that could not be here today, is now twenty-three years old and has served two tours in Iraq with the United States Marines. He and his fellow marines are defending our country against today's terrorists as I stand in front of you, a victim of a terrorist act that occurred twenty-seven years ago. My son has asked me questions that I cannot answer for him, but I beseech you to answer for him today. Questions in regards to terrorism and justice, such as these:

When a person aids and conspires with terrorists, is that person as guilty as a terrorist who commits the act?

If a terrorist evades capture for twenty-three years, does the passing of time cause a terrorist's sentence to lessen in this state?

Does the life of a victim and the lives of his family mean less to the justice system than the defendant that sits before you?

You have the power to provide answers to these and many other questions today when you deliver Miss Olson's sentence. I hope that justice will be served today. I hope that the questions of my young marine will be answered, inspiring him and his fellow marines to defend our country with the absolute knowledge and confidence that any form of terrorism will never be tolerated by our nation.

Judge Larry Fidler sentenced Soliah to fifteen years for her part in the attempted murder of LAPD officers. She also received four years for committing a bank robbery in April 1975, in which a bank customer was killed and a pregnant bank employee was beaten so severely that the employee suffered a miscarriage. I believe Soliah only served nine years of her sentence.

In 1980, the department formed the K-9 unit. Two friends of mine, Jay Moberly and John Lopata, joined the unit and asked me if I was interested. I was and joined the unit in June 1981. For the next seventeen years of my career, and with four different dogs, I searched for every type of felony suspect, from murderers of police officers to burglars to stolen-car suspects.

l to r: John Hall, "Chas," Mark Mooring, "Blue," Paul Stropkai, "Friday," Donn Yarnall, "Popeye," Ron Ryan, "Erko," Dan Hart, "Lasso," Mike Long, "Duke," Jay Moberly, "Elka," and Joe Vita, "Jake:" Metropolitan Division K-9 Unit, 1984

One night, Jay and I were working morning watch. We were the K-9 units for the city. Two Southwest Division officers working morning watch stopped a Cadillac with four suspects on Martin Luther King Boulevard. As the officers began to exit their patrol car, the suspects opened fire at the officers and then sped away. A pursuit ensued, and during the pursuit, the suspects continued shooting at the officers, with one suspect rising through the sunroof and shooting. At one point, the suspects stopped their car and fled on foot. It was in an area of apartment buildings. A perimeter was set, and we were requested to do a search. At the command post, we set up a tactical plan on how we would search for the armed suspects with officers who would be part of our search team. We began our search at the alley where two of the shooters had last been seen. Jay released his dog, Elka, with the command to find the suspects. As Elka entered the alley, she gave an alert that told us a suspect was close by. The dog worked her way to an open carport and located an armed suspect hiding underneath a car parked in the first stall of a parking area. The suspect was lying on his back with his gun in his right hand. Elka grabbed the suspect by his left leg and distracted him as Jay and I approached the

John Hall, left, with Chas, apprehending armed felony suspect

suspect's right side. I dropped into a prone position with the shotgun as Jay continued forward. As I activated the flashlight attached to the shotgun, I saw that I was staring down the barrel of the suspect's gun. I yelled, "Gun!" Jay fired, and I let one shotgun round go, and we put the suspect down. Other K-9 units were called in from home to continue the search for the additional suspects, but they had escaped.

In June '88, I was home on vacation when I was notified to respond to a command post in North Hollywood Division. A police officer had been killed. I rolled Code 3 from home to the command post, where I met Jay, who had been working the morning watch. Jay told me that James Beyea and his partner had responded to a burglar alarm at a closed business. Beyea had gone in foot pursuit of a suspect and caught him, and in the struggle, the suspect had gained control of Beyea's gun. He'd shot Beyea once in the groin, stepped back, and shot him again in the head. As Beyea's partner was coming to his aid, the suspect had taken a shot at him, missed, and taken off on foot between some houses.

My dog Liberty, a Rottweiler, and I were an hour into the search when we entered the backyard of a vacant house. Liberty picked up a scent and followed it from the rear fence to a broken window next to a side door of the house. Liberty and I searched the interior of the vacant house and found no one. However, she continued to go back to the rear bedroom and gave a high alert. This meant something or someone was above us.

A ladder was retrieved from the garage of the house, and we placed it under the entrance to the attic. I contacted the command post and asked for additional flashlights and an attic mirror. With the lights placed strategically around the crawl space, I scanned the attic by looking through the mirror but saw no one. I climbed into the attic and spotted a suspect on his back about ten to fifteen feet from me. As he began to sit up, I ordered him to put his hands up. He said, "The guy you want is downstairs. He's hiding in a cubbyhole."

I said, "You mean the guy who shot the officer?"

He replied, "Yeah, the guy that shot the cop—he's downstairs."

As I yelled to the officers below me, "Watch out—somebody's downstairs," I saw the suspect's hand drop, and he started to grab something next to him. I realized he was grabbing a gun. I fired and put him down. He had Officer Beyea's gun. Liberty had done her job well in finding him. There was no one else hiding in the house.

On March 22, 1989, I was at home and received a call that a perimeter had been set in Pacific Division for suspects who'd crashed a stolen car during a police pursuit and shot at the officers while running away. It was a little after nine o'clock at night. Little did I know, Liberty would not be returning home with me. Liberty's life would end while saving my life. Liberty had been with our family since she was eight weeks old. She was now five years old and ninety-five pounds and had been working as a police K-9 for two years. Liberty had been involved in 250 searches and had captured 115 suspects. While I was grabbing my gear, Liberty made her usual rounds to each of our children to get her pet and a hug before heading out the door.

When we got to the command post, a search team was waiting for us. I went through a tactical briefing with each member of the team. There was a six-square-block perimeter, and there were other K-9 officers already searching. When we started the search, as was typical, Liberty was out front. We started moving up the block, and as we got to the second-to-the-last house, Liberty started giving me a high alert on the next house, which had an unattached, open garage. Liberty went into the garage. There was a laundry room at the back of the garage, with the laundry-room door open and a window on the far side. Liberty went into the laundry room and started barking; she had a suspect. I got to the door. I could see the back end of Liberty; she had somebody right up against the washer. Two rounds went off almost simultaneously. One hit Liberty and entered her lung. The

Liberty
K9-40
04/29/1986 - 03/22/1989

second one hit me in my left arm, breaking both bones, causing me to drop my flashlight and shattering the bulb. The only light was the muzzle flashes from the suspect firing at me and me firing at him.

I realized that the airship was orbiting over me, and every time the airship's light came across that back window, it flashed, which illuminated the suspect for a fraction of a second. When it flashed, I could see Liberty was still in the fight. She was biting the suspect as he shot at me, causing him to miss me five times. Because of her, and even though she was fatally wounded, he was never able to get an accurate shot at me. I was braced against the wall of the doorjamb, and as that light came around and flashed, I could see him. I fired and put him down. I called Liberty, and she came out and lay down in the driveway. I did a tactical one-handed reload on my gun, and I walked back into the laundry room to take the gun away from the suspect I'd just shot, when a second suspect popped up. I thought it was the first suspect. I put him down too. I went back to Liberty and put her head in my lap. Liberty died that night saving my life.

To acknowledge Liberty's courage and heroic actions, the department created the Liberty Medal. The medal is awarded to dogs or horses on the department that are injured or killed while protecting their partners or citizens that we serve. Liberty was obviously the first to receive the award, but three other K-9 dogs that had died in the line of duty before Liberty have since been awarded the medal. Liberty has become a part of department history, and she will remain forever in the thoughts of me and my family.

In May '97, two detectives with the Glendale Police Department—Charles Lazzaretto and his partner, Art Frank—went to a warehouse in Chatsworth on a follow-up to a domestic-abuse investigation. The warehouse was a front for a porno-video film-production company. An employee escorted the detectives past the front office and into the warehouse. Once inside the warehouse, the detectives were met with gunfire. Lazzaretto was hit and fell on the warehouse floor, and his partner put out a help call. Two LAPD officers were wounded trying to get to Lazzaretto. K-9 units, including me, responded, and we put a team together to attempt another rescue. This time, we would place a police dog out front to locate and divert the killer's attention while we completed the rescue. As the K-9 team approached the front of the building, some SWAT team officers arrived and replaced the K-9 backup team. We entered the building with my dog Saber, a German shepherd. We were still in the front office area when two shots rang out. The bullets missed Saber, but we now knew the suspect was in the same area as the downed officer. The SWAT search team moved forward, putting

John Hall with K-9 Saber prior to second entry of warehouse to capture shooting suspect of Det. Lazzaretto

out heavy firepower, while an additional team of officers completed the rescue of Lazzaretto. Sadly, it was too late. The paramedics at the command post determined that Lazzaretto had died in the warehouse. Saber and I went back into the warehouse with SWAT. Saber located the suspect in a loft just above where Detective Lazzaretto had been lying on the floor. The suspect had fatally shot himself.

When I retired, Saber became our family dog until he passed away. After Liberty and before Saber, I got Recon, a Rottweiler. He was a great work dog, but he was not a good family dog. When the earthquake occurred in '94, all the walls in my backyard and my neighbors' backyards came down. Recon was in the backyard at the time and took control of about six neighbors' backyards. He wouldn't let the neighbors back in; their yards became *his* backyards. I found a home for him. He spent the rest of his days out in Malibu with a nice couple. He enjoyed life to the end.

After that foot pursuit on my month out from the academy, I was excited, and I said to myself, *This is my career for the rest of my life. Every night, this is what I'll be doing.* I was so right. My thirty-one-year career was an incredible—just an absolutely incredible—adventure.

Michael Albanese

Birthplace: Van Nuys, California
Career: 1971–2008
Rank at Retirement: Lieutenant II
Divisions: West Los Angeles, Communications, Seventy-Seventh Street, Wilshire, Narcotics, Hollywood, Metropolitan

My decision to come on the department had its genesis in my childhood. I'd wanted to go into law enforcement as long as I could remember. My grandfather, Robert McGarry, and his brother, Paul, came on the department in the 1920s. They would visit us together and talk about the early days of police work. Their stories were absolutely mesmerizing, and some I recall to this day. Gilbert Reyes, my father's best friend, was also on the department. He and his wife were godparents to me and my sister. Gilbert was killed on the job in a traffic accident when he stopped to help a motorist. His death had a huge impact on our family.

I entered the academy in August 1971, the day before I turned twenty-two. I was pleased that my grandfather was still alive to attend my academy graduation; that was a big deal for him. He passed away a couple years after that, but he remained a driving force in my life and profession. Uncle Paul lived until he was eighty-nine years old, passing away in 1988. When he died, I went to his funeral in uniform, and there were a couple of older retirees from the department who had worked with Paul. They came up to me and said, "It is so great that the department sent a uniformed officer to the funeral." I didn't have the heart to tell them I attended because he was my uncle. Of course, they would not have known that, since my name is Albanese and his was McGarry.

Paul McGarry   *Robert McGarry*

Michael Albanese, with grandfather Robert McGarry: academy graduation, 1971

My time in the academy was pretty uneventful. We had a small class, due in part to the draft and the Vietnam War. Richard Beach and I were the last two to retire from our class, reminiscent of the last man standing. I think Richard retired a couple of months after I did.

Upon graduation, I was assigned West Los Angeles Division. The first night at roll call, I was just trying to figure out what to do. I went to the back row, corner pocket, and tried to get as small as I could. Some motor officers provided me an escort to the front row and told me that I was to remain in the front row until I was told otherwise. I understood that: "Front row, keep your mouth shut." As a rookie officer, I worked morning watch; there were only four units. The division was huge geographically, and there was just nothing going on. I had grand expectations as far as police work, and there was no criminal activity happening—at least not that I witnessed. After all the stories I had heard from my grandfather, it was disappointing and a real letdown.

Within a few months, I was wheeled to Communications. It was like going to purgatory, but I did my requisite six months there. After an officer's tour was up at Communications, he had the opportunity to make three choices of divisions to transfer to. I thought, *I'll just go to Seventy-Seventh Division.* I reasoned that was where I would fight crime and see what police work was all about. I had no clue what I was about to embark on!

I loved working Seventy-Seventh. The energy was great; the community was terrific because they knew if we weren't there, it would have been disastrous and catastrophic for them. The community was effusive with gratitude that police were there. About 5 percent had disdain for the police, but the rest of the community, I found, just loved the police. On my first day at Seventy-Seventh, I showed up in my Porsche. I had come from the beach, and while bringing my gear in, Louie Villalobos and Steve Stear said, "Who are you?" There were no Porsches there, and no one showed up in flip-flops.

I just told them, "I live at the beach, and this is how I am going to show up." There were some great folks there, such as Steve, Louie, Bill Duffy, Jerry Bennett, and Jerry Mulford, and we developed enduring and deep friendships.

One time, I put out a help call in Seventy-Seventh. It was at Ninety-Sixth and Compton. It was a problematic residence, and my partner and I got into a good-sized donnybrook. The suspect had done something that necessitated us to stop and detain him. The next thing we knew, we were fighting him and his two brothers. Then we had the whole family on top of us. I was able to put out a help call, and we were still in the mix when four Metro guys showed up and took care of business. That was it. We dusted ourselves off, and we secured our arrestee. I thought, *Okay, I want to be like those guys.* I put Metro Division in my sights.

A notable character, Tookie Williams, terrorized Seventy-Seventh Division. He was a pretty big guy and a supreme thug. But Tookie was terrified of Louie Villalobos and Jerry Mulford—I mean terrified of them. Louie was a pure street cop. He had done two tours in Vietnam and came from modest means. What scared Tookie most was that Louie wasn't afraid of him at all. Louie would get right in his face, and Tookie would drop his head in submission. It was just fascinating to watch those dynamics. Because of Louie and Jerry, it would be safe for the rest of us, especially when walking a footbeat in the projects. Those were interesting times as far as the gang activity though. Even as young police officers, we could see that if we could get more resources, we could eliminate the gang problem. There was reluctance in the city to devote money for more resources, the thinking being that gang activity was a passing fad. For most of us who worked on the streets, the reality was that the gang problem wasn't going anywhere.

Louie Villalobos

One night, I was working with Louie, and we responded to the help call when Ted Severns got shot. He and Bobby Yarnell made a stop on a guy, and he came out shooting. Ted was shot in the stomach, but he was able to get back to the car and put out a help call. Bobby engaged the suspect and killed him. The scene was chaotic. When we arrived, the ambulance had not yet made its way to Severns. This was at a time in law enforcement when everybody drove directly to the scene, causing gridlock in the street. That was a huge learning curve for me that I found useful in years to come. Ted survived and went off the job medically for a while but then came back and had a fine career.

From patrol, I went to Seventy-Seventh Vice. I worked with my classmate Roosevelt Josephs, and we mainly worked the bookmakers. There was no way we were able to operate some bookmakers. We looked like salt and pepper, and we weren't fooling anyone. So we would go to the cash rooms, sit down, and play dominos to stop their action. There were two bookmakers in particular, one at Ninety-Second and Central and one at 120th and Avalon. Big Man, weighing in at a mere four hundred pounds, ran book at Ninety-Second Street. He once told us that if we ever nailed him for bookmaking, he would "kiss every dog's backside along 103rd Street"—he was that confident we would never catch him! At 120th and Avalon, the bookmaker's name was Prince. He had a restaurant, and it really upset him when we would come in, because he knew that we weren't going to leave anytime soon. That was the one way we could essentially put either of them out of business. Now, for some people, that may not make sense. But it made a lot of sense to us. After about a day or two, they would close up shop and move, or they would have to get out of the bookmaking business altogether.

On another occasion, we got a complaint of a bingo game at a church on Vermont at about Eighty-Eighth Street, where it turned into Los Angeles County. Part of the church property was on the county side, and the other part was on the city side. But the bingo game was played on the city side, so we got the complaint. We met with the monsignor, and he was not happy with us, because we were going to shut down his bingo game. He said the game money helped underwrite expenses at the church and school and was essential to their survival. There was no wink and nod, but instead, it was more strategic. We told him that if he moved the game twenty feet, into the county, we had no enforcement powers. They moved, we left, and they continued their bingo game. We found the whole encounter pretty humorous because my partner and I had both gone to Catholic schools, and here we were, trying to tell a priest we were going to shut his game down!

A few years later, I went to Seventy-Seventh Narcotics. I had also applied to Metro in the meantime. At Narcotics, I worked with Ron Gilbert, Roger Gouge, Dick Elliot, Jimmy Ball, and Jim Segars, who got stuck with me as a trainee. It was a really good group of folks with a great work ethic. This was at the beginning of the epidemic use of PCP. We were hitting these PCP labs with no safety equipment. We took deep breaths and then just hit the door and ran in. In such a small unit like ours, when we worked a case and had a warrant to serve, we'd just get whoever was working, and we'd say, "Okay, we're going to serve a warrant," and that was it. SWAT, still in its formative years, was not part of the equation yet for serving warrants.

In March '78, I finally transferred to Metropolitan Division. It was a pivotal decision that had huge implications for the rest of my career with LAPD. A year later, in 1979, I was accepted into the SWAT unit—a big deal for me at the time, as that was the job I'd wanted since my early days in Seventy-Seventh. The mission of SWAT was appealing. It was, and remains, the last phone call—after SWAT, there was no one else to call to receive aid. A group of highly trained, capable men were responsible for resolving a crisis. You relied on your intellect and training as well as your police sense and your gut instincts. The exposure to crises was ever present and required great discipline and sacrifices from everyone in the unit. Callouts varied from light-weight barricaded suspects to dramatic, compelling hostage-taking incidents where lives hung in the balance from the moment you arrived until the situation was resolved, either peacefully or by force. I remained in SWAT from '79 to '88 as a police officer and relished every minute of my time there. I matured as an officer and was given an opportunity to develop as a leader among my peers. Soon I became a team leader, and also had a collateral duty as a crisis negotiator. Negotiating an incident became a task I found particularly satisfying, as I had countless opportunities to negotiate with suspects as well as victims, often while they were in grave peril. Again, these incidents shaped how I would later oversee the unit when I came back as a sergeant, then as a lieutenant.

Charles "Chic" Daniel, Michael Albanese, and Steve Beidle

As a new member of the SWAT team, your big moment came on your first entry. If you did well and established yourself, that was a benchmark day for you. On my first entry, it was a hostage-taking incident—domestic violence driven. A jilted husband had taken his wife hostage at a business in Harbor Division, and the whole neighborhood was gridlocked. We were waiting for our assignments, and Jack Johnson, the team leader, announced his entry team, and I was part of the five-man entry team. My inclusion was more position driven than personality or proficiency, because the weapon that I carried was a shotgun, and Jack needed a shotgun guy. When he called my name, I just about fell over. I started second-guessing myself. Before we moved from the command post, I put as much ammo into my pockets as I could possibly carry. I didn't know what I was expecting, but whatever was coming, I was going to be ready.

Now that we were moving, my adrenaline was racing, and I tripped and fell, and ammo went everywhere. One of the guys who had come into the unit the same time I had, Chic Daniel, was looking at me like *Better you than me.*

I was trying to pick up the ammo, and thankfully, Jack was gracious about it. He said, "Don't worry about that. We need to get over here." That spoke to how composed those folks were in the middle of a crisis: "Well, let's not worry about that. We need to focus on this." It also established the tempo as far as how we were going to manage the crisis. As it turned out, our entry team had a critical position, because if the suspect reached a certain threshold, we were going to knock him down. He ultimately surrendered, and the incident ended peacefully. The negotiator was effective to encourage surrender. We debriefed afterward, and again, it was a different tone than I was accustomed to, because they were all serious and consummate professionals. Everyone was self-effacing, genuine, and dedicated to the mission.

The SWAT unit at the time was underequipped, lacking modern weaponry and sorely lacking in sophisticated devices and skill sets to face the perils on the horizon. The Summer Olympics of 1984 in Los Angeles changed all that. Prior to the preparations for the Olympics, we had only one training day a month, with the majority of our time dedicated to crime suppression. We would be assigned to a problem area in the city of Los Angeles with the intention of reducing a particular crime problem and then deploy from there to any SWAT incident that might occur.

Beginning in 1980, with the Olympics just four years away, we elevated our training and our tactics as a SWAT team. The focus was on hostage-rescue tactics. The training and preparation for the Olympics ultimately took over our lives. The Olympics also presented the opportunity to get new equipment; the equipment we had was essentially salvaged weapons from various sources. When the department took weapons into custody, if usable, specific types of weapons were offered to Metro Division. The weapons were refurbished and assigned to SWAT officers. The Olympics brought significant funding, and we went from using piecemeal equipment to having the best equipment. We had parity with the FBI's Hostage Rescue Team. The impetus of these changes dated back to the 1972 massacre at the Olympics in Munich, Germany. In the intervening years, the United States had never hosted the summer Olympics. Now it was a big deal. The security aspect associated with policing the Olympics required a much higher skill set than in years prior.

In '83, we were immersed in our preparations for the Olympics when we had a hostage-taking incident in Wilshire Division that lasted nearly sixteen hours. I was part of the negotiating component, and I negotiated with the suspect for that entire incident. This was a meaningful test of the negotiation process; however, this particular

Michael Albanese, front row, center, right: Metropolitan Division SWAT team, 1984

crisis ultimately required deadly force against the suspect while successfully rescuing two hostages. Our suspect was implicated in several murders, and it became apparent he had no intention of surrendering. For our unit, this was a reality check on what we might face the following year, and at the least, it built our confidence that we could operate at a high level of stress. Fortunately, the Olympics in Los Angeles were uneventful as related to criminal or terrorist activity, but the residents of Los Angeles now had a marquee SWAT team that was unparalleled in the US law-enforcement community.

After ten years in Metro, I elected to promote to sergeant, with the hopes of one day returning to SWAT as a supervisor. My first assignment as a sergeant was Wilshire Division patrol. After the previous decade in Metro, it was a challenging transition, principally because the mission of patrol was quite different from the SWAT mission. As a field supervisor, I had greater responsibility to manage people rather than responding to crises.

Right before Thanksgiving in 1988, there was one particularly difficult incident. There was a traffic-accident call at the La Brea on-ramp to the Santa Monica Freeway. I had heard a couple of officers requesting a supervisor and additional units. I could hear distress in their voices, and I thought something was not right. There were four fatalities. Body parts were strewn all over the freeway. It was a horrific scene. At that time, I had more than seventeen years on the job, so I was a veteran. I had two concerns. First, I was concerned about these young officers being exposed to this carnage and how they would overcome the tragedy. The second concern was who was going to handle the traffic-accident investigation. I thought this was going to fall back on us, and it required more expertise than either the patrol officers or I had. Gordon Graham, a CHP sergeant, showed up and said, "We got it."

I said, "That's great. I've got two kids here that I need to take care of." I ended up kind of triaging the two officers and some of the other folks who were there. It was horrific—it really was. I don't think folks realize the devastation and visual images from accidents that officers are going to be exposed to. Some law-enforcement agency always had to take care of the investigation and be the caretaker. That usually fell to us, but in this case, the CHP officers were the heroes.

In '89, I made detective, and I went to the Major Violators Section of Narcotics Division. I was looking for relief from being the morning-watch sergeant. I had a family, and sleeping during the day wasn't happening. The change normalized my life for a while. We worked on some big-time investigations and were part of a federal task force. I was a new detective without any lead at all in any of these investigations; I was just part of the investigative component and was given orders to follow, and I was good with that. There was some heavy lifting with these investigations—writing warrants and evidence seizures. I had never before seen the amount of narcotics and money associated with these investigations. Brian Murphy, my boss, was a great guy to work for. He was a hoot. He was knowledgeable about how the drug cartels worked, how they were structured, and how they marketed themselves. He was great on informant management, which is a big deal, because you can really put your organization at risk if your intel is not spot-on. Brian understood how to manage a large-scale undercover operation and recognized opportunities for larger seizures and convictions where some of us would have been more shortsighted. He had really a good grasp of narcotics enforcement, and it was an opportunity for me to learn. I loved working for the guy, because he knew how to take care of his troops.

Det. Brian Murphy

The following year, I made my way back to Metro as a sergeant and was assigned to the Mounted Unit. Then after nine months, I went back to SWAT as a sergeant. I was assigned to SWAT during the riots in '92. The city was unraveling, and you had an organization that was trying to figure out what to do. At the command post at Fifty-Fourth and Arlington, my boss told me, "I need you to get up in the airship, get over Florence and Normandie, and start calling out what you're seeing. Then call out how we can get into the intersection safely and stabilize the intersection."

I was up in the helicopter, and I was communicating and directing the ground units when the pilot said, "Did you feel it? We're hit. We're hit." All of a sudden, I could feel the bucketing of the airship, and I believed we were hit, that we had taken a round. The pilot said, "We're losing power. We need to set it down."

There was nothing I could do to help. I couldn't be an advocate for myself, and I couldn't save myself—I couldn't do anything. I still had my boss yelling at me, because he wanted eyes on, as they were getting ready to make a move. I told him, "The helicopter is hit, and we're going down."

I threw the radio on the seat, and I thought, *I'm going to die in the riots.* The observer was looking for a place to set the helicopter down, and he saw a big parking lot at Slauson and Western. He said, "Set it down there." They radioed that we were coming in hot. We came down and started bouncing up and down until we landed. Once we were on the ground, some security officers came running over, and they posted up around our helicopter. I didn't know who they were or where they had come from, but I thought, *Whoever made that call was brilliant.* Another helicopter came in for me, and I went back up—probably the bravest thing I did that night.

Eventually, we set down in a school playground at Eighty-Eighth and Vermont. I needed to get back to the command post, so I got into my unmarked police car, and as soon as I made my first turn out of the school, the rioters started throwing rocks and shooting at me. I turned out my lights, took out my .45, took about a half a can of Copenhagen, stuck it down my cheek, and just drove full throttle to the command post. When I arrived, they asked, "What happened to the car?"

About this time, the SWAT mission had become a rescue operation. My boss told me our first mission was to rescue firemen taking rounds at the Ralphs market on Vermont at Vernon. We got there, and there were fire department rigs there but no firefighters. They had abandoned their rigs and gone to a house around the corner for cover. We brought in other patrol units, and it took about forty-five minutes to recapture Vermont and Vernon and rescue the firefighters.

We were heading back to the command post when help calls came out at 112th and Central. There was a fire, the fire department was there, and there was an ongoing gun battle. Some Southeast Division officers encountered some armed individuals and got into a gun battle but ran out of ammo. They left to regroup and were requesting help when some Metro officers happened on to the same suspects, and they got in a gun battle as well. The plan was to get the fire department out, then get the Metro officers out, and then regroup. I went back to where the fire guys were, and I said, "This is how we are going to extricate ourselves from this." I told them the plan, and all the firefighters were looking at me as if what I was saying was biblical.

One battalion chief said, "We can't leave until I collect all my hoses."

I said, "You're kidding me, right?"

He said, "No. The hose has brass, and we have to account for it, and I need to recover the hoses."

I said, "Here's the deal. I don't care a rip about your hoses or the brass. The city is burning—consider it collateral damage. You have two choices. You can stay here on your own, or you can just cut the hoses and we'll get you out of here."

All the firefighters were saying, "Cut the hose!" Reasonable heads prevailed, and we got everyone out of danger.

One of SWAT's most memorable warrant services was on Damian Williams for his attack on Reginald Denny, which occurred at the beginning of the riot. All we were going to do was secure the location and take Williams into custody. That was our function as a SWAT team. We were going to surround, contain, announce, and hope that it didn't become a barricade situation. Chief Gates was with me, and while we waited, we had an opportunity to talk. He was a legend in my eyes, and it was a memorable encounter. When we served the warrant, Williams was cooperative, so as we approached him to take him into custody, I stopped everyone and said, "Chief, do you want the honors?" So Gates handcuffed him. I told him, "Now, just remember the last arrest you made, you made with me."

On the morning of February 28, 1997, I was at the academy, doing a pre-watch workout. I was getting ready to go for a run when Donnie Anderson drove up. He told me, "They got a shoot-out going on in North Hollywood at a Bank of America." I saw a couple of other guys, and I told them to get in their cars, drive around the academy, and start picking up the guys that were on a run and deploy everybody to North Hollywood. Donnie Anderson, Rick Massa, Steve Gomez, Pete Weireter, and I motorcaded from the academy to North Hollywood. We were the first Metro folks to arrive at the scene. It was absolute chaos. Rounds were going off all over the place, people were screaming, and people had gone to the ground.

I told Donnie, Rick, and Steve, "Just get close, and get eyes on the bank. Call out what you're going to need, because we've got other Metro folks inbound." I told Pete to set up a rescue effort. I started moving up on foot toward the bank, trying to connect up with the incident commander, Lieutenant Nick Zingo. I couldn't reach him, so I grabbed somebody else's radio to let Nick know some Metro folks were moving up close to the crisis site. The other thing I was trying to do was broadcast to the inbound Metro folks what was unfolding and where we needed to deploy them. What we didn't need was everyone arriving en masse and blocking any rescue effort.

The rounds exchanged were voluminous. If I had closed my eyes and just had a visual image of a shooting range, it would have sounded like a SWAT training day with our shoulder weapons. I was talking to Donnie Anderson on the radio, and I heard him say, "We're at the bank. We may have contact." Then I lost radio communication with him.

The two suspects separated, with one suspect, Lawrence Phillips, on foot, headed toward the neighboring homes. He was walking eastbound on Archwood, exchanging rounds with patrol officers. At one point, he self-inflicted and went down. The patrol officers saw Donnie, Steve, and Rick in their black-and-white, with their SWAT helmets on, and the officers connected the dots. They were waving feverishly toward where the other suspect, Emil Matasareanu, had driven in a white vehicle. At that moment, he was trying to hijack a Jeep pickup truck. He was transferring weapons and money from the back of the white car into the Jeep. That was when Donnie saw him and yelled out, "Suspect!"

This was unbelievable, not only as an act of courage but also as an act of superb tactical acumen in a split-second decision. Donnie, as the driver, realized that if he closed the distance and went directly to the threat, it would limit the suspect's field of fire. Matasareanu saw them and started shooting at their police car as they got closer and closer. While they were driving toward Matasareanu, Steve was leaning out the front passenger side, actually popping a couple of rounds at Matasareanu. That brushed Matasareanu back, and I think Matasareanu realized that these were different folks on the scene, with different weapons, and it was a game changer. Donnie just drove in hot, stopped, and a hellacious gun battle ensued. Remarkably, the entire shooting was broadcast live on local television, so the outcome was well documented. Matasareanu succumbed to his injuries and died at the scene.

Michael Albanese, left: SWAT command post, Bank of America robbery. "There were countless acts of heroism that day—it was a good day for LAPD."

A team went into the bank to secure the folks who had witnessed the robbery. As a group, I have never seen so many folks so visually traumatized after an incident. They didn't say anything when asked, "Are you all right?" They would just nod their heads, speechless because of what they witnessed—not only the scene inside but also the initial gun battle with the patrol officers outside the bank. Once we secured those folks and the two suspects, it took nine hours to search the area northeast of the bank to ensure that there were no other suspects or injured persons. There were countless acts of heroism that day—it was a good day for LAPD.

In 1999, I made a decision to promote—this time to the rank of lieutenant. It was a hard decision since, once again, I would be leaving the SWAT unit with no guarantee I would ever return. At the time, there was only one lieutenant assigned to the SWAT unit, so all the factors would have to align for me to be considered. Upon promotion, I went to Hollywood Division and then back to my beloved Seventy-Seventh. Then in 2000, remarkably, I was able to return to Metro as the

SWAT OIC. It truly was the pinnacle of my law-enforcement career. I held that position from May 2000 to the end of 2008, when I retired.

The thing about working SWAT was that it was seductive and it was addictive. From mission to mission, whatever the circumstance or whatever the problem was, SWAT was it. We used our intellect, our physicality, our equipment, all our resources—everybody—to collectively manage and resolve the incident in the hopes that there was a safe outcome for everybody. It was a high-risk business with no guarantees that there would be a good outcome. All the folks in SWAT knew it was a high-risk business. Even after SWAT incidents where officers were shot or injured, all they were looking forward to was the day when they could come back to work. Folks embraced the mission, and that was the addictive, seductive part.

My career started slowly, but it became a journey of excitement to match what I had sensed from my grandfather's stories, although he'd served a different community of folks. Over the nearly nine decades that encompassed our years of service, Los Angeles changed radically. It was a smaller city, everybody knew each other, and the crime that occurred then was nothing like the crime we have now. There was civility and respect for law enforcement back then. Officers told people once to do something, and they would do what they were told. It was just different when they were doing police work in the '20s, '30s, and '40s. They really just had a car, used call boxes, and carried revolvers. Back then, a piece of paper with a phone number would be the linchpin to a good investigation. But if I learned anything from my grandfather directly, it was how he conducted himself, how he carried himself, and how he respected everyone and had a deep commitment to live a moral life with integrity. I don't know if I was able to garner any of those attributes, but hopefully I did.

Steve LaRoche

Birthplace: Winnipeg, Canada
Career: 1973–2001
Rank at Retirement: Lieutenant II
Divisions: Rampart, Communications, Wilshire, Metropolitan, Southwest,
    South Bureau CRASH, Training, Internal Affairs, Van Nuys, Hollywood

I wanted to be a police officer for as long as I can remember, and I had a number of influences. We lived in Eagle Rock, and my next-door neighbor, Ralph Bailey, was on LAPD. He was a guy I really looked up to. He was big in martial arts and would come home at midnight or one o'clock in the morning, and I would hear him punching a piece of padded wood. He would do that for two hours almost every night. After I came on the job and later went to Metro Division in '79, Ralph was still on the job, working Metro as a team leader. He worked a different platoon, and we would chat occasionally. He retired not too long after that. I really admired him and always will.

One day, an officer from Highland Park Division came to my high school just before I graduated. He talked about the LAPD student worker program. After I graduated, I went to a local college, and I also applied to the student worker program. You had to be a college student with a full load of classes. You could only work twenty hours a week for the department during school, but you could work full-time during the summer. I was accepted into the program, and I did that for two and a half years. When student workers turned twenty-one years of age, they were done with the program, and were expected to go in the academy. In '73, I turned twenty-one in mid-October, and by the end of October, I was in the academy.

Steve LaRoche receives diploma from Chief Ed Davis, 1973

As a student worker, I worked four different places. Metro was the first place I worked, and it was at the old Georgia Street station. As much as I wanted to be a policeman when I got there, that was the only thing I wanted to do after that. I was there for a year. In '72, I transferred to Traffic Enforcement Section, then to Highland Park detectives, and from there to Newton detectives. I had the benefit of a lot of experience before I got to the academy.

My academy class was the first unisex class; there were three females. Everybody was looking at our class because we were the first class that was going to certify females for the field. Of the three females, two were policewomen from LAPD, and the third one was from the outside. Ultimately, two dropped out. Pat Berry, one of the policewomen, graduated and had a fine career.

On our ride alongs, I went to Northeast Division, formerly Highland Park Division. On my first ride along, it was a Friday afternoon on night watch, and I showed up at the station in my uniform. I was wearing a police-officer badge, something no one had seen before except our class. At roll call, someone noticed it, and when roll call was over, you would have thought I was holding a press conference. I had twenty policemen standing all around me, looking at my badge, making comments. The comments were not that flattering, such as "I don't care what they do—they'll never make me wear one of those" and "I'm not giving up my policeman badge." It was such a new thing.

After graduation, I went to Rampart Division. One night, I was working with John Tanner. John ultimately retired out of motors, but he was one of my training officers. We booked an arrestee downtown, gassed the car, and were leaving Parker Center. It was about four thirty in the morning. There was a shooting call that came out at a restaurant at Ninth and Figueroa. Although it was Central Division, it was on the way back to Rampart, so we went to the shooting call. A guy and his girlfriend had finished eating, come outside, and gotten into their car. They were both Asian, and he owned a big restaurant in Chinatown. He had been behind the wheel, and before he'd been able to start the car, a guy had walked up on the driver's side with a sawed-off shotgun and ordered him to roll down the window, but he'd refused to do it. The suspect fired a round right through the window of the car. The guy was hit on his left side with buckshot and glass, and she had been hit as well. They were both in the car when we got there. They weren't dead, but he was really messed up. He was unconscious, and the paramedics were working on him. There were a couple of witnesses, and we got a brief, obscure description of the shooter. One witness said he'd gone north, and the other one said no, he'd gone south. There was not a lot to work with; John just kind of guessed the guy probably had gone south. We got in the car and drove down the street, just looking for a guy running. It was getting light out, and we went down this one street and looked to the west. We saw somebody about a block and a half away. As we got closer, we realized it was not the guy—he didn't fit the description. John, who was just a good basic street cop, said, "Yeah, that's not the guy, but let's talk to him."

John asked the man, "Hey, did you see a guy running through here?"

"In fact, yeah, I did see a guy about five minutes ago running that way." He fit the description.

"Okay, thanks."

We made the turn, went a couple of streets, and saw someone else on the corner. He was not the guy—he didn't fit the description—but we decided to try the same thing and see if he knew anything. "Yeah, I did see a guy come by here, and I saw him go that way, and he's running," the man told us. Long story short, we had about three witnesses along the way, and we got all the way to Vermont and Adams. We were a long way from the scene of the shooting. We were about to cross the intersection, going west, and we saw the suspect a block south on Vermont, making a quick turn west onto a side street. We came around the corner, and this guy was still running! He had weeds in his hair because he'd been crawling through the brush, and he was dirty. We detained him, and we started checking him out. He had fresh cuts on his hands, and in the cuffs of his pants, he had shattered glass from the window of the car. He was booked and convicted and went to prison. The restaurant owner survived, and the shotgun was recovered. When we arrested the suspect, he had a big, fresh cut in the webbing of his hand. The shotgun was a single-barreled shotgun, and the forestock was missing. There was a piece of jagged steel halfway up the barrel that had held the forestock. We surmised that there had been no forestock when he'd fired the shotgun and that was how he'd cut the webbing of his hand. It was probably the best arrest I ever made. I didn't make it, but I was following the lead of my partner, going off his experience. I had good training officers, and I learned from all of them.

I was off probation, and I was wheeled to Communications Division at Parker Center. I hated life when I saw my name on the transfer, but once I got there, I found out how much I didn't know. It turned out to be a good experience, and I learned a lot. From there, I went to Wilshire.

Not long after I got to Wilshire, I was working midday watch, and they assigned me as a one-man car. I was following a traffic violator and ran his license plate on the radio. Before I could get a return on his plate, he pulled over. This was near Highland and Eighth Street. I put my red lights on, and as soon as I got out of the car, the guy punched it and took off. There was a guy and a girl in the car. I went in pursuit, and I was driving, broadcasting, and it was daytime traffic. We went into Rampart Division, and he T-boned a car coming north on a green light. He was going east through a red light. No sooner had he T-boned

John Tanner, back row, second from left: "It was probably the best arrest I ever made."

this car than he was out and running. I chased him with the car down an alley and caught him. He had stolen the car during a robbery. There was a purse on the front seat from another robbery. The guy was a seventeen-year-old kid, and the girl was a sixteen-year-old runaway. Another unit took the two to the station. I impounded the stolen car, and I drove back to the station.

As I walked into the back of the station, a help call went out at the Bank of America on Larchmont: "Officer needs help—shots fired." Everybody was running out of the station. My sergeant, Dick Eyster, came running out the back door. I jumped in his car with him, and Dominic Runci was in the backseat. We drove Code 3 to this help call at the bank. We got there, and Dominic and I got out of the car; we were a few houses south of the bank. I grabbed some citizens to get them out of the way and off the street. The bank was on a corner, and the air unit was overhead. The air unit had actually put out the help call. This was before we had individual radios. About two minutes after we got there, on the far side of the bank—the parking-lot side—the two suspects came out with three female hostages. They loaded up in one of the hostage's little four-door Fiat, and one of the suspects was driving. Off they went. Dick was the only officer in a police car when that started, so off he went in pursuit. Everybody else scrambled and jumped in their cars, and now we had a big pursuit going. Dominic and I went into the bank. There were a number of people who'd been shot, and a bunch of money and a gun were lying on the floor. It was a mess! In the parking lot where the suspects had traded shots with officers Ray Hernandez and Jimmy Copeland, there were a couple of screaming kids who had been left in cars while their moms were in the bank. It was pretty bad. I learned later that during the pursuit, the suspect in the backseat was firing shots at Dick. The suspects ultimately crashed the car, one of the suspects was shot and killed, and the other one was taken into custody. One of the hostages was also shot and killed. This happened in the early part of '76.

I worked the Wilshire Special Problems Unit for a while with Rick Lawin. We had fun and a chance to do some police work. We worked mostly in plainclothes, sometimes in uniform in a plain car. One night, John Waddell and Jack Erickson saw a guy sitting outside of his apartment building. John and Jack were wearing plainclothes. They decided they wanted to talk to the guy—I don't remember why—but there had been many robberies recently in that area. The guy took a barricaded position behind a tree, pulled a gun, and started shooting at them. They fired back and hit him once. The guy took off on foot, and he finally was caught almost a mile away in Rampart Division. He was an ex-con just out of prison. In court, the suspect claimed he hadn't known they were policemen. That defense got John upset. However, what really upset him was he had received a letter from the DA's office saying that the DA's office had investigated the shooting and that they hadn't found any criminal charges to charge against John and Rick. John got that letter, and he quit the job. I remember him being so frustrated. John felt like "Here's a bad guy, he tries to kill me, I defend myself, and the DA is telling me, 'We decided you're not the bad guy.'" John said, "There's something wrong with this," and he left the job. Times were changing.

At Wilshire, I became a training officer, but I wanted to go to Metro. I'd been there as a student worker, and I had told myself, "If I'm going to be on the police department, that's the place to work." I applied and was accepted to Metro. To this day, I think the world of the guys and gals on LAPD, but the guys who were at Metro were exceptional. I had a great time there, but not without controversy. I went to Metro to get my equipment two or three days before the transfer. I met with my lieutenant, Art Melendrez. He told me, "Welcome aboard. Glad you made it. I don't know what you've been hearing about Metro, but here's what's going on." Long story short, they were in the middle of a personnel complaint, and as I later found out, the complaint was right in the middle of the platoon, where I was going, and had divided the platoon in half. I was assigned to a three-man car, so on any days that all three of us were working, I worked with somebody else. My two partners were on one side of the issue, and when I worked with someone else, they were on the other side of the issue. Everyone was upset; no one was happy. This was not really what I had thought I was signing on to. I didn't want to be there, and it wasn't fun.

Then something happened, and everyone was brought back to reality. I was off on this particular night, but C Platoon was working Southeast Division, and there was a PCP suspect in a parking lot, holding a shotgun. The drug PCP was prevalent at the time. The police were called, and Metro officers, including Jerry Wallace, a team leader, responded. Jerry was a super guy and a real gentleman. All of the officers, including Jerry, were in positions of cover, trying to deal with this guy. At some point in the back-and-forth exchange, the guy wanted to hand the shotgun over to somebody or put it down. Whatever he did or said caused a police officer to leave a position of cover. When he left his position of cover, Jerry saw this and went to support whatever the officer was doing or about to do. The suspect turned the shotgun around quickly and fired a round. The round hit Jerry in his hand. The suspect was shot and killed. About a week later, we were in roll call, and Jerry came in. His hand was all bandaged up, and we could see a little bit of blood still soaking out. He came in and made a speech. This officer had just lost his hand, and he was talking about being a policeman and what a great job it was and about being in Metro. He said the injury was nothing and that when he healed up,

Jerry Wallace: "This officer had just lost a hand, and he was talking about being a policeman and what a great job it was ..."

he would be back on the job. Well, he never did come back. He bled blue, and he made a huge sacrifice. His speech, I thought, brought these guys back to reality. There were much bigger things than this little beef going on. That was the way I took it. Jerry changed the tone for many people.

I took the sergeant test, and in the meantime, I applied to SWAT and was accepted. I was there for about two years and was fortunate to have been there. I got to do stuff that I'd never thought I'd ever be able to do—the training, the schooling, and the assignments. I was a sniper the whole time I was there, and I worked for Sergeant Charlie Schoppner. Back then, SWAT handled the dignitary-protection details. I worked a number of dignitary-protection details, including one for President Ronald Reagan in 1980, when he was running for his first term as president of the United States. He and Mrs. Reagan were friendly and really treated us well. He won the election, and the following morning, he was going to make his first press conference to the world media at the Century Plaza Hotel. I was assigned to a position behind the stage. I was in uniform, and I was there with a Secret Service agent. President Reagan was getting ready to go out and give the press conference, and he and his entourage were standing in a little huddle. They were right behind me. I could hear the conversation, and I remember thinking at the time, *I can't believe I'm even standing here. This is amazing.*

Steve LaRoche and President Ronald Reagan

When I was a student worker and was first assigned to Metro on Georgia Street, SWAT was in existence, but it was a city-wide bunch of guys who would get together occasionally and train. While I was there as a student worker, Metro decided to assign a full-time platoon as SWAT. Bob Smitson was brought in as the lieutenant, and Larry Graham was one of the officers. When the platoon was put together, they provided tactical training to all the patrol divisions throughout the department. I volunteered to help, and I was both a hostage and a suspect. One time, Larry Graham posed as a suspect and held me as a hostage with a gun to my head. As a student worker, I was thinking, *This is great!* They didn't have to pay me for this; I'd just do it. Later, when I came to SWAT, Larry was still there.

We had a callout in Hollywood one morning at the Time Motel on Western above Sunset. There were two male suspects—an adult and a juvenile—and they had robbed a doughnut shop in Hollywood. After the robbery, they went to this motel. Somebody saw them robbing the motel office and flagged down a motor officer. The motor officer rolled up on his bike, and the suspects came out and shot him in the leg.

Georgia Street police station, circa 1980s

They went back into the office of the motel and barricaded themselves. The night-watch component of SWAT set up a perimeter and got things going. At about two or three in the morning, they called the dayside, which I was on, and said, "Be here at six o'clock to relieve these guys." We went out there at six in the morning and relieved them, and they were still trying to negotiate with this adult suspect. I was there as a sniper, along with Rich Durup. He was another sniper, and we were up in separate windows of a building behind this motel. The adult suspect was planning to come out with some female hostages and leave in a car. Jeff Rogers, our lieutenant, gave us a green light to take this guy out when he emerged. Just before he did come out, Jeff also gave a green light to anybody who had a clear shot. Where we thought the suspects were going to come out, they didn't. The suspects came out some other doorway that neither Rich nor I could see from our position. John Helms, a great guy, ended up shooting this adult as he came out. The juvenile suspect ran back into the motel. The assault team threw gas, went in, and pulled the hostages out. The juvenile suspect was arrested while trying to escape.

On New Year's Day 1981, a guy was robbing the Ralphs supermarket at Third and Vermont. Somebody called the police, and the guy was now trapped inside the market. He took the store manager hostage and was in a room upstairs. We responded, and there were negotiations going on with this guy. At one point, we heard shots inside the office. He killed the manager, and then he shot himself. It was one of those times you asked yourself, *What do we do? Should we have rushed the office?* Well, if we rushed the office and that happened, it was the wrong thing to do. So we were going with this plan to try to draw him out, but the guy didn't wait. It was tragic.

In '81, I made sergeant and went back to Wilshire. One night, a lady was in her small house, asleep. She had two little boys, and they were asleep in their bedroom. She woke up, and there was a guy standing in her bedroom. She instinctively leaped up and ran out of the house. Well, as odds would have it, as she ran out into the street, there was a black-and-white police car driving down the street. A perimeter was set, and a couple of units were there. We decided to go in and get the boys out, and then we needed to find the suspect. We couldn't call the dogs—the K-9 units—because we had two kids in the house, and this was not a SWAT caper—not yet anyway. We went in the house, extracted the two boys, and did a search. We narrowed the search down to the last room—her bedroom. We went in the bedroom and lifted up the mattress, and the guy was on the floor underneath the bed. He had a small, short-handled sledgehammer in his hand. The guy was just out of prison and had been in prison for rape, I believe. We surmised that was what he was doing there. The mother was lucky. The police just happened to be right there on the street.

I swear, how could this happen twice in one's career? A transfer came out, and it listed six sergeants on long-term loan to Communications Division, including me. So there I was again, going to Communications. I did my six months, and I went back to Wilshire. I was there for about a month and was transferred again because I was now on the wheel. I went to Southwest Division. It was a hot division where crime was out of control, drugs were out of control—everything.

Steve LaRoche, second from right, practicing rappelling out of a helicopter

One night at about four in the morning, Tom McMullen and his probationer, Greg Cottrell, and Sergeant Mike Evers either got a call or were flagged down, but a woman said she'd had a dispute with her boyfriend and he had threatened her with a gun. The three of them did a follow-up to where the guy lived. It was a place with several cottages; some of the cottages faced each other, and a couple more were at the back of the property. This was near Forty-Second and Menlo. As they approached the front door, the door flew open, the guy stepped out with a gun, and they started trading shots at close range. The probationer immediately grabbed his radio and requested backup. I was the watch commander and heard his request, but I could also hear the shots going off. I told Communications to upgrade that to a help call, and we all responded. In this exchange of gunfire, Officer McMullen was shot in the hand, and the suspect retreated into the cottage. McMullen was down. When we got there, I made radio contact with him, and he said, "I'm hit, but I'm okay."

"Okay. Can you get out of there?"

He said, "I'll just crawl out."

He came out, and we sent him to the hospital. We requested SWAT. They came out, and Sergeant Frank Hancock, a funny and great guy, was the SWAT supervisor. At one point, they decided they were going to try to breach the door and get a look inside. The entry team went up to the door. Randy Walker was the team leader. They had to push hard on this door with a pole, because the guy had a mattress up against the door. The suspect opened fire from inside, and Randy was hit in the shoulder and in the facemask. They had masks on because they'd been shooting gas in there. The round that hit the mask splintered off and tore into his scalp. I saw Randy come staggering out; he was holding his shoulder, and he went to his knees. Then it was as if World War III opened up. I mean, they opened up on this place. There was no response from the suspect, and things quieted down. They put smoke in, and smoke takes away the oxygen, so anyone inside either comes out or doesn't. The other thing about smoke is that it burns very hot, so we had the fire department there. The cottage caught fire, and when they put the fire out, they found the suspect's body. He had been shot multiple times in the exchange with SWAT. SWAT was a dangerous job. You see them go on mission after mission, but then you realized they were not invincible. Those injuries put Randy off the job for a while. McMullen fully recovered, and today he's a lieutenant.

I was working South Bureau CRASH during the riots in '92. One day, we responded to a call from the National Guard at 103rd and Central at a shopping center. They had come under fire. After we resolved that, a National Guard lieutenant approached me and said, "Sergeant, I need to ask you a question."

"Okay."

"What are our rules of engagement?"

I said, "What did they tell you?"

He said, "They just sent us out here."

I thought, *This is not good.* These guys didn't know what to do, and they were all scared. Not that we weren't scared, but at least we were used to the area. I told them, "Well, defend yourselves. If you are shot at, you shoot back if you've got a clear target. You got to do what you have to do to survive." I told them that it was out of control and that they should take care of themselves and handle what they could handle.

When I graduated from the academy and went to Rampart, I was listening to these sergeants who had a lot of time on, and they had figured out when was the best time to retire, considering benefits, taxes, and everything else. They said the best time to retire was at twenty-seven and a half years—anything after that, and you were going to lose money. That stuck with me. So twenty-seven and a half years to the day, I retired, and that was April 2001. It wasn't easy. I had a great job; I was back at Metro as a lieutenant, and I was working with great people. There were a few things that happened, though, that helped make it easier to come to the decision to retire. I was dismayed beyond belief about the LA Lakers riot after the championship final game. I was in the middle of that, and that never should have happened. I went to a short briefing at the command post before the basketball game, and a captain from Central Division was giving the briefing. I was throwing out a couple of questions, such as what the traffic plan was going to be if it went sideways. I was told we didn't need one. On the night of the event, I had my Metro platoon, and Ron McCall had another platoon, and they staged us in a fenced-in parking lot a block or two south of the Staples Center. "That's where you are, and we'll call you if we need you" was what we were told.

We were down there for the entire game. My cell phone rang, and it was my wife calling me. She was at home. She said, "Where are you guys?"

"What are you talking about?"

"Do you know they're burning a black-and-white police car in front of Staples?"

"No." This was the first I was learning of it. Off we went, and I mean, it was hard to do anything except try to push people out. We had what I would call legitimate people trying to get out, and then we had these knuckleheads who were just raising hell. And here was this black-and-white police car on fire, and the command post was within sight of it. I don't know what they were doing; I never did hear from them. We just went out and started our own mission. I got hold of the captain of Metro, and he activated the division.

Now other Metro lieutenants were calling me. "Where do you want us? Where do you want us to come in?" We were trying to run this operation from inside this mess. We finally got a squad of motors behind our platoon to try to keep our backs clear enough that we could work and push people and get the others deployed. It was crazy! When it was all over, I never heard anything else about it. You know, where was the investigation? What did we learn there? Well, that captain was promoted. I just had to shake my head.

Then there was the Rampart scandal. As the administrative lieutenant at Metro, I was getting notifications and paperwork to assign people home who were being investigated. That wasn't fun, but then when I later learned how that investigation was being handled, I just thought this was insane. The department was taking action to its detriment on a proven liar's word. I learned that a number of the allegations were based only on the word of a liar. The Board of Rights was a system the department had created and refined over the years. Either they had a preponderance of the evidence or they did not. On the Rampart boards, where was the fairness? There was no fairness there.

Those kinds of things were in the back of my mind and allowed me to say, "You know what? I can go. I'm ready." That was it. I had a great career and a lot of fun, and I would not trade a minute of it—mostly not a minute.

Isaiah "Ike" Williams

Birthplace: Oxnard, California
Career: 1975–2005
Rank at Retirement: Sergeant I
Divisions: Narcotics, Wilshire, West Los Angeles, Southeast, Pacific

I grew up in the Aliso Village projects on the east side of Los Angeles. I was the oldest of seven kids. In the projects, there were heroin addicts shooting up in stairwells and alcoholics drinking and lying out on the yard. A few that we knew died, including one whose nickname was "Rock-Bottom" because of all the cheap wine he used to drink. All the stuff was there for me to go sideways, but I didn't fall for it. Neither did my brothers and sisters. My parents' teachings, the organizations we were involved in, attending church—all of that helped us keep a straight line with not too many screwups. I was in every organization you could think of—Boy Scouts, YMCA, Military Cadet Corps, Woodcraft Rangers, and others.

We had one car. If I went downtown, I walked because I didn't want to take the bus and lose a quarter. I would walk by Parker Center, and at times, I would see motor officers all lined up, having an inspection in the parking lot. I'd watch them, and I thought that was pretty neat, seeing that many policemen at one time. The old Hollenbeck Division station was right near my house, and I would go into the station and look at the pictures of suspects that were on a wall.

When I went to college, I studied architecture and drafting for a year, and I liked it. But I didn't like the fact I would be working inside a building every day. I also took a police science course, and it just clicked. The instructors were good, and I had the opportunity to talk to cops who were in the class. I went to college for a year but decided to go into the army. I became a K-9 dog handler for three years. When I

Ike Williams, right, K-9 handler, US Army

got out of the army, I went back to college and took more police science classes. In '74, I applied to LAPD, and I went into the academy in January 1975.

The first day of the academy, we were all lined up in the gym. Terry Speer gave a speech. He essentially said, "Look, some of you people don't want to be here, and we don't want to have to fire you later on, so why don't you save us the trouble and just quit now?" Seven people quit right then. They actually quit after all they'd had to go through to get there. I always shook my head about that. My academy experience was outstanding. Because of my military experience, everything they were doing, I understood why they were doing it. All the yelling was just to get our minds right. It was similar to the military because the military always said, "Look, we're going to get the civilian out of you. You start thinking like a civilian and you'll get killed." To be a policeman was the same way. They didn't want us acting like civilians, because we might misconceive something out there and assume that Jimmy Joe was our friend when he was not. I understood that, so I didn't have a problem with it.

Near graduation, officers from Narcotics Division approached some of us about working undercover. I thought it sounded interesting, so I, along with a few others, volunteered. When I went to Narcotics Division, it was an environment that I understood. It was easy for me just to blend in and become invisible. I knew how to play the game and not run my mouth. When I started, the detectives had an informant introduce me to a bunch of players. Once I bought from him, the

*Ike Williams, Narcotics
Division*

others knew I was cool, and then I could go out by myself and buy. One dealer in Central Division was cautious. He wouldn't let anybody do business with him unless the person shot heroin right in front of him. I couldn't do that, so I asked him, "Hey, man, where's your bathroom?" I made it for the door and disappeared because that deal wasn't going to work out.

I also worked Ocean Front Walk in Venice Beach. There was a group selling drugs, but everybody gave me the cold shoulder. I thought I wasn't going to get any buys, and I wasn't sure what to do. Then I decided I'd just pass out in front of them. I pretended to pass out right in the middle of Ocean Front Walk. These dealers came over, and one said, "Hey, man, what's going on?"

"I'm having a fit. I had this coke; it was good, and I got to have some more."

From that encounter, they turned me on to a guy who was selling cocaine, and I bought from him. That set me up on Ocean Front Walk. I was buying everything. To them, I never had a money problem, and I was not begging for anything. I would tell them some of the drugs were for a girl who wanted to get high too. It worked out really well. On our roundup, I must have arrested half of those on Ocean Front Walk who were dealing. Everybody in court was looking at me cross-eyed.

I'd been around them all the time, and I'd gotten to the point where I'd been in their houses and knew their mothers and their fathers. It was a neat job, and I enjoyed it. But the first time I had to turn somebody in, I felt like an informant. It was funny—I was a cop, and I felt like an informant because I had to drop a dime on this guy.

When it was time to leave Narcotics, I transferred to Wilshire Division. I was still on probation, and I was not remembering much from the academy. The first day in patrol, it was good to be in uniform. I remember standing in front of the mirror and thinking, *I'm a cop!* I felt like a policeman. I was working with a couple of old-timers, Al Mack and Dick Bowman. They were good for me because they were moving slower, and I was just starting. They broke me in. When I went to nights, it was fast paced, and I started messing up. I was told, "You're a good narcotics officer, but you're not making it as a street cop; you probably ought to resign." That hurt. I remember going home upset and depressed. I realized I had to really tighten things up, because I knew I could do the job. I told myself that I had to be the first one at the call, I had to make my own observations, and I had to react as though I were working by myself. That affected me the rest of my career. Later, when I became a training officer, with every probationer I ever worked with, I was up-front with them. I kept my ratings from probation and showed them to any probationer who was having a problem. The probationers didn't know whose name was on the rating, and I just showed them the negative part. Some of the comments on the ratings were "This guy screwed up," "I feel like I'm working by myself," and "He probably shouldn't be on the job." The probationers would read that and say, "Yeah, this guy is screwed!" I would then tell them that the ratings were mine. That helped them realize they could overcome poor performance.

Then I had Sam Layton, Jerry Glade, and Frank Mika as training officers. They were good training officers. Sam was pretty easygoing; he understood. He took me under his wing and helped me work through it. Jerry was hard core. He had come from Seventy-Seventh Division, and he was great on tactics. Jerry was open with me. He would tell me, "You're moving too slow." I thought he was mean, but then as I improved, I realized where he was coming from. Frank was just really relaxed. His confidence level was through the roof. Whenever he talked to suspects, he would talk to them as if he knew the guys, even if he

Sgt. Frank Mika

didn't know them. I never saw Frank too worked up about much of anything. In roll call, he'd be rattling off stuff, and everybody'd just stop and listen. I was a boot, and I was thinking, *There's guys with fifteen years on, and everybody's listening to this guy.* He was really good on tactics, like Jerry. Frank would have me crack the door on a vehicle stop before we even came to a stop. When we were getting ready to slow down, my door was already cracked, and I was ready to step out. He wanted me out of that car quickly.

I used that technique during an off-duty incident that I was later commended for. On that incident, I was with my girlfriend, but it was as if Frank were in the car with me. I saw an accident, and I jumped out before I even realized what was going on. I got out and did everything I needed to do. That was primarily from the training I had received. Those guys had prepared me so well that I moved on impulse. That training affected my whole career, because everything I did after that was quick. I can't thank Sam, Jerry, or Frank enough for what they did for me.

This accident occurred while I was off duty. I was on the Harbor Freeway, southbound, near Manchester, when all of a sudden, I saw cars going horizontally westbound. It happened so quickly. Some car hit another car, and they ran into the freeway embankment, and one of the cars caught fire. I pulled right over, and it was as if I went into work mode. I ran over to the car that was burning, and a mother and a couple of kids were in the front seat. I pulled them out. Then she told me her husband was in the backseat. Smoke was all over, the car was on fire, and I couldn't even see the backseat. Sure enough, he was there; he'd been knocked out during the accident. He would have burned up if she hadn't said anything. I couldn't get in—the back doors were jammed. So I climbed in through the window. His feet were wedged up under the front seat, and his body was like dead weight. I was having a hard time trying to pull him out, and I thought I may not be able to get him out. But I managed to get his upper body near the window. I climbed out, and I pulled him through the window. I got him to the ground, but he was not breathing, so I gave him CPR. What was amazing about it—I still remember it now—was that everybody was still driving. No one stopped to get out of his or her car and check on these people. It wasn't until I was doing CPR that people started showing up. The guy came to, and now the rescue ambulance and the CHP were arriving. I went back to my car and was ready to leave when a CHP sergeant came over and took my information. I didn't think anything of it and left.

Some days later, one of my sergeants came to me and said, "Hey, I heard about what you did on the freeway."

"You did? It was nothing."

"Well, it must have been something, because the CHP sergeant wrote a big letter about it, and they're going to write you up for the Medal of Valor."

I thought, *Well, okay*. It didn't register, because it was a side issue. My issue was I wanted to be a good street cop. I just thought, *Okay, I did my part, but I need to do better on these reports and all this other stuff*. I was proud of what I had done, that I had reacted as quickly as I had. I took it as a service I was supposed to do. In fact, I treated everything I ever did on the job that way. I was supposed to do that. I didn't look at it as if I should be getting anything special. Other policemen had done similar things. But I couldn't live off that; I needed to move forward.

Ike Williams, back row, far right: Medal of Valor ceremony, 1977

Now I was working the Wilshire Crime Task Force. It was a unit that worked specific crime problems. One night, my partner, Jay Moberly, and I saw three possible robbery suspects walking on Fifth at Ardmore. We were working a robbery problem, and we had information on some male blacks who were committing the robberies. We stopped them and searched them, and everybody's pockets were filled with jewelry. Then there was a radio broadcast of a robbery that had just occurred a few buildings away. Another unit responded to the call as we kept these guys detained. It turned out some girl had answered her door thinking it was her boyfriend. These three came in, beat her up, stabbed her in the eye, and ransacked the house. They had taken her jewelry, and we'd just happened to stumble onto it. They had jacked her up bad, and she lost her eye. It was a good observation arrest. Jay and I were a good team, and we made a lot of arrests. We worked together for quite a while until he became a training officer.

In '77, I was working with Greg Meyer, who later made captain. We were at Third and Fairfax when we were flagged down. A man said his wife was having a heart attack. She was sitting in their car, and she was pale. Greg called for an RA, and I gave the lady CPR. The RA unit showed up and took her to Cedar-Sinai Medical Center. She survived and contacted the captain at Wilshire and told him she wanted to speak to me. Sam Layton and I went to the hospital, and she and her family thanked me for saving her life. I didn't think anything of it. Again, I took it for what it was. It was my job—something I'd always done. I was helping them out. I was happy for them. But I didn't think too much of it other than she felt grateful. Her daughter wrote me a letter thanking me, and I still have it.

I was working the night David Kubly was killed. He was working a report car by himself when he saw a car speeding down Crenshaw Boulevard. He went in pursuit, and the suspects' car crashed into the Pep Boys Auto Parts store at Twenty-Eighth and Crenshaw. David didn't know it, but the guy in the car had just committed a robbery up in Hollywood. When the guy got out of the car, he shot David as David was getting out of the police car. David's bullet-proof vest was on the front seat. When we got there, officers were trying to put David into their police car. Somebody was saying to wait for the ambulance unit, and they did. David was talking, so I was shocked when we learned later that he had died. That taught me that unless the hospital was right next door, wait for the ambulance. If they had taken him in the police car, there would have been no medical treatment. He could have died just riding to the hospital. At least the paramedics put a pressure suit on him and stabilized him for a while to give him a chance. It was a huge perimeter because we thought the guy had run. All he'd done was run a short distance and hide behind somebody's house in a storage shed, where he hunkered down for the whole night. He was found the next morning when a lady saw blood on the shed in her backyard. He had the gun with him. David was only working by himself because his partner had taken the day off for some reason.

For the 1984 Olympic Games, the department put together a counterattack team. A few people were picked from each division. Dave Lowenthal and I were selected from Wilshire. We were sent to Camp Pendleton, and we trained with M16 rifles and with SWAT. During the Olympics, we were not called out for anything. I was also a member of the Wilshire Division Special Events Team. It was a cadre of personnel to work a command post for any special event held in Wilshire. In fact, when Pope John Paul II came to Los Angeles, we were assigned to work with him during his visit to Wilshire. I never applied for any of these details. My name just always seemed to be thrown in. I was always proud of that.

One night, I was working with a probationer, and we responded to back up officers on a call. When we got there, a suspect was pointing a knife at these young officers. The family was yelling, "Don't shoot. Don't shoot him."

The officers were about ten to fifteen feet away from the guy. I started talking to the guy, telling him to drop the knife. The guy was worked up about something. I told him, "It isn't worth dying over. We can help you, but the way you're going with this thing—pointing a knife at the officers—is not going to help the situation. You got your mother and your sister over here. They don't want you to die. And you're going to die for what? Once you're dead, we're going to do some paperwork, and we move on." I kind of broke it down to him as if it were something really simple. He dropped the knife, and everything was good, and the family was really happy. It didn't become a disaster. I always tried to talk to people as if they were family or friends. I didn't get all sanctimonious about it, and I tried to not be too official about it. That way, someone hopefully would understand what the real deal was.

I did twenty years in patrol. I didn't leave patrol because I was burned out. I left because my time was up. The kids of guys I had worked with were now on the job. "What's your name?"

"Johnson."

"Johnson? Are you Tim Johnson's son?"

"Yes."

I realized, *Ike, your time is gone, man.* Also, there was nothing else challenging. I needed to be in another position. I took the sergeant test, made it, and went to Southeast Division. I didn't think the job as a supervisor was hard at all. To me, everything those guys would call me for, I had already done a thousand times.

Southeast was the type of environment I had grown up in; I was familiar with it. That wasn't a big deal. There was nothing in Southeast that I found shocking. I worked morning watch, and the guys were good. As a sergeant, I tried to stay ahead of stuff. That was my job, and I took that seriously. When officers had personal issues that concerned them, I tried to assist them in working things out. I had learned from my own experience as an officer that just because an officer was at work did not mean that he was mentally there. Mental errors could get an officer injured or killed. The environment for a street cop was unforgiveable if he was careless. In '86, when I was at Wilshire, I arrested a female for shoplifting. At the station, I allowed her to stand too close to me unhandcuffed. She attempted to remove my gun from my holster, and a struggle ensued for the control of the weapon. My weapon never left the holster, but it took the assistance of other officers to control her. The incident shook me up. About that time, I had also made some mental and tactical errors in the field that no one knew about. I couldn't put my finger on what was happening, so I figured maybe I needed a break from working the field. I asked the watch commander to put me on the desk. He thought I was overreacting to the incident, but I did work inside for a few weeks. I later went back out in the field, and I was fine. I never had similar moments again. Now that I was a supervisor, it was important for me to remember that experience in the interests of my officers.

One time, I responded to a situation of a citizen complaining that an officer had beaten him up and cursed him out. It was hectic—the family was there, and everybody was yelling and screaming. The officer was arguing with them even after I got there, so I had to get him under control. It was important that I stayed calm, because this situation was out of control. I told the officer to go back to the station and cool off, that I was going to talk to the people. I calmed them down by not arguing with them on who was right or wrong. Once I did my investigation, it wasn't what the citizen had claimed. But that was a classic example of what I knew my job to be: to take care of my people and hopefully prevent them from getting into trouble.

After a year, I wheeled from Southeast to Pacific Division. It was about five o'clock in the morning, and I was on Jefferson Boulevard, waiting at a red light. A car went through the red light and collided with another car, and that car went over onto its side. I checked on both drivers. The first guy seemed to be all right, but the driver of the second car had been knocked out from hitting the windshield. His car was burning. I was pulling on the guy to get him out, and I saw a gun on his hip. He turned out to be a parole officer. I never had a chance to talk to him; he was unconscious the whole time. I pulled him away from his vehicle, which was now fully engulfed in flames. The ambulance arrived and took care of him. I started directing traffic as the traffic unit arrived and started their traffic investigation. Again, I didn't think too much of it. The fire department sent a letter to the chief about what I had done, and I was recommended for the Police Star.

But that was pretty much how my career had gone. I never got caught up in things; my whole deal was just service. This is probably the first time I have ever talked to anybody about any of this stuff. To be honest about it, that's why I've kept these things in a notebook here at home. If somebody asked, "What did you do?" I'd just say, "Well, read that."

When I came on the department, there was an interest in setting up a karate team. I started martial arts when I sixteen years old. Well, it just so happened that a few guys I had known previously in martial arts were now on the department, including Ray Sua. At the Police Olympics, we cleaned up. We were good. Ray and I fought in the same weight class for a while. Sometimes we'd just bow out depending on who was doing the best. We'd say, "Okay, you can take it. I'll take second." I was in the Police Olympics from '78 to '93. I was forty-four years old when I finally gave it up. I also became a member of the department ski team. Yeah, snow skiing. I took medals in that too.

Ray Sua, standing, far left, Ike Williams, standing, far right: LAPD Martial Arts team

Michael Neel

Birthplace: Los Angeles, California
Career: 1975–2009
Rank at Retirement: Detective II
Divisions: Pacific, West Los Angeles, Hollenbeck, Narcotics, Internal Affairs,
    Southern California Drug Task Force

When I got out of high school, I planned to be either a geologist or a paleontologist, but I was a C student in junior college. The Vietnam War was at its peak in 1968, and I said, "What the heck— I'm going to go see what this is all about." I joined the Marines for a two-year enlistment, and I ended up going to Vietnam right away. When I came home, the Marines didn't want regular infantrymen hanging around; all we'd do was get into trouble, so I was out after only eighteen months. I went back to junior college and worked for a department store as the manager in men's clothing. Dick Ruza, a motor cop for LAPD, worked off duty as our security guy. When he'd go after a shoplifter, I'd go with him. On one particular day, Dick went after a guy, and the guy was badmouthing him. I said something to the guy, and he said, "You know what? You're not even a cop. I can tell he's a cop, but you're not a real cop," even though we were dressed about the same. That kind of stuck in my craw. So Dick convinced me to be a reserve officer.

I went through the LAPD Reserve Academy in 1972. We had basically the same training as a regular academy class. When I graduated, I went to Pacific Division and worked a variety of details. I worked almost every weekend, and I loved it. My wife finally said, "If you're going to work so much, why don't you just get paid for it?"

I said, "You know, that's a good idea."

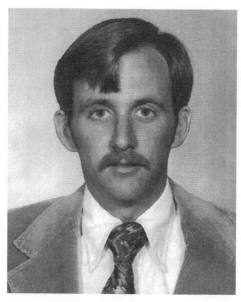

Mike Neel

I applied, was accepted, and entered the academy in August 1975 to become a police officer.

When I graduated, I was sent right back to Pacific Division. They were already used to seeing me there, and I knew almost all the officers and the sergeants. My second week in Pacific, both my training officers were off, and Sergeant Andy Andrews, who probably had twenty-five to thirty years on at that time, said in roll call, "Neel, your partners are off. You'll be working the U-car." Because I was on probation, he couldn't put me in a U-car—a report car—but he did. He was used to seeing me as a reserve officer, and I didn't say anything. We were halfway through the night shift, and I wrote some parking citations down on Ocean Front Walk. As I drove off, some lady cut in front of me, and we had a traffic accident. I had to ask for a traffic unit. You should have heard the hooting and hollering that went over the radio about that. The next thing I knew, I got a call: "Go to the station and see the watch commander."

I walked in, and Sergeant Andrews was sitting there, and he said, "Neel, why didn't you say something? You should have never been out there by yourself. Now go back out there, but you're not going to do anything."

"Yes, sir."

Frank Galvan and I were working together in Pacific; I'd just gotten off probation, and he'd been there awhile. We had a female mental one night, and we took her over to Van Nuys to a place for people with mental problems. We delivered her, and then we were southbound on Van Nuys Boulevard, heading back to the freeway. Neither of us knew the area. We were stopped at a traffic light when a pickup truck pulled up next to us with six people—guys and girls—in the bed of the truck. One was sitting in a rocking chair, and they were all taking drinks out of a bottle of whiskey. They were drunk as skunks. We were in a black-and-white, and they started shouting profanities at everybody. I said, "Frank, we can't ignore this."

He said, "Yeah, you're right. We can't."

So we turned the red lights on, they turned, and we stopped them behind some closed businesses off Van Nuys Boulevard. We told Communications Division we had a drunk driver with multiple drunk suspects. I requested a Van Nuys unit to meet us, and I gave her our location. She put out the call. We got everybody out and had them all put their hands on the bed of the pickup truck, standing in a horseshoe configuration around the bed of the truck. There were two girls and four guys in their late teens or early twenties. The guys were pretty well put together. We took opposite sides and waited. We didn't want to search them yet until another unit got there, but one guy kept going down to his boot, and I told him several times, "Don't go in there."

Frank got on the radio: "Where's that unit?"

Finally, this unit showed up—two great big guys with hash marks up and down their sleeves. They sized up the situation, and we didn't need to tell them what was going on. The one officer walked around and came up to the guy who kept going to his boot. He said, "Where did you get that nose? In a joke shop?" and the fight was on. We ended up arresting six people for being drunk in public, for assaulting a police officer—for everything you can imagine. The guy who'd kept going for his boot had a dagger in it. At the Van Nuys station, the officers apologized to us for taking their time. They'd thought it was just a meet the unit, not a backup or anything. But they'd sized up the situation right when they'd gotten there, and they were just what we needed. The one who'd had a knife in his boot was seventeen years old, so we had to call his father. The kid was on probation for rape. I was the one who'd choked this kid out and handcuffed him. His father, a lawyer, told the desk officers he wanted to talk to the officers who'd arrested his son. I walked out and said, "I'm the one who arrested him."

He said, "I just want to know—how many of you did it take to arrest him?"

I said, "Me."

He said, "I don't believe you."

The choke hold was a wonderful thing back then before it was outlawed. When we got back to Pacific Division, it was seven or eight o'clock in the morning, and the watch commander said, "I'm never putting you two together again." Frank and I would work narcotics for years together later in our career.

I wheeled to West Los Angeles Division, and after a short time there, I transferred to Hollenbeck Division. Hollenbeck was like heaven. I probably had the best time of my life there working patrol, a special problems unit, and detectives.

Lynn Cummings and I were paired up for a month because her training officers went on vacation and the two guys I was with were also on vacation. We went to a burglary radio call where the crime had already occurred and the family had come home. Lynn was taking the burglary report, and I said, "I'm going to walk the alley and see if anybody else saw anything."

Frank Galvan and Mike Neel: "The watch commander said, 'I'm never putting you two together again.'"

The alley was at the top of the hill, and there were houses down below, in line with the house we were taking the report from. This was at a time when it was mandatory for officers to wear their hats. Well, I never wore mine, so right away, I was in violation because I didn't have my hat on. I was looking over a wall into the backyard of this house below the alley. All anyone could see from the house was my head because of the wall. There were two teenage girls in the yard. I said, "Hey, have you seen anybody up in this area in the last couple of hours?"

They said, "What? Just a minute," and they went inside.

A few minutes later, an old man appeared in the yard, and he said, "What do you want?" And he pulled a gun out and shot at me. He didn't know I was a cop, because I was not wearing my hat, and all he could see was my head. I ducked down so that I wouldn't get shot at again, and I went back into the house. Thank goodness it was a small gun—a .25 auto.

I said, "Come on, Lynn. We got to go."

She said, "Well, I'm taking this report."

I said, "Lynn, we have to go right now. Some guy just shot at me." She looked at me with a blank stare. I said, "Come on, Lynn. Let's go!"

She finally got up, we got in the car, and we requested another unit. I knew this guy was old, so we weren't going to set up a command post or anything. We drove down into the cul-de-sac, and we got on the public-address system and told the people in the house to come out. The girls came out, and I said, "I was up there, and somebody just shot at me."

"That was you?"

I said, "Yeah. Where's the person that shot at me?"

One girl said, "That's our neighbor. We went and got him because we didn't know what you wanted."

He was a retired sheriff, about eighty-five years old, and he and his wife came out together. I told the wife to go in and get the gun, and she did. We took the gun, took all his information, and left. Later, I said to Lynn, "I come in and tell you I've just been shot at. What was going through your mind? You weren't moving."

She said, "Mike, when you told me that, my ass just sucked up the cushion of the couch. I couldn't move."

Lynn Cummings

About two months later, we were back with our regular partners, and Lynn got a call—"Gang members with guns"—to the rear of a place on Chicago Street. This was before we had portable radios. We did have what we called little cheaters, on which we could hear radio calls but couldn't broadcast. We got to the location of the call the same time as Lynn and her partner. I had a shotgun, and she had a shotgun. Our partners went up to the front of the house to contact the person who'd called, and Lynn went down one side of the house, and I went down the other side. We made eye contact when we got to the alley. I looked down the alley, and I didn't see anything. I heard on the cheater that my partner and I had gotten a Code 2 call. I turned around and walked back out to my partner. Lynn, thinking I was still there, walked up the alley, and she found six gang members around a car. She drew down on them with her shotgun and said, "Don't move. Do exactly what I say and nothing else." She looked around, didn't see me, and yelled, "Neel!" All these gang members went down to their knees. She said to them, "I told you not to move! Get up!" So they all got up. She yelled again, "Neel!" Down they went again. Lynn was getting nervous, and she had a shotgun in her hand. One gang member said, "Lady, just tell us what you want us to do." Well, she finally figured out I wasn't there anymore. Her partner reached her, and the gang members didn't have any guns. That was the famous "Neel" story. Lynn later became the first female to go to Metro Division.

Rod Osler and I became partners in the Special Problems Unit. Rod was a Montana boy, built like a lumberjack, big and strong. I was skinny and fast, so they called us Laurel and Hardy. Rod and I got a radio call of a man causing a disturbance at a liquor store. Rod was driving, and when we got there, I got out of the car first. It was one of those liquor stores with an all-glass door. Well, the glass was gone. I walked inside, and a huge black guy was pressing the clerk against the wall with the candy counter. I ran up, jumped on his back, and put a bar arm on him, and the fight was on. He was going through the whole liquor store, knocking everything off the shelves, with me holding on for dear life, trying to choke him out. Rod came in and struck him with his baton as hard as he could. Well, long story short, the guy took a nosedive. He went out, and he was on the ground. It took two pairs of handcuffs—we couldn't put his arms together with one pair of handcuffs because he was so big. When we finally got him in the police car, he was thanking Rod and me for saving his life. Apparently, he'd been drinking across the street in the bar, and there had been nothing but Mexicans in there. He'd started spouting off; they'd gotten in a big fight with him and chased him out into the street. They'd had knives, and he'd run into the liquor store. The guy in the liquor store wouldn't help him. His mood had changed, and he'd gone after the liquor store guy. Now we had him in custody, and we were his best friends. We booked him for being drunk. This guy worked in a wrecking yard, and he could pull a whole engine by himself out of a car. He had the most incredible build I'd ever seen on a guy.

Manny Hernandez and I were also partners in the Special Problems Unit. He had about two years on me. We put a ton of people in jail, including some bank robbers. Maybe that was because of our ties with all the hypes. The majority of my arrests in Hollenbeck were hypes. Hypes had to commit crimes to support their habit. I learned early on that if you arrested a hype, you're arresting a burglar or a receiver of stolen property. We would turn hypes into informants who would give us information on other people.

Manny Hernandez   *Mike Neel*

We arrested a kid once for being under the influence. We were told later by an informant that this kid robbed banks and scored his dope at Lefty's, which was two blocks from the station. One day, we heard a radio call of a robbery at a bank, and the description of the suspect matched this kid. We headed over and staked out Lefty's. They called the owner "Lefty," but her name was Evelyn. We arrested over four hundred hypes out of her place. Well, sure enough, here came this guy; he ran into Lefty's, and he had purple dye all over him. We knocked on the door. "Who is it?" Evelyn asked.

I said, "This is Neel, Evelyn."

"What do you want?"

"I want the guy that just ran in there with all the money and the purple dye on him."

She said, "He's not here."

I said, "Evelyn, if you don't get him out, I'm coming in, and I'll arrest everybody in the place for being under the influence."

Out the door he came. The detectives made thirteen bank robberies on him.

I made detective in '87 and worked Juvenile Narcotics for six months, the Marine Smuggling Squad for almost three years, and a number of years at a federal narcotics task force. On one case with the federal task force, we were working a Colombian drug supplier. He had two houses, and we were going to serve a search warrant at both places. We divided into two teams. We served a search warrant at one house and recovered fifty kilos of cocaine. When we were done, I went to the suspect's main house, where the other search warrant had been served. I said, "What did you guys get?"

They said, "We didn't get anything. There's nothing here."

I said, "Well, I can't believe that there's nothing here. This is the crook's main house. There should at least be money here."

The guy's wife was arrogant, telling us that there was nothing there and that she was going to sue us. I interviewed some of the co-conspirators and told them, "Hey, look, you're going to take all the heat, and the main guy's basically getting away with it." I said, "I know that there had to be money or something in his house."

This one guy kept making his eyes go up as if he were looking up, but he wouldn't say anything. The narcotics dog had also alerted in the garage; he had been jumping up and scratching at the wall, right below the main crook's master bedroom. I went to the supervisor and said, "I know we already did the search warrant, and it's done. But I want to write another search warrant and put all the different reasons that I think that there's more dope or money in this house."

He said, "Well, if you think you can make it fly with the judge."

I wrote another search warrant and got it signed.

The next day, I told the wife we had another search warrant for the house. We split up where we were going to search, and I went to the master bedroom. I figured that was where the money would be. I had a DEA agent right next to me, and we were at the sink in the master bedroom. I opened the medicine cabinet, and there must have been twenty bottles of perfume. I took all the perfume out and put it in the sink. Then I took the screws out of the medicine cabinet, and I pulled the medicine cabinet out. I looked, and there was nothing there. I put the medicine cabinet back on, and I put the screws back in. But I thought there was something wrong. I started taking the screws out of the medicine cabinet again. The DEA agent said, "You just did that."

I said, "Something's telling me that there's something here."

I pulled it out, and the bottom two-by-four—the cross-frame member—should have had two nails to toenail it in, right? The holes were there, but there were no nails. I lifted the board up, and there was a string attached and two nylon socks on the string. We pulled that out, and there was $500,000, right above where the dog had alerted. The dog had been getting the scent coming down the wall. I called the group supervisor and said, "I've recovered five hundred thousand dollars. What do you want me to do with the female?"

He said, "Book her."

I just grinned at her, and we booked her too.

We were involved in an investigation with two other police departments on some Colombians living in Orange County. One of the suspects owned an upholstery business. We watched them for about a month. One night, we followed these suspects to their homes. It was about seven o'clock at night, we were already on overtime, and there was nothing remarkable happening. We left the location, and we were debriefing. My supervisor called and told me he'd just gotten word that the suspects were going to pick up five hundred kilos of cocaine at a shopping center. The suspects had left their house, so we set up at the shopping center. Twenty minutes later, the crook showed up. He met with these Mexican guys, and they were given a key to a van. They got in this loaded-down van, went to the upholstery shop, and unloaded. They left and made another pickup and took it to the main crook's house. Now we had two places under surveillance, and we'd been working for almost twenty hours. We made a deal with the other agencies involved in the investigation, and they maintained the surveillance until we picked it up again at five o'clock in the morning. We resumed the surveillance, and I went past the upholstery shop, where there shouldn't have been any cars; a worker's car was there. I called up the night surveillance supervisor and said, "When did that car arrive?"

"That car didn't come in."

I said, "Oh, oh."

We made a decision to take it down. The worker was inside the upholstery shop, putting cocaine into black plastic bags and coating the bags with axle grease to throw off narcotics dogs. We were waiting for the search warrant. I was sitting at this guy's desk in the upholstery shop, and a trash can was right next to me. I looked over at the trash can, and there was a piece of paper with numbers scribbled on it. On the paper, there were three columns of writing. One column added up to 500, another added up to 410, and a third column added up to 260. I called the detective writing the search warrant. I said, "I think you're going to get another 260 kilos that you don't even know about yet."

We served the search warrant, and 410 kilos was recovered at the crook's house, and 500 kilos was recovered in the upholstery shop. During our search of the upholstery shop, another detective and I were standing on top of the ceiling of the interior office of the shop. I said, "By what's on this tally sheet, there's got to be another 260 kilos. Where the hell would it be?"

My partner said, "Well, maybe we're standing on it."

There was plywood nailed down on top of the rafters over the interior office. We took off the plywood, and there it was—260 kilos. We ended up with almost twelve hundred kilos. Sometimes you lucked out. The suspects went to prison.

I had this one informant, one of the best informants I'd ever had with LAPD. He was a truck driver, and his route was across country. He told me he was always being approached by people wanting him to take dope or dope money for them across country. One day, he called and said, "They want me to pick money up and bring it back."

"Well, what are we talking about?"

He said, "It sounded like one hundred thousand dollars."

I said, "All right. Pick it up, and let me know when you got it."

A little later, I got another call from my informant, and he said, "Well, it's not a hundred thousand; it's a million."

Mike Neel: "Well, maybe we're standing on it."

That changed everything. My boss sent me and my partner, Brian Agnew, to meet with my informant and two DEA agents. The next day, my informant delivered the money, and he was given $10,000 by the crook. We did a search warrant at the location where my informant dropped the money off, and it was a typical flophouse. The million dollars, minus the ten thousand, was sitting on a pool table. When all was said and done, we recovered $4.8 million. We estimated that at least $20 million to $30 million had passed through this house. That was my informant's first case—a pretty good one.

On this one case, we recovered thousands of pounds of cocaine and marijuana and millions of dollars. Barry McCaffrey, the director of the Office of the National Drug Control Policy, the nation's "drug czar," came to Los Angeles from Washington, DC, to present us with plaques of recognition for this case. But they didn't notify us in advance. We were in the field, and they called us in. Our captain and our lieutenants were in the audience, in addition to some DEA bigwigs and district attorneys for this presentation. We formed a line, and they brought us up one at a time, and we had our picture taken with McCaffrey as he presented plaques and shook our hands. I was standing in line, and I had my "Billy Bob" teeth that I used sometimes for undercover purposes. My partner was next to me and said, "You haven't got a hair on your ass if you don't wear those when McCaffrey makes the presentation."

I was called up next, and I had my "Billy Bob" teeth in. I walked up and looked at McCaffrey, he looked at me, and I grinned with my "Billy Bob" teeth. They were horrible to look at. He turned to the camera, and I spit them out. The picture was taken with him and me and my regular teeth. The people in the audience just cracked up. McCaffrey never did realize that those weren't my regular teeth. One of the Metro guys who knew me and was part of the security detail for McCaffrey called me later and said, "Hey, all McCaffrey could talk about the rest of his trip was why doesn't LAPD have a dental plan?"

I had a dope case that started in Chino Hills, and we ended up getting twenty kilos of cocaine and quarter of a million dollars. From there, we did a search warrant in Ontario, and we got another two kilos. The whole case ended up in court in San Bernardino with a jury trial. My partner, Rich Biestros, a sheriff, and I went to court for five days. On the next-to-last day of testimony, they interrupted our trial

Mike Neel and Brian Agnew with recovered $4.8 million.

and brought in a guy from the Aryan Brotherhood for sentencing. He was going to be a third-striker for petty theft with a prior. He'd done all these other crimes, but the last thing he had done was steal three pairs of Levi's jeans from JC Penney. Our judge was going to sentence him and told our jurors to go into the hall. Well, they all went into a waiting room that had glass windows that looked right at the courtroom. They went in there because it was only going to take a few minutes. Rich started to walk out, and I said, "Rich, don't go."

Two people in the courtroom were obviously friends of this guy who was about to receive his sentence. The bailiff for the court was about sixty-five years old, and the judge had polio and used crutches and a wheelchair. The defendant was with his attorney, and he had a comic book in his hand. He was wrapping it tightly as the judge was talking to him. The judge asked him a question, and the guy was looking around. The judge said, "Are you paying attention to me?" The bailiff went up to the defendant, and the defendant stabbed the bailiff in the eye with the rolled-up comic book. Well, over the gate I went. I put a choke hold on him, and down to the floor the defendant went. We rolled him over and held him until other bailiffs came in and took the defendant back into confinement. The jury was glued to the windows.

The judge brought the jury back in, and he admonished the jury. He said, "Did you witness what went on here?" They all said they had. "Well, these officers are officers of the court. They are here to protect the court. You saw what this gentleman did to the bailiff. These officers took the appropriate action. Do you have any prejudice toward them?" No. No. No.

One day, my wife and I left a shopping center and headed for the freeway. We stopped at a red light, and I saw a white Buick Riviera with two gangsters in it. Then there was a brand-new Honda to its left with another gang member. The guy in the Honda handed a slide hammer to the guys in the Buick. I told my wife, "These guys just stole that car." I said, "Grab a piece of paper, and copy this down." I told her the license numbers to both cars and the descriptions of the guys. When we got home, I called the detectives for the police department, identified myself, and asked, "Do you have a stolen-vehicle problem with Hondas in your area?"

He said, "Yeah, we're losing ten a week, and we're finding them dumped up in this other area.

I said, "Well, here's my story," and I told him what I had seen.

He said, "This is too good to be true." The Honda had been stolen minutes before I'd seen it. It was found stripped a week later.

I ended up identifying three of the suspects, and they went to jail. About six weeks later, I went to the preliminary hearing. I got up on the stand to testify, and I was able to put it all together. The defense attorney wanted to question me to determine my experience to justify my actions toward his client. "How long have you been a policeman?" It was about eighteen years or something like that. "Well, do you have any expertise in the area of autos?"

I said, "I worked Hollenbeck Autos for two years as a trainee. We arrested hundreds." And I continued on. He didn't want to hear any more.

The suspects were held to answer and eventually convicted and went to state prison. The judge said, "Detective, good work. I just want these people here to know that even when you're not working, you're working."

My career with LAPD was awesome. How many people can say they worked for the same employer for thirty-five years and looked forward to going to work every day? I worked toward my interest, which was narcotics enforcement. I figured out how to promote to the point I was comfortable and still be able to do the work I loved in the field. I was fortunate to have worked a federal narcotics task force for fourteen years, conducting numerous investigations in most major cities in the United States. I probably would not have experienced what this great country has to offer had it not been for my career in law enforcement.

Stacey Morris

Birthplace: Los Angeles, California
Career: 1977–2007
Rank at Retirement: Detective II
Divisions: Devonshire, Communications, Wilshire, Juvenile Narcotics, West
    Bureau Violent Crimes Task Force, West Los Angeles, Training, North
    Hollywood, Bunco-Forgery, Newton, Commercial Crimes

We had a barricaded suspect, and the guy was shooting shotgun blasts right over our heads. We were behind a black-and-white, and I remember being on my knees, holding my gun in my hand, going, *Dear God, why am I not at home barefoot and pregnant? I should have listened to my mom.* Then you put it out of your mind. You tell yourself, *You're an officer. Do your job.* We kept the suspect contained, and eventually, SWAT went in and got the guy.

I was one of the first Jewish girls on the job. My parents wanted me to go to school; marry a nice, rich doctor; settle down; and have kids, like other Jewish girls. I turned out to be the black sheep by going into law enforcement. My family was a little upset with that; they had different expectations for me. I was seventeen years old and working at a Sizzler restaurant in Sherman Oaks, and occasionally, officers came in to eat. One day, Officer Mark Leap came in with his partner. They talked to me about getting a job with the police department. When I left work, I found they had left a flyer on my car. In '73, I applied to be a clerk typist, and the department hired me. I worked the morning watch in the Records and Identification Division at Parker Center.

Stacey Morris LAPD cadet identification card

Then I was accepted into the police cadet program. The cadets worked full-time, wore khaki uniforms, and did the same duties as property officers and jailers. The only difference was that we were paid less. My first assignment was Property Division, which was also at Parker Center. One of my jobs was to file the packages of narcotics. The narcotics were kept in a walk-in safe, and I was in there filing the packages. I was a young kid from the San Fernando Valley, and I had never been around this kind of stuff before. I was then transferred to Jail Division at the Van Nuys station. That was where I really got to learn what police work was about—every night, searching women and fighting the women. The officers would bring in drunk drivers who, it seemed, were either nurses or teachers. They would say, "You're not touching me," or "You're not gonna search me," and the fight was on. Every night, we were choking someone out; it was crazy. When it was quiet, maybe on a weekend, we used to take the prisoners out to a patio area. We wrapped Kotex napkins around our hands, and we'd play handball with the prisoners in the courtyard.

Sometimes we'd be searching someone, and then I'd have to tell the officers, "Wrong side, guys," because we had a female impersonator. Sometimes it wasn't until they were naked that we'd discover which side they needed to be on. One night, we had one woman who didn't want to be searched. We were trying to hold her legs apart, because we had to do complete strip searches in those days. We had to call a probationary officer in from the men's side, and we told him to hold her legs. He had to hold her legs apart as she was struggling, and his face was practically in her crotch. This poor kid, just coming on the job, brand new, was now holding this woman's legs apart so that we could search her. I'll never forget the look on his face.

In the jail, I worked with a lot of policewomen. One was Sergeant Grace Lindsay. She wore these little glasses, but she was tough as nails. One day, we had someone who was giving us problems. Grace came in, took off her glasses, set them down, and then put a C-clamp on this woman. Once the woman cooperated, Grace put her glasses back on and walked out. I thought, *God bless her!*

When cadets turned twenty-one, they had to leave the cadet program. I applied to the department to be a police officer, passed everything, and went into the academy in March 1977. During the hiring selection process, there was only one list. It wasn't women, it wasn't Hispanics, it wasn't African Americans—it was just one list. I wasn't selected just because I was a female. I was selected because I had earned it. I was proud of that.

After graduation, I was assigned to Devonshire Division, which was not one of my three choices. At the time, the department wanted at least a couple of women in each patrol division. I argued that my badge said "police officer," not "female police officer." They

Stacey Morris, with academy classmates,
two-on-one self-defense drill

Mary Weisser and Stacey Morris: academy graduation, 1977

said they didn't care, that they needed a woman in each division. At Devonshire, some of the male officers had never worked with a woman in a patrol car. They went home and talked about us to their wives, some of whom became jealous. Another problem was that some male officers started having feelings for us. One officer was writing me love letters, and another officer said he was falling in love with me. I had to tell them, "Listen, you don't understand." Some didn't know the difference between love and friendship. About a year later, the department initiated a program on partner relations that I was involved in. We taught officers the difference between respect and caring and emotional love. Some of the male officers just did not know how to work beside us.

Female officers were unique to the citizens too. One time, we were going through some park at nighttime. I was on our car's public-address system, telling a guy who was riding a motorcycle to pull over and get off the bike. He stopped and got off the bike, and he was laughing. I said, "What are you laughing at?"

He said, "You should have heard yourself—'Get off the bike!' You know, high pitched." He said, "When a woman yells, her voice goes up!"

What could I do? My partner and I started laughing too. The truth was the truth.

Another time, we stopped another guy, again on a motorcycle. He got off his bike and had his hands to his sides, and he was shaking. I said, "What are you shaking for?"

He said, "I'm afraid of a woman with a gun."

I said, "What?"

"I'm afraid of a woman with a gun."

"Okay, fine." Because we were so new, the public really hadn't become aware of us. There were probably twenty female officers in the field at that time.

My partners learned that because of my experience in the jail, I was able to handle myself. I remember one time, Michael Hohan and his partner got a call of a family dispute, and I told my partner, "Let's go by there."

When we got there, I could see Mike in the middle of a crowd. He was holding a suspect who had assaulted him. He was surrounded and getting pummeled by these people. All I remember was grabbing my baton and just swinging at anyone I could until I could get to Mike. One of Mike's eyes was closed shut, and he didn't know where he was going. I grabbed him, and we got him out of there. What came out of the incident was that a female officer would actually fight. Honestly, I don't think the people in the crowd even noticed that I was female. Some officers told me, "You did a great job. We're proud of you."

At the hospital, the captain and the commander said to me, "We want to thank you for saving the officer's life." From that incident, I finally got the respect—or at least some respect—that I felt I deserved.

In '78, I wheeled to Communications Division at Parker Center. When officers finished their tours at Communications, they put in for three divisions and hoped to get one of their choices. I was sent to Wilshire Division in July '79. "I didn't put in for Wilshire," I said.

"You're a female."

"No, I'm a police officer."

"Yes, but you're a female."

When I got to Wilshire, Captain Joe De Ladurantely called me into his office and said, "I hear you're not happy about being here."

I said, "No, I'm not. My badge says 'police officer,' not 'female.'"

He said, "Yes, but you're here now, and we'll make things good for you." As it turned out, he didn't have to do anything. I worked with some great officers at Wilshire, and that was where I learned what police work was really about. I worked with one old-timer, Sam Bass, whom we called "Smiley." He'd been working Wilshire for many years. He knew the suspects, and he knew how to talk to them. Another officer was Joe Curreri. Joe was one of the first officers who actually treated me as a partner, not as a female.

One sergeant, though, had never been around female officers, so he was trying to be protective of me. I was working by myself, and I stopped a guy. The sergeant said, "Why are you stopping this guy?"

I said, "For a traffic violation."

He said, "You're a female."

I said, "I'm glad you noticed."

"It's unsafe."

"But I'm an officer." That was how it continued for us until about 1980, when the department made a push to hire more female police officers.

Narcotics Division approached me to work an undercover assignment in the Juvenile Buy Program. I accepted and was placed in a high school for three months. The problem was, I was twenty-five years old, and I was well endowed. I had to find clothes to fit that didn't make me stand out. So I wore overalls. My undercover name was Ann. At first, they enrolled me at this one high school because I had never been in that area before. We thought no one would know me. The first day in class, some kid turned around and said, "You know, you look like this female officer that worked Parker Center." Right out of the blue. He was a student worker for the department.

I was then placed in another high school. You know, when you go through high school normally, you're doing the best you can. Here, I was trying to be somewhat bad. I tried to take the English tests, and I was failing—not intentionally. I just couldn't pass the tests. I realized how much I had forgotten, or maybe the kids were just much smarter than I was. It played well for my undercover work though. I did my drug buys, and after fourth period, I'd go to a fast-food place across the street and continue buying drugs there. I did well.

We had what was called a "round up," and the kids I bought from were arrested. I would be at a location, and I had to identify them. There was one guy who was not a student, but I bought from him at the fast-food place. He was told he was under arrest for selling drugs

*Stacey Morris with other undercover juvenile narcotics officers,
l to r: Charles Anderson, Steve Richards, Mike Sullivan, John
Whipp, and Ruben Holguin*

to an undercover officer. He said, "I didn't sell drugs to an undercover officer." Then he saw me standing there. He said, "Ann! Ann! Tell them I didn't." Then he looked down and saw my badge. "Officer Ann, Officer Ann, tell them I didn't sell to an undercover officer." This guy was wacked-out. "Officer Ann, okay, fine."

I arrested one girl's father for narcotics. She came to me after court and said, "I want to thank you for arresting my father. It helped out the family." That made me feel good. I guess in this job, if you can help one person, change one person's life, then maybe at the end of the day, you can look back and know you had done a good job. On this job, you don't get a lot of thanks. But I got it from a suspect's kid, and that was nice.

Female officers were often asked to work extra details. When I first came on, I was a decoy for the Hillside Strangler case. I had just graduated from the academy, and I was working Devonshire Division. The detectives put me on a bus bench in Eagle Rock to see if the suspects would approach me. I apparently fit the bill, being a female with blonde hair. I had a wire, and I was on this bus bench for two nights, but nothing happened. As I was sitting on this bench, I was thinking, *What do I do if this guy comes up? What if there is more than one?* Honestly, I felt as if I were flying by the seat of my pants.

If anything happened, I was hoping my training would kick in. A couple of months later, they did arrest the suspects, Angelo Buono and Kenneth Bianchi.

I applied and was selected for a training-officer position at West LA Division. While there, Wells Fargo Bank wanted some officers to work undercover as bank tellers as a second job for robbery suppression. Two other officers and I were selected. We actually worked as bank tellers, but we were armed. The people in the bank knew we were officers, but none of the customers knew. As bank tellers, though, we still had to balance at the end of the day. Asking police officers to do math wasn't the greatest thing, but I balanced. A customer walked up to the counter and asked if he could conduct a transaction—deposit some money or something—and I said, "Let me see your ID."

He said, "You know, you sound just like a cop." I had to tweak my approach a little. Fortunately, there were no robberies while I was there. The bank experience would prove beneficial for me later in my career.

While at West LA, I got a vice spot. Nick Barbara was my supervisor, and Ed Oliver was my partner. One night, Nick was driving, I was hiding in the trunk of the car, and he approached a prostitute on La Cienega Boulevard. I had a radio, and I was holding the trunk lid down so that I could jump out if Nick got a violation. As he approached the prostitute, she jumped into the car in front of him, and they took off. Nick said, "Get outta the car—quick!"

I said, "I don't have time. Take off."

Nick was driving like a bat outta hell following this car, going over bumps and around corners. I didn't know where we were, and I was just going all over the trunk. We got the girl, and we got the john, but we ended up somewhere in South LA. That wasn't the first time I was in the trunk as an overhear officer. Normally, we'd get the violation, and then I'd jump out. One time, I didn't jump out as quickly as I had hoped. I kinda tripped over and fell. Sometimes I was in the backseat trying to hide, and I'd pop up and say, "Hi!"

Just before the '84 Olympics, Ad Vice Division wanted to close down all the outcall prostitution services. Ad Vice created a fictitious company called Express West. Express West would handle credit-card invoices for each outcall service for a fee. Each service was required to place on each invoice the customer's name, address, phone number, and driver's license number. They had to call in for an authorization number, and every prostitute would put her name on the receipt. One of the detectives, using the name Dave, acted as the manager of the company. Carol Aborn and I were the bookkeepers. Every week, someone from a service would come into our Express West office and talk to Dave, and he'd go through every receipt with them as if it were a business. He essentially got them admitting that the money was earned through prostitution. When the Olympics were about to start, Dave set up a party. He told all of the services that he wanted all the prostitutes to come to the party. When they walked in, all of the prostitutes were arrested, and search warrants were served on the outcall-service locations. The operation closed down almost every outcall service in the city of Los Angeles. Some of these customers were spending thousands and thousands of dollars on prostitutes. It was amazing. We were actually getting calls from men who were asking, "What's this?" in reference to a charge on their credit-card statement listed as "Party Company, so and so." They were asking, "What is Express West? I never use Express West."

We would say, "You know, you had a party."

And the guy would say, "I never had a party."

"Nooo, you had a *party*."

The guy would go, "Ohhh."

When my vice tour ended, I transferred to North Hollywood Division patrol as a training officer. One night, Louis Varga and I saw a car drive into a convenience-store parking lot. There was tape over the rear license plate, covering the license number. Great detective work, you know—ding-dong, could be a robber. We stopped the guy, we got out, and I told the guy, "Let's see your hands."

He opened the door, and then he shut it and took off. The pursuit was on, and we eventually went over the hill into Hollywood. The guy crashed at the corner of Franklin and Highland, and he bailed out. Louis went in foot pursuit. He ran down Highland and then into an alley. I saw Louis throw his baton, his flashlight, and something else at him, and I was laughing, because what more was he going to throw at this guy? The air unit was overhead. I was in the car, and I came around onto Highland and then onto a side street to cut the suspect off. The suspect was running on the sidewalk, and somehow he ran into the front fender of the police car. He staggered back, and then he ran into the back of the car. He fell down, and we took him into custody. He

Stacey Morris

had a gun, he was on parole, and he had committed multiple robberies. He was high on PCP, and he didn't realize he'd run into the car. I was told by the air unit, "That was great driving. It was amazing how many times the guy ran into your car."

In '85, I worked an off-duty job with some detectives from the Financial Crimes Section of Bunco-Forgery. They told me that I should apply for a detective trainee position, and I did. I was selected over another due to my experience working the bank teller position with Wells Fargo. I knew about deposits and credit cards and the security features of a bank. I was assigned downtown, working the NSF, nonsufficient funds, section. The majority of forgers weren't bad people. A lot of them had had some form of education. There was a thought process behind the forgery. It wasn't just going in, pointing a gun, and walking out.

Probably one of the best cases I ever had was on a suspect from Puerto Rico. I'd been looking for him for almost ten years, and twice I'd had him portrayed on *America's Most Wanted*. He was a quasi-attorney. He would call up a parish priest or a minister in Los Angeles and say, "I'm an attorney. I'm coming to Los Angeles from

Puerto Rico, and I'm looking for the heir to an estate. I need someone to drive me around that needs a little extra money." The priest would put him in touch with some person in need. He would get friendly with these people and be invited to their house for dinner. At their house, he would steal their personal checks. He would represent the stolen checks to others as checks from his clients. He'd say, "I have checks from my clients. Will you deposit these checks into your account, and I'll give you five hundred dollars?" He would write checks for $1,200, $1,800, or $2,000. They would deposit the checks, and he would let them keep $500, and they'd give him the difference. He'd say, "Take me back to the Biltmore Hotel. I'm going to change clothes, and we'll go out for dinner." The people would take him to the hotel and sit there waiting for him, but he had already left.

He did this all over the country, using different names, and he was wanted in seven or eight states. He was arrested once in Texas and escaped by pretending to have a heart attack. When an ambulance was transporting him, he jumped out of the ambulance and escaped. Finally, he was arrested in Puerto Rico. Juan Baello and I went to Puerto Rico and brought him back. This guy would do anything to get out of jail. He was in our jail, calling the FBI and the LA sheriffs, telling them he knew about homicides, bombings, and terrorists groups. When we went to court, the FBI and the LA sheriffs were saying they wanted to talk to this guy. I told them all he wanted was to get out of jail and he would say anything. They talked the judge into releasing him into FBI custody, and the FBI put him in a hotel. During the night, he walked out. That was it. They didn't call us for three months to tell us he'd walked out; they were too embarrassed to tell us that they'd lost him. He was supposed to plead guilty on our case, and they were going to bring him back in six months for sentencing. If the information he had proved to be good, they would talk to the judge and get his sentence reduced. That was the deal. I kept telling them that he was going to do everything he could to get away from them. I was so mad.

When I was promoted to detective at the end of '89, I went to Newton Division and, six months later, Commercial Crimes Division. I was working Commercial Crimes when the riots occurred in '92. I remember walking out of the office as the riots were starting, and I was thinking to myself, *Why are they letting me go home?* The next morning, I was called at home to come in. I thought, *Why didn't the*

Detectives Phil Wright, Stacey Morris, Pat Green, and Bob Hansen:
Forgery Division, 1996

department mobilize us and keep us at work? I felt let down by the department, both for the community and for the officers. We were sent to Wilshire Division in uniform, four of us to a car. We were in Wilshire for five days. On Western Avenue, there were Koreans shooting at looters who were stealing stuff out of their stores. At first, we were ducking behind walls because we didn't know whom they were shooting at. They were trying to protect their property, and I felt good that they were willing to do that. Rocks were thrown at our police cars. It was mayhem. Once the riots slowed down, we were essentially doing traffic enforcement. We'd look around at buildings smoldering, and we couldn't understand why they were burning their own community. It didn't make any sense to destroy your own homes, your markets, and your shopping centers. But that was what happened.

One of the last cases I handled involved a suspect named Arnel, a Filipino. I arrested Arnel four or five times. Just before I retired, we arrested Arnel again. I said, "Hi, Arnel. You remember me?"

He said, "Yeah, but you've gained weight."

I just laughed. Okay, the truth hurts. I told him, "Yeah, I gained a little weight. It won't affect the sentencing, you know." When the suspects start realizing you're gaining weight, maybe it's time to do something different.

In reflection, I had the best job in the world. I'm proud that everything I did was on my own merit. And even though I didn't follow their initial expectations, my parents were proud of me too. And speaking of their expectations, yes, I did marry a doctor and settle down!

Patricia "Patty" Fuller

Birthplace: Huntington Park, California
Career: 1984–2009
Rank at Retirement: Police Officer III + I
Divisions: Rampart, Newton, Air Support, Bomb Detection K-9 Unit

One night, I left the "doghouse," which was the office for the Bomb Detection K-9 Unit, and got on the freeway. My partner, Don Bender, another handler with his dog, was behind me. We would follow each other home because we lived in the same neighborhood. All of a sudden, a car in front of me spun out of control, hit the guide rail, and flipped over. Don stopped traffic, and I ran over to assist the driver. This young lady was upside down in her car, held by her safety belt, and there was gas pouring all over the place. She was almost losing consciousness. I reached in, grabbed her hand, and said, "You're going to be okay; I won't leave you."

She squeezed my hand and said, "Please don't leave me."

There was obviously some head trauma, and I didn't want to move her. I held her hand until the fire department came. They got her out and took her to a hospital. Somehow that story was published and played on a local radio station. Later, there was a sign on a billboard at that spot that said, "Officer Fuller held the hand of a woman trapped in a car." I was just doing my job. I would expect somebody to do the same for my family members or me. That was what I always said: "Treat them the way your family members would want to be treated."

At first, I wanted to be a veterinarian, but we had *Adam-12*, then *Police Story*, and then *Policewoman* on television. I was intrigued and decided that was what I wanted to do—I wanted to be a police officer. I wanted to be Angie Dickinson and work vice and do all of that stuff. Eventually, I did, but it wasn't in the nice clothes or in the nice area. I used to mimic, "One-Adam-12, 1-Adam-12. See the woman." I was too short to be an officer, so I applied to become an RTO, a radio-telephone operator. I was hired in August 1977 and was an RTO until 1984, when I became a police officer. I actually worked with Sharon Claridge, the original voice from the *Adam-12* series. She was an instructor in Communications Division.

In RTO training, there was a Geiger-type counter to track the level of our voices. We could not get excited. We would be written up if the needle went to the excited level. I'd just take a big, deep breath and say, "All units. Officer needs help. Shots fired," and give the location. One night, a Harbor Division unit broadcasted, "Shots fired—officer down." On this call, it was at 1300 Ross Place. I was brand new at the time, and I was a little shaky. I put it out as Roth Place and not Ross Place. They were strict. I was told, "You cannot miss anything, because it's somebody's life out there."

RTOs were sometimes confronted with unusual situations. We'd get a voice on the radio saying, "Hello, hello." I would think, "What is that?" On this one occasion, it was a citizen. I put the frequency on standby. I said, "Citizen on the radio, go ahead." He'd start to talk and cut out, and I had to say, "Hold the button in. Tell me what you have. Is it an emergency?"

A motor cop had crashed, and this citizen had gotten on the radio and said, "Yes, I have this motorcycle. He crashed."

"Where are you, sir?" He gave me the location, and I yelled out, "Ambulance!"

One time, I had an officer say, "I'm having a baby."

"Repeat."

"I'm having a baby."

And then you would figure it out. "Okay, do you need an ambulance?"

For some of the boot officers, we had to drag it out of them or help them along, "What are you requesting?" If an officer gave me a bad time, I'd tell my relief, "Give him a traffic accident—something." They would quickly learn to be nice to their RTO.

There were a number of RTOs married to police officers. We all knew that if a uniform that had stars or bars came through Communications and talked to a senior RTO or sergeant and then an RTO was pulled from her position, it was not good. A couple of times that happened. One

Two RTO's working their assigned divisions.

night, an RTO was working Harbor Division and South Traffic Division frequencies when an officer put out a help call: "Officer needs help—officer down." At the time, her fiancé was working Harbor Division and in the field. She broadcasted the help call; she was professional and calm while handling the emergency. When the situation allowed, she went on her break and did not appear overtly worried. She came back from her break, now knowing that her fiancé had been involved in the incident, and she continued to work the frequency. She said, "I'm not going to let it bother me, because I know he's in good hands. There are good hospitals, and he works with good officers." A short time later, a captain and a couple of officers came to get her to take her to the hospital. Her fiancé did not make it. That was how it was. RTOs had to be cool and calm while working their positions, especially during an emergency, and with the knowledge that the emergency could involve them personally.

One night, I was working next to Laura Robles. She was bilingual and working the Northeast and Hollenbeck frequencies. All of a sudden, she started speaking Spanish. Then just as suddenly, she broke into English: "All units. Officer needs help." She kept putting it out— English, Spanish, English, Spanish. After a short while, they went to a different tactical frequency. She said, "That was a hard one."

"What happened?"

She said, "He was a brand-new guy. I knew it when I sat down. He had an accent. Well, when he put out the help call, he broke down, and he reverted to Spanish." She said, "I had to put it out in Spanish so he would calm down, and then the other units were saying, 'What's going on?' I broadcasted in English for them." Luckily, Laura was on that frequency and could do that for that officer.

In '83, the department lowered the height requirement to become a police officer. I applied, passed all the testing, and entered the March '84 academy class. We graduated early because of the 1984 Olympics. We were only in the academy for three months, and we were sent to the Olympic venues for traffic control. We had no radios. I remember we were directing traffic, and a citizen called over one of my classmates to a bus. My classmate went on the bus, and he said to me, "Come here, come here." He was as white as a ghost. He said, "There's a guy in there that's been shot."

I went on the bus, and because of the stories that I'd known as an RTO about the different people who frequented Central Division, I said, "He's not shot. It's a stoma from a colostomy." I said, "Don't get near him, because he will throw that colostomy bag at you." It stunk, and there were flies, and people were starting to puke on the bus. I got on the Gamewell and asked for a Central patrol unit to handle the drunk. My classmate thought for sure that was his first shooting scene.

One night, I was working with Ernest Dunton, a civilian traffic control officer, and we were directing traffic at Washington and Vermont. Ernest and I took turns directing traffic. It was his turn, and all of a sudden, here came a car, and I could hear it screaming. It was a little yellow station wagon, and this guy literally ran into Ernest. His body flew up into the air and came down on the windshield, and he was carried on the car for a block. The suspect jerked the wheel, and Ernest fell off the car. I went running to him, and he was all twisted up. I got on the radio—we had radios by then—and I said, "Requesting an ambulance. I have a traffic officer down." I gave the suspects' info and the direction they had gone. Rampart officers caught the suspects. My RTO experience came into play. I could rattle off all this stuff without getting upset and nervous. Ernest was in bad shape, very bad shape. After that, the civilian traffic control officers were given reflector vests.

After the Olympics, I was assigned to Rampart Division. My training officer was Louie Lozano. He was big and tall, and I was five foot four. He grabbed my days-off sheet, looked me up and down, and said, "Last female I had, I tried to fire."

I thought, *Oh, this is going to be good.*

Patty Fuller receives diploma from Chief Daryl Gates, 1984

Louie and I turned out to be good partners.

My first dead-body radio call was off Echo Park Avenue, and it was an infant. Louie and I walked into this apartment. I was looking around, and I didn't see a baby. There were two people sitting on a couch, and the place was a mess; clothes, food, and cockroaches were all over the place. Louie asked, "Where's the child?"

The baby was in all these nasty, dirty clothes. I looked around some more and saw hype needles. At first, we thought that the mother or whoever had mixed up the baby formula using a dirty spoon with heroin and that was probably how the baby had died. We found out later the baby had died from SIDS. I was taking notes while Louie went outside. I could tell something was different about him. Later on, he said, "I have to commend you on how you handled that infant-death call." He said, "You didn't fall apart, but it will get harder."

I knew what he meant, because as years went by and I saw more little victims, I changed. At first, I thought, *How did this happen?* Then after a while, I thought, *My God, how many of these do I have to see before something is done?* The one thing that would bring me back when I saw these horrible things was the thought that I had done my job. I couldn't dwell on it.

After probation, I transferred to Newton Division, where I spent eleven years. On my first day, I knew it was home. I eventually worked with Hugh O'Gara on 13A61. Hugh had worked Newton for a long time. He had such a commanding presence, and everybody knew him. We worked together like hand in glove. The gang bangers would call us "Lurch" and "Little Bit" because he was so big. Hugh was at Newton so long that when he retired, the number of his basic car, 13A61, was retired as well. There is no more 13A61. He was a policeman's policeman.

We had a child-abuse case one time in which the child had third-degree burns on the buttocks area and the private area and down the

Patty Fuller, front: Newton Division inspection

legs. The hospital was not equipped for burn cases, so the little girl was taken by ambulance to the burn ward in Van Nuys. We had the mother with us. She did not speak English, and she had another child with her, a seven-year-old. She was also pregnant. The doctor at the burn ward told us he thought the little girl had been burned by hot water. The detectives arrived, and they told us to go to the house to see what we could find. We went to the house, and in the bathtub was a five-gallon bucket with water in it. I felt the water, and it was still scalding. I thought, *Tap water can't get that hot.* We went in the kitchen, and there were pots of water that she had been boiling. That was what the mother had done. The child had been placed in the bucket and burned up to her waist area. We arrested and booked the mother. Later, I got a call from the prosecuting attorney. She told me the mother had lost her pregnancy in jail. I commented, "Well, it's too bad the judge can't order her to get her tubes tied or some sort of birth control."

The attorney said, "That's the first thing that I'm going to ask the judge."

I went to court and testified about what we had found in the home. The attorney told the judge, "Because of the circumstances and that there were other children, I'm requesting the court order the mother to have her tubes tied."

Naturally, the judge said, "That's against the first amendment, blah, blah, blah." But the attorney did ask, and that surprised me. Most attorneys wouldn't have the fortitude to do that.

Some follow-ups weren't so successful. It was Christmas Eve, and my partner, Porfirio Navarro, and I got a call to go to Children's Hospital on another child-abuse case. This little boy's skull had been fractured, and he was being kept alive for organ donation. The mother and the boyfriend were there. Naturally, at first, we assumed the boyfriend had done it. The child-abuse detective met us. Porfirio spoke Spanish, so he stayed there to talk to the mother and the boyfriend, and I went with the detective to do a follow-up to the residence. On our way over there, I was thinking the address sounded familiar. We drove up, and I told the detective, "Sir, I was here a couple of weeks ago, but I don't quite remember which apartment."

He said, "Well, let's go to the apartment and see."

It was the same apartment. I told the detective we had been there to keep the peace when the social workers had released a little three-year-old boy into the mother's custody. We didn't know the background of the case. It turned out the little boy had been in his mother's way with the new boyfriend. So she had shaken him and pounded his head on a porcelain toilet. I hadn't recognized the little boy because of his injuries; he was so bloated from the medication and what they were doing to keep his vital organs alive for donation.

One time, I backed a Central Division unit—Wolf Dietzman and his partner—on a child-abuse-in-progress radio call. When we arrived, a lady came out and said, "He's doing something to his kid, and we don't know what it is, but the kid's screaming."

We could hear his screaming. At the door, Wolf shouted, "Police!" and the kid screamed louder. Well, they kicked the door in. Wolf was the first one in. He took the child in his arms, and my partner and Wolf's partner had this guy on the bed, pinned down, handcuffing him. I looked, and this little boy didn't have a diaper on. He had a bloody little butt, and there was blood on the sheets. This guy had been sodomizing the child. I had to gather the sheets, the clothing, and the suspect's underwear. I later called Wolf at the hospital, and he said, "Patty, the baby just clung to me." Wolf told me, "If that baby would have gone to you, I would have killed the son of a bitch."

We saw a lot of horrible things. It made me appreciate how my parents had raised me, what I had, and how bad I felt for what others didn't have.

There was an old black gentleman in Newton—Clifford Goodwin— who was ninety-six years old and played the piano. He lived on Fifty-First Street, near Avalon Boulevard. When his wife died, we went to the call for a death investigation. I was talking to him in his little apartment, and he was in a daze. He said, "Yep, that was my Minerva. She was such a kid at ninety-four." He was beside himself.

I said, "Do you have any family I could call?"

"No. Minerva was all I had."

He was wearing a sports jacket with Los Angeles City pins on it. I found out he was a retired City Parks employee, and he worked South Park. I told him my mom had grown up in the '40s and spent her teens in a house on Park Front Walk. Park Front Walk was a row of houses that faced South Park. He said, "What was your mom's name?"

I said, "Patricia, like my name."

He said, "Where did she live?"

I told him the address.

He said, "Was there a big peach tree out in front of her house?"

I said, "You know, Clifford, I don't know that, but I'll ask my mom."

He said, "Did she look like you?"

I said, "Well, I guess."

I talked to my mom the next day, and she said, "We had the only peach tree on the row." Clifford had remembered my mom and where she had lived. I felt so bad for Clifford that I went to check on him later, and he became my little guy that I adopted. He was almost blind, and he didn't have anybody else. I took him Christmas presents every year—flannel pajamas and socks. I would check on him and take him meals. I even took him to the eye doctor on my off-duty time for his glaucoma surgery. Later, when I went to Air Support Division, I would have Hugh check on him. One Christmas, I called Hugh and asked him if Clifford had gotten his gift. He was silent. I said, "Hugh, did Clifford pass away?"

He said, "Yeah, I didn't want to tell you." He said, "But he was taken care of." Clifford was 102 years old when he passed away.

Donna Cox and I were working Narcotics one day when I saw a guy with a gun in his waistband on Fifty-Ninth Place. I said, "Donna, that guy in the plaid shirt has a gun."

We stopped, I got out, and I drew down on him. I said, "Put your hands up." My intent was "Put your hands up, get on the ground, and keep your hands away from the gun." But he kept walking toward me. "Get your fucking hands up."

He didn't want to do that. He went for the gun and brought it up. It was like slow motion as I fired. Then it looked as if tomato paste came out of his shirt, and he kind of collapsed. I could smell the gunpowder. All of a sudden, everybody started coming out of the woodwork, and we put out a help call. The guy was okay. The round had hit him right in the stomach because when his gun had come up, I had been watching his hand. During the investigation, they asked me, "Okay, what did he look like?"

Well, he was ten feet tall, and he was carrying a bazooka—that was what it had looked like to me.

They said, "What did the gun look like?"

I said, "It looked like a big-ass chrome forty-five."

It turned out that it was a replica of a .45. It was a pellet gun. At the time, I was not going to say to the guy, "Time out. Excuse me. Oh, that's a pellet gun. That's not the real thing." At the scene, once other officers were there, and as we were waiting for the detectives, I went across the street to a muffler shop and called the station. We did not have cell phones then. I said to Sergeant Barry Ross, the watch commander at Newton, "Sarge, there's been a shooting here."

He said, "Holy jump to Jesus. Well, who's involved?"

I said, "Me."

He said, "Were you the shooter?"

I said, "Yeah."

He said, "Holy jump to Jesus." That was his favorite phrase. He said, "Well, who're you working with?"

"Donna Cox."

"They sent two women out?" That was Barry; he just went on and on. He said, "Well, are you going to come to the station?"

I said, "Yeah."

"Who's transporting?"

I said, "Annette."

He said, "You know what? I just can't win. I can't win."

I was kicked in the stomach once during a fight. I didn't think anything of it when I was fighting. When it was over, Sergeant Jim Smalling said, "Are you okay, Patty?"

My nametag was hanging, I was dirt from one end to the other, and my uniform was ripped. I said, "Yeah." Because one of the officers had used chemical spray on the suspect, I told the sergeant, "I have another uniform I'll put on while they're getting him situated."

While I was changing, I went to the bathroom. "Oh, this isn't good." How do you tell a male sergeant who was not used to working with females that you were bleeding internally? I said, "Hey, Sarge. You know, I think I am hurt a little bit." I literally had a shoe print on my stomach.

He said, "What's wrong?"

I said, "Well, I'm bleeding."

"From where?"

I said, "You don't want to know." He looked at me, and I said, "I think I need to get checked out, because it's not my time."

He said, "Okay, I'll take you to the hospital."

He took me over to the hospital. The suspect had hit me so hard that I had hematomas in my uterus, so that got me the night off.

Then I got a spot in Newton Vice. It wasn't glamorous, it wasn't in a nice area, and I was the only female. One time, we were working a prostitution-enforcement task force. I was wearing a wire, and I was standing on the corner of Forty-Ninth Street at Broadway. It was December, and I was freezing. My supervisor and a couple of other officers were close by. I was getting violations all night long. Then one car came up with Georgia plates; it was a green Buick Regal with a black guy in it. He gave me a violation, and I told him, "Go around into the alley."

The guy drove off, and I gave my signal. I was waiting for the next violation, and all of a sudden, I heard sirens. My sergeant grabbed me and said, "Get back to the command post." Our chase car, Abe Barron and Bill Reiner, had stopped the suspect in the Buick, put him in plastic handcuffs, placed him in the backseat of their black-and-white, and parked the guy's car. Abe, rest his soul, went to get in the black-and-white to sit behind the driver. When he opened the door, the suspect, who had popped the plastic handcuffs, went immediately for Abe's gun. Bill put out a help call. We were on a different frequency, so we didn't know what was going on until we heard the sirens. The suspect had Abe's gun partly out of the holster, and he and Abe were struggling over it. Bill couldn't shoot, because Abe would've been in the way. Bill used his flashlight and conked the guy over the head, and they subdued him. The suspect had just gotten out of prison. Bill messed up his elbow really bad during the fight, and he now has a plastic elbow because of it. Abe was later killed in a traffic accident while working the Northeast Division Unsolved Murder Squad. He was a good guy and fun to work with. That flashlight saved both officers.

I took an oral interview for Air Support Division, got a loan and then a permanent position as an observer. Again, being an RTO helped me because in the helicopter, we listened to avionics frequencies as well as our department frequencies. One night, we responded to a burglary call in Southwest Division. I saw the burglar—he was on the roof, and then he jumped off the roof. He was running, and I told the units, "Shop 502, hold your position, and I need a unit at the far end of this street."

Bob Baker and Patty Fuller

I was watching the burglar running, and I saw him looking back, and he hit a clothesline. *Boom*—he went down. He got up, and then he ran into a bougainvillea bush—and you know that hurt. He climbed over a block wall fence, and on the other side, there was a Rottweiler waiting for him. Now he was fighting with this Rottweiler. He got away from the Rottweiler, and his clothes were ripped. My partner and I were laughing because this guy was just running into one obstacle after another. He climbed one more fence, and I told the officers, "He's running right toward you."

Well, then a Chihuahua came at him. The officers came around the corner, and the guy just dropped and put himself in a felony prone position, and they hooked him up. The Chihuahua was just circling and yapping. The sergeant at the scene later called me and said, "Were you working?"

"Yes, sir."

"I want your name and serial number."

"Okay."

"This arrestee was claiming that the officers beat him."

I started laughing.

He said, "What's so funny?"

I said, "It was all self-inflicted. I can tell you exactly what happened. He's probably got a mark around his neck because he was clotheslined, he should have scratches from a bougainvillea bush, and he should have some dog bites." I said, "All of his injuries were sustained prior, because when the officers got there, he gave himself up." I thought that was funny.

Pilot Bob Baker was my Hugh O'Gara at Air Support Division. He told me he wanted to go to Special Flights before he retired in a year. I told him I wanted a bomb-dog-handler spot. He said, "Well, maybe we'll both get lucky," and we did. He went to Special Flights, and after five years at air support, I got a spot with the bomb K-9 unit.

My first bomb dog was Amber, a little black Lab. She was the littlest dog in the unit. We did a lot of work together; then she got a little spot on her, and it ended up being a mast cell tumor. We had it removed, but it affected her stamina. A dog searching for bombs has to be able to work a certain amount of time without tiring out. She couldn't do that, so she was retired and given to me. Then I got Nero, a big Belgian Malinois. His name was Nero, but he was nicknamed "Mr. Grinch." I went from working with the littlest dog of the unit to the biggest dog.

Mr. Grinch's primary training had been for military; he was supposed to go to Bosnia, but he wasn't aggressive enough. He had been sent to the civilian side for police work and cross-trained in bite work and bomb detection. He could smell minute traces of explosives; his nose was that good. He had previously worked with the New York Port Authority and had done searches of the Twin Towers during the aftermath of a bombing in 1993 and many searches thereafter. When the New York handler promoted to sergeant, Mr. Grinch was returned to the training facility in Texas, and I was chosen as his new handler.

There was a case involving the leader of the Jewish Defense League. The FBI was working a sting on him. It was my understanding that he wanted to get hold of explosives to blow up some places. The investigation had been going on for a few months when an undercover agent made an exchange with the suspect. We were at the place where the exchange occurred to conduct a search. I mentioned to my supervisor, Frank Long, that the FBI guys who had cleared the house were, in the eyes of Mr. Grinch, dressed in big, giant bite suits. I wondered how my dog was going to react. There was also a German shepherd on the property, and my dog was a dogfighter. Well, Mr.

Amber

Grinch was all business. He bypassed all the FBI guys and the other dog. We went in and started searching, and all of a sudden, he dragged me to a closet in a bathroom off a bedroom. He found something, and he sat. "Good boy, good boy. Let's go. Come on, buddy," I said.

I got him out of there. He had found a cache of weapons and a large amount of smokeless powder. Then we did a search of the garage, and he was sniffing. I told Frank, "Sarge, you know what? He didn't go final. He didn't sit down, but there was something in there." Frank checked with the FBI. The table that Mr. Grinch was sniffing and sniffing was where the undercover agent had made the exchange. The scent was faint, but he knew something had been there.

Eventually, the time came to retire Mr. Grinch. I had his hips examined to see if he could stay on the job until I retired, but the veterinarian found a tumor. It was hemangiosarcoma. Like Amber, he was retired to me. He had chemotherapy and lasted four more years than he should have. We had worked together for eight years. When I was in the K-9 bomb unit, I dealt with the VCA Animal Hospital. The VCA Animal Hospital put together a donation in his name to UC Davis. The vet at the VCA said, "That's the hardest one I've ever had to do." Mr. Grinch was like a legend there. They loved him. The New York

Patty Fuller and "Mr. Grinch"

Port Authority put a donation together in his name and donated it to Cornell University. After Mr. Grinch went, Amber was never the same. Then it came her time. Both had sixteen good years.

There were so many things on the department for a young officer to do. I felt that every door was open; all I had to do was knock. I was fortunate to work some good details. My career was a good one, but it was fast—very fast—and I miss it.

When I was an RTO and listened to the things happening in the field, I often wondered, *What does it look like?* When I became a police officer, I thought, *Okay, this is what it looks like.* It was like finding the piece to a puzzle that was missing.

Tribute

Author academy class, March 1975: Dan Miller, holding flag; Sgt. Ken Dionne, third row, third from left; Bob Jarvis, third row, far right; author, seated, far right

Gary Hein

A special tribute to my academy classmates, particularly Dan Miller, and to my instructors, including Sergeant Ken Dionne and Bob Jarvis, all of whom provided me inspiration to survive, excel, and graduate from the academy. To those I worked with during my career, I humble myself before you in respect and devotion. One special person, Gary Hein, a relative by marriage and an LAPD officer for more than twenty years, encouraged me to come on the department and provided me advice throughout my career. At the beginning of the academy, he told me, "Don't drop out of any runs." I took from that advice to be prepared, be committed, and do the job. I followed that advice till the day I retired.

Photo Credits

Note: All photos, unless indicated below, were from the officers in the book or were considered public domain.

The following photos were courtesy of:

Affree Family 225
Associated Press 131
Burgoyne Family 100
Cochran Family 170
Conrad Family, Huntington
    Library 290
Cooper Family 318
Corbis Images 103
David Davis 206
Davis Family 139
DeLadurantey Family 220
Franceschini Family 236
Gail Ryan 25
Glenn Grossman 251, 289, 362,
    395
Greenwell Family 329
Hamilton Family 269
Howlett Family 40
Isbell Family 73
John Rieth 187
Kensic Family 199
King Family 164
KTLA Archives 41
Lee Family 304

Lonshoremen's and
    Warehousemen's Memorial
    Association 3
Los Angeles Police Department
    115, 314
Los Angeles Police Beat Magazine
    9, 121, 137
Los Angeles Public Library
    Special Collections 26, 28,
    37, 46, 58, 114, 143, 145,
    151, 159, 160, 161, 213, 261,
    319, 326, 339, 373, 419
Marshall Family 326
Mika Family 383
Moon Family 10
Much Family 150
Murphy Family 358
North American Association of
    Uniform Manufacturers
    and Distributors 253
Palmer Family 233
Piepenbrink Family 68
Posner Family 100
Russell Family 269

Los Angeles Police Department Rank Structure

Prior to 1971
Chief of Police
Assistant Chief
Deputy Chief
Inspector
Captain
Lieutenant
Sergeant
Policeman

After 1971
Chief of Police
Assistant Chief
Deputy Chief
Commander
Captain I, II, III
Lieutenant I, II
Sergeant I, II,
Detective I, II, III
Policeman I, II, III

Note: In 1973, the designation Policeman changed to Police Officer

Los Angeles Police Department Patrol Divisions Map

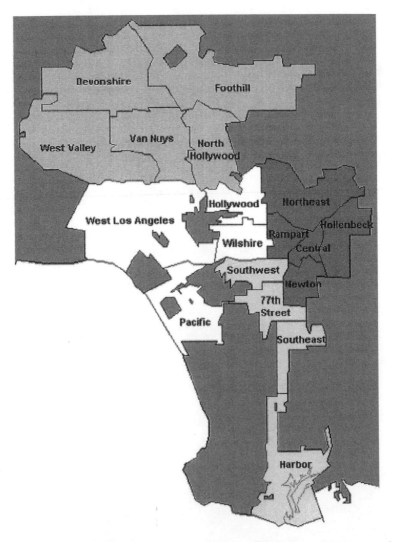

Note: Southeast Division was previously part of 77th Street Division; and Pacific Division was previously named Venice Division.

Index

Made in the USA
San Bernardino, CA
10 January 2015